Praise for Jim Highsmith's
Agile Project Management, Second Edition

"This second edition is a remarkable palimpsest that overlays critical enterprise aspects such as scaling agile, governing agile projects, and measuring agile performance onto its original, award-winning agile project management foundation. If you're an agile manager or executive seeking a holistic understanding as well as the critical details of agile project management—this edition will be a very valuable addition to your bookshelf."

—*Sanjiv Augustine, President, LitheSpeed and Author of Managing Agile Projects*

"Jim continues to successfully communicate complex project management concepts and interactions in an easily digestible manner. The breadth and depth of practical agile experience, insight, and guidance is immense. In typical fashion, he tempers 'agile religion' with the reality that agile development is not right for every situation or everyone."

—*Robert Holler, President and CEO of VersionOne*

"This book is one of the very best on the topic of agile methods for project management, offering profound concepts and actionable guidelines. Stressing the need to abandon the old paradigm of "following a plan with minimal changes," in favor of "adapting successfully to inevitable changes," this book is one of those rare books suitable for both novice and seasoned project managers."

—*Alexander Laufer, Director, Center for Project Leadership, Columbia University author,* Breaking the Code of Project Management

"Jim's second edition is a timely update that extends this decade's progress to the Project and Program Managers making the transition to agile project management. This edition expands on the topics of governance and performance management, helping PMs shape new models of adaptability, serving teams and continuous value delivery. It addresses the critical questions that PMs face in release planning, backlog preparation, capacity planning, and risk reduction. Jim knows how to talk to project managers, detailing agile phases that lead to adaptable learning and creating greater value in spite of high expectations and constraints. This is the one handbook on agile project management I would recommend for any business or technical leader who has a hand in the agile community."

—*Ryan Martens, CTO & Founder, Rally Software*

"Envisioning a different way of working begins with a shift in thinking. Jim Highsmith shares an exciting vision and the new way of thinking behind the Agile Revolution in his latest book, *Agile Project Management*. Through storytelling and examples, Jim draws us into appreciating a new way of fostering creativity and innovation. This is required reading for anyone looking for a fresh perspective that can change the way teams develop new products.

Antoine de Saint-Exupery once said, 'If you want to build a ship, don't drum up people together to collect wood and don't assign them tasks and work, but rather teach them to long for the endless immensity of the sea.' Agile Project Management helps us chart a course along those lines. There's no doubt that great products and a new way of how teams work together will be the result."

—*Michael Mah, Director, Benchmarking Practice, Cutter Consortium and Managing Partner, QSM Associates Inc.*

"I have always considered the first edition of Jim Highsmith's *Agile Project Management* to be the source for information on agile project management and good project management in general. In the second edition, Jim has done a great job of extending coverage to the key aspects of spreading agile thinking to portfolio management and the rest of the organization. Again, a must have for a project, program, or portfolio manager's book shelf."

—*Kent J. McDonald, Program Manager*

"It's been almost twenty years since Jim and I first started to collaborate. Jim was always fond of saying that more has been written about Software Development than is known. In this second edition of *Agile Project Management*, Jim's writing has finally caught up with all that needs to be known. The rest is up to you and your experiences."

—*Sam Bayer, Ph.D., CEO b2b2dot0*

"When Jim's first APM book hit the shelves five years ago it added much needed structure to project and product release planning levels. His APM principles and practices have been widely and successfully adopted worldwide. In this edition Jim adds many new insights, values, principles, and practices based on his extensive experience helping large enterprises scale their agility across projects, programs, products, and divisions. This latest edition is chock full of valuable new ideas and practical applications."

—*Ken Collier, Ph.D., Agile Consultant and Author*

"In this new mainstream world of agile adoption, Jim walks a wonderful and generous line for new and seasoned project managers alike. Jim still has the beginner agile project manager in mind, offering his very clear ideas backed by immediately applicable practices. He continues his agnostic view of agile by sticking to tools for the project manager, regardless of any particular agile framework or method. In this second edition, Jim has remained vigilant to the agile project manager's success, adding thought-provoking guidance for the bigger agile world."

—*Jean Tabaka, Agile Fellow, Rally Software*

"No one makes agile project management as clear, compelling, and real as Jim Highsmith—and without coming off as a cheerleader. His models of agile project management just make sense and important—no, essential—agile nuggets can be found on every page. In particular, Chapter 13, "Beyond Scope, Schedule, and Cost: Measuring Agile Performance," is required reading. I'm recommending it to all my clients. So read *Agile Project Management* if you value performance over politics."

—*Christopher Avery, Ph.D., Leadership Mentor, www.ChristopherAvery.com*

"Jim challenges conventional wisdom and provides excellent examples of the leadership mindset shifts needed to successfully implement *Agile Project Management* for products. A must read for all product and project managers."

—*Ron Holliday, Vice President, Financial Services, Fidelity Investments*

"There is no better source of wisdom on agile project management than Highsmith's second edition. A master of explaining all sides of a story, Highsmith helps you understand exactly why traditional project management fails to deliver in a competitive world and how agile management provides a faster, more adaptive and customer-focused process. I love Jim's real-world stories of companies that are thriving with agile, his in-depth coverage of essential agile management practices, and his innovative ideas on agile governance."

—*Joshua Kerievsky, Founder, Industrial Logic, Inc.*

Praise for Jim Highsmith's
Agile Project Management

"Jim Highsmith is one of a few modern writers who are helping us understand the new nature of work in the knowledge economy. A transition—from industrial-age thinking to management more suited to reliable innovation—is well underway. But few people yet understand the implications of this shift. *Agile Project Management* explains what's going on with startling clarity. Perhaps more importantly, it provides the vital management structure and practical advice that will support ongoing innovation in your company."

—Rob Austin, Assistant Professor, Harvard Business School

"There is a lot of attention these days being given to whether organizations are harvesting the maximum benefits from their IT investments. This book is totally in alignment with that theme and should be a must-read for all project participants who are passionate about their projects delivering 'value for money.'

"The one constant in the vast majority of large projects I see in my role as Project Management Practice Manager for Fujitsu Consulting is change. Yet, true to the observations that Jim has made in this book, the majority of these projects have been executed as if change is not the norm and as if the project initiators were 'seers' who could foretell the future with a high degree of certainty. These projects were run on the basis of traditional project management practices, where, simplistically speaking, the project plan was 'king,' and performance was measured and couched in terms of 'delivery to plan.'

"In the past 12–18 months, Fujitu Consulting has seen the potential benefits of adopting more 'Agile' approaches in the way we deliver and manage some of our projects and have encouraged our clients to embrace an 'adaptive' project culture."

—Karen Chivers, Senior Consulting Director and Project Management Practice Manager, Fujitsu Consulting (Asia Pacific)

"There is a common set of values that all the Agile methods share, and, in this book, Jim Highsmith uses those values plus his knowledge of the Agile methods to present a common framework for Agile project management. Jim shows us what an Agile approach to project management is about—the essential insights and experiences—plus he expertly combines tools and techniques with proven project management value, those of his own and those from other methods, into this framework."

—*Jeff De Luca, Project Director, Nebulon Pty. Ltd. (Australia)*

"Jim's book, *Agile Project Management*, addresses one of the key questions asked when adopting an Agile software development methodology, 'How do you manage the project?' He spends a lot of time on the values and principles needed to be successful in a less bureaucratic development environment. It requires individual discipline and a substantial mindset shift by all parties. He has done an excellent job of documenting the behaviors that will create a winning team, no matter what process is being used. I applaud Jim for creating a book that will help take the Agile movement to a new level."

—*Christine Davis, Visiting Scientist, Carnegie Melon University/
former Executive Vice President and General Manager, Raytheon*

"Welcome to the second generation of Agile methodologies! *Agile Project Management* is an Agile methodology thoughtfully built on the key ideas and experiences of other AMs. The result is a coherent whole, from principles to practices. If your job is to deliver serious software, keep this book at hand on your library, since in the next ten years you will use it too many times!"

—*Michele Marchesi, Professor of Software Engineering,
University of Cagliari, Italy*

"The world of product development is becoming more dynamic and uncertain. Many managers cope by reinforcing processes, adding documentation, or further honing costs. This isn't working. Highsmith brilliantly guides us into an alternative that fits the times."

—*Preston G. Smith, Founder and Principal of New Product Dynamics/
Coauthor,* Developing Products in Half the Time

"Finally a book that reconciles the passion of the Agile software movement with the needed disciplines of project management. Jim's book has provided a service to all of us.

"Agile software development is largely a grass-roots movement that focuses on reliably delivering software products in a dynamic world. To date, much of the Agile literature has focused on the engineering practices that support an Agile philosophy, and thus the coverage of project management has been limited. In this book, Jim Highsmith addresses project management in the Agile environment. He doesn't limit this coverage to simply making a case for a new style of project management. Rather, Jim also offers a practical framework and supporting practices that project managers can use to help software development teams be more productive and reliably deliver products that add business value."

—*Neville R(oy) Singham, CEO, ThoughtWorks, Inc.*

"Software development is a human activity, although we sometimes try to deny that fact by wrapping high ceremony processes and tools around our teams which, if unleashed, can produce some truly amazing things. Jim knows this all too well from his broad experience in working with a variety of projects, and that experience shines through in this very pragmatic and much needed take on Agile project management."

—*Grady Booch, IBM Fellow*

"Agile methods, whether for software development, project management, or general product development, are the ideal approach for building things where change is a risk factor. Everywhere? Highsmith clearly shows how iterative development methods can be successfully applied to project management generally. It is truly groundbreaking when methods refined in the software space can actually inform other disciplines."

—*Charles Stack, Founder and CEO, Flashline, Inc.*

"This is the project management book we've all been waiting for—the book that effectively combines Agile methods and rigorous project management. Not only does this book help us make sense of project management in this current world of iterative, incremental Agile methods, but it's an all-around good read!

"Many IT organizations have made a mess of Agile methods and component development. Organizations that abandoned waterfall methods for undisciplined software hacking have given Agile methods a bad reputation in some businesses. A cure for these woes can be found in Jim Highsmith's new book. You really can combine the benefits of Agile methods with project management disciplines. Jim shows us the way."

—*Lynne Ellyn, Senior VP & CIO, DTE Energy*

"Jim Highsmith's *Agile Project Management* is a refreshing change in the flow of project management books being published today. The book combines project management theory and practice cast in common-sense terms in a manner valuable to both the student and user. The author's recasting and renaming of the phases of a project life cycle adds an approach likely to be emulated in the future literature in this discipline.

"His treatment of the general principles to be followed in the Agile Revolution for new product development provides a model of behavior valuable to the enlightened scholar and practitioner of the project management process."

—*Dr. David I. Cleland, Professor Emeritus, Industrial Engineering Department, School of Engineering, University of Pittsburgh*

"Product development in the 21st century must move from the world of structure and compliance to one of agility and rapid learning. As a result, project management must change from the administration of tasks to the flexible balancing of possibilities against constraints—'managing on the edge of chaos,' as the author puts it. This book explains the process of doing just that and should be the foundation for change—readable, full of logic, and a sound process."

—*Michael Kennedy, President, Product Development Solutions/ Author,* Product Development for the Lean Enterprise

"This is a wonderful and highly practical book. Within hours of putting it down I was putting some of its advice into practice. It's a highly thought-provoking book that argues, for instance, that agility is more attitude than process and more environment than methodology. Because of the complexity of today's software projects, one new product development project can rarely be viewed as a repeat of a prior project. This makes Highsmith's advice to favor a reliable process over a repeatable one particularly timely and important."

—*Mike Cohn, President, Mountain Goat Software/ Author,* User Stories Applied: For Agile Software Development

"Jim's book removes the mystery around Agile project management and its associated techniques while providing a framework of discipline that can be easily applied to any high-tech development and is not limited to software development."

—*Ken Delcol, Director, Product Development, MDS SCIEX*

"Iterations are clearly the best way to create the innovative products that customers want to buy. *Agile Project Management* contains a wealth of ideas and insights about how to make a flexible product development process work."

—*Michael A. Cusumano, Professor, MIT Sloan School of Management/Author,* The Business of Software

"Practical and provocative advice allows the reader to examine Agile project management in unusual depth, which is what sets this book apart. Jim opens the gateway to the clockworks of Agile project management and does it using a great storyline that takes you all the way through the journey. A must-have for any leadership collection."

—*Wes Balakian, PMP, Chairman and Executive Advisor, PMI eBusiness SIG/President TSI*

"*Agile Project Management* is the first book to successfully bring together the theory of complex adaptive systems and the practice of project management in a usable, 'how-to' format. The book offers a range of concrete suggestions including, my favorite, how to develop a product vision statement by creating a prototype of the final package. Agile project management also helps the project manager with issues of scalability through offering specific suggestions on tailoring the APM approach and by devoting an entire chapter to managing the large team. If you're looking for practical suggestions on how to deliver the best product you can given the normal constraints of time and budget, then APM is one book you absolutely want to have on your book shelf."

—Donna Fitzgerald, Partner, Knowth Consulting/former Project Director for Project Management Software, Oracle

"In this landmark book, Jim Highsmith catapults project management into the 21st century. The book's a goldmine of the essential principles and practices you need to succeed in delivering innovation and business value on any new product venture."

—Doug DeCarlo, Principal, The Doug DeCarlo Group

"Jim Highsmith has done a great service in this book by providing an easy-to-read and valuable reference for project managers who want to foster greater agility through a common-sense set of practices."

—Kevin Tate, Chief Product Architect, Alias

Agile Project Management

Creating Innovative Products,

Second Edition

The Agile Software Development Series

Alistair Cockburn and Jim Highsmith, Series Editors

Agile software development centers on four values identified in the Agile Alliance's Manifesto:

- Individuals and interactions over processes and tools
- Working software over comprehensive documentation
- Customer collaboration over contract negotiation
- Responding to change over following a plan

The development of Agile software requires innovation and responsiveness, based on generating and sharing knowledge within a development team and with the customer. Agile software developers draw on the strengths of customers, users, and developers, finding just enough process to balance quality and agility.

The books in The Agile Software Development Series focus on sharing the experiences of such Agile developers. Individual books address individual techniques (such as Use Cases), group techniques (such as collaborative decision making), and proven solutions to different problems from a variety of organizational cultures. The result is a core of Agile best practices that will enrich your experience and improve your work.

Titles in the Series:

Steve Adolph, Paul Bramble, Alistair Cockburn, and Andy Pols; *Patterns for Effective Use Cases;* 0201721848

Alistair Cockburn; *Agile Software Development, Second Edition;* 0321482751

Alistair Cockburn; *Crystal Clear;* 0201699478

Alistair Cockburn; *Surviving Object-Oriented Projects;* 0201498340

Alistair Cockburn; *Writing Effective Use Cases;* 0201702258

Anne Mette Jonassen Hass; *Configuration Management Principles and Practice;* 0321117662

Jim Highsmith; *Agile Software Development Ecosystems;* 0201760436

Jim Highsmith; *Agile Project Management;* 0321219775

Craig Larman; *Agile and Iterative Development;* 0131111558

Dean Leffingwell; *Scaling Software Agility;* 0321458192

Mary Poppendieck and Tom Poppendieck; *Lean Software Development;* 0321150783

Jean Tabaka; *Collaboration Explained;* 0321268776

Kevin Tate; *Sustainable Software Development;* 0321286081

Agile Project Management

Creating Innovative Products,

Second Edition

Jim Highsmith

✦ Addison-Wesley

Upper Saddle River, NJ • Boston • Indianapolis • San Francisco
New York • Toronto • Montreal • London • Munich • Paris • Madrid
Cape Town • Sydney • Tokyo • Singapore • Mexico City

The publisher offers excellent discounts on this book when ordered in quantity for bulk purchases or special sales, which may include electronic versions and/or custom covers and content particular to your business, training goals, marketing focus, and branding interests. For more information, please contact:

    U.S. Corporate and Government Sales
    (800) 382-3419
    corpsales@pearsontechgroup.com

For sales outside the United States please contact:

    International Sales
    international@pearsoned.com

Library of Congress Cataloging-in-Publication Data

Highsmith, James A., 1945-

  Agile project management : creating innovative products / Jim Highsmith.

    p. cm.

  Includes bibliographical references and index.

  ISBN-13: 978-0-321-65839-5 (pbk. : alk. paper)

  ISBN-10: 0-321-65839-6 (pbk. : alk. paper)

  1. Software engineering. 2. Agile software development--Management.

I. Title.

  QA76.758.H54 2010

  005.1--dc22

            2009019147

ISBN-13: 978-0-321-65839-5
ISBN-10: 0-321-65839-6

Text printed in the United States on recycled paper at RR Donnelley, Crawfordsville, Indi

Nineth Printing February 2016

Editor-in-Chief
Karen Gettman

Executive Editor
Chris Guzikowski

Senior Development Editor
Chris Zahn

Managing Editor
Patrick Kanouse

Project Editor
Mandie Frank

Copy Editor
Margo Catts

Indexer
Tim Wright

Proofreader
Kathy Ruiz

Publishing Coordinator
Raina Chrobak

Cover Designer
Louisa Adair

Compositor
Mark Shirar

To Wendie, Debbie, and Nikki

Contents

Acknowledgments

All books are collaborative efforts, and this one is no exception. Many people have contributed ideas, reviews, comments, and inspiration that have helped me turn my ideas about agile project management into the reality of this book.

Although I take full responsibility for the content of this second edition book, I had a wonderful group of advisors and reviewers who contributed significant time and effort to turning my drafts into a final product. I owe a tremendous thanks to Ken Collier for long conversations over morning coffee, and to Kent McDonald, Israel Gat, Jean Tabaka, and Sanjive Augustine. Israel Gat, in particular, provided a valuable senior executive's perspective.

Many people contributed to the material in this book. They include Mike Cohn, Ken Delcol, Jeff DeLuca, Luke Hohmann, J. R. Jenks, Martyn Jones, Michael Mah, Anne Mullaney, Michele Marchesi, Lynne Nix, Norm Kerth, Scott Ambler, Doug DeCarlo, Ed Yourdon, Josh Kerievsky, Borys Stokalski, Peter George, Bartek Kiepuszewski, Tim Lister, Kent Beck, Donna Fitzgerald, Glen Alleman, Todd Little, Rob Austin, Ken Orr, Don Olson, Tom DeMarco, Sam Bayer, Kevin Tate, Gary Walker, Paul Young, David Spann, Alistair Cockburn, Pollyanna Pixton, Ole Jepsen, Greg Reiser, Roy Singham, Robin Gibson, Lynda Belhoucine, Bob Charette, Christopher Avery, and Preston Smith.

Special thanks goes to Karen Coburn, president of the Cutter Consortium, for her support and permission to include material I wrote for various Cutter publications in this book.

Finally my thanks to executive editor Chris Guzikowski at Addison-Wesley for his support and encouragement.

About the Author

Jim Highsmith directs Cutter Consortium's agile consulting practice. He has over 30 years experience as an IT manager, product manager, project manager, consultant, and software developer.

Jim is the author of *Agile Project Management: Creating Innovative Products*, Addison Wesley 2004; *Adaptive Software Development: A Collaborative Approach to Managing Complex Systems*, Dorset House 2000 and winner of the prestigious Jolt Award, and *Agile Software Development Ecosystems*, Addison Wesley 2002. Jim is the recipient of the 2005 international Stevens Award for outstanding contributions to systems development. He is also co-editor, with Alistair Cockburn, of the Agile Software Development Series of books from Addison Wesley.

Jim is a coauthor of the *Agile Manifesto*, a founding member of The Agile Alliance, coauthor of the *Declaration Interdependence* for project leaders, and cofounder and first president of the Agile Project Leadership Network. A frequent speaker at conferences worldwide, Jim has published dozens of articles in major industry publications.

Jim has consulted with IT and product development organizations and software companies in the U.S., Europe, Canada, South Africa, Australia, Japan, India, and New Zealand to help them adapt to the accelerated pace of development in increasingly complex, uncertain environments. Jim's areas of consulting include the areas of Agile Software Development, Project Management, and Collaboration. He has held technical and management positions with software, computer hardware, banking, and energy companies. Jim holds a B.S. in electrical engineering and an M.S. in management.

Foreword

We live in an era characterized by information overload. This statement itself is now a cliché. However, it bears repeating because in virtually every field we are still drowning in information and struggling for meaningful knowledge. Even in the relatively nascent field of agile project management and development we already need to filter "noise," connect the dots, and integrate diverse disciplines. Jim Highsmith's *Agile Project Management* is a timely book for the drowning agilist in need of insights that make Agile principles actionable.

The first challenge of the struggle with information is to keep up with and not become overwhelmed by the state of the art. The coming of age of agile methods has led to exponential growth of publications on the subject—books, essays, conference proceedings, blogs, wikis, and, yes, tweets. This fast growth is compounded by the accelerating pace of new practices that get introduced by enthusiastic communities of agilists. Putting our hands around the Agile topic nowadays requires a significant investment of time and effort. Agile Project Management fully covers the whole agile landscape, in depth, in a single, easy-to-read volume.

The second level of information explosion is the day-to-day struggle of the agilist to keep the artifacts produced by the software engineering process at the just-enough level. This is not merely a matter of keeping the template zombies in check. As agile methods get mainstream traction, it's hard to resist the temptation to add "just one more artifact" to fit in with established portfolio management and life cycle processes. Blind adherence to additional process and documentation requirements can often be problematic, but is especially troublesome when such processes fail to take into account how elegant and powerful agile principles can be in sticking to the bare minimum. Jim Highsmith's book demonstrates how to maintain the effectiveness of software development without sacrificing efficiency of ideation, design, coding, and testing. It guides the reader to the point at which the code starts speaking for itself louder and clearer than any verbose reports about the code.

Agile project management will appeal to both novice and expert in just about any discipline that touches agile methods. It reaches a rare level of broad applicability by emphasizing principles over practices. The book does not dogmatically tell the reader what to do in a "one size fits all" manner. Rather, it gives the reader the tools to observe, characterize, and analyze his or her particular circumstances and then to determine the appropriate method to practice. It teaches the practitioner how to implement agile as a process platform, how to tailor his or her agile work to business needs, corporate cultures, and project imperatives in a way that prescriptive advice can never accomplish. Moreover, it explains how the process platform could and should be used by both customer and vendor.

If I were to choose a subtitle for the book, I would pick the phrase "The Thinking Man's Guide to Agile Project Management." The book challenges the reader to look at what he or she is practicing through fresh eyes. In the course of so doing, the reader will assimilate the critical role agile plays in fostering innovation and creating value through affordable experimentation. He or she will develop the ability to facilitate the application of agile at the enterprise level by balancing empowerment, performance management, and governance considerations on a large scale.

How appropriate it is that Agile Project Management is being published at a time when the macro-economic situation poses so many formidable challenges. The book clearly articulates the "secret sauce" for corporate success amidst the crisis: relentless innovation through impassioned employees. Applied in this manner, agile can become a core discipline, revolutionizing the product life cycle all the way from inception through evolution to eventual retirement, and transforming the company all the way from the R&D lab through its value chain partners to the customer.

Israel Gat
Senior Consultant, Cutter Consortium
July 2009
Austin, Texas

Preface

When the Manifesto for Agile Software Development (www.agilealliance.org) was written in spring 2001, it launched a movement—a movement that raced through the software development community; generated controversy and debate; connected with related movements in manufacturing, construction, and aerospace; and been extended into project management.

The impetus for this second edition of *Agile Project Management* comes from four sources: the continuing pace of business change, the maturing of the agile movement over the last five years, the trend to large and distributed agile projects, and the formation of a project management organization for agile leaders (the Agile Project Leadership Network).

An article titled "There Is No More Normal" introduces a series of Business Week articles on game changing ideas. It quotes John Chambers, CEO of Cisco Systems, "Without exception, all of my biggest mistakes occurred because I moved too slowly."[1] If there is no more normal then adapting to change, quickly becomes a requisite skill for improving organizational performance. Agile project management enhances a team and an organization's ability to deal with change and the abnormal.

The essence of this agile movement, whether in new product development, new service offerings, software applications, or project management, rests on two foundational goals: delivering valuable products to customers and creating working environments in which people look forward to coming to work each day.

Innovation continues to drive economic success for countries, industries, and individual companies. Although the rates of innovation in information technology in the last decade may have declined from prodigious to merely lofty, innovation in areas such as biotechnology and nanotechnology are picking up any slack.

[1] McGregor, Jena. "There Is No More Normal," *Business Week* (March 23 and 30, 2009).

New technologies such as combinatorial chemistry and sophisticated computer simulation are fundamentally altering the innovation process itself. When these technologies are applied, the cost of iteration can be driven down dramatically, enabling exploratory and experimental processes to be both more effective and less costly than serial, specification-based processes. This dynamic is at work in the automotive, integrated circuit, software, and pharmaceutical industries. It will soon be at work in your industry.

But taking advantage of these new innovation technologies has proven tricky. When exploration processes replace prescriptive processes, people have to change. For the chemist who now manages the experimental compounding process rather than design compounds himself, and the manager who has to deal with hundreds of experiments rather than a detailed, prescriptive plan, new project management processes are required. Even when these technologies and processes offer lower cost and higher performance than their predecessors, the transformation often proves difficult.

Project management needs to be transformed to move faster, be more flexible, and be aggressively customer responsive. Agile Project Management (APM) answers this transformational need. It brings together a set of principles, practices, and performance measures that enable project managers to catch up with the realities of modern product development.

The target audience for this book is leaders, those hardy individuals who shepherd teams through the exciting but often messy process of turning visions into products—be they software, cell phones, or medical instruments. Leaders arise at many levels—project, team, executive, management—and APM addresses each of these, although the target audience continues to be project leaders. APM rejects the view of project leaders as functionaries who merely comply with the bureaucratic demands of schedules and budgets and replaces it with one in which they are intimately involved in helping teams deliver products.

Four broad topics are covered in Agile Project Management: opportunity, values, frameworks, and practices. The opportunity lies in creating innovative products and services—things that are new, different, and creative. These are products that can't be defined completely in the beginning but evolve over time through experimentation, exploration, and adaptation.

The APM values focus helps create products that deliver customer value today and are responsive to future customer needs. The frameworks, both enterprise and project, assist teams in delivering results reliably, even in the face of constant change, uncertainty, and ambiguity. Finally, the practices—from developing a product vision box to participatory decision making—provide actionable ways in which teams deliver results.

In this second edition of *Agile Project Management*, the five major new or updated topics are agile values, scaling agile projects, advanced release planning, project governance, and performance measurement. Chapters 2–4 have been rewritten around three summarizing value statements: delivering value over meeting constraints, leading the team over managing tasks, adapting to change over conforming to plans. The "Scaling Agile Projects" chapter has been completely revised to reflect the growth and development of the agile movement over the past five years. A new chapter has been added to encourage teams to place more attention on release planning. Finally, chapters on the organizational topics of project governance and changing performance measurement have been added.

In the long run, probably the most important addition is the new perspective on performance measurement. We ask teams to be agile, and then measure their performance by strict adherence to the Iron Triangle: scope, schedule, budget. This edition of APM proposes a new triangle—an Agile Triangle, that consists of value, quality, and constraints. If we want to grow agile organizations, then our performance measurement system must encourage agility.

Finally, although Agile Project Management can be applied to a wide range of product development efforts—and examples of this range are included, the book's primary product emphasis is software development.

Jim Highsmith
July 2009
Flagstaff, Arizona

Introduction

Agile Project Management (APM) contains four focal points: opportunities created by the agile revolution and its impact on product development, the values and principles that drive agile project management, the specific practices that embody and amplify those principles, and practices to help entire organizations, not just project teams, embrace agility.

Chapter 1, "The Agile Revolution," introduces changes that are occurring in product development—from cell phones to software—and how these changes are driving down the cost of experimentation and fundamentally altering how new product development should be managed. The chapter outlines the business objectives of APM and how organizations need to adapt to operating in a chaotic world.

Chapters 2–4 describe the values and principles that actuate APM. These core agile values are articulated in the *Declaration of Interdependence* and the *Manifesto for Agile Software Development*. For clarity and simplicity, three summarizing core values—Delivering Value over Meeting Constraints, Leading the Team over Managing Tasks, Adapting to Change over Conforming to Plans—are introduced, and each is discussed in a chapter.

Chapters 5–10 cover APM frameworks and individual practices. Chapter 5 describes both an agile enterprise framework (Project Governance, Project Management, Iteration Management, Technical Practices) and the phases in the Agile Delivery Framework (Envision, Speculate, Explore, Adapt, Close). Chapters 6–10 identify and describe the practices in each of the phases. Chapter 8 covers advanced release planning and includes a section on value point calculation.

Chapter 11, "Scaling Agile Projects," examines how agile principles are used, together with additional practices, to scale APM to larger projects and larger teams. Scaling covers both organizational and product-related practices.

Chapter 12, "Governing Agile Projects," begins the transition from topics about agile projects to agile organizations. This chapter addresses the key management and executive issues around project governance and the need to separate governance from delivery operations.

Chapter 13, "Beyond Scope, Schedule, and Cost: Measuring Agile Performance," continues the emphasis on agile organizations. It raises the issue that measuring success based on scope, schedule, and cost must change. The Agile Triangle, introduced Chapter 1, is examined in detail as a new way of thinking about performance measurement to encourage agility.

Chapter 14, "Reliable Innovation," underscores how APM helps address the changing nature of new product development, summarizes the role of the agile project leader, and reflects on the need for conviction and courage in implementing agile project management.

Conventions

One presentation technique used in this edition is highlighting key points or quotes in a box and italicizing the statement as illustrated.

> *Presented in a box and words italicized.*

The Agile Software Development Series

Out of all the people concerned with agility in software development over the last decade, Alistair Cockburn and I found so much in common that we joined efforts to bring to press an Agile Software Development Series based around relatively light, effective, human-powered software development techniques. We base the series on these two core ideas:

- Different projects need different processes or methodologies.
- Focusing on skills, communication, and community allows the project to be more effective and more agile than focusing on processes.

The series has the following main tracks:

- *Techniques to improve the effectiveness of a person who is doing a particular sort of job.* This might be a person who is designing a user interface, gathering requirements, planning a project, designing, or testing. Whoever is performing such a job will want to know how the best people in the world do their jobs. *Writing Effective Use Cases* (Cockburn 2001) and *Patterns for Effective Use Cases* (Adolph et al. 2003) are individual technique books.
- *Techniques to improve the effectiveness of a group of people.* These might include techniques for team building, project retrospectives, collaboration, decision making, and the like. *Collaboration Explained* (Tabaka 2006), *Improving Software Organizations* (Mathiassen et al. 2002) and *Surviving Object-Oriented Projects* (Cockburn 1998) are group technique books.
- *Examples of particular, successful agile methodologies.* Whoever is selecting a base methodology to tailor will want to find one that has already been used successfully in a similar situation. Modifying an existing methodology is easier than creating a new one and is more effective than using one that was designed for a different situation. *Scaling Lean & Agile Development* (Larman 2008), *Scaling Software Agility* (Leffingwell 2007), *Crystal Clear* (Cockburn 2004), *DSDM: Business Focused Development* (DSDM Consortium 2003), and *Lean Software Development: An Agile Toolkit* (Poppendieck and Poppendieck 2003) are examples of methodology books.

Three books anchor the Agile Software Development Series:

- This book, *Agile Project Management*, goes beyond software development to describe how a variety of projects can be better managed by applying agile principles and practices. It covers the business justification, principles, and practices of APM.
- *Agile Software Development Ecosystems* (Highsmith 2002) identifies the unique problems in today's software development environment, describes the common principles behind agile development as expressed in the *Agile Manifesto*, and reviews each of the six major agile approaches.

- Alistair's book, *Agile Software Development* (Cockburn 2006), expresses his thoughts about agile development using several themes: software development as a cooperative game, methodologies as conventions about coordination, and families of methodologies.

You can find more about Crystal, Adaptive, and other agile methodologies on these Web sites:

- www.alistair.cockburn.us
- www.jimhighsmith.com
- www.agilealliance.org
- www.apln.org

Chapter 1

The Agile Revolution

Product development teams are facing a quiet revolution in which both engineers and managers are struggling to adjust. In industry after industry—pharmaceuticals, software, automobiles, integrated circuits—customer demands for continuous innovation and the plunging cost of experimentation are signaling a massive switch from anticipatory to adaptive styles of development. This switch plays havoc with engineers, project managers, and executives who are still operating with anticipatory, prescriptive mindsets and processes geared to a rapidly disappearing era.

> *Symyx (a medical instrument company) creates and operates highly integrated, complete workflows that enable scientists to explore their ideas to discover and optimize new materials hundreds to thousands of times faster than traditional research methods. These workflows consist of robotics that synthesize arrays of materials on a miniaturized scale, creating hundreds to thousands of tiny experiments on one silicon chip. These materials are then rapidly screened in parallel for desired physical and functional properties, including chemical, thermal, optical, electronic, or mechanical attributes. The results are captured in database systems for mining large sets of data to help scientists make well-informed decisions on the next steps of the discovery process.[1]*

Symyx boasts that its instruments speed drug company testing performance 100 times at 1% of the cost of traditional research. Drug companies used to *design* compounds for specific purposes by having scientists pore over how to make just the right one. Today they generate tens of thousands of compounds and then test them quickly using ultra-sophisticated, ultra-speedy

---

[1] Formally listed on the Symyx web site, www.symyx.com.

tools such as mass spectrometers. *New product development economics are at work here.*

In mid-2002, when Alias Systems (now part of Autodesk) of Toronto, Canada, started developing Sketchbook Pro©, a software package to be announced concurrently with the launch of Microsoft's Tablet PC operating system, the product management and software development team didn't begin with a lengthy product planning effort. The team's marketing and product strategy evolved over several months, but its product development effort began early, and in parallel, with the strategy process. The team had a vision—an easy-to-use consumer-focused sketching product worthy of a professional graphics artist—and a deadline, the November Microsoft launch date. The product evolved in two-week iterations. For each iteration, a short planning session identified features to be developed. Then, within the constraints of "platform" architecture, the operating system, and Tablet PC computers, the product evolved—iteration by iteration. In the end, the product was delivered on time, met high quality standards, and continues to be successful in the marketplace. The product wasn't planned and built; it was envisioned and then it evolved. Alias didn't start with architectures, plans, and detailed specifications; it began with a vision followed shortly by the first iteration of the product. The product, the architecture, the plans, and the specifications evolved as the team adapted to the ever-unfolding reality of the market and the technology.

With Sketchbook Pro©, the team literally didn't know past the next iteration which features would be included in subsequent development iterations. Team members did have a clear product vision and a business plan. They did have a general idea about what features were needed in the product. They did have active involvement from product management. They did have an absolute time deadline and resource expenditure constraints. They did have an overall product platform architecture. Within this vision, business objectives and constraints, and overall product roadmap, they delivered tested features every two weeks and then adapted their plans to the reality of actual product testing. The team's process was one of evolution and adaptation, not planning and optimization.

In the automobile industry, BMW uses simulations to improve car crashworthiness. It ran 91 simulations and conducted just two real crashes. The results were a 30% improvement in design effectiveness and simulated crash tests that took 2.5 days versus 3.8 months (for simple tests)—and the 91 simulations cost less than the two real crashes (Thomke 2003).

All these approaches to product development point to a very critical issue. When we reduce the cost of experimentation enough, the entire economics of how we develop products changes—it switches from a process based on anticipation (define, design, and build) to one based on adaptation (envision, explore, and refine). When the cost of generating alternatives plunges and the cost of integrating them into a product is low, then great products aren't built, they evolve—just like biological evolution, only much, much faster than in nature. Biological evolution begins with experimentation (mutation and recombination), exploration (survival of the fittest), and refinement (producing more of the survivors). Increasingly, product development processes are being built using this biological metaphor.

Time is also a driving factor in new product development (NPD). In the short and intense decade of the 1990s, the average new product time to market in the US dropped from 35.5 to 11 months (Wujec and Muscat 2002). "Corporations everywhere are engaged in a new products war," says NPD expert and author Robert Cooper. "From soup to nuts, from can openers to automobiles, companies are at a competitive war with each other—and the advance troops are product development teams. On this new product battlefield, the ability to mount lightning attacks—well-planned but swift strikes—is increasingly key to success.... And mobility or speed enables lightning strikes designed to seize windows of opportunity or to catch an enemy off guard" (Cooper 2001).

Uncertainty, shrinking time schedules, and the need for iterative exploration are not restricted to new product development. New business practice implementations, such as those fostered by customer relationship management (CRM) installations, are often fraught with uncertainty of a different kind. The high rate of failures reported in CRM implementations can, in part, be attributed to anticipatory (plan-driven) project management approaches that failed to "explore" into the uncertainty caused by major business process changes. Companies tried to plan and do when they needed to envision and explore. As authors Preston Smith and Guy Merritt (2002) write, "Innovative product development depends on exploring the uncertain to add product value and maintain competitive advantage."

But innovation and faster development aren't good enough. Companies have to deliver better products geared to what customers want at the time of shipment, which may or may not resemble what the team guessed they wanted when the project was initiated. Companies that have the ability to quickly and inexpensively evolve a product closest to the end of the development lifecycle will have a tremendous competitive advantage.

> *Ultimate customer value is delivered at the point-of-sale, not the point-of-plan.*

So why isn't every company doing this? For most companies there is a great gap between needing and delivering new products. NPD is a multifaceted and extremely difficult challenge. The Product Development and Management Association (PDMA) estimates newly launched product failure rates of around 59%, which has changed little from the early 1990s. Also, cancelled or failed (in the market) products consumed an estimated 46% of product development resources (Cooper 2001). Yet some companies are consistently more successful than others, and a growing number of these successful companies are practicing agile methods.

The product development efforts targeted by agile methods include new products[2] and enhancements to products in the domains of

- Commercial software products
- Industrial products with embedded software (from electronics equipment to autos)[3]
- Internally developed IT projects

The key point is that opportunity, uncertainty, and risk reside in the proposed product—not in the approach to project management. Our approach to project management needs to fit with the characteristics of the product to improve our chances of capitalizing on the opportunity by systematically reducing the uncertainty and mitigating the risks over the life of the project.

Companies need results from their high-pressure product development efforts, but they shouldn't come at the expense of quality. John Wooden,

---

[2] In Robert Cooper's (2001) definition, new product development applies to products that have been on the market five years or less.

[3] For hardware development a good reference is *Flexible Product Development: Bringing Agility for Changing Markets*, by Preston Smith (2007).

the legendary basketball coach of UCLA whose teams won 10 national championships, used a saying with his teams that applies to product development: "Be quick, but don't hurry." In other words, do the right things, but learn how to do them quickly. Strip away the overhead, the non-value-adding activities. Create quality products *and* do it quickly. Agile development focuses on speed, mobility, *and* quality. To accomplish this, individuals and teams must be highly disciplined—but with self-discipline rather than imposed discipline.

> *Anyone who practices ad hoc development under the guise of agile methods is an imposter.*

There is no reason to think the changes in the next ten years will be of less magnitude than those of the previous ten, although the emphasis will likely change from pure information technology to the integration of information and biotechnology. The underlying codes of information technology are zeros and ones. The underlying codes of biotechnology are A, T, C, and G (the components of DNA). When biological codes can be reduced to computer codes, as in the Human Genome Project, and then be manipulated by computer programs (as is happening), the potential impact on product development of many types is staggering. Drug companies, for example, are beginning to simulate the impact of drugs on the human body. "New materials, programmed molecular factories, and self-organizing fabrication processes could change the cost and performance characteristics of everything from drugs to dragsters, paint to plastics, china to chairs" (Meyer and Davis 2003). Scientific and technology advances in the coming decade and beyond will continue to irrevocably alter product development processes, and those changes, in turn, will cause us to rethink the management of those processes.

Linear thinking, prescriptive processes, and standardized, unvarying practices are no match for today's volatile product development environment. So as product development processes swing from anticipatory to adaptive, project management must change also. It must be geared to mobility, experimentation, and speed. But first of all, it must be geared to business objectives.

Agile Business Objectives

Building innovative products, processes, and business models requires a new approach to management in general and project management in particular. There are five key business objectives for a good exploration process such as Agile Project Management (APM):

1. *Continuous innovation*—to deliver on current customer requirements
2. *Product adaptability*—to deliver on future customer requirements
3. *Improved time-to-market*—to meet market windows and improve return on investment (ROI)
4. *People and process adaptability*—to respond rapidly to product and business change
5. *Reliable results*—to support business growth and profitability

Continuous Innovation

As discussed in the opening section, developing new products and new services in today's complex business and technology world requires a mindset that fosters innovation. Striving to deliver customer value, to create a product that meets today's customer requirements, drives this continuous innovation process. Innovative ideas aren't generated in structured, authoritarian environments but in an adaptive culture based on the principles of self-organization and self-discipline.

Product Adaptability

No matter how prescient a person, a team, or a company, the future will always surprise us. For some products, changes in the market, technology, or specific requirements happen weekly. For other products, the timeframe for incorporating changes varies from months to years. With the pace of change increasing and response time shrinking, the only way to survive is to strive for product adaptability—a critical design criterion for a development process. In fact, in an agile project, technical excellence is measured by both capacity to deliver customer value today *and* create an adaptable product for tomorrow. Agile technical practices focus on lowering technical debt (improving the ability to adapt) as an integral part of the development process. In an agile project, developers strive for technical excellence, and project leaders champion it.

Improved Time-to-Market

As the statistics for rapidly shrinking product development times indicate, reducing delivery schedules to meet market windows continues to be a high-priority business goal for managers and executives. The iterative, feature-based nature of APM contributes to improving time-to-market in three key ways: focus, streamlining, and skill development.

First, the constant attention to product features and their prioritization in short, iterative timeboxes forces teams (product management and developers) to carefully consider both the number of features to include in the product and the depth of those features. Constant attention reduces the overall workload by eliminating both marginally beneficial features and marginal requirements of those features. Second, APM—like its lean development counterparts—streamlines the development process, concentrating on value-adding activities and eliminating overhead and compliance activities. Third, APM focuses on selecting the right skills for project team members and molding them into productive teams.

People and Process Adaptability

Just as products need to adapt to marketplace reality over time, so do people and processes. In fact, if we want adaptable products, we must first build adaptable teams—teams whose members are comfortable with change, who view change not as an obstacle to resist but as part and parcel of thriving in a dynamic business environment. The APM principles and framework encourage learning and adapting as an integral part of delivering value to customers.

Reliable Results

Production processes are designed to be repeatable, to deliver the same result time after time after time. Good production processes deliver the anticipated result, for a standard cost, within a given time—they are predictable. Exploration processes are different. Because of the uncertainty surrounding requirements and new technology, exploration projects can't deliver a known, completely pre-specified result, but they can deliver a valuable result—a releasable product that meets customer goals and business requirements as they become known. Good exploration processes can deliver innovation reliably—time after time. But while performance measures for production processes can be based on actual scope, cost, and schedule versus their predicted values, exploration processes need to be measured differently.

> *A repeatable process is one in which doing the same thing in the same way produces the same results. One that is reliable delivers regardless of the impediments thrown in the way—reliability means constantly adapting to meet a goal.*

Confusion about reliable and repeatable has caused many organizations to pursue repeatable processes—very structured and precise—when exactly the opposite approach—mildly structured and flexible—works astonishingly better for new product and service development. If your goal is to deliver a product that meets a known and unchanging specification, then try a repeatable process. However, if your goal is to deliver a valuable product to a customer within some targeted boundaries, when change and deadlines are significant factors, then reliable agile processes work better.

Agility Defined

There is no *Agility for Dummies*. Agility isn't a silver bullet. You don't achieve it in five easy steps. So what is it? For myself, I've characterized agility in two statements:

"Agility is the ability to both create and respond to change in order to profit in a turbulent business environment.

Agility is the ability to balance flexibility and stability" (Highsmith 2002).

In an uncertain and turbulent world, success belongs to companies that have the capacity to create change, and maybe even chaos, for their competitors. Creating change disrupts competitors (and the entire market ecosystem); responding to change guards against competitive thrusts. Creating change requires innovation: developing new products, creating new sales channels, reducing product development time, customizing products for increasingly smaller market segments. In addition, your company must be able to respond quickly to both anticipated and unanticipated changes created by your competitors and customers.

An example of a product development effort in which all the aspects of agility come into play is that of small, portable DNA analyzers. These instruments can be used for analyzing suspected bioterror agents (e.g., anthrax), performing quick medical diagnoses, or undertaking environmental bacterial analysis. These instruments must be accurate, easy to use, and reliable under wide-ranging conditions, and their development depends on breakthroughs in nanotechnology, genome research, and microfluidics. Developing these leading-edge products requires blending flexibility and structure, exploring various new technologies, and creating change for competitors by reducing delivery time. These are not projects that can be managed by traditional, prescriptive project management methodologies.

Some people mistakenly assume that agility connotes a lack of structure, but the absence of structure, or stability, generates chaos. Conversely, too much structure generates rigidity. Complexity theory tells us that innovation—creating something new in ways that we can't fully anticipate (an emergent result) occurs most readily at the balance point between chaos and order, between flexibility and stability. Scientists believe that emergence, the creation of novelty from agent interaction, happens most readily at this "edge of chaos." The idea of enough structure, but not too much, drives agile managers to continually ask the question, "How little structure can I get away with?" Too much structure stifles creativity. Too little structure breeds inefficiency.

This need to balance at the edge of chaos to foster innovation is one reason process-centric methodologies often fail. They push organizations into over-optimization at the expense of innovation. Agile organizations don't get lost in some gray middle ground; they understand which factors require stabilization and which ones encourage exploration. For example, in a high-change product development environment, rigorous configuration management stabilizes and facilitates flexibility just as a focus on technical excellence stabilizes the development effort. The concepts and practices described in this book are designed to help teams understand this balancing between flexibility and stability.

Agile Leadership Values

Agility is more attitude than process, more environment than methodology. In 1994 authors Jim Collins and Jerry Porras (1994) wrote *Built to Last*, a book based on their research that set out to answer the question, "What makes the truly exceptional companies different from the other companies?" One of their core findings was that exceptional companies created a foundation that didn't change and strategies and practices that did: "Visionary companies distinguish their timeless core values and enduring purpose, which should never change, from their operating practices and business strategies (which should be changing constantly in response to a changing world)."

> *"In high-performance teams, "the leaders managed the principles, and the principles managed the team." Carl Larson and Frank LaFasto (1989).*

I think one reason the agile movement has grown in recognition and use during the last decade is that the founders of the movement stated explicitly what we believed in the *Manifesto for Agile Software Development* and subsequently the *Declaration of Interdependence*. We stated our core values and enduring purpose. Why teams exist, what we intend to build, whom we build it for, and how we work together form the core principles of APM. If we want to build great products, we need great people. If we want to attract and keep great people, we need great principles.

We live in an age in which the volume of available information stupefies us. On any relatively interesting subject we can find thousands of Web pages, tens—if not hundreds—of books, and article after article. How do we filter all this information? How do we process all this information? Core values and principles provide one mechanism for processing and filtering information. They steer us in the direction of what is more, or less, important. They help us make product decisions and evaluate development practices.

Principles, or "rules" in complexity theory terminology, affect how tools and practices are implemented. Practices are how principles are acted out. Grand principles that generate no action are mere vapor. Conversely, specific practices in the absence of guiding principles are often inappropriately used. Although the use of agile practices may vary from team to team, the principles are constant. Principles are the simple rules of complex human adaptive systems.

There are two primary sources for agile values, the *Declaration of Interdependence*, shown in Figure 1-1 and authored by the founding members of the Agile Project Leadership Network (www.apln.org) and the *Manifesto for Agile Software Development* shown in Figure 1-2 authored by many of the founding members of the Agile Alliance (www.agilealliance.org). The *Declaration of Interdependence* was developed with project leaders in mind, whereas the *Agile Manifesto* (the oft-used short name) was developed with software development in mind.

The Declaration of Interdependence

We increase return on investment by making continuous flow of value our focus.

We deliver reliable results by engaging customers in frequent interactions and shared ownership.

We expect uncertainty and manage for it through iterations, anticipation, and adaptation.

We unleash creativity and innovation by recognizing that individuals are the ultimate source of value, and creating an environment where they can make a difference.

We boost performance through group accountability for results and shared responsibility for team effectiveness.

We improve effectiveness and reliability through situationally specific strategies, processes, and practices.

©2005 David Anderson, Sanjiv Augustine, Christopher Avery, Alistair Cockburn, Mike Cohn, Doug DeCarlo, Donna Fitzgerald, Jim Highsmith, Ole Jepsen, Lowell Lindstrom, Todd Little, Kent McDonald, Pollyanna Pixton, Preston Smith and Robert Wysocki.

Figure 1-1
The Declaration of Interdependence

Figure 1-2
The Agile Manifesto

> **The Agile Manifesto**
>
> We are uncovering better ways of developing [products] by doing it and helping others do it. Through this work we have come to value
>
> *Individuals and interactions over processes and tools*
> *Working software over comprehensive documentation*
> *Customer collaboration over contract negotiation*
> *Responding to change over following a plan.*
>
> That is, while there is value in the items on the right, we value the items on the left more.
>
> ©2001 by Kent Beck, Mike Beedle, Arie van Bennekum, Alistair Cockburn, Ward Cunningham, Martin Fowler, James Grenning, Jim Highsmith, Andrew Hunt, Ron Jeffries, Jon Kern, Brian Marick, Robert C. Martin, Steve Mellor, Ken Schwaber, Jeff Sutherland, and Dave Thomas.

> *The core value of an egalitarian meritocracy runs deep in the agile movement. It is surely not the only core value that can produce products, but it is a core value that defines how the majority of agilists view themselves.*

Over the years, the manifesto statements have been misinterpreted, primarily in confusing less important with unimportant: "This should not be construed as indicating that tools, process, documents, contracts, or plans are *unimportant*. There is a tremendous difference between one thing being more or less important than another and being *un*important" (Highsmith 2000). Tools are critical to speeding development and reducing costs. Contracts are vital to initiating developer-customer relationships. Documentation aids communication. However, the items on the left are the *most* critical. Without skilled individuals, working products, close interactions with customers, and responsiveness to change, product delivery will be nearly impossible.

While drinking coffee and talking agile with colleague Ken Collier one morning, the topic turned to project management, or more precisely, agile project leaders. We were discussing the problems we had encountered with aspiring agile project leaders (managers, scrum masters, etc.) who just didn't get the transition to self-organizing teams. Ken recalled a couple of cases in which the leaders seemed to buy into the general ideas of agile related to iterations and story planning, but were still micro-managing their teams. As Ken was talking, I jotted down "task" management versus "team" management as differing management styles. "Team managers" enable teams to self-manage their own tasks to facilitate the completion of features. "Task managers" focus on task completion as a measure of how well the team is conforming to the project plan. "Team managers" assist their teams (and the broader project community) remain coordinated and effective so that they can succeed. "Task managers" *oversee* teams to ensure that they remain "productive," on task, and don't lag behind the plan.

Later, on a beautiful afternoon bike ride, this discussion evolved into asking myself the question, "What traits differentiate an agile leader from a traditional (or non-agile) leader?" Furthermore, could this differentiation be boiled down into a couple of traits or value statements? Although the task-versus-team component seemed an important one, it wasn't enough. In the end, I proposed three critical values that both summarize those in the *Agile Manifesto* and *Declaration of Interdependence* and highlight key values for agile leaders:

- Delivering value over meeting constraints (Value over Constraints)
- Leading the team over managing tasks (Team over Tasks)
- Adapting to change over conforming to plans (Adapting over Conforming)

I used the agile manifesto format because, for example, although conforming to plan may be a reasonable strategy in some circumstances, adapting to change is usually more important. It is not a matter of either/or, but a matter of emphasis, of primary style. Both agile and traditional managers plan; it's how they view plans that differs.

> *A traditional project manager focuses on following the plan with minimal changes, whereas an agile leader focuses on adapting successfully to inevitable changes.*

I've worked with some team leaders who are good team managers, but overly conforming, and others who are good at adapting, but poor at self-organizing team leadership. A good agile leader must be both. Unfortunately, I've found a fair number of teams and their leaders who say, "we are agile," but they exhibit neither team leadership nor an adapting mindset. These are teams who think agile is about some group of practices. Both agile and traditional leaders need to utilize risk management practices, for example, so it is difficult to say "this set of project management practices is agile; this other set is not agile." A particular set of practices can help evaluate mindset, but they are indicators, not determinants. I remember arguments like—"code reviews are not agile, pair programming is agile." But I've worked with very agile teams who used code reviews, and questionably agile teams who used pair programming. Agility is principally about mindset, not practices.

Too often project managers (and those above them) focus on the usual constraints of time and cost. There are times when value doesn't seem to matter at all—it's schedule, schedule, schedule, as if value will take care of itself. Then there are those who focus on scope and detailed requirements, but not the end goal of value. For many managers, the traditional project management iron triangle dominates—scope, schedule, cost. Nowhere in that triangle are either quality (particularly technical quality that is a key determinant of continuous value), nor feature value itself. The assumption gets made that delivering on scope, schedule, and cost means delivering value. But that can be a false assumption because a "requirement" may get thrown into the project without respect to value. Given that studies show over 50% of software functionality is rarely or never used, the idea that focusing on scope and requirements yields value is mistaken.

These three leadership values work together. For example, if your primary project management style is conformance to plan, then the plan will be viewed as a collection of well-defined—and infrequently changing—tasks. Managing tasks rather than people and teams is a natural outgrowth of a focus on conforming to plans. Conversely, viewing a project as dynamic and ever changing means that the ability to adapt is paramount, and adapting relies on innovative thinking and deep understanding of the goal. How goals are reached change often during the project, making detailed task lists less than useful in reaching those goals.

Just because these three value statements are simple doesn't mean they are simple to implement. In fact, they are often very difficult to implement, as any behavioral change can be. Giving up detailed task management can be wrenching for project managers, making them feel disconnected from something concrete and left to manage intangibles. They fear giving up deterministic plans can lead to fluidity, frustration, and the feeling of loss of control.

In looking at whether these three main traits—Value, Teams, Adaptation—cover all bases, one might question the lack of a customer-oriented value. But, between collaborating with customers (Team) and delivering value to customers (Value), I felt that customer focus did not need to become a fourth differentiating category (as in the Agile Manifesto). The other reason I left it out was that my focus was on differentiating traits, not identifying important traits. Getting close to customers is a critical business trait, whether a company is agile or not. It seemed to be important, but not as differentiating as the other three.

So a good set of questions to determine whether a project leader—or even an individual contributor—has an agile mindset might be, "In what specific ways and with what practices do you focus on value first and constraints last?" "In what specific ways and with what practices do you manage teams rather than tasks?" "In what specific ways and with what practices do you adapt to change rather than conform to plans?" Try these out in your organization to get a feel for your agile maturity.

Agile Performance Measurement

One of the key goals of this second edition of *Agile Project Management* is to discuss performance measurement issues and introduce the Agile Triangle as a replacement for the traditional Iron Triangle of project management.[4] If change, adaptation, and flexibility are the trademarks of agile projects, and conforming to plan is the trademark of traditional projects, then why do we still measure success on agile projects using the traditional framework? This may be the key reason that thwarts wider agile adoption in organizations: Agile teams are striving to meet one set of goals and managers and executives are measuring against another set. Until this gap is bridged, agile project management and development will be relegated to "just another technical approach" status.

Measuring success it tricky. Motorola's ill-fated, multibillion-dollar satellite-based Iridium project was a spectacular failure in the market.

---

[4] I had many conversations with colleague David Spann about changing performance measures. My thanks to David for his contribution to this discussion.

Meanwhile, the movie *Titanic*, which was severely over budget and schedule—and viewed by early pundits as a $200 million flop awaiting release—was the first movie to generate over $1 billion in worldwide revenue. By common constraint-based project management measures of success—scope, cost, and schedule—*Titanic* was a failure. Within some circles, Iridium was considered a success because it fulfilled the original specifications. Using the agile triangle, the Titanic project would be considered a success—it delivered value even though it exceeded its constraints. Iridium would have been considered a failure because it failed to deliver value, even though from a technical perspective it succeeded.

So to attain significant levels of improvement in an organization, we have to address how performance is measured. Figure 1-3 shows the transition to a new way of measuring success. The traditional iron triangle of project management, the left-most triangle, consists of scope, schedule, and cost. In many cases scope was the primary driver (because the false assumption was made that scope was known early in the project) and cost and schedule varied—although many managers attempt to lock down all three dimensions.

The second triangle represents an early view of measuring agile development where schedule was fixed (timeboxed) and scope was allowed to vary—that is, time was used as a fixed constraint. Unfortunately, this second triangle still conforms to the existing iron triangle measures. Success, in many organizations and perpetuated by research organizations like the Standish Group, is still viewed as conformance to cost, schedule, and scope. If conformance to plan defines success, then how will agile projects that adapt continuously ever be deemed successful?

This brings up the third triangle in Figure 1-3, the Agile Triangle. The measures here are value (to the customer), quality (required to deliver continuous value to the customer), and constraints (scope, schedule, and cost). Constraints are still important project parameters, but they are not the project's goal. Value is the goal and constraints may need to be adjusted as the project moves forward to increase customer value. Schedule might still be a fixed constraint, but then scope could be adjusted to deliver the highest value within the schedule constraint. If we want adaptability we must reward it. Adjusting constraints to meet value or quality goals helps organizations meet this need. To summarize:

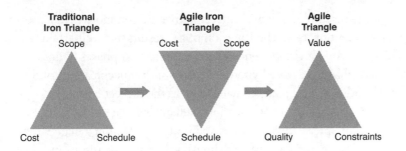

Figure 1-3
The Evolution to an Agile Triangle

- *Value goal*: Build a releasable product
- *Quality goal*: Build a reliable, adaptable product
- *Constraint goal*: Achieve value and quality goals within acceptable constraints

Chapter 13, "Beyond Scope, Schedule, and Cost: Measuring Agile Performance" addresses this topic in detail, with special consideration of why focusing on quality—advocated by all, implemented by few—is critical to value delivery. Also, Chapter 8, "Advanced Release Planning," addresses the need for calculating value points for product features. If we are serious about focusing on value, then we have to move from qualitative value determination to a more quantitative one.

The APM Framework

Project management processes and performance measures are different for exploration- and experimentation-based approaches than they are for production- and specification-based ones. Production-oriented project management processes and practices emphasize complete early planning and requirements specification with minimal ongoing change. Exploration-based processes emphasize nominal early planning, good enough requirements, and experimental and evolutionary design with significant ongoing learning and change. Each approach has its place, but the lifecycle framework for the one has a very different flavor from the other. Within a four-layer enterprise agile framework (described in Chapter 5, "An Agile Project Management Model" the APM delivery approach consists of five phases, each with supporting practices: Envision, Speculate, Explore, Adapt, and Close.

These phases resemble a scientific investigative process more than a production management process. The Envision phase results in a well-articulated business or product vision—enough to keep the next phases bounded. In the Speculate phase, the team hypothesizes about the specifications of the product and builds a release plan, knowing that as the project continues both technology and customer specifications will evolve as new knowledge is gained. The Explore phase then becomes an iterative operation in which the features and stories are implemented. In the Adapt phase, the results of these experiments are subjected to technical, customer, and business case review, and adaptive actions are incorporated into the next iteration.

Within this general APM framework, a set of recommended practices enable and guide the successful completion of the work effort. Some of these practices are simple and straightforward, like the product vision box and project data sheet. Customer focus groups, iterative planning, workload self-management, and participatory decision making help grow an agile, adaptive culture. Values and guiding principles describe the *why* of APM, and practices describe the *how*.

Performance Possibilities

So, what are the possibilities of agile development? Quite a number of surveys and studies have been done about agile software development, most of which are anecdotal or qualitative surveys. One of the most comprehensive surveys has been done annually by Version One. Highlights of their 3rd Annual State of Agile Development, released in the fall of 2008 include:

- "Teams practicing Agile Development are getting larger and more distributed.
  - 32% of respondents are from development groups with over 250 people
  - 76% of respondents are from development groups with over 20 people
- Agile development is delivering meaningful and measurable business results. Respondents reporting specific improvements greater than 10% include:
  - Increased Productivity – 89% of respondents
  - Reduced Software Defects – 84% of respondents

- Accelerated Time-to-Market – 82% of respondents
- Reduced Cost – 66% of respondents"

Figure 1-4
Metrics Summary

Metrics Summary

- In one organization agile methods helped reduce defect levels by 83% over previous non-agile projects.
- In two software companies, the productivity index numbers recorded for their project were among the highest recorded in a data base of 7,500 projects.
- Agile teams have shattered the previous formula from traditional projects that doubling staff increased defects by 2-6 times. Agile teams can increase staff without a corresponding increase in defects.
- Immature agile teams, those that fail to do comprehensive automated testing, improve schedule performance, but do not reduce defect levels from the norm.
- Mature agile teams, who do comprehensive automated testing, improve both schedule performance and reduce defect levels.
                                        --Source Michael Mah, Cutter Study

Although qualitative surveys such as this provide useful information, a series of quantitative studies done by colleague Michael Mah, Managing Partner of QSM Associates, provide a better picture of the possible. For example, 89% of the respondents to the VersionOne survey reported increased productivity, but Mah's work provides a look at the magnitude of the improvement, as summarized in Figure 1-4.

Tables 1-1 and 1-2 summarize two of Mah's studies.[5] The first shows improvements at a scientific instrument company between several pre-agile projects and several agile ones. The most important figure is the 84% defect reduction, which drove the other improvements. The second figure, widely reported, is from BMC Software, Inc. This data was from a team of about 100 engineers, distributed across multiple locations. They were able to deliver with a 68% schedule improvement over norms by doubling normal staffing levels (at a somewhat lower overall cost because of the shorter schedule). The most significant number is actually the 11% reduction in defects, because of the long-time norm from Mah's database of projects that doubling staff results at least quadrupling defects. Projects from BMC Software and Follett Software, two participants in Mah's study, scored in the top 5% of 7,500 projects from across the world in their overall productivity index.

[5] Michael Mah. "How Agile Projects Measure Up, and What This Means to You." Cutter Agile Product and Project Management Executive Report, vol. 9, no.6, September, 2008.

The bottom line—agile methods have the potential to make a huge difference in competitive advantage. They can produce orders of magnitude improvements in productivity, quality, and schedule compression, which in turn can change entire business models.

Table 1-1
Scientific Instrument Company: Improvements in Performance[6]

	Previous Performance	Current Performance	Percent Improvement
Project Cost	$2.8 Million	$1.1 Million	61%
Project Schedule	18 months	13.5 months	24%
Cumulative Defects	2,270	381	83%
Staffing	18	11	39%

Table 1-2
BMC Software: Improvements versus Industry Norms[7]

	Industry Average	Current Performance	Improvement
Project Cost	$5.5 Million	$5.2 Million	-$.3Million (-5%)
Project Schedule	15 months	6.3 months	-8.7 months (-58%)
Cumulative Defects	713	635	78 (-11%)
Staffing	40	92	+52 (+130%)

Agile projects still fail; there is no silver bullet—even agile methods. If we believe the Agile Manifesto principle that individuals are more important

[6] Michael Mah. "How Agile Projects Measure Up, and What This Means to You". Cutter Agile Product and Project Management Executive Report, vol. 9, no.6, September, 2008.

[7] Michael Mah. "How Agile Projects Measure Up, and What This Means to You." Cutter Agile Product and Project Management Executive Report, vol. 9, no.6, September, 2008.

than process or tools, then failures are more apt to come from having the wrong people than from using the wrong process. Nevertheless, process isn't unimportant and Mah's comprehensive metrics studies show that agile processes improve performance.

Final Thoughts

The objective of this book is to outline the values, principles, and practices of Agile Project Management—to describe what I believe constitutes a better approach to project management. I hope you will find that the concepts and practices of APM will help you achieve your goals of delivering innovative products to customers and improving your work environment.

Many, if not most of the practices of APM are not new. Iterative lifecycle development, for example, has been around since the 1950s (Larman 2004). Good practices for building a project community have developed steadily over the years. Fundamental project management practices have evolved, and many are useful in fast-moving, rapidly changing projects.[8]

So is APM new? Well, yes and no. Complex Adaptive Systems theory tells us that biological agents evolve by recombining existing building blocks until a different organism emerges. APM involves carefully selecting existing building blocks—practices that have proven useful to teams in the past—and linking these practices to core values and a conceptual framework that draws on CAS theory as its foundation. The "combination" of all these building blocks—practices, values, and conceptual framework—result in Agile Project Management. APM draws on a rich project management legacy, but it is very selective about which parts of that legacy it incorporates. APM also draws on a rich legacy of management, manufacturing, and software development literature and practice that incorporates a worldview and ideological foundation better suited to mobility and speed.

APM isn't for everyone or every project; it is *not* a universal best practice. APM works well for certain problem types, in certain types of organi-

---

[8] For an excellent mapping of traditional and agile project management practices see *The Software Project Manager's Bridge to Agility,* Michele Sliger and Stacia Broderick, 2008.

zations, with people who have a particular cultural perspective, and for leaders who have a certain worldview. It thrives in innovative cultures and on projects in which speed, mobility, and quality are all key to success. APM is not defined by a small set of practices and techniques. It defines a strategic capability to deliver releasable products, to create and respond to change, to balance flexibility and structure, to draw creativity and innovation out of a development team, and to lead organizations through turbulence and uncertainty. People are guided by their value systems, so creating an agile team depends on aligning with a value system—which is why implementing APM will be nearly impossible for some teams and organizations. APM is value driven because people are value driven. A team can employ agile practices, but it won't achieve the potential benefit of agile development without embracing agile values and principles.

Chapter 2

Value over Constraints

The agile value "Delivering Value over Meeting Constraints" provides a focus for rethinking how we measure performance on projects. Although constraints such as cost and time are important, they should be secondary to creating value for customers. All too often, we focus on what is easily measurable and ignore really important characteristics that are harder to quantify. Agile development attempts to change that bias and focus on the most important things, and value is at the top of that list.

Traditional project managers tend to focus on requirements as the definition of scope, and then concentrate on delivering those requirements. Agile project leaders focus on delivering value and are constantly asking questions about whether different renditions of scope are worth the value they deliver. Traditional teams also focus on delivering to scope, schedule, and cost constraints. The traditional rationale goes that development teams have no control over outcomes or value, therefore they should not be held accountable for them. However, when a development team is divorced from outcomes they become fixated on requirements, requirements that should change as projects progress, but often don't because they are deemed a critical piece of performance measurement. When teams are focused on outcomes, even those over which they have minimal control, they are more apt to deliver true business value.

Outcomes indicators include product vision, business objectives, and capabilities (high-level product functionality), not detail requirements. These outcome characteristics define a *releasable product* and quality objectives define a *reliable and adaptable* (works today, easy to enhance) product. These are the critical value traits, then teams need to strive to meet constraints—scope, schedule, and cost—but as secondary in importance to the value components. In many, if not most, agile projects schedule becomes the most critical constraint and is timeboxed (fixed) and scope varies.

Project leaders need to focus on value in several ways: value determination (with product owners), value prioritization (backlog management), and value creation (iterative development). Although value determination lies primarily with business managers and product management, project leaders often have some involvement in cost/benefit analysis or value judgments (particularly in product companies). Value prioritization again lies more with product managers, but project leaders are involved (particularly in the case of non customer-facing or technical stories). Value prioritization also involves managing the product backlog. Value creation, within the development team, involves activities such as collaborating with customers, running customer focus groups, and technical debt reduction (which addresses quality and long-term value delivery). There are many ways in which the project leader can foster a value-oriented perspective within the team. It's a far cry from the traditional—scope, schedule, cost—fixation.

Continuous Flow of Customer Value

> *"We increase return on investment by making continuous flow of value our focus." (The Declaration of Interdependence)*

There are a couple of key terms in the return on investment principle—continuous flow and value. Value deals with business or organizational outcomes, which is most often related to financial gains (or potential financial gains as would be the case with an objective such as increasing market share). Continuous flow reflects the need for leaders to view value over time—during both the current and future projects. Software in particular needs to change at the pace of business. Delivering version 1 of the software in a timely manner is important, but even more important may be delivering a high-quality product that is easily adaptable to future needs.

A benefit of continuous feature delivery is that for some products, software being a good example, incremental releases can provide early benefits.

Rather than wait 12 or 18 months for new software features, incremental delivery can deliver features to customers quarterly or even more frequently. Incremental releases can favorably alter ROI calculations because they allow product managers to address opportunities that would be lost by waiting 18 months. However, some products that can be developed iteratively using simulations or prototypes are very difficult to release incrementally (medical instruments for example). As the battle over Web browsers showed in the late 1990s, customers sometimes don't want to assimilate new product releases every three to four months.

Customers and product managers drive agile development. The product team (customers, product managers, product specialists) and the development team form a partnership in which each has specific roles, responsibilities, and accountabilities. In highly volatile, ambiguous, and uncertain new product development efforts, the customer-developer relationship needs to be as collaborative as possible.

Customers define capabilities that provide value and the business objectives that assist in quantifying that value. Today, value arises from implementing capabilities as they evolve over the life of a project. After a product has been initially delivered, future benefits are a function of how quickly and cost effectively the product can be adapted to new capabilities that arise. Products that meet today's customer requirements but cannot adapt easily to future needs are doomed to short life spans.

> *The formula for success is simple: deliver today, adapt tomorrow.*

Although this may appear to be a simple principle it is one that must be emphasized over and over lest team members forget. When organizations get bigger and administrivia increases, when compliance activities take a larger and larger portion of a team's time, when the communications gap between customers and team members widens, and when project plans focus on interminable intermediate artifacts, delivering something useful to the customer gets lost.[1]

---

[1]In this book, the term "customer" represents a wide range of entities—commercial business-to-business customers, retail consumers, and customers internal to an organization. The people included in each of these instances vary from organization to organization. I will use the terms "product team" to represent of all the potential combinations of customers and others such as executives who approve purchase and product managers, who coordinate customer interactions with development organizations.

The goal of a project team is to deliver value to customers. In defining customer value, one question always comes to the fore, "Who are the customers? Are they users of the product, or managers, or other stakeholders?" A direct answer is that the *customer* is the individual or group that uses the created product to generate business value or, in the case of retail products, the person who uses the product. Customers define value and are the judges of user experience. This definition separates customers from other stakeholders, so in this book the word "stakeholders" represents these other individuals associated with the project who may assist in defining business objectives or constraints.

If we want products that deliver outstanding customer value, then we must have a customer-developer partnership, one with responsibilities and accountability on both sides (and similar relationships with key suppliers). Agile teams constantly seek customer involvement and are always asking the question, "Is what we are doing useful in meeting your business goals?"

The success of any product involves meeting expectations—those of the ultimate customer, those of stakeholders, and those of the team itself. There is a big difference between requirements and expectations: Requirements are tangible, expectations intangible. Yet ultimately it is the intangible expectations against which actual results will be measured. Cultivating committed customers and stakeholders means involving them in dialogue about both requirements and expectations. As colleague Ken Delcol comments, "This also includes the Kenny Rogers school of managing the communications with customers and stakeholders—know when to hold, when to fold, when to walk away, and when to run. Project leaders must have the business savvy to understand this."

There are three particularly important issues involved in delivering customer value: focusing on innovation rather than efficiency and optimization, concentrating on execution, and lean thinking.

Innovation

> "We live in a time where creativity, innovation, and imagination drive the world." (Tom Wujec and Sandra Muscat 2002)

Innovation drives companies. The core ideology at 3M has always emphasized innovation. In early 2003 General Electric changed its motto to,

"Explore Imagination at Work." Jeffrey Immelt, chairman and CEO of GE, placed a high priority on innovation and new business. "The companies that know how to develop things are ultimately going to create the most shareholder value. It's as simple as that," says Immelt (Budeir 2003). In 2009, the imagination slogan still introduces GE on the first page of its Web site. Many companies have innovation initiatives; fewer are willing to create processes and practices that directly support those initiatives. Switching from delivering documentation artifacts—characteristic of a serial development style—to delivering iterative versions of the real product is one of those mind and practice shifts that supports innovation.

Innovation usually offers the highest levels of value creation in a company's project portfolio. Innovation may come in the form of new products, new business models, new processes, or new performance initiatives. Creating new products and services differs from making minor enhancements to existing ones. The first must focus on innovation and adaptability, whereas the second usually focuses on efficiency and optimization. Efficiency delivers products and services that we can think of. Innovation delivers products that we can barely imagine. Efficiency and optimization are appropriate drivers for a production project, whereas innovation and creativity should drive an exploration-type project. A production mindset can restrict our vision to what appears doable. An exploration mindset helps us explore what seems impossible.

Optimization implies that we already know how to do something but that we now need to improve it. Innovation implies that we don't know how to do something, and searching for that knowledge is paramount. No project, no product development effort is all one way or all the other, but project leaders (team members, customers, and executives) should understand this fundamental difference when deciding how to plan and manage projects. APM's core purpose of creating innovative new products and services means dealing with constant technological and competitive change, generating novel ideas, and continually reducing product development schedules.

Execution

When project leaders focus on delivery, they add value to projects. When they focus on planning and control, they tend to add overhead.[2]

A quick review of the general management literature uncovers hundreds of books on leadership and strategy, but interestingly enough, very few on how to actually execute. Ram Charan, a distinguished author and consultant to CEOs, echoes this observation. "As I facilitated meetings at the CEO and division levels, I watched and studied, and I saw that leaders placed too much emphasis on what some call high-level strategy, on intellectualizing and philosophizing, and not enough on implementation" (Bossidy and Charan 2002).

With respect to project management, Greg Howell and Lauri Koskela (2002) argue that traditional project management practices focus too much on management-as-planning and a thermostat model for control, and not enough on what the major project management focus should be—execution.

According to Howell and Koskela, the common project management approach is composed of three processes that exchange information—planning, controlling, and executing. In construction projects, they see several troubling aspects of traditional planning. First, the motivation for planning often comes from outside the project; that is, plans are developed to satisfy legal, regulatory, or management requirements rather than being based on the work that needs to be accomplished. Second, the motivation to plan often relates more to the desire for control than the needs of actual work execution, perhaps because the people planning the work are not involved in the doing of the work. This happens constantly in software development, where the task-based planning that project managers use for control has little relationship to how software engineers really work. Third, planning and control become the focal points; execution is considered of minor importance, and legitimizing the project takes precedence over producing results.

Control has historically centered on correction rather than learning, because plans were viewed as reasonably correct, and translating the plan into action was considered a simple process. Witness the conventional "wisdom" that construction itself (carpentry, electrical, plumbing, etc.) is merely manual,

---

[2] Ken Delcol observes, "The reality in NPD is that you need both, and the trick is balance, which changes through the development lifecycle. Most people don't get this."

mechanical work without much decision making or creativity (just follow the plans) or that software programming is just coding what's specified. If plans are viewed as correct, then control focuses on fixing mistakes and explaining discrepancies, not learning something new that might legitimately alter the plans.

APM is an execution-biased model, not a planning-and-control-biased model. In APM, the project leader's primary role is to facilitate creation of a product vision and guide the team toward making that vision a reality, not to develop plans and schedules and control progress such that the "plan" is implemented. However, we need to interpret the foregoing ideas carefully—APM is *not* an anti-planning model. Planning (and control) is an integral part of APM; it is just not the focal point. As with many aspects of agile development, there is a wide gap between one thing being *less* important than something else and being *un*important.

Once teams focus on execution, the critical next step concentrates on value-adding activities, those that assist the team in delivering results, rather than those that merely ensure compliance.

Lean Thinking

Many of the ideas of the agile movement first arose within lean manufacturing, which began in the automotive industry in Japan in the 1980s. One of the fundamental tenets of lean manufacturing is the systematic elimination of waste; that is, any activity that doesn't deliver value to the customer. One way to streamline projects (doing fewer things, doing the right things, eliminating bottlenecks) involves differentiating between delivery activities and compliance activities and applying appropriate strategies to each.

Whereas lean manufacturing ideas have been used a while, lean product development ideas, especially those of Toyota, have gained less recognition. The Toyota development system offers huge potential productivity gains by eliminating non-value-adding compliance activities—many organizations stand to increase their productivity *three to four times*! Allen Ward popularized many of the ideas from Toyota's lean product development system. When Ward asked Toyota's American engineers and managers how much time they spend adding value (i.e., actually doing engineering work), their response averages 80%. The same question asked of engineers and managers at American automobile companies averages 20%. How can you compete with companies that are getting four times as much value-adding work from their development engineers (Kennedy 2003)? Maybe if the American auto companies employed more lean thinking the industry would be much better off today.

Try this survey in your organization, but be prepared for a shock. Ask your entire staff or your project team, including managers, how much time they spend doing engineering or development activities—how much time do they spend adding value to the customer? How many of your "improvement" initiatives (CMM, ISO, Six Sigma, TQM, BPR) have just added layer after layer of forms, procedures, meetings, and approvals to teams trying desperately to produce something useful? Too much structure not only kills initiative and innovation, it consumes enormous chunks of time. The fundamental issue is not that these initiatives are valueless, because they are not, but that they fundamentally value process over individual knowledge and capability.

The issues surrounding delivery versus compliance activities have special significance for project leaders. First, project leaders need to analyze project activities to maximize time spent on delivery. Second, project leaders must analyze their own activities to determine whether they are contributing to delivery or compliance. For example, when a project leader creates a status report for management, she is "complying" with a management dictum. However, when she is coordinating the activities between two feature teams or assisting a team in reaching a critical design decision, she is contributing to delivery—she adds value to the delivery process.

Iterative, Feature-Based Delivery

> *If you want to innovate, you have to iterate!*

Traditional waterfall methods deliver value at the end of the project, often months or years after the project begins. Agile projects can deliver value quickly and incrementally during the life of the project. Capturing value early and often can significantly improve a project's return on investment, and utilizing iterative, feature-based delivery is the cornerstone practice in making that happen.

Agile development and project management stress delivery of versions of the actual product, or in the case of high-cost materials, effective simulations or models of the actual product. Finishing a requirements document verifies that a team has successfully gathered a set of requirements. Completing and demonstrating a set of working product features verifies that the development team can actually deliver something tangible to the customer. Working features provide dependable feedback into the development process in ways that documentation cannot.

The serial, or waterfall, development life cycle has been under attack for years. For example, Donald Reinertsen (1997) writes, "The vast majority of academic literature on product development is skewed towards the sequential approach. This is in striking contrast to the enormous shift that has taken place in managerial practice towards a more concurrent approach."

In the software development field, the attack on waterfall approaches goes back decades, as thoroughly documented by Craig Larman (2004). As Larman recalls, a 1970 paper by Winston Royce was credited with starting the "waterfall" trend. In fact, Royce was an advocate of iterative development for anything more than simple projects. The reliance on waterfall development in software began to change in the late 1980s with the introduction of Spiral (Barry Boehm) and Evolutionary (Tom Gilb) models. In the early 1990s the move to iterative models increased with the introduction of Rapid Application Development (RAD) and then accelerated with the rise of agile methods in the last decade.

But even though waterfall approaches have been attacked as too simplistic, not only do they continue to be widely used, they continue to influence contracting procedures and executive perspectives. So to respond to the widespread misinformation about waterfall development, teams that practice APM need to understand how iterative, feature-based delivery is critical to innovative product development.

The iterative piece of agile can be defined by four key terms: iterative, feature-based, timeboxed, and incremental. *Iterative* development means that we build a partial version of a product and then expand that version through successive short time periods of development followed by reviews and adaptations. *Feature-based* delivery means that the engineering team builds features of the final product or, particularly with industrial products, at least a close representation of the final product (such as a simulation model).

Iterations are constrained to produce a result within a certain period of time—a timebox (as short as 1–4 weeks for software). *Timeboxes* force closure;

they force us to make something concrete, often before we are quite ready. *Incremental* development means that we build these products such that they could be deployed at the end of one or more of the iterations. For software companies, iterative development and incremental delivery have become a competitive advantage.

Short, timeboxed iterations are a fixture of APM. However, iterations are only half the story—features, rather than tasks, are the other. Customers don't understand, nor do they care about, the engineering tasks required to build a DVD player or an automobile. They do, however, understand the features of each of those products.

If we are to build products that deliver value each and every iteration, then the highest-level concern in the process must be features about which the customer or product manager can say, "Yes, that is the feature we want, and it is valuable." Saying to the customer at the end of milestone 1, "Yes, we finished the relational database schema," or "We got the CAD drawings of the fluid transfer valve done" just doesn't work. This information isn't something the customer can relate to, much less make a priority decision about.

The feature delivery approach helps define a workable interface between customers and product developers. Customers get to schedule and prioritize features; engineers figure out what tasks will be necessary to deliver those features and what it will take in terms of time and cost. This feature-based approach applies to everyone else, too. Senior management is restricted to feature management, rather than task management; they can cut features but not tasks (testing for example).

For projects and products in which the requirements can evolve over time, it is critical that the results reviewed by customers during the development process be as close to the actual product as possible. Customers have a very difficult time visualizing from documents how a product will function, which is why in industry after industry companies have embraced modeling, simulations, and prototyping to improve the feedback loop from customers to the development teams. Development and product teams also need common ground, a shared space in which to discuss, debate, and decide on critical product feature issues. Features indicate real, not artificial, progress. Project teams, product managers, customers, and stakeholders are thus forced to confront the difficult tradeoff decisions.

Iterative development, when accompanied with reasonable end-of-iteration reviews—product, technical, process, team—is also self-correcting. Probably the most important aspect of self-correction is customer feedback on the product as it evolves. As these evolutionary changes get incorporated in later iterations, the customer's confidence in the product grows, or conversely, it becomes clear that the product isn't working and should be abandoned—early.

Driving exploration is critical, but knowing when to stop is also. Product development is exploring with a purpose, delivering value within a set of constraints. Frequent, timeboxed iterations compel the development and product teams and executives to make difficult tradeoff decisions early and often during the project. Feature delivery contributes to realistic evaluations because product managers can look at tangible, verifiable results.

> *In my early years of iterative development, I thought timeboxes were actually about time. What I came to realize is that timeboxes are actually about forcing tough decisions.*

If a team plans to deliver 14 features in an iteration and it can produce only 10, then the development team, product team, and possibly the executive sponsor must face the shortfall and decide what actions to take. Many factors will influence the decision making—whether this iteration is early in the project or late, whether the shortfall will impact the delivery date or product viability (every product has set of features that constitute the minimum viable set)—but the salient point is that these decisions are addressed frequently in an agile project.

All too often, sequentially developed products reach the final stages only to discover major problems when the options available are limited. By forcing difficult decisions early and often, timeboxed feature delivery gives the team more options for solving problems. Iterations allow you to manage risk sooner—you do not have to build the whole product to find out whether you can meet a particular specification or overcome a sticky design problem.

Technical Excellence

Agile developers are dedicated to technical excellence—not because of aesthetics (although that may be a rationale for some), but because a dedication to technical excellence delivers customer value. Project leaders must be champions of technical excellence; they must support and advocate technical excellence while maintaining a watchful eye on other project objectives.

High quality ensures that companies will be able to deliver value in the future. Many software products suffer from technical debt, the accumulation of problems caused by poor quality practices. Few products today, particularly industrial products, are one-shot wonders. Products evolve over time, improving constantly. For example, the Boeing 747 passenger jet has been in existence for more than four decades, but the 747-400 planes rolling off the assembly line today are much different than the 100 series planes first put into service in January 1970.

In discussing the Toyota lean product development system, Michael Kennedy (2003) laments that in too many organizations project management has become focused on administrative excellence rather than technical excellence. He goes on to state that one of the four pillars of the Toyota system is an "Expert Engineering Workforce," which encourages both technical excellence and individual responsibility.

Some critics consider agile methods to be ad hoc, undisciplined, and, ultimately, technically inferior. They are wrong—there is a big difference between discipline and formality. First, for traditionalists, who thrive on process, procedure, and documentation, the informality of agile methods is interpreted as undisciplined. Nothing could be further from reality. Discipline is doing what you said you would do. Using this definition, many organizations with elaborate formality fail—they have volumes of processes, procedures, forms, and documents that are systematically ignored. Agile organizations have less-elaborate formal structures, but they tend to follow the ones they have.

Second, the difference of opinion isn't over *whether* technical quality is important but over *how* technical quality can be achieved. Critics say, "Agile development ignores design." What they are really objecting to is the lack of extensive up-front design, believing that it is the only valid design process. Agile developers believe that iterative, emergent design and frequent feedback yield superior designs. So again, it's not a question of design versus ad hoc development, but a disagreement over design approach.

As a software development consultant, I've never encountered a successful software company (although my sample size is limited) in which the team and project leaders were not technically savvy. Whether a company is building electronic instrumentation, jet engines, or pure software products, project leaders need specific technical expertise to adequately manage projects. Championing technical excellence requires that the project leader, and team members in general, understand what technical excellence means—in the product, the technology, and in the skills of the people doing the work. They must understand, within the context of their specific product, the difference between excellence and perfection. No company can afford to produce a *perfect* product, but building a product that delivers customer value and maintains its technical integrity is essential to commercial success and the technical team's satisfaction.

One of the reasons project leaders (in their role as decision makers or influencers) need a technical background is that while technical excellence is a laudable goal, there may be considerably different approaches to achieving that excellence. Should the software team focus on refactoring, automated testing, and simple design? Extensive front-end modeling? Or some balance of the two? Project leaders need to be involved with the team in debating and deciding on the technical approach to development, as well as keeping the team aware of the business objectives as technical issues are decided. The project leaders may not make the decision, but they should be knowledgeable enough to steer the interactions between team members, make sure project data (e.g., architectural platform constraints) are fully understood by the team, and keep the team on track in making timely technical decisions. Poor technical decisions often manifest over time as process problems and people then get busy trying to fix unbroken processes.

Project leaders must champion technical excellence because therein lies the key to adaptability and low-cost iteration that drive long-term product success. Project leaders are jugglers, always keeping multiple balls in the air. They must be aware, for example, of the point at which their team starts tipping the balance from technical excellence to perfection. They must be aware when the product manager pushes too hard for speed and features over adaptability. Helping teams find and maintain these balance points is nearly impossible unless the project leader has the necessary technical background. The project leader doesn't have to *be* a technical guru, but he has to know enough to converse with one.

Simplicity

> *"When you want your boat to go fast, it is easier to cut anchors than add horsepower."* (Luke Hohmann)

If you want to be fast and agile, keep things simple. Speed isn't the result of simplicity, but simplicity enables speed. Furthermore, keeping things simple reduces costs and therefore adds value. If you want to be slow, rigid, and expensive, pile on the bureaucracy. A friend who once worked for NASA relayed the story of his team's unique software design criterion—least impact on documentation. The documentation revision process was so onerous and time consuming that minimizing the documentation changes became the major design objective. This is a clear example of how compliance work not only impedes delivery by draining away engineering time, it even undermines technical design decisions. Large portions of the productivity gains from agile methods come not from doing things better, but from not doing them at all.

> *Simplicity—the art of maximizing the amount of work not done—is essential.* (The Agile Manifesto)

When you simplify processes by taking out the detail task-based structures and compliance activities, you force people to think and to interact. Neither they nor their managers can use structure as a crutch. Although some structure aids agility, the overabundance of structure in many organizations gives people an excuse not to think, or bludgeons them into not thinking. Either way, people feel their contributions are devalued, and they lose any sense of personal responsibility or accountability for results.

Generative Rules

Simple principles (or rules) are one facet of "swarm intelligence" from complexity theory. This is the idea that the right set of simple rules, applied within a group of highly interactive individuals, generates complex behaviors such as innovation and creativity. Jim Donehey, former CIO of Capital

One, used four rules to help ensure everyone in his organization was working toward the same shared goals:

1. Always align IT activities with the business.
2. Use good economic judgment.
3. Be flexible.
4. Have empathy for others in the organization (Bonabeau and Meyer 2001).

Do these four rules constitute everything that Doneney's department needed to do? Of course not, but would a 400-page activity description get the job done? What Donehey wanted was bounded innovation—a department that thought for itself in a very volatile business environment, but also one that understood boundaries.

One of the key concepts of agile project management is that the practices, when driven by guiding principles, are generative, not prescriptive. Prescriptive methodologies attempt to describe every activity a team should do. The problem with prescriptive approaches is that people get lost. They have much to choose from and so little guidance as to applicability that they have trouble eliminating extraneous practices from their projects.

A set of generative practices is a minimal set that works well together as a system. It doesn't prescribe everything a team needs to do, but it identifies those practices that are of high value and should be used on nearly every project. By employing these practices, teams will generate other necessary supporting practices as part of their efforts to tailor and adapt the set to fit their unique needs. For example, when a team needs configuration control, members will figure out a minimum configuration control practice and use it.

Starting with a minimal set of practices and judiciously adding others as needed has proven to be more effective than starting with comprehensive prescriptive practices and attempting to streamline them down to something usable (Boehm and Turner 2003). Agile methods don't attempt to describe *everything* that any development effort might need in thousands of pages of documentation. Instead they describe a minimal set of activities that are needed to create swarm intelligence.

Developing a useful set of rules is not a trivial exercise because the right combination can often be counterintuitive. Apparently minor changes can have unforeseen results. Changing one practice, without understanding the interactions and the concepts of swarm intelligence, can cause an agile system to react in unforeseen ways. The guiding principles of APM, and its practices, constitute a set of rules that have been shown to work together well.

Barely Sufficient Methodology

When deciding on process, methodology, practices, documentation, or other aspects of product development, the admonition to simplify steers us toward bare sufficiency, toward streamlining, toward implementing "a little bit less than just enough." Simplicity needs to balance the need for speed and flexibility with retaining enough stability to ward off careless mistakes. Barely sufficient does not mean *in*sufficient. It does not mean "no documentation" or "no process." Furthermore, barely sufficient for a 100-person project will be very different from barely sufficient for a project of only 10 people.

John Wooden's admonition to his basketball teams seems appropriate here: "Be *quick*, but don't hurry." As author Andrew Hill (2001) recounts his playing days with Wooden, he enriches the meaning of the phrase, "Life, like basketball, must be played fast—but *never* out of control." In product development, lack of quickness results in competitive disadvantage, whereas hurrying causes mistakes. Balancing, one of the keys to agility, was part of Wooden's coaching technique. As Hill writes, "Wooden's genius was in helping his players find and maintain that razor's edge between quickness and hurrying." Finding that razor's edge isn't easy. If it was, everyone would be doing it.

An engineer who hurries to design a feature but fails to adequately review or test it creates defects that ultimately slow the project. Delivery activities done quickly and effectively speed projects, whereas overemphasis on compliance activities acts as a speed break. Selecting the activities that absolutely, positively have to be done, and doing them well, contributes to quickness. Sloppy execution of those key activities can be the consequence of hurrying.

One of the competitive advantages of finding this balance, of being quick without hurrying, is that it can force the competition into hurrying. This is actually one of the potential dangers of implementing agile methods. Less disciplined organizations and teams may confuse quickness with hurrying and misunderstand the foundational work, experience, and dedication it takes to balance on the edge. Wooden used the fast break to increase the tempo of the game enough that the opponent was pressured into hurrying. Because of his team members' discipline and work ethic, they could play faster than opponents but still be in control. Teams can use the same strategy.

> *Leaders who can coax simplifications out of the complexity, who can institute just enough process, who can find that razor's edge between quickness and hurrying have a much better chance of success.*

Delivery versus Compliance

Simplicity also means reducing overhead. APM is first and foremost about delivering value to customers. Too many project managers, too many project office members, too many organizations have drifted toward compliance as their primary, if often implicit, focus. Compliance activities, at their best, attempt to mitigate the risk of mistakes, fraud, poor performance, and financial overruns. Managers want reports. Accountants want numbers. Auditors want sign-offs. Governmental agencies want documents. Standards groups want proof of compliance. Legal departments want everything. Failure to differentiate between delivery and compliance results in ever-increasing compliance work—producing documents for regulators, lawyers, or management—while delivering products falls to secondary priority.

A very simple but infrequently used method of distinguishing delivery from compliance activities is to ask those doing the work, "Does this activity help you deliver customer value, or is it overhead?" Unfortunately, many managers and process designers don't like the answers they receive.

In one of my favorite books, *Systemantics: How Systems Work and Especially How They Fail*, John Gall (1975) warns against the rising tide of "systemism"—"the state of mindless belief in systems; the belief that systems can be made to function to achieve desired goals." Gall's point is that "the fundamental problem does not lie in any particular system but rather in *systems as such*." These systems become the goal rather than the means to a goal.

Adherents of these "systemisms" would argue that implementing these programs *should not* result in losing track of the primary goal (results rather than process). But Gall points out how this subversion becomes inevitable through two of his axioms: 1) "Systems Tend to Expand to Fill the Known Universe" and 2) "Systems Tend to Oppose Their Own Proper Functions"(Gall 1975).

Consider, for example, the rounds of procedures and mounds of documentation that are required to gain International Organization for Standardization (ISO) certification. I worked with a company that had workaround after workaround to circumvent its processes. Changing the standard processes was so burdensome ISO that everyone used workarounds. However, they did have one solution for the volumes of process documents—a sophisticated automation system in which just the list of processes went on for page after page after page. I examined an auditor's report (ISO certification requires periodic audits) of some 10 pages that were filled with compliance issues such as failures to sign or date a form or the absence of some document. There was not a single substantive delivery issue mentioned in the report! Managers had to spend time analyzing this audit report and then writing another report about how they would keep these terrible things from happening again, when of course their only concern was to placate the auditors, not to make meaningful improvements in the system.

Clearly, this company's ISO "system" had run amok. However, the system had become so ingrained in the company—and maintaining certification such a mantra—that getting out from under the burden was proving exceedingly difficult. This illustrates Gall's first axiom, which says systems tend to expand to fill the known universe. After they are underway, systems become very difficult to change, and compliance, not delivery, becomes the goal. At the point where employees are trying to deliver results, these systems are almost universally hated because they impede progress. The systems, as Gall says, inevitably tend to oppose their own proper functioning.

Project leaders need to relieve the team from as much compliance work as possible, even if that means taking on the tasks themselves. Several years ago, when talking to a project leader of a very successful CMM Level 5–certified software development organization, I asked him about all the documentation, metrics, and reporting work that went into certification. "Oh," he said, "I take care of most of that myself. The development team needs to concentrate on the real work."

It is important to note that there are good reasons for some compliance activities. Every organization, every company, every team has legitimate compliance issues. For example, in the automotive industry, an enormous volume of documentation must be retained for potential product liability lawsuits and government crash investigations. In the pharmaceutical industry, companies may decry US Food and Drug Administration (FDA) inefficiencies, but few consumers would want to buy drugs unfettered by federal regulation. Executives have a responsibility to shareholders, employees, and customers to exercise oversight, which may take the form of audits, project status reports, purchasing policies, or certifications. For necessary compliance activities, the strategy should be to minimize them and *get them off the critical path and the critical people.*

Final Thoughts

Traditional project management methods focus on adhering to plans for scope, schedule, and cost. But this formula often causes teams to deliver lower value. Plans rapidly go out of date, but business goals and objectives tend to remain—how to meet them changes. By focusing on value, both current and future, teams can align themselves with the goals of the organization much more effectively. Whether it's explicit valuing of product capabilities (Chapter 8), embracing technical excellence (Chapter 9), or changing measures of success (Chapter 13), defining practices that help teams deliver on "value over constraints" will be a major theme of this book (see Figure 2-1).

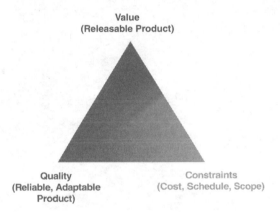

Value
(Releasable Product)

Quality
(Reliable, Adaptable
Product)

Constraints
(Cost, Schedule, Scope)

Figure 2-1
The Agile Triangle

Chapter 3

Teams over Tasks

Agile leaders *lead* teams, non-agile ones *manage* tasks. How many project managers spend hours detailing tasks into Microsoft Project and then spend more hours ticking off task completions? Unfortunately, many project managers like this task oriented-approach because it is concrete, definable, and completion seems finite. Leading teams, on the other hand, seems fuzzy, messy, un-definable, and never complete. So naturally some people gravitate to the easier—managing tasks.

APM focuses on team management, from building self-organizing teams to developing a servant leadership style. It is both more difficult, and ultimately more rewarding than managing tasks. In an agile project the team takes care of the tasks and the project leader takes care of the team. This chapter has four major themes related to building teams: leadership, building self-organizing teams, collaboration (including decision making), and customer collaboration.

Leading Teams

> *"You cannot manage men into battle: You manage things…you lead people." (Admiral Grace Hopper)*

Most projects are overmanaged and underled. What is the difference between project management and project leadership? Although there is an elusive line between them, the core difference is that management deals with complexity, whereas leadership deals with change. Without adequate management, complex projects rapidly descend into chaos. Plans, controls, budgets, and processes help project managers stave off potential project-threatening complexity. However, when uncertainty, risk, and change are prominent, these practices are insufficient and adaptation practices are required.

Leaderless teams are rudderless teams. Leaders who want to create adaptive, self-organizing teams steer rather than control—they influence, nudge, facilitate, teach, recommend, assist, urge, counsel, and, yes, direct in some instances. Project leaders should be both managers and leaders, with the importance of the latter escalating rapidly as the exploratory nature of projects increases. Good leadership contributes significantly to project success. As authors Carl Larson and Frank LaFasto (1989) point out, "Our research strongly indicates that the right person in a leadership role can add tremendous value to any collective effort."

At any organizational level people are leaders not because of what they do, but because of who they are. Authoritarian managers use power, often in the form of fear, to get people to do something their way. Leaders depend for the most part on influence rather than power, and influence derives from respect rather than fear. Respect, in turn, is based on qualities such as integrity, ability, fairness, truthfulness—in short, on character. Leaders are part of the team, and although they are given organizational authority, their real authority isn't delegated top-down but earned bottom-up. From the outside, a managed team and a led team can look the same, but from the inside they feel very different.

> *A leader's real authority isn't delegated top-down but earned bottom-up.*

Project managers who are effective at delivering in complex situations—planning in detail, creating organizational positions and roles, monitoring through detailed budget and progress reports, and solving the myriad day-to-day project problems—don't like change. Change leads to paradox and ambiguity, and these managers spend enormous energy trying to drive ambiguity and change out of their projects.

Leaders, as opposed to managers, encourage change—by creating a vision of future possibilities (which may be short on details), by interacting with a large network of people to discover new information that will help turn the product vision into reality, and by creating a sense of purpose in the endeavor that will motivate people to work on something outside the norm.

Leaders who steer rather than command are not abdicating decision making. Self-directing (as opposed to self-organizing) teams—those that theoretically don't have a single leader—tend to drift and procrastinate, which is not appropriate for fast-moving product development teams. Steering means the manager makes unilateral decisions at times, makes decisions with team involvement at times, but primarily delegates decisions to the team.

Projects, like organizations, need both leaders and managers. Unfortunately, it is often difficult to find both skill sets in the same person. And since creating a project budget is more tangible than, say, resolving the ambiguity of trying to satisfy conflicting customer needs, project management training tends to focus on tangible practices and tools. Growing leadership skills in managers is clearly possible, but it requires a dedication to understanding the differences between the two roles.

As authors Phillip Hodgson and Randall White (2001) observe, "Leadership is what crosses the frontier between what we did yesterday and what we'll do tomorrow. We'll argue…that the real mark of a leader is confidence with uncertainty—the ability to admit to it and deal with it." The authors pose six questions in Figure 3-1 that illustrate the damaging illusions of our 20th-century approaches to management.

Figure 3-1
Management Illusions

Management Illusions

- Why do you believe you are in control?
- Why do you behave as if you can predict the future, its consequences, and outcomes?
- Why do you think that because you've done it before and it worked that it will work again?
- Why do you believe everything important is measurable?
- Why do you think that words like leadership, management, and change have the same meaning for everyone?
- Why do you think that reducing uncertainty will necessarily increase certainty?

Hodgson and White 2001

Agile project leaders help their team balance at the edge of chaos—some structure, but not too much; adequate documentation, but not too much; some up-front architecture work, but not too much. Finding these balance points is the "art" of agile leadership. Although books like this can help readers understand the issues and identify practices that help, only experience can refine a leader's art. High-uncertainty projects are full of anxiety, change, and ambiguity that the team must deal with. It takes a different style of project management, a different pattern of team operation, and a different type of project leader. I've labeled this type of management *leadership-collaboration*.

A leadership-collaboration management style creates a certain kind of social architecture, one that enables organizations and teams to face the volatility of their environment. Such a social architecture resonates with concepts such as egalitarianism, competence, passion, self-discipline, and self-organization.

> *"Commanders know the objective; leaders grasp the direction. Commanders dictate; leaders influence. Controllers demand; collaborators facilitate. Controllers micro-manage; collaborators encourage. Managers who embrace the leadership-collaboration model understand their primary role is to set direction, to provide guidance, and to facilitate connecting people and teams" (Highsmith 2000).*

Jim Collins (2001) has a similar concept he refers to as a "culture of discipline," meaning self-discipline, not imposed discipline. In discussing company growth and the frequent imposition of "professional management" to control that growth, Collins says, "The company begins to hire MBAs and seasoned executives from blue-chip companies. Processes, procedures, checklists, and all the rest begin to sprout up like weeds. What was once an egalitarian environment gets replaced with a hierarchy. They create order out of chaos, but they also kill the entrepreneurial spirit. The purpose of bureaucracy is to compensate for incompetence and lack of discipline."

> *"In the Chaordic Age, success will depend less on rote and more on reason; less on the authority of the few and more on the judgment of the many; less on compulsion and more on motivation; less on external control of people and more on internal discipline" (Dee Hock 1999).*

The agile movement supports individuals and teams through dedication to the concepts of self-organization, self-discipline, egalitarianism, respect for individuals, and competency. "Agile" is a socio-technical movement driven by both the desire to create a particular work environment and the belief that an adaptive environment is critical to the goal of delivering innovative products to customers.

Building Self-Organizing (Self-Disciplined) Teams

Self-organizing teams form the core of APM. They blend freedom and responsibility, flexibility and structure. In the face of inconsistency and ambiguity, the teams strive to consistently deliver on the product vision within the project constraints. Accomplishing this requires teams with a self-organizing structure and self-disciplined individual team members. Building this kind of team is the core of an agile project leader's job.

A simple definition of a team is that it has a defined goal, consists of two or more people, and requires coordination among those people (Larson and LaFasto 1989). Beyond this definition, there are numerous variations in team composition and structure. In a self-organized team, individuals take accountability for managing their own workload, shift work among themselves based on need and best fit, and take responsibility for team effectiveness. Team members have considerable leeway in how they deliver results, they are self-disciplined in their accountability for those results, and they work within a flexible framework.

Self-organizing teams are not, as some perceive, leaderless teams. Any group left to its own devices will self-organize in some fashion, but to be effective in delivering results, it needs to be steered in the right direction.

> *Self-organizing teams aren't characterized by a lack of leadership, but by a style of leadership.*

There is a big difference between the terms "self-organizing" and "self-directing." Self-directing usually implies self-led, as various team members assume the leadership role depending upon the situation. The self-directing model runs counter to much research that indicates good leaders are a major ingredient of project and organizational success (Larson and LaFasto 1989).

Creating a self-organizing team entails

- Getting the right people
- Articulating the product vision, boundaries, and team roles (Chapter 6)
- Encouraging collaboration (next section)
- Insisting on accountability
- Fostering self-discipline
- Steering rather than control (leadership section)

Ultimately, APM is about people, their interactions, and creating an environment in which individual creativity and capability erupts to create great products. It's people, not processes, that build great products.

Get the Right People

The organization, through the project leader or other managers, has the responsibility to staff the project with the right people. Getting the right people means finding those with appropriate technical and behavioral skills. The project leader should have the authority to reject any team member that other managers might want to assign, unilaterally, to the project.

Companies often issue flowery statements about how important their people are and then tie them down with unyielding procedures and forms. In the 1990s business went through a period of infatuation with process—much of it under the banner of business process reengineering (BPR). Process literally became more important than people. BPR proponents thought that structured processes would somehow make up for mediocre individual capabilities, but no process can overcome the lack of good engineers, product managers, customers, and executives.

The agile value of people over process drives the need to get the right people. Process proponents argue that a good process will compensate for less capable staff, and therefore getting the right people isn't as critical to success as getting the right process. Agilists believe that process can provide a common framework within which people can work effectively, but it cannot replace capability and skill. Products are built by capable, skilled individuals, not by processes. Effective project leaders focus on people, product, and process—in that order. Without the right people, nothing gets built. Without a laser focus on product value, extraneous activities creep in. Without a minimum process framework, there can be inefficiency and possibly a little chaos.

Insist on Accountability

Responsibility and accountability create self-organizing teams that work. The Declaration of Interdependence contains the principle, "We boost performance through group accountability for results and shared responsibility for team effectiveness." When an individual commits to delivering a particular feature during an iteration he accepts accountability for that delivery. When the team commits to a set of features by the end of the milestone, all members of the team accept that accountability. The product manager agrees to be accountable for providing requirements information to the team. The project leader agrees to be accountable for resolving impediments to team progress. When a team member commits to provide some information to another the next day, he has agreed to be accountable for that action. When team members commit to each other, when the team commits to the customer, when the project leader commits to provide the team with a particular resource, they are all agreeing to be held accountable.

In addition, every team member has a responsibility to improve teamwork. And it is incumbent on each and every team member and the project leader to hold each other to commitments. Trust is the foundation of collaboration, and meeting one's commitments is core to building trust, and in so doing building effective teams.

Foster Self-Discipline

Self-discipline enables freedom and empowerment. When individuals and teams want more autonomy, they must exercise greater self-discipline. One of the acute dangers of process-centric development and project management is that they reduce any incentive for self-discipline. When managers impose discipline through process—"follow this process or else"—they stifle initiative and self-discipline. These same managers then turn around and complain, "Why doesn't anyone around here take any initiative or accept any responsibility?" Imposed-discipline teams accomplish things. Self-disciplined teams accomplish near-miraculous things.

Self-disciplined individuals

- Accept accountability for results
- Confront reality through rigorous thinking
- Engage in intense interaction and debate
- Work willingly within a self-organizing framework
- Respect colleagues

Dialogue, discussion, and participatory decision making are all part of building self-discipline. A series of words scattered throughout Jim Collins's book *Good to Great* (2001) create an image of the rigorous thinking and debate that are core to self-discipline—truth and brutal facts; dialogue and debate, not coercion; a penchant for dialogue; questioning. Collins found that individuals in great companies were extremely interactive, engaging in debates that often lasted a long time.

Self-discipline is also built on competence, persistence, and the willingness to assume accountability for results. Competence is more than skill and ability; it's attitude and experience. Get the right people involved, and self-discipline comes more easily. Get the wrong people, and imposed discipline creeps in, destroying trust and respect. "The point is to first get self-disciplined people who engage in very rigorous thinking, who then take disciplined action within the framework of a consistent system," says Collins (2001). One reason would-be agile teams don't succeed is that they fail to realize the self-discipline required. There is no binary switch to go from no discipline to self-discipline; it's a journey that some individuals get right away, whereas others need to take a longer trip.

Agile teams don't blossom automatically from good intent. Growing and maturing effective agile teams takes time and dedication to building relationships and encouraging collaboration. This is the most important task of the project leader and individual team members also.

Encourage Collaboration

The capability of self-organizing teams lies in collaboration—the interaction and cooperation of two or more people to jointly produce a result. When two engineers scratch out a design on a whiteboard, they are collaborating. When team members meet to brainstorm a design, they are collaborating. When team leaders meet to decide whether a product is ready to ship, they are collaborating. The result of any collaboration can be categorized as a tangible deliverable, a decision, or shared knowledge.

Ultimately, unique, talented, and skilled individuals—individually and collectively—build products and services. Processes provide guidance and support, and tools improve efficiency, but without the right people who have the right technical and behavioral skills, all the processes and tools in the world won't produce results. Processes (in moderation) and tools are useful, but when critical decisions must be made, we rely on the knowledge and capabilities of individuals and the team to overcome obstacles.

The quality of results from any collaboration effort are driven by trust and respect, free flow of information, debate, and active participation—bound together by a participatory decision-making process. When any of these components is missing or ineffective, the quality of the results suffers. In a collaborative team, one of the key leader roles involves facilitating, coaching, cajoling, and influencing the team members to build healthy relationships.

At the core of healthy team relationships is trust and respect. When team members don't respect the knowledge and capabilities of others, meaningful debate falters. The line between confidence and arrogance can be awfully narrow, and individuals sometimes bluster to cover up lack of knowledge. The project leader helps meld a group of people into a working team by working through these types of issues—and getting the wrong people off the team when necessary.

Complex systems, such as large project organizations, thrive on interaction and information flow. Project leaders should be constantly asking questions such as, "Are the right people coordinating with each other about the right things at the right times?" and "Is the right information available at the right time?" These are critical questions whose answers can help the team operate smoothly or bog the team down. The design engineer who fails to include the ideas of the manufacturing engineer ends up with products that are too expensive to make. Software engineers who fail to work closely with QA build code that is difficult and expensive to test. Too little coordination and information, and teams will diverge so far that integration becomes a nightmare (hence the need for frequent integration). Too much coordination and information flow, and teams become mired in constant meetings and information overload.

Participatory Decision Making

Decision making is the heart and soul of collaboration. Anyone can sit down and chat about a product design. Collaboration means working together to jointly build a feature, create a design, or write a product's documentation. Collaboration is a joint effort. So whether you are designing with another individual or struggling with feature priorities or deciding to ship, there are literally thousands of decisions, large and small, to be made over the life of a project. How a team makes those decisions determines whether the team is a truly collaborative one. Some teams are driven to quick decisions by a senior technical individual, while others are driven by those with the loudest voice. Neither situation is conducive to true collaboration.

Several years ago, I wrote an article on distributed decision making. In researching that article, I reviewed six books on project management and found only one paragraph on decision making. Many, if not most, process-centric approaches to project management seem to spend no time on decision-making processes. But for all the general neglect, team decision-making capabilities are absolutely critical to successful project management, agile or otherwise. From feasibility go/no-go decisions, to whether or not to release a product, to each and every minute design choice—the way teams make decisions has a major impact on their performance.

Leadership is also critical to good decision making. In product development work there are thousands of decisions to be made—and the information available to make those decisions often remains fuzzy. Customer preferences may be fuzzy. The new technology being used may be untried, and therefore fuzzy. For every clear decision to be made, ten others require "fuzzy" logic. Teams can become paralyzed by this fuzziness and oscillate back and forth over decisions. When all the discussion, debate, and dialogue have reached an impasse—when the ambiguity of the situation overwhelms the decision-making capability of the team—the leader often has to step in and say, "Well, the direction isn't abundantly clear, but we're going East." An effective leader "absorbs" the ambiguity, takes responsibility for the decision, and allows the team to get on with its work. Knowing when and how to carry this off is one mark of an effective leader.

There are two words that engineers seem to hate most, maybe because they see a relationship between the two—politics and compromise. Compromise results from win-lose thinking, in which I am right and you are wrong. An alternative model is win-win thinking, in which reconceiving replaces compromise.[1] Reconceiving means combining ideas to create something better than any individual could create on her own. It isn't giving up, but adding to. Innovation and creativity are emergent, not causal, properties of teamwork. There is no set of steps that guarantees innovation; it *emerges* from a melding of gradually expanding ideas that are the results of interaction. In this process, pieces of your ideas and pieces of mine contribute to the eventual solution. This process of melding ideas, of subjecting them to discussion, of analyzing them in the light of our product's vision and constraints, is not a process of compromise, but one of reconceiving.

Compromise polarizes. Reconceiving unites.

However, win-win or reconceiving should not imply consensus decision making. Participation doesn't mean consensus either. Self-organizing teams have leaders who make unilateral decisions on occasion, but their primary style is inclusive, to encourage wide participation in decision making to make the best decisions. Self-organized teams have a lot of discretionary decision-making authority, but it is balanced with that of the project leader. As in other areas, balance is the key to agility in decision making.

---

[1] Colleague Rob Austin originated the use of the word "reconceive" in this way.

Shared Space

"The biggest single trend we've observed is the growing acknowledgment of innovation as a centerpiece of corporate strategies," says Tom Kelley (2001), general manager of IDEO, one of the world's leading industrial design firms. IDEO uses a combination of methodologies, work practices, culture, and infrastructure to create an environment conducive to innovation. Its methodology includes understanding the issues, observing real people, visualizing through the use of simulations and prototypes, evaluating and refining the prototypes, and implementing the concept. The use of prototypes, simulations, and models has a profound influence on IDEO's entire product design process.

"Virtually every significant marketplace innovation in this century is a direct result of extensive prototyping and simulation," says Michael Schrage (2000). His investigation into the world of prototypes—starting with his work at the Media Lab at MIT—led him to a startling conclusion: "You didn't have to be a sociologist to realize that the Lab's demo culture wasn't just about creating clever ideas; it was about creating clever interactions between people." Shared space leads to shared experience.

Innovation cannot be guaranteed by some deterministic process—innovation is the result of an emergent process, one in which the interaction of individuals with creative ideas results in something new and different. Demos, prototypes, simulations, and models are the catalysts for these clever interactions. They constitute the "shared space" (Schrage's term) in which developers, marketers, customers, and managers can have meaningful interactions.

Shared space has two requirements—visualization and commonality. One of the common problems in the product development field has been that requirements documents had neither quality. When engineers moved to conversations with customers around prototypes and working features rather than documents, the quality of the interactions increased dramatically. Visualization drives industrial design today. For example, Autodesk, whose software builds special effects for movies—*Lord of the Rings*, *Spiderman*, *Harry Potter*—also provides sophisticated software to industrial designers who need to visualize their products early in the development process.

Commonality means that the prototype needs to be understood by all parties that have a stake in the development effort. So, for example, although electrical circuit diagrams might help electrical and manufacturing engineers communicate, they don't create a shared space for marketing or customer representatives. Project leaders need to be aware, at each stage of the project, of who needs to interact at that stage and what the shared space needs to be for that to happen.

Customer Collaboration

APM depends on effective customer collaboration. The customer or product team should be an integral part of any agile development effort. Although the development and customer staffs have different roles, the more they consider themselves a single team, the more effective they will be.

A partial list of customer team responsibilities indicates how involved they are in an agile project (these responsibilities are further described in Chapter 6):

- Create and manage the feature/story backlog
- Set priorities in release and iteration planning
- Identify and define features/stories
- Define acceptance criteria
- Review and accept completed features and stories
- Interact on a continuous basis with the development team
- Accept accountability for results and adapting constraints

Achieving this level of customer-development team collaboration is often difficult and therefore a barrier to more effective agile implementation. Going "agile" often points out inadequacies in customer/product team staffing levels and the need to identify specific roles with the product team, such as product manager and product specialist.

No More Self-Organizing Teams?

Self-organizing teams are at the core of agile management, but the concepts have become corrupted—and counterproductive—in parts of the agile community. Although self-organizing is a good term, it has, unfortunately, become confused with anarchy. Why has this occurred? Because there is a contingent within the agile community who encourage an anarchistic management style and have latched onto the term *self-organizing* because it sounds better than anarchy. As larger and larger organizations are implementing agile methods and practices, the core of what it means to be agile—an empowering organizational culture—may be lost because large organizations will reject the cultural piece of agile.

So how do we bring the concept of self-organizing back from the brink of anarchy and return it to the realm of empowering, servant leadership (rather than no leadership)? In *Adaptive Software Development*, I used the term *Leadership-Collaboration management* to replace the concept of Command-Control management. This book went into great depth about the concepts of leaders (as in a person) and leadership (as in any team member can provide situational leadership) as an active part of an agile team and what that leadership model looked like. In his book, *Managing Agile Projects*, Sanjiv Augustine (Augustine 2005) also addresses this issue and calls for management to have a "Light Touch." I hope that the descriptions of leadership and adapting teams in this chapter will help put self-organizing in the right perspective.

There are several issues in returning self-organizing to usefulness. First, we need to get away from the idea that agile teams are leaderless or that leadership revolves around the team depending on the situation (this type of situational leadership does occur, and often, but it does not replace a designated leader). There is just too much experience and management literature that shows that good leaders make a big difference. The anarchists want to eliminate leaders and merely go with situational leadership. However, a large contingent in the agile community think the right approach is to change the style of leadership, not to eliminate leaders. It's easy to rail against poor managers and advocate eliminating them. It's much harder to work with organizations to change their leadership style to one that supports an agile environment.

Second, some advocates of empowering self-organizing teams have gotten carried away. They forget that in the management literature empowerment is a fancy term for delegation—basically delegation of decision making authority. Does empowerment mean that teams get to make any and all decisions related to their project? If five teams are working on a project, do each of them get to make architectural or development infrastructure decisions independently? Self-organization means that to the extent possible, decision making is delegated to individual teams. However, delegating decisions in an organization isn't a simple task—it requires tremendous thought and some experimentation. In larger teams and multi-team projects, we must convey the right mix of delegation of decision making to teams while retaining appropriate decision-making authority with the appropriate leader.

Although agile leaders may be "light" in terms of top-down decision making, they are heavy in articulating goals, facilitating interactions, improving team dynamics, supporting collaboration, and encouraging experimentation and innovation. These characteristics of a leader are more critical to success than decision-making authority, but decision making is still an important piece of the leader's role.

Leading is hard. If it was easy every company would be "great," to use Jim Collins' term (*Good to Great 2001*). Anarchy isn't the answer; it's merely a simplistic solution to a very complex problem: managing organizations. What we need are good leaders. What we need is a better leadership style. What we need are managers and leaders who work hard at empowering their teams to the right extent.

Final Thoughts

Agile leaders manage teams and the teams manage their own tasks. Agile leaders articulate project goals and objectives, the product vision, key capabilities, and constraints, and then encourage team members to deliver them—figuring out the details of how to accomplish the tasks on their own. This approach to project management gives the team flexibility to adapt rather than blindly follow a set of predetermined tasks—it encourages the team to self-organize to find the best way to accomplish their project goals.

Chapter 4

Adapting over Conforming

> *A traditional project manager focuses on following the plan with minimal changes, whereas an agile leader focuses on adapting successfully to inevitable changes.*

Traditional managers view the plan as the goal, whereas agile leaders view customer value as the goal. If you doubt the former, just look at the definition of "success" from the Standish Group, who has published success (and failure) rates of software projects over a long period of time. Success, per the Standish Group is "the project is completed on time and on budget, with all the features and functions originally specified."[1] This is not a value-based definition but a constraint-based one. Using this definition, then, managers focus on following the plan with minimal changes. Colleague Rob Austin would classify this as a dysfunctional measurement (Austin 1996)—one that leads to the opposite behavior of what was intended.

When customer value and quality are the goals, then a plan becomes a means to achieve those goals, not the goal itself. The constraints embedded in those plans are still important; they still guide the project; we still want to understand variations from the plans, but—and this is a big but—plans are not sacrosanct; they are meant to be flexible; they are meant to be guides, not straightjackets.

---

[1] Standish Group. Chaos Reports
(http://www.standishgroup.com/chaos_resources/chronicles.php).

Both traditional and agile leaders plan, and both spend a fair amount of time planning. But they view plans in radically different ways. They both believe in plans as baselines, but traditional managers are constantly trying to "correct" actual results to that baseline. In the PMBOK[2], for example, the relevant activity is described as "corrective action" to guide the team back to the plan. In agile project management, we use "adaptive action" to describe which course of action to take (and one of those actions may be to correct to the plan).

The agile principles documents—the Agile Manifesto and the Declaration of Interdependence—contain five principle statements about adaptation, as shown in Figure 4-1.

Figure 4-1
Adaptive Principle
Statements

Adaptive Principle Statements

(DOI) We expect uncertainty and manage for it through iterations, anticipation, and adaptation.

(DOI) We improve effectiveness and reliability through situationally specific strategies, processes, and practices.

(AM) Responding to change over following a plan.

(AM) Welcome changing requirements, even late in development. Agile processes harness change for the customer's competitive advantage.

(AM) At regular intervals, the team reflects on how to become more effective, and then tunes and adjusts its behavior accordingly

DOI=Declaration of Interdependence. AM=Agile Manifesto

These principles could be summarized as follows:

- We expect change (uncertainty) and respond accordingly rather than follow outdated plans.
- We adapt our processes and practices as necessary.

The ability to respond to change drives competitive advantage. Think of the possibilities (not the problems) of being able to release a new version of a product weekly. Think of the competitive advantage of being able to pack-

[2] The Project Management Institute's *Project Management Body of Knowledge*, known as the PMBOK.

age features so customers feel they have software specifically customized for them (and the cost to maintain the software remains low).

Teams must adapt, but they can't lose track of the ultimate goals of the project. Teams should constantly evaluate progress, whether adapting or anticipating, by asking these four questions:

- Is value, in the form of a releasable product, being delivered?
- Is the quality goal of building a reliable, adaptable product being met?
- Is the project progressing satisfactorily within acceptable constraints?
- Is the team adapting effectively to changes imposed by management, customers, or technology?

The dictionary defines *change* as: "To cause to be different, to give a completely different form or appearance to." It defines *adapt as*: "To make suitable to or fit for a specific use or situation." Changing and adapting are not the same and the difference between them is important. There is no goal inherent in change—as the quip says, "stuff happens." Adaptation, on the other hand, is directed towards a goal (suitability). Change is mindless; adaptation is mindful.

> *Adaptation can be considered a mindful response to change.*

The Science of Adaptation

Former Visa International CEO Dee Hock (1999) coined the word "chaordic" to describe both the world around us and his approach to managing a far-flung enterprise—balanced on the precipice between chaos and order. Our sense of the world dictates management style. If the world is perceived as static, then production-style management practices will dominate. If the world is perceived as dynamic, however, then exploration-style management practices will come to the fore. Of course, it's not that simple—there is always a blend of static and dynamic, which means that managers must always perform a delicate balancing act.

In the last two decades a vanguard of scientists and managers have articulated a profound shift in their view about how organisms and organizations evolve, respond to change, and manage their growth. Scientists' findings about the tipping points of chemical reactions and the "swarm" behavior of ants have given organizational researchers insights into what makes successful companies and successful managers. Practitioners have studied how innovative groups work most effectively.

As quantum physics changed our notions of predictability and Darwin changed our perspective on evolution, complex adaptive systems (CAS) theory has reshaped scientific and management thinking. In an era of rapid change, we need better ways of making sense of the world around us. Just as biologists now study ecosystems as well as species, executives and managers need to understand the global economic and political ecosystems in which their companies compete.

"A complex adaptive system, be it biologic or economic below, is an ensemble of independent agents

- *Who interact to create an ecosystem*

- *Whose interaction is defined by the exchange of information*

- *Whose individual actions are based on some system of internal rules*

- *Who self-organize in nonlinear ways to produce emergent results*

- *Who exhibit characteristics of both order and chaos*

- *Who evolve over time"* (Highsmith 2000).

For an agile project, the *ensemble* includes core team members, customers, suppliers, executives, and other participants who interact with each other in various ways. It is these interactions, and the tacit and explicit information exchanges that occur within them, that project management practices need to facilitate.

The individual agent's actions are driven by a set of internal rules—the core ideology and values of APM, for example. Both scientific and management researchers have shown that a simple set of rules can generate complex behaviors and outcomes, whether in ant colonies or project teams. Complex rules, on the other hand, often become bureaucratic. How these rules are formulated has a significant impact on how the complex system operates.

Newtonian approaches predict results. CAS approaches create emergent results. "Emergence is a property of complex adaptive systems that creates some greater property of the whole (system behavior) from the interaction of the parts (self-organizing agent behavior). Emergent results cannot be predicted in the normal sense of cause and effect relationships, but they can be anticipated by creating patterns that have previously produced similar results" (Highsmith 2000). Creativity and innovation are the emergent results of well functioning agile teams.

An adaptive development process has a different character from an optimizing one. Optimizing reflects a basic prescriptive Plan-Design-Build lifecycle. Adapting reflects an organic, evolutionary Envision-Explore-Adapt lifecycle. An adaptive approach begins not with a single solution, but with multiple potential solutions (experiments). It explores and selects the best by applying a series of fitness tests (actual product features or simulations subjected to acceptance tests) and then adapting to feedback. When uncertainty is low, adaptive approaches run the risk of higher costs. When uncertainty is high, optimizing approaches run the risk of settling too early on a particular solution and stifling innovation. The salient point is that these two fundamental approaches to development are very different, and they require different processes, different management approaches, and different measurements of success.

Newtonian versus quantum, predictability versus flexibility, optimization versus adaptation, efficiency versus innovation—all these dichotomies reflect a fundamentally different way of making sense about the world and how to manage effectively within it. Because of high iteration costs, the traditional perspective was predictive and change averse, and deterministic processes arose to support this traditional viewpoint. But our viewpoint needs to change. Executives, project leaders, and development teams must embrace a different view of the new product development world, one that not only recognizes change in the business world, but also understands the power of driving down iteration costs to enable experimentation and emergent processes. Understanding these differences and how they affect product development is key to understanding APM.

Exploring

Agility is the ability to both create and respond to change in order to profit in a turbulent business environment (from Chapter 1). The ability to respond to change is good. The ability to create change for competitors is even better. When you create change you are on the competitive offensive. When you respond to competitors' changes you are on the defensive. When you can respond to change at any point in the development lifecycle, even late, then you have a distinct advantage.

> *Adaptation needs to exceed the rate of market changes.*

But change is hard. Although agile values tell us that responding to change is more important than following a plan, and that embracing rather than resisting change leads to better products, working in a high-change environment can be nerve-wracking for team members. Exploration is difficult; it raises anxiety, trepidation, and sometimes even a little fear. Agile project leaders need to encourage and inspire team members to work through the difficulties of a high-change environment. Remaining calm themselves, encouraging experimentation, learning through both successes and mistakes, and helping team members understand the vision are all part of this encouragement. Good leaders create a safe environment in which people can voice outlandish ideas, some of which turn out not to be so outlandish after all. External encouragement and inspiration help teams build internal motivation.

Great explorations flow from inspirational leaders. Cook, Magellan, Shackleton, and Columbus were inspirational leaders with vision. They persevered in the face of monumental obstacles, not the least of which was fear of the unknown. Magellan, after years of dealing with the entrenched Spanish bureaucracy trying to scuttle his plans, launched his five-ship fleet on October 3, 1519. On September 6, 1522, the Victoria, last of the ships, sailed into port without Magellan, who had died in the Philippines after completing the most treacherous part of the journey. The expedition established a route around Cape Horn and sailed across the vast Pacific Ocean for the first time (Joyner 1992).

Great explorers articulate goals that inspire people—goals that get people excited such that they inspire themselves. These goals or visions serve as

ADAPTING OVER CONFORMING

a unifying focal point of effort, galvanizing people and creating an esprit de corps among the team. Inspirational goals need to be energizing, compelling, clear, and feasible, but just barely. Inspirational goals tap into a team's passion.

Encouraging leaders also know the difference between good goals and bad ones. We all know of egocentric managers who point to some mountain and say, "Let's get up there, team," when everyone else is thinking, "Who is he kidding? There's not a snowball's chance in the hot place that we can carry that off." "Bad BHAGs [Big Hairy Audacious Goals], it turns out, are set with *bravado*; good BHAGs are set with understanding," says Jim Collins (2001). Inspirational leaders know that setting a vision for the product is a team effort, one based on analysis, understanding, and realistic risk assessment, combined with a sprinkle of adventure.

Innovative product development teams are led, not managed. They allow their leaders to be inspirational. They internalize the leader's encouragement. Great new products, outstanding enhancements to existing products, and creative new business initiatives are driven by passion and inspiration. Project managers who focus on network diagrams, cost budgets, and resource histograms are dooming their teams to mediocrity.[3, 4]

Leaders help articulate the goals; teams internalize them and motivate themselves. This internal motivation enables exploration. We don't arrive at something new, better, and different without trial and error, launching off in multiple new directions to find the one that seems promising. Magellan and his ships spent 38 days covering the 334 miles of the straits that bear his name. In the vast expanse of islands and peninsulas, they explored many dead ends before finding the correct passages (Kelley 2001).

Magellan's ship Victoria sailed nearly 1,000 miles, back and forth—up estuaries that dead-ended and back out—time and time again. Magellan (his crew, actually) was the first to circumnavigate the globe. But Magellan

---

[3] This sentence should not be interpreted as saying these things are unimportant, because properly used, each can be useful to the project leader. It is when they become the focal point that trouble ensues.

[4] Ken Delcol observes, "Most PMs are not selected for their ability to inspire people! Leadership and business influencing skills are hard to establish in an interview. Most managers have a difficult time identifying and evaluating people with these skill sets."

would probably have driven a production-style project manager or executive a little crazy, because he surely didn't follow a plan. But then, any detailed plan would have been foolish—no one even knew whether ships could get around Cape Horn; none had found the way when Magellan launched. No one knew how large the Pacific Ocean was, and even the best guestimates turned out to be thousands of miles short. His vision never changed, but his "execution" changed every day based on new information.

Teams need a shared purpose and goal, but they also need encouragement to adapt—to experiment, explore, make mistakes, regroup, and forge ahead again.

Responding to Change

> *We expect change (uncertainty) and respond accordingly rather than follow outdated plans.*

This statement reflects the agile viewpoint characterized further by

- Envision-Explore versus Plan-Do
- Adapting versus anticipating

In *Artful Making*, Harvard Business School professor and colleague Rob Austin and his coauthor Lee Devin (2003) discuss a $125 million IT project disaster in which the company refused to improvise and change from the detailed plan set down prior to the project's start. " 'Plan the work and work the plan' was their implicit mantra," they write. "And it led them directly to a costly and destructive course of action....We'd all like to believe that this kind of problem is rare in business. It's not."

Every project has knowns and unknowns, certainties and uncertainties, and therefore every project has to balance planning and adapting. Balancing is required because projects also run the gamut from production-style ones in which uncertainty is low, to exploration-style ones in which uncertainty is high. Exploration-style projects, similar to development of the Sketchbook Pro© product introduced in Chapter 1, require a process that emphasizes envisioning and then exploring into that vision rather than detailed planning and relatively strict execution of tasks. It's not that one is right and the other wrong, but that each style is more or less applicable to a particular project type.

Another factor that impacts project management style is the cost of an iteration; that is, the cost of experimenting. Even if the need for innovation is great, high iteration costs may dictate a process with greater anticipatory work. Low-cost iterations, like those mentioned earlier, enable an adaptive style of development in which plans, architectures, and designs evolve concurrently with the actual product.

Product, Process, People

Faced with major redirection in release 2.0 of their product, the Sketchbook Pro© team introduced in Chapter 1 delivered the revised product in 42 days. As I quip in workshops, "I know teams who would have complained for 42 days with comments such as: "They don't know what they want. They are always changing their minds." Adaptability has three components—product, process, and people. You need to have a gung-ho agile team with the right attitude about change. You need processes and practices that allow the team to adapt to circumstances. And you *need* high quality code with automated tests. You can have pristine code and a non-agile team and change will be difficult. All three are required to have an agile, adaptable environment.

The barrier to agility in many software organizations is their failure to deal with the technical debt in legacy code. The failure is understandable because the solution can be costly and time consuming. However, failure to address this significant barrier keeps many organizations from realizing their agile potential. It took years for legacy code to degenerate; it will take significant time to revitalize the code. It requires a systematic investment in refactoring and automated testing—over several release cycles—to begin to solve the problems of years of neglect.

Barriers or Opportunities

One of the constant excuses, complaints, or rationalizations about some agile practices are "They would take too much time," or "They would cost too much." This has been said about short iterations, frequent database updates, continuous integration, automated testing, and a host of other agile practices. All too often companies succumb to what colleague Israel Gat calls the "new toy" syndrome—placing all their emphasis on new development and ignoring legacy code. Things like messy old code then become excuses and barriers to change. Some activities certainly are cost-prohibitive, but many of these are artificial barriers that people voice. Experienced agilists turn these barriers into opportunities. They ask, "What would be the benefit if we *could* do this?"

Working with a large company—and a very large program team (multiple projects, one integrated product suite) of something over 500 people—several years ago we wanted them to do a complete multi-project code integration at the end of every couple of iterations. The reply was, "We can't do that, it would take multiple people and several weeks of time out of development." This was from a group who had experienced severe problems in prior releases when they integrated products very late in the release cycle. Our response was, "What would the benefit be if you could do the integration quickly and at low cost?" and, "You don't have a choice; if you want to be agile you must integrate across the entire product suite early and often." Grumbling, they managed the first integration with significant effort, but with far less time than they anticipated. By the time 3–4 integrations had occurred, they had figured out how to do them in a few days with limited personnel. The benefits from frequent integration were significant, eliminating many problems that previously would have lingered, unfound, until close to release date.

Most, but not all, of the time perceived barriers to change (it costs too much) really point out inefficiencies—opportunities to streamline the process and enhance the organization's ability to adapt. Agile development demands short-cycle iterations. Doing short-cycle iterations demands finding ways to do repetitive things quickly and inexpensively. Doing things quickly and inexpensively enables teams to respond to changes in ways they never anticipated previously. Doing things quickly and inexpensively fosters innovation because it encourages teams to experiment. These innovations ripple out into other parts of the organization. Lowering the cost of change enables companies to rethink their business models.

Reliable, Not Repeatable

Note that the word "repeatable" isn't in the agile lexicon. Implementing repeatable processes has been the goal of many companies, but in product development, repeatability turns out to be the wrong goal; in fact, it turns out to be an extremely counterproductive goal. *Repeatable* means doing the same thing in the same way to product the same results. *Reliable* means meeting targets regardless of the impediments thrown in your way—it means constantly adapting to meet a goal.

Repeatable processes reduce variability through measurement and constant process correction. The term originated in manufacturing, where results were well defined and repeatability meant that if a process had consistent inputs, then defined outputs would be produced. Repeatable means that the conversion of inputs to outputs can be replicated with little variation. It implies that no new information can be generated during the process because we have to know all the information in advance to predict the output results accurately. Repeatable processes are not effective for product development projects because precise results are rarely predictable, inputs vary considerably from project to project, and the input-to-output conversions themselves are highly variable.

Reliable processes focus on outputs, not inputs. Using a reliable process, team members figure out ways to consistently achieve a given goal even though the inputs vary dramatically. Because of the input variations, the team may not use the same processes or practices from one project, or even one iteration, to the next. Reliability is results driven. Repeatability is input driven. The irony is that if every project process was somehow made repeatable, the project would be extremely unstable because of input and transformation variations. Even those organizations that purport to have repeatable processes are often successful not because of those processes, but because of the adaptability of the people who are using those processes.

> *At best, a repeatable process can deliver only what was specified in the beginning. A reliable, emergent process can actually deliver a better result than anyone ever conceived in the beginning. An emergent process can produce what you wish you had thought about at the start if only you had been smart and prescient enough.*

Herein lies a definitional issue with project scope. With production-style projects, those amenable to repeatable processes, scope is considered to be the defined requirements. But in product development, requirements evolve and change over the life of the project, so "scope" can never be precisely defined in the beginning. Therefore, the correct scope to consider for agile projects isn't defined requirements but the articulated product vision—a releasable product. Product managers may be worried about specific requirements, but executives are concerned about the product as a whole— Does it meet the vision of the customer? When management asks the ever-popular question, "Did the project meet its scope, schedule, and cost targets?" The answer should be evaluated according to the vision, value, and totality of the capabilities delivered. That is, the evaluation of success can be encapsulated in the question "Do we have a releasable product?" not on whether the set of specific features defined at the start of the project was produced.

Agile Project Management is both reliable and predictable: It can deliver products that meet the customer's evolving needs within the boundary constraints better than any other process for a given level of uncertainty. Why does this happen? Not because some project manager specified detailed tasks and micromanaged them, but because an agile leader established an environment in which people wanted to excel and meet their goals.

Although APM is reliable, it is not infallible, and it cannot eliminate the vagaries of uncertainty, nor the surprises encountered while exploring. APM can shift the odds toward success. If executives expect projects to deliver on the product vision, within the constraints of specified time and cost, every time, without fail, then they should be running an assembly line, not developing products.

Reflection and Retrospective

Adapting requires both a certain mindset and a set of skills. If we are to be adaptable, then we must be willing to seriously and critically evaluate our performance as individual contributors and as teams. Effective teams cover four key subject areas in their retrospectives: *product* from both the customer's perspective and a technical quality perspective; *process*, as in how well the processes and practices being used by the team are working; *team*, as in how well the group is working as a high-performance team; and *project*, as in how the project is progressing according to plan. Feedback in each of these areas—at the end of each iteration and at the end of the project—leads to adaptations that improve performance. The "how to" of retrospectives and reflection is covered in Chapter 10, "The Adapt and Close Phases."

Principles to Practices

> *We adapt our processes and practices as necessary.*

Ultimately, what people *do*, how they *behave*, is what creates great products. Principles and practices are guides; they help identify and reinforce certain behaviors.

Although principles guide agile teams, specific practices are necessary to actually accomplish work. A process structure and specific practices form a minimal, flexible framework for self-organizing teams. In an agile project there must be both anticipatory and adaptive processes and practices. Release planning uses known information to "anticipate" the future. Refactoring uses information found later in the project to "adapt" code. Ron Jeffries once said, "I have more confidence in my ability to adapt than in my ability to plan." Agilists do anticipate, but they always try to understand the limits of anticipation and try to err on the side of less of it.

Final Thoughts

Developing great products requires exploration, not tracking against a plan. Exploring and adapting are two behavioral traits required to innovate— having the courage to explore into the unknown and having the humility to recognize mistakes and adapt to the situation. Magellan had a vision, a goal, and some general ideas about sailing from Spain down the coast of South America, avoiding Portuguese ships if at all possible, exploring dead end after dead end to finding a way around Cape Horn, then tracking across the Pacific to once-again known territory in the Southeast Asia archipelagoes. Great new products come from similarly audacious goals and rough plans that often include large gaps in which "miracles happen," much like the miracle of finding the Straits of Magellan.

Chapter 5

An Agile Project Management Model

The first edition of this book introduced an agile process framework that focused on major project phases. However, as agile methods have spread to larger projects and larger organizations over the last five years, a more encompassing enterprise framework has become necessary. In an organization that spans multiple countries, for example, not all projects will be agile projects and even if they were, some locations may use different agile methods than others. It isn't rare for one organization location to use Scrum, another Extreme Programming (XP), and yet another Feature Driven Development (FDD). Furthermore, this multiplicity of approaches should not be discouraged! It may well be that a location in China can get good support (training, coaching, etc.) for Scrum, whereas another in Australia can get good support for FDD.

One of the tenets of agile development is adapting to different situations. One of the six principles of the Declaration of Interdependence is, "We improve effectiveness and reliability through *situationally specific* strategies, processes, and practices." It is therefore difficult to make a compelling argument for standardizing on a single agile method across a multinational organization. However, utilizing a common framework within which individual choices can be made does appeal to larger organizations.

An Agile Enterprise Framework

The overall Agile Enterprise Framework is shown Figure 5-1. The Portfolio Governance layer can offer some common checkpoints, and the Project Management layer can offer guidance to managing a variety of projects. The differentiation between the Project Management and Iteration Management layers can offer insight into differences between running a project and creating a release plan versus the day-to-day management of a short iteration. Finally, separating the Iteration Management layer from Technical Practices can assist in melding a core of technical practices into several project or iteration management approaches.

Figure 5-1
An Agile Enterprise
Framework

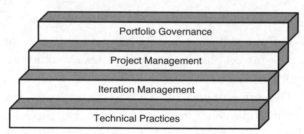

This structure facilitates organizations in building hybrid agile methods to suit their specific needs—positioning different agile methods for each layer. The framework encourages flexibility at the lower tier (technical practices) and less flexibility at the upper tier (project governance). This structure recognizes that no one agile method covers all the tiers—that in fact, all agile methods used in organizations are hybrids. For example, one organization might use APM for the Project Management layer (plus parts of the PMBOK), Scrum for Iteration Management, and selected XP practices in the Technical Layer. By drawing on the strengths of several agile methods, companies can build highly effective hybrid methodologies, or build several hybrids for different parts of the organization.

Portfolio Governance Layer

Large companies have hundreds, if not thousands, of projects—some agile, some traditional; some using one agile method, some another agile method, some a hybrid of agile and traditional methods. Even when an organization has committed to a major agile transformation there will be a several-year transition period when there will be a mix of methods used. What executives need is a common framework for evaluating all these projects; a framework that addresses the major executive concerns—investment and risk. Executives want to know the value of the project (in terms of ROI), and the certainty or uncertainty of obtaining that ROI. Executives don't really care whether a requirements document has been finished; they want to know about project progress, investment, and risk. No matter what the project type—agile or otherwise—a governance mechanism can be created that addresses these two key project status attributes. Chapter 12, "Governing Agile Projects," addresses the Portfolio Governance layer in detail.

Project Management Layer

Many people think about project versus iteration management as dealing with stakeholders external to the core team versus dealing with internal core team members. Although that is part of the differentiation, it is only half. The other critical differentiation between these two is managing the release versus managing the iteration. A full project release plan, described in Chapters 7 and 8, involves creating a vision for both the product and the team, developing the project scope and boundary components, and developing an overall feature release plan.

Project management also includes working with stakeholders and suppliers outside the core team. Therefore, the Project Management layer focuses on overall project/release activities, assisting coordination among multiple feature teams, and managing the project externals. In addition, project management practices such as risk analysis or contract management practices, that are useful in a variety of projects, agile or not, can be brought into this layer (they may come from sources such at the Project Management Institute's *Project Management Body of Knowledge*).

A quick note here is that the Project Management and Iteration Management layers can have the same leader or different leaders, depending on the project's size. For example, a large project with four teams might have an iteration manager for each team and one overall project leader.

Iteration Management Layer

Iteration management focuses on planning, execution, and team leadership during short individual iterations. The reasons for separating the Iteration and Project Management layers were outlined in the last section, basically separating release and iteration work and internal and external management activities.

Technical Practices Layer

Technical practices, in software projects, run the gamut from continuous integration to pair-programming, from test-driven development to refactoring. Hardware projects might employ a range of engineering practices, from electrical to mechanical. Although this book focuses more on the other three layers, the foundation of effective project delivery lies in the technical arena. In implementing agile methods in a wide variety of organizations, transforming technical practices are critical. For example, continuous integration and ruthless automated testing are core agile software practices that can't be left out.

Another reason for separating out a Technical Practices layer is to make APM more amenable to a variety of project and product types. Although I've had difficulty getting electrical or mechanical engineers to warm up to pair programming, equivalents of agile software practices have proved useful in a wide variety of product development areas. Furthermore, except for potentially longer iteration lengths in hardware projects, the Governance, Project, and Iteration layers work for companies wanting to apply agile methods to non-software projects.

An Agile Delivery Framework

Process may not be as important as people, but it's far from unimportant. Process has gotten a bad rap in agile circles as being static, prescriptive, and difficult to change. Process, per se, doesn't have to be negative, but it must be tied to business objectives. If the objective is repeatable manufacturing, then a prescriptive process may be completely justified. However, if the objective is reliable innovation, then the process framework must be organic, flexible, and easy to adapt. An agile delivery framework needs to embody the principles described in the previous chapters. In addition to supporting business objectives, the framework needs to:

- Support an envision, explore, adapt culture
- Support a self-organizing, self-disciplined team
- Promote reliability and consistency to the extent possible given the level of project uncertainty
- Be flexible and easy to adapt
- Support visibility into the process
- Incorporate learning
- Incorporate practices that support each phase
- Provide management checkpoints for review

The APM model's structure—Envision-Speculate-Explore-Adapt-Close—focuses on delivery (execution) and adaptation (see Figure 5-2). It is based on a model first described in *Adaptive Software Development* (Highsmith 2000).

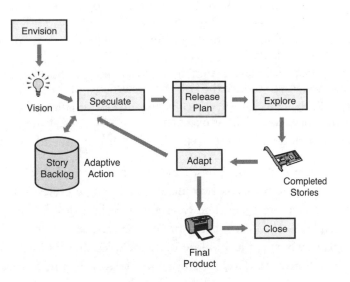

Figure 5-2
The APM Delivery Framework

The departure from traditional phase names—such as Initiate, Plan, Define, Design, Build, Test—is significant. First, Envision replaces the more traditional Initiate phase to indicate the criticality of vision. Second, a Speculate phase replaces a Plan phase. Words convey certain meanings and visual images that arise from systematic use over time. The word "plan" has become associated with prediction and relative certainty. "Speculate" indicates that the future is uncertain. Many traditional project managers faced with uncertainty try to "plan" that uncertainty away. We have to learn to *speculate* and *adapt* rather than *plan* and *build*.

Third, the APM model replaces the common Design, Build, Test phases with Explore. Explore, with its iterative delivery style, is *explicitly* a nonlinear, concurrent, non-waterfall model. Questions developed in the Speculate phase are "explored." Speculating implies the need for flexibility based on the fact that you cannot fully predict the results. The APM model emphasizes execution and it is exploratory rather than deterministic. A team practicing APM keeps its eyes on the vision, monitors information, and adapts to current conditions—therefore the Adapt phase. Finally, the APM model ends with a Close phase, in which the primary objectives are knowledge transfer and, of course, a celebration.

To sum up, the five phases of agile project management are

1. *Envision*: Determine the product vision and project objectives and constraints, the project community, and how the team will work together
2. *Speculate*: Develop a capability and/or feature-based release plan to deliver on the vision
3. *Explore*: Plan and deliver running tested stories in a short iteration, constantly seeking to reduce the risk and uncertainty of the project
4. *Adapt*: Review the delivered results, the current situation, and the team's performance, and adapt as necessary
5. *Close*: Conclude the project, pass along key learnings, and celebrate.

Figure 5-2 identified all the phases and shows the flow of work; Figure 5-3 shows the same activities as two major collaborative cycles—an Envision cycle and an Explore cycle. The Envision cycle includes the Envision and Speculate phases (product vision, project objectives and constraints, and release plan), whereas the Explore cycle includes the Explore and Adapt phases (iteration plan, develop, and review/adapt). Figure 5-3 emphasizes cycles rather than flow and indicates that all or part of the Envision cycle may be executed multiple times during a project. For example, a revised release plan might (and should) be constructed every iteration or two. In a longer project, the entire Envision cycle results might be revised periodically.

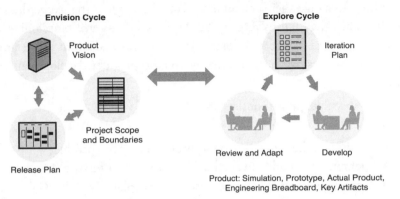

Figure 5-3
APM's Envision and Explore Cycles

Envision Cycle

Product Vision

Project Scope and Boundaries

Release Plan

Explore Cycle

Iteration Plan

Review and Adapt

Develop

Product: Simulation, Prototype, Actual Product, Engineering Breadboard, Key Artifacts

Phase: Envision

The Envision phase creates a vision for the product teams that covers what, who, and how. Absent a vision, the remaining activities in getting a project off the ground are wasted effort. In business-speak, vision is the "critical success factor" early in a project. First, team members need to envision *what* to deliver—a vision of the product and the scope of the project. Second, they need to envision *who* will be involved—the community of customers, product managers, team members, and stakeholders. And, third, the team members must envision *how* they intend to work together.

Phase: Speculate

The word "speculate" first calls to mind an image of reckless risk-taking, but actually the dictionary definition is "to conjecture something based on incomplete facts or information," which is exactly what happens during this phase.[1] The word "plan" has come to connote certainty and prediction, whereas the more useful definition, for exploratory projects at least, is spec-

[1] *Encarta® World English Dictionary*, 1999, 2000 Microsoft Corporation.

ulating or hypothesizing based on incomplete information. Colleague Ken Delcol makes a great observation: "People believe when they plan that they introduce certainty, which is far from the truth. What they introduce is something to gauge their performance by. Then, when the gauge does not reflect reality, they fail to replan." APM consists more of envisioning and exploring than planning and doing—it forces us to confront the reality of today's precarious business and highly volatile product development environments.

The Speculate phase consists of:

- Gathering the initial broad requirements for the product
- Defining the workload as a backlog of product features
- Creating a iterative, feature-based release plan
- Incorporating risk mitigation strategies into the plan
- Estimating project costs and generating other required administrative and financial information

Phase: Explore

The Explore phase delivers product stories. From a project management perspective there are three critical activity areas during this phase. The first is delivering planned stories by managing the workload and using appropriate technical practices and risk mitigation strategies. The second is creating a collaborative, self-organizing project community, which is everyone's responsibility but is facilitated by the project and iteration leaders. The third activity is managing the interactions among customers, product management, and other stakeholders.

Phase: Adapt

Control and correction are common terms applied to this lifecycle phase. Plans are made, results are monitored, and corrections are made—implying that the plans were right and the actual results, if different from the plan, are wrong. "Adapt" implies modification or change rather than success or failure. In projects guided by the Agile Manifesto value that "responding to change is more important than following a plan," attributing failure to variation from the plan isn't productive. A purely ad hoc process fails to learn from its mistakes, whereas the incorporation and retention of lessons learned are key pieces of APM.

In the Adapt phase the results are reviewed from customer, technical, people and process performance, and project status perspectives. The analysis looks at actual versus planned, but even more importantly, it considers actual versus a revised outlook on the project given up-to-the-minute information. The results of adaptation are fed into a replanning effort to begin the next iteration.

After the Envision phase, the loop will generally be Speculate-Explore-Adapt, with each iteration successively refining the product. However, periodically revisiting the Envision phase may be necessary as the team gathers new information.

Phase: Close

Projects are partially defined by the presence of both a beginning and an end. Many organizations fail to identify a project's end point, often causing perception problems among customers. Projects should end—with a celebration. The key objective of the Close phase, and the "mini" close at the end of each iteration, is learning and then incorporating that learning into the work of the next iteration or passing it on to the next project team.

Not a Complete Product Lifecycle

One caveat to the agile delivery framework presented in this chapter and expanded upon in subsequent chapters is that it does not define a complete product lifecycle. The front and back of a product lifecycle, the early conceptualization phase and the later deployment phase, are not included in this agile framework because they are outside the scope of this book, not because they are unimportant.

Selecting and Integrating Practices

The next several chapters describe specific practices for each of the APM delivery framework layers. These practices should be considered a "system of practices," because as a system, they reinforce each other as they align with agile principles. But they do more than align; they implement. Principles without practices are empty shells, whereas practices without principles tend to be implemented by rote, without judgment. Without principles, we don't know *how* to implement practices—for example, without a Simplify principle we tend to overdo the formality and ceremony of almost any practice. Principles guide practices. Practices instantiate principles. They go hand in hand.

Aligning principles and practices prompts the realization that the holy grail of "best practices" is a sham. A wonderful practice for one team may be a terrible practice for another. Practices are just practices—various ways of carrying out some goal. A practice is only good or bad within some context, which might include principles, problem type (e.g., exploratory), team dynamics, and organizational culture.

> *There is no such thing as a best practice. There are only good practices for a given situation.*

The practices in the following chapters have proven useful in a variety of situations. Some could be useful in production-style projects, just as practices not included may be very useful in agile projects. In selecting and using these practices, and others, these guiding principles apply:

- Simple
- Generative, not prescriptive
- Aligned with agile values
- Focused on delivery (value adding), not compliance
- Minimum (just enough to get the job done)
- Mutually supportive (a system of practices)

Few, if any, of the practices described in the following chapters are new. Some of them are variations on a theme of practices described by others. Some are well known, others not so well known. For example, risk management practices are widely described in the project management literature, whereas others, like participatory decision making, are not. Therefore, common practices such as risk management are briefly described and other resources are referenced; decision making is described in detail.

Judgment Required

Because of product and project management's long history of favoring serial development processes, any illustration like that shown earlier in Figure 5-2 might be interpreted as one of a serial process. However, although a project may follow the general sequence of Envision, Speculate, Explore, Adapt, and Close, the entire model should be considered fluid. The wording of production-style models implies linearity and repeatability—Initiate, Plan, Define, Design, Build, Test—while the APM terms were selected to imply iterative evolution—Speculate, Explore, Adapt.

An overemphasis on linearity leads to stagnation, just as an overemphasis on evolution leads to endless, and eventually mindless, change. With either model, development team members, product team members, and executives need to exercise judgment in its application.

One of the most common questions about APM is, "What about the planning, architecture, and requirements phases?" The simple answer is that these things are activities and not phases. An agile approach can easily include as much time for these activities as a conventional serial phase approach does, *but* the activities are spread across multiple iterations and many stories.

A second area of concern is the risk of rework in agile development if the initial architecture work (the discussion in this section could refer to architecture, plans, or requirements) misses a critical item. But there is an equal if not greater risk in serial development that often goes unnamed—that of getting the up-front architecture wrong. In a serial process, the validation of the early architecture decisions comes late in the project lifecycle, when the actual building occurs. By that time, a tremendous amount of time and money have been spent. Changing the architecture then becomes a major, and costly, decision—if it is possible at all.

> *All work should be evolutionary, even architecture development.*
> *Getting up-front architecture wrong in serial development usually*
> *means poor long-term adaptability because no one can stomach*
> *changing architecture late in a project.*

Project Size

The core values and principles of APM are applicable to projects of any size. Similarly, the practices described in the next chapters are applicable to projects of any size. However, for teams that exceed 100 or so people, additional practices or extensions to the described practices may be necessary—some of which are described in Chapter 11. As teams get larger, more documentation, additional coordination practices, increased ceremony, or other compliance activities (financial controls, for example) are usually needed. However, even these expanded practices should still be governed by APM's values and principles. For example, the principle of Simplify still applies to a large project; it just means to employ the simplest practice that works for a team of 150 rather than one of 15.

A 500-person team can't be as agile as a 10-person team, but it *can* be more agile than a competitor's 500-person team. By focusing on value, delivery, self-organization, and self-discipline, even larger teams burdened with complex coordination issues can readily adapt to business, technology, and organizational changes.

An Expanded Agile Delivery Framework

Figure 5-4 shows an expanded version of the Agile Delivery Framework. At this level, it identifies practices and becomes, in effect, the beginning of a hybrid methodology. It breaks the Explore phase into detail about the work done during an iteration. The expanded framework also shows specific practices in each of the other phases. In the next several chapters, the practices outlined in this overview of the agile framework are presented in detail.

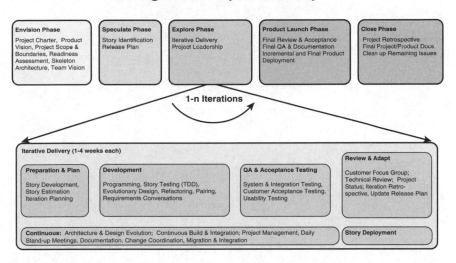

An Agile Development Lifecycle

Figure 5-4
An Expanded APM
Delivery Framework

Final Thoughts

An agile framework, just like an agile project, should be balanced between structure and flexibility. As the number and size of agile projects undertaken in an organization grow, there needs to be a common framework, some common guidelines, a few standard practices, and of course a set of common values. At the same time, a project team in Beijing, China, and another in Seattle, Washington, have different team members and different environments, so they need the freedom to adapt from the common framework and practices. The "art of agility" comes into play here—the ability to balance flexibility and structure. It takes effective leadership and agile experience to discover the best balance point for each organization.

Chapter 6

The Envision Phase

It's the vision thing again! Visioning and goal setting have been identified time after time as key ingredients of project success.

> *"It is rare to discover anything in the realm of human behavior that occurs with great consistency....Therefore, it was surprising to find that in every case, without exception, when an effectively functioning team was identified, it was described by the respondent as having a clear understanding of its objective" (Larson and LaFasto 1989).*

But how does this need for a clear vision jibe with the exploratory nature of product development, which we have just gone to great lengths to describe as volatile and fuzzy? This apparent dichotomy is resolved when you consider that although the details of requirements and design can be volatile, the overarching business goal or product vision must be clear. In fact two critical aspects of a vision are clarity and an elevating goal that makes a difference and conveys a sense of urgency to the project. Absent a clear vision, the exploratory nature of an agile project will cause it to spin off into endless experimentation. A clear vision must bound exploration.

If everyone knows that creating a clear, compelling vision is so critical to project success, then why do so many teams suffer from lack of vision? The answer is that creating a clear, compelling vision is hard—it takes work, and it takes leadership. In the process of developing a new product there are so many options that creating a clear path forward can be daunting. This is one activity in which effective leaders lead—they help cut through the ambiguity and confusion of creating an effective vision. Compounding the problem, there is no fixed rule for creating a good vision. It's one of those "I'll know it when I see it, but I can't describe it" phenomena, in part because the essence of a good vision is the teams's articulation of it.

Figure 6-1 depicts the evolution of a project plan—from vision, to scope, to release—utilizing three simple but powerful practices: the vision box, the project data sheet, and the release plan (accomplished in the Speculate phase). Each of these artifacts is simple in concept, powerful, and low ceremony (informal), and operates on the principle of limited "real estate." The vision box exercise forces the team to condense information about a product vision onto two flip chart pages (front and back of a box). The project data sheet forces the team to condense key project scope and constraint information into a single page. Story cards force the team to condense the key information about a story onto a single index card. Limiting the space in which we record information requires focus and selection: It demands collaboration and thinking, and it compels the team to make effective tradeoffs.

Figure 6-1
The Evolution of a
Project Plan

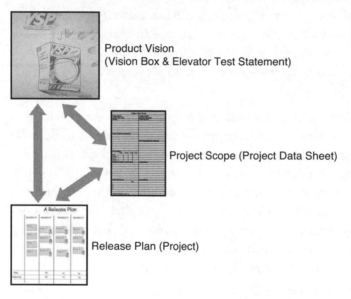

Product Vision
(Vision Box & Elevator Test Statement)

Project Scope (Project Data Sheet)

Release Plan (Project)

This chapter approaches the Envision phase as it would unfold for a new product and a new project, so the activities would need to be selected and adapted for other situations. For example, for a software product enhancement release, the vision should be done for the enhancement theme, not the overall product. A preliminary vision box and project data sheet could also be developed in a conceptualization phase early in a product life cycle.

A Releasable Product

In Chapter 1, the foundation for agile project success was defined as

- *Value goal*: Build a releasable product
- *Quality goal*: Build a reliable, adaptable product
- *Constraint goal*: Achieve value and quality goals within acceptable constraints

These are strategic goals, not specific requirements. They help teams and management answer the key questions at the end of every iteration: "What defines a releasable product?" and, "What is keeping us from releasing this product today?" These are very different from: "Are we conforming to our plan?" Circumstances, say a revised business objective, may lead to a "releaseability" answer that differs substantially from the plan. For example, the decision to release a product at an industry conference might alter the definition of minimal acceptable release capabilities. Focusing on the strategic releaseability question, rather than looking at a detailed requirements checklist, provides the entire project community with the right incentives to adapt to a changing environment.

One release criteria for a product is that features or stories are "done-done"—done from both a development perspective (coded, unit tested, etc.) and a product team perspective (acceptance tested). The project community and the organization define what production quality—done-done—means. For a life-critical medical device the quality threshold would be higher than for video games. Nonetheless, for a specific project defined production quality is a given, not a tradeoff option.

In looking at the three areas that define a releasable product, information from the product vision box and project data sheet (PDS, both to be defined in this chapter) can be used:

- *A releasable product*: product vision box; PDS—Project objective statement, business objectives, capabilities, capability value (defined in Chapter 8)
- *A reliable, adaptable product*: PDS—Quality objectives
- *Within acceptable constraints*: PDS—Tradeoff matrix (scope, schedule, cost)

Negative answers to the releasable question can be caused by a variety of factors: a missing capability, a key capability that wasn't mature enough, too much accumulated technical debt, or too many unfixed defects. These negative answers then become inputs to adapting strategies for subsequent iterations.

Using this "releasable" product approach, progress discussions with executives take on a different flavor. They revolve first around value, objectives, key capabilities and what has been delivered to date on the project (refer to the parking lot diagram in Chapter 10, Figure 10-2) and quality issues. These discussions set a context for talking about cost and schedule, whereas in many non-agile environments, cost and schedule progress dominate.

Envisioning Practices

The purpose of the Envisioning phase is to clearly identify what is to be done and how the work is to be accomplished. Specifically, this phase answers the following questions:

- What is the customer's product vision?
- What are the key capabilities required in the product?
- What are the project's business objectives?
- What are the project's quality objectives?
- What are the project constraints (scope, schedule, cost)?
- Who are the right participants to include in the project community?
- How will the team deliver the product (approach)?

For small projects, much if not most of the work of the Envision and Speculate phases can be accomplished in a single "kickoff" chartering session. For larger projects, chartering, requirements-gathering, additional training, resource procurement, and architectural work may take longer and can be included in an Iteration 0 (see Chapter 7 "The Speculate Phase"). For large-to medium-sized projects, there is normally a debate and discussion period required to obtain agreement about the product vision. During the Envision phase the vision constantly evolves based on new information. After the

Envision phase it needs to be reviewed periodically for any changes and to ensure that the team continues to understand the vision.

Although there are other important aspects of initiating a project, such as budgets, staff organization, and reporting needs, without a commonly held vision the project will falter. Without a vision, "initiation," on its own becomes bureaucratic and sterile.

The Envision phase defines the beginning of a project for which the kick-off event might be the approval of a feasibility study. Many companies conduct feasibility and marketing studies prior to initiating development projects, whereas others use only brief project requests. Envisioning should involve the development and product team members in this process, normally using a series of collaborative meetings.

In the Envision and Speculate phases of APM it is particularly important to remember that

- The team members should constantly ask the question, "What is the barely sufficient process and documentation that we need?"
- All the practices related to "how" a team delivers are tailored and adapted to improve performance as the project progresses.
- The project community will also evolve its teaming practices.

The practices explained in this chapter fall into four categories: visions for product, project, community, and approach.

- Product Vision
  - Product vision box and elevator test statement
  - Product skeleton architecture and guiding principles
- Project Objectives and Constraints
  - Project data sheet
- Project Community
  - Get the right people
  - Participant identification
  - Customer team-development team interface
- Approach
  - Process and practice tailoring

Product Vision

A product vision (defined by a product vision box and elevator test statement) galvanizes members of the product team into focusing their often disparate views of the product into a concise, visual, and short textual form. These two project artifacts, and the product roadmap, provide a "high concept" of the product for marketers, developers, and managers. Although a preliminary product vision may have been done during a conceptualization phase, few members of the delivery team are usually involved in that process. Teams may take that vision as input, but it's critical that the team revisit that preliminary work.

Innovation, creating emergent results that we cannot predict, requires an evolutionary process that can accommodate exploration and mistakes. A good product vision remains relatively constant, whereas the path to implement the vision needs room to wander. Emergent results often come from purposeful accidents, so managers must create an environment in which these accidents can happen. Mountain climbing is a good analogy for this process. The goal remains getting to the top of the mountain, a fixed point. The goal may also be bounded by constraints, such as only having food for nine days. Every climbing team has a route plan for gaining the summit. Every climbing team also alters its route plan on the way to the top—sometimes in minor ways, sometimes in major ones—depending on conditions.

Similarly, every product needs a marketing theme, a crisp visual image and capability description whose intent is to draw customers into further investigation. In this design-the-box exercise (developed originally by colleague Bill Shackelford), the project and product teams create a visual image of the product (vision does imply "visual," after all). For software and other small products, the image should be the product package. For larger products—automobiles or medical electronics equipment, for example—the vision could be a one- to two-page product brochure or one to two Web pages.

In the design-the-box activity, the entire team, including product team members customers, breaks into groups of four to six people. Their task is to design the product box—front and back. This involves coming up with a product name, a graphic, three to four key bullet points on the front to "sell" the product, a detailed feature description on the back, and operating requirements. Figure 6-2 shows a sample vision box developed during a chartering session.

Figure 6-2
Product Vision Box
Example

Coming up with fifteen or twenty product capabilities or features proves to be easy. Selecting the three or four that would incent someone to buy the product is difficult. Usually this involves an active discussion about identifying the real customer. Even with a simple product, the vision boxes can vary quite a bit among teams. Presentations by each of the groups are then followed by a discussion of how the different focal points can be reduced to a few that everyone agrees upon. A lot of good information gets generated by this exercise—plus, it is fun and helps build team cohesion.

In addition to the vision box, the team concurrently develops a short statement of the product's positioning using an "elevator test statement"—a couple of sentences that indicate target customer, key benefit, and competitive advantage:

For midsized companies' distribution warehouses *who* need advanced carton movement functionality, *the* Supply-Robot *is a* robotically controlled lifting and transferring system *that* provides dynamic warehouse reallocation and truck loading of multisized cartons that reduces distribution costs and loading time. *Unlike* competitive products, *our product* is highly automated and aggressively priced.

The elevator test statement—an explanation of the project to someone within two minutes—takes the following format:
- *For (target customer)*
- *Who (statement of the need or opportunity)*
- *The (product name) is a (product category)*
- *That (key benefit, compelling reason to buy)*
- *Unlike (primary competitive alternative)*
- *Our product (statement of primary differentiation) (Moore 1991)*

The product vision box and elevator test statement vividly depict a product vision. They emphasize that projects produce products. Some projects (e.g., internal IT projects) may not create products for the external market, but viewing them as products for an internal market keeps the team grounded in a customer-product mindset. Whether the project results involve enhancements to an internal accounting system or a new digital camera, product-oriented thinking reaps benefits.

Finally, with several hours of active product vision discussion recorded on flipcharts, the team can construct a good outline for a short one- to two-page product vision document. This might include the mission statement, pictures of the "boxes," identification of target customers and each of their needs, the elevator test statement, customer satisfaction measures, key technology and operational requirements, critical product constraints (performance, ease of use, volumes), a competitive analysis, and key financial indicators.

For a four- to six-month project, this visioning exercise might take half a day, but it will pay big dividends. Recently, a client reported that spending three to fours hours for a visioning session brought a group with widely different ideas about product direction into alignment. The more critical the delivery schedule and the more volatile the project, the more important it is that the team have a good vision of the final desired outcome. Without this vision, iterative development projects are likely to become oscillating projects, because everyone is looking at the minutiae rather than the big picture.[1]

Companies doing new hardware development have a range of other "visioning" tools available to them, some of which significantly reduce the cost of experimentation and cycle time. One example is AliasStudio, a graphics software product from Autodesk, which industrial design firms use to "sketch" new product ideas. The use of AliasStudio precedes (and feeds) CAD/CAM tools, making it possible to explore product possibilities visually, as shown in Figure 6-3.

Figure 6-3
A Product Vision
(Courtesy of
Autodesk)

[1] Ken Delcol comments, "This statement is true regardless of the development approach. The joy of the iterative approach is that if you are lacking a vision, it should become obvious sooner than in the case of the traditional approach. The traditional approach creates the illusion that a vision exists for a number of months before someone figures out what is going on."

The next step, a prototype or working model, is the realm of companies such as Stratasys. Its fused deposition modeling (FDM) system creates plastic models from a downloaded 3D drawing (analogous to a 3D copy machine that creates plastic parts). Figure 6-4 shows an example of the parts produced. The model is built layer by layer from the bottom up. These parts can be used to construct working models quickly and cost effectively. Bell & Howell used FDM to create a new top-of-the-line scanner, building working prototypes from parts created by FDM. Both the design cycle and product part count were reduced by 50%. Using early lifecycle visioning tools such as AliasStudio that can feed data to automated prototyping tools such as FDM can greatly reduce cycle time and experimentation costs.

Figure 6-4
A Plastic Prototype of a New Scanner Design (Courtesy of Stratasys, Inc.)

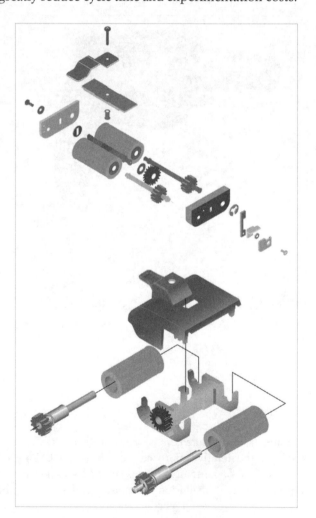

Although these practices provide a high-concept vision of the product, for complicated projects the vision may need to be supplemented with additional concept documents and financial analyses. However, without a high-concept vision, these other supporting practices tend to grow large and unfocused. A 25-page vision document subverts the whole meaning of a concise vision. For larger products and projects, an overall product vision can also be supplemented with vision statements for the major components. Each component team should participate in this visioning process for its own area.

Product Architecture

The objective of product architecture is to depict the internal plumbing of the project—a design that facilitates exploration and guides ongoing product development. An early "skeleton" product architecture guides both the technical work and may guide the organization of people who carry out the technical work. It is intended to communicate the larger context to the development team, not lock in a design.

> *In agile development, architecture is a guide, not a straightjacket.*

Software projects might utilize domain models of business areas (participants and capabilities) and technical block-diagram conceptual models. Agile modeling encourages early architectural "sketches" to create an overall vision of approach and help determine cost and schedule estimates, followed by architecture and design evolution. Architecture and design aren't one-time activities in agile development, but ongoing activities that occur every iteration as architectures and designs evolve (technical architecture evolution is a difficult concept for engineers whose experience has been to design and fix the architecture early in the development process). This evolution must, however, take into account the cost of change. So, for example, a platform architecture decision, such as which database management system to use, probably wouldn't evolve (too costly to change), whereas database schemas (application architecture) would evolve. Obviously, if major architecture changes continue through iteration after iteration, something is probably wrong.

Although in general agile practices encourage change and adaptation, certain changes have greater impact and require careful coordination. For example, in automobile design the transmission and drive train components have a certain well defined interface. Changes within the component that don't change the interface can be handled less formally than those that affect the interface. It is not a matter of control—who gets to make the decisions—as much as it is a matter of coordination—making sure the team understands the total impact of a change and which groups are affected. A poor technical architecture makes this change coordination job difficult. Astute teams will recognize when excessive time spent on cross-component coordination or integration points to poor architectural decisions that need to be remedied.

In general, technical architectures utilize some combination of platform, component, interface, and module architectures. A new sport utility vehicle may begin with a "truck" or a "car" platform. A software product may utilize a Windows or a Mac platform, or both. The SUV has components such as a body, drive train, and engine. A software component may have application programming interfaces (APIs) that specify how other components are to interact with it. A multifunction PC device may have printer, scanner, and faxing components, each of which has subordinate modules (which in this case include integrated circuit boards).

A feature breakdown structure (FBS) can be used to depict a product architecture model in either software or hardware projects (see Figures 6-5 and 6-6). Many architectural representations are useful for technical teams, but the FBS serves to communicate between customer and development teams and acts as a bridge between the Envision and Speculate phases. The FBS identifies a backlog of features from which release and iteration plans will be developed.

Figure 6-5
Software Feature
Breakdown Structure
(CRM)

• Sales Management (Business Area)
  – Prospecting (Capability)
    • Create sales person log on (Story)
    • List leads for the sales person
    • Display individual lead detail
  – Territory Management
  – Sales Analysis
• Marketing
  – Lead Generation
  – Lead Follow Up
  – Advertisement Placement
  – Call Center Service

- KIT Vacuum Pump (Group)
- Control Panel
- Electrical
  - Power Cable Assembly
  - Vacuum System (Component)
    - Tray (Feature)
    - Base Unit
    - Fan
    - Vacuum Chamber
    - Card Cage
  - Gas Control
- System Electronics
  - Vacuum Gauge Module
  - System Control Module
  - Exciter Module
  - Amplifier Module

Figure 6-6
Hardware Feature
Breakdown
Structure—Mass
Spectrometer

One of the reasons project leaders need technical domain experience as well as project management skills is that they need to understand the interactions between technical architecture, project organization, and planning. Poor technical structures can cause organizational problems, just as poor organizational structures can sometimes result in bad technical decisions. Poor organizational structures can make release planning and roadmap development difficult.

Finally, in many projects, the team structure and the technical architecture are decided upon in the beginning and are thereafter fixed. Colleague Mike Cohn comments, "This is a real problem with staffing large projects too quickly. If you have 20 people on a project that needs 5 to start with, you have a tendency to want to find work for the other 15 so as not to be inefficient. This means that the system gets partitioned along the skill sets of the 20 developers rather than along boundaries appropriate for that project."

A better model would be for the human organization and the technical architecture to co-evolve over the early phases of the project. It may appear beneficial, with a large project, for the project feature teams to be aligned with the major product components. In automobile design we might have body, frame, drive train, engine, and electronics feature teams. Although this organization may be useful later in the project, a small core team that covers all components may work better in the beginning. The core team develops the overall architecture and, very importantly, the interfaces. After the interfaces have been specified through interaction and debate, feature-based teams may work better (note that component or feature-teams are cross-functional in terms of engineering disciplines). The core team may evolve into a part-time architecture and integration group that coordinates among feature teams. Another advantage of this approach comes from the cross-functional relationships that are built in the early project stages and that facilitate coordination as people are dispersed from their initial assignments into various feature teams.

Guiding Principles

A second piece of the architectural guide is, appropriately enough, a set of guiding principles (GPs) to assist development teams in "molding" the product to meet customer preferences. Just as agile values and principles guide people in their development efforts, guiding "product" principles assist in steering the product's evolution in the desired direction.[2] GPs are usually not measurable requirements or constraints but conceptual guides. For example, defining the ubiquitous phrase "user friendly" in measurable terms may be difficult. However, a GP stating that "The target user for this medical device, an entry-level medical technician, should be able to use the basic features of the product with minimal training" would help steer a development team in its user interface design. A guiding principle for this book was to focus on delivery rather than compliance practices. Another was a constraining GP—keep the length under 350 pages.

GPs can be used early in a project before specific requirements or design decisions have been made. For example, an early GP might be, "Maximize the employment of reusable components and services to speed development." That GP could then be used as a consideration in design, where it might be a criteria for selection of a technology platform. An early GP may evolve into a specific requirement later. In the case of the medical device mentioned earlier, after several iterations of experimenting the minimal training GP might be supplemented with specific user interface design requirements and measurable training objectives.

Although some GPs may be developed during project envisioning, they often emerge over early development iterations. Each principle should be described in a sentence or two, and the total number for a project, at any one time, should number in the single digits.

---

[2] Colleague Kevin Tate introduced me to this idea of guiding principles. It is further explained in his book *Sustainable Software Development* (Tate 2006).

Project Objectives and Constraints

The product vision establishes a baseline for what the product team, in conjunction with sponsors and the development team, desire in a product. Product visions outline a somewhat unconstrained goal, but a project also needs to establish objectives and constraints. A project needs to have articulated business objectives (which are different than the customer's product vision), quality objectives, and a defined set of capabilities that begin to bound the scope of a releasable product.

A project's scope and boundaries can be documented in a single-page project data sheet that conveys the essence of how a project will deliver on the product vision. This section describes the project data sheet and its components.

Project Data Sheet

A project data sheet (PDS) is the second major envisioning practice in the evolution of a project plan (refer to Figure 6-1). Although the product vision is an expansive view of what the product could become, the project vision bounds product development with objectives and constraints. Colleague Mike Cohn defines product vision as the "should haves" and the project scope as the "will haves." Eventually the product "should have" 234 features; however, for this project (release 1.0), it "will have" 126 features. A PDS, as shown in Figure 6-7, is the minimum documentation for a project's objectives and constraints.

> *A project data sheet (PDS) is a single-page summary of key business and quality objectives, product capabilities, and project management information. It is a simple document with a powerful impact whose condensed format appeals to the entire project community and constantly reminds them of the strategic aspects of the project.*

Figure 6-7
Project Data Sheet

Project Data Sheet	
Project Name: CRM Development	Project Leader: Braxton Quivera
Project Start Date: 3/1/2009	Product Manager: Roger Jones
Clients:	Executive Sponsor: Andrian Poledra
Marketing	
Call Center	Quality Objectives:
Sales	Defects: 25% under industry average
Accounting	All Severity 1 & 2 defects fixed
	Comprehensive automated testing implemented
	Overall McCabe Cyclomatic Complexity < 10
	Quality Assessment > 4 (reliability & adaptability)
Project Objective Statement:	
The objective is to build a web-based CRM	
application that includes sales tracking, order	Performance Guidelines:
management, Sales Management, and Marketing.	Call Center volume of 3,500 calls per day
The system needs to be operational by 9/30/09 and	Worldwide web access
cost less than $2.5 million.	<1/2 day training required
Business Objectives:	
Better customer service	
Reduce paperwork	Architecture Guidelines:
More accurate order processing	Integrate effectively with ERP system
Overall ROI > 14%	Maximize reusable components

Trade-Off Matrix:				
	Fixed	Flexible	Accept	Target
Scope		x		12,500 FP
Schedule	x			=/- 6 weeks
Cost			x	+/- $.5 M

Project Delay Cost per Month: $50,000
Exploration Factor: 8

Capability:	Major Project Milestones:	
Sales Management	Marketing except Call Center	9/30/09
Sales Analysis	Call Center	1/15/10
Prospecting	Sales Management	3/30/10
Territory Management	Order Management	6/30/10
Marketing	Issues and Risks:	
Lead Generation	Development costs are difficult to calculate.	
Lead Follow Up	Sales staff reluctant to embrace new system.	
Advertisement Placement	Requirements agreement among user groups	
Call Center Service	appears it may be difficult.	

Sections of the PDS include a combination of the following, depending on organization and project type:

- *Clients/customers*: A list of the key clients or customers.
- *Project leader:* The name of the project leader
- *Product manager*: The name of the product manager (product owner)
- *Executive Sponsor:* The person who has decision-making responsibility over the project plan and constraints

- *Project objective statement (POS)*: A specific, short (25 or fewer words) statement that includes important scope, schedule, and cost information (see Figure 6-8)
- *Business Objectives*: The overall financial and business reasons for undertaking this project
- *Tradeoff matrix:* A table that establishes the relative priorities of the project constraints—scope, schedule, and cost (see Table 6-1)
- *Exploration factor*: A measure (1–10) of the risk and uncertainty of the project
- *Delay cost*: The daily, weekly, or monthly cost of project delay (particularly useful when schedule is a high priority)
- *Capabilities*: A list of the key capabilities (or features)
- *Quality Objectives*: Quantitative and qualitative quality goals for a releasable product
- *Performance/quality attributes*: A list of the key performance and quality attributes of the product
- *Architectural Guidelines*: Key architectural guidelines that shape design decisions
- *Issues/risks*: Factors that could adversely impact this project

---

Project Objective Statement

POS: To provide an online automated athletic membership services system that includes court scheduling, billing, and member service charges. The system needs to be operational by 6/30/10 and cost less than $150,000.

Figure 6-8
Project Objective Statement

Table 6-1
Tradeoff Matrix

	Fixed	Flexible	Accept
Scope	X		
Schedule		X	
Cost			X

Tradeoff Matrix

The tradeoff matrix helps the development team, the product team, and the executive stakeholders manage change during a project. The trade-off matrix informs all participants that changes have consequences and acts as a basis for decision making. The trade-off matrix indicates relative importance of the three constraints (scope, schedule, cost) identified on the agile triangle (value, quality, constraints). If a team must adapt to inevitable changes, then they need to know which dimensions offer the most flexibility.

> *"When a project starts, it is important that the project plan represents a healthy balance between value, quality, and constraints. The tradeoff matrix comes into play when this balance is upset." —Ken Collier*

The rows of a project trade-off matrix, as shown in Table 6-1, depict the key constraints on a project—scope, delivery schedule, and cost. The columns display the relative importance of each dimension and are labeled Fixed, Flexible, and Accept. Fixed means that the dimension—schedule, for example—is fixed or constrained and that tradeoff decisions should not impact performance in that dimension. Fixed also connotes that the dimension in question has the highest priority. Flexible is one step down from Fixed; the dimension is still very important, but not important enough to trade off for the Fixed dimension. Accept indicates that the dimension—cost, for example—has a wider range of acceptable tolerance. In fact, as the importance goes from Fixed, to Flexible, to Accept, the tolerance for variation increases.

In the matrix, each column can each contain only one check mark. If the highest priority is scope (Fixed), then everything else takes lower priority. Schedule might be designated as the second-highest priority (Flexible). Similarly, the team would strive to meet the acceptable (Accept) tolerance on total project cost.

Many managers and executives consider project success to be on time, on budget, and on scope. They define each characteristic with no tolerances and then fantasize that the team can respond to all manner of business change without project changes. Software engineering metrics expert Capers Jones (2008) points out that it is common for customers "to insist on costs and schedules that are so far below U.S. norms that completion on time and within budget is technically impossible." If these three characteristics are all top priority, then how do teams make hard tradeoff decisions? Executives and customers put teams into an impossible position by demanding that they respond to change while failing to give them reasonable tolerances for dealing with those changes.

If a customer executive asserts that the delivery schedule is of paramount importance, then he should also be willing to prioritize other characteristics—to say, for example, that cutting features would be preferable to slipping the schedule. The team strives to meet all the goals, but it also needs to know the relative importance of the key characteristics to make informed day-to-day and end-of-iteration decisions.

Another powerful piece of information that can assist teams in making project decisions is delay cost. I once worked with a team for which the calculated delay cost was nearly a million dollars a day in lost revenue. Knowing this cost drove much of the decision making on the project and helped ward off the constant flow of new features from marketing. When stakeholders insist that schedule is the most critical element of a project, having them calculate a delay cost puts the criticality of the schedule in perspective.

Exploration Factor

An exploration factor acts as a barometer of the uncertainty and risk of a project. Big projects are different from small projects; risky projects are different from low-risk ones. One issue in selecting project management practices and processes is the particular problem domain in which the team has to operate. An exploration factor of 10 indicates a highly exploration-oriented (high-risk) problem domain, and a 1 indicates a very stable (low-risk) problem environment. It is important to identify the various problem domain factors, but it is even more important to tailor processes and practices to the problem and to adjust expectations accordingly.

> *Articulating an exploration factor helps considerably in managing customer and executive expectations.*

The exploration factor is derived from a combination of the volatility of a product's requirements (ends) and the newness—and thus uncertainty—of its technology platform (means). The exploration factor matrix shown in Table 6-2 shows four categories of requirements volatility: erratic, fluctuating, routine, and stable. "Erratic" requirements depict a situation in which the product vision is understood, but the business or product requirements are fuzzy. An example would be a version 1.0 new product development effort in which features are unfolding as the project goes forward. In this case, the requirements might change drastically as the project proceeds, not from poor requirements definition but from evolving knowledge of the product. Fluctuating requirements would be one step down in uncertainty. While an erratic problem space might experience requirements change of 25%–50% or more, a fluctuating one might be more sedate at 15%–25%. Table 6-3 summarizes these percentage change guidelines. A routine categorization would apply to a wide range of projects in which up-front requirements gathering yields a reasonably stable baseline for further work, whereas a stable environment might be something like a federally mandated change to payroll withholding rates that is well defined and unlikely to change.[3] These categorizations can also be applied to specific capabilities or features during release planning.

Table 6-2
Project Exploration Factors

Product Require-ments Dimension	Product Technology Dimension			
	Bleeding Edge	Leading Edge	Familiar	Well-known
Erratic	10	8	7	7
Fluctuating	8	7	6	5
Routine	7	6	4	3
Stable	7	5	3	1

[3] Ken Delcol comments, "This guides the PM in both how the project and individual requirements should be managed. For example, erratic requirements need a more iterative approach and should be planned that way up front, regardless of the overall state of the remaining requirements. Not all requirements fall into the same bucket. The trick is to realize which requirements are key to overall product success—there is no point rushing forward to specify the stable requirements when critical, high-risk requirements are erratic or fluctuating!"

Table 6-3
Requirements Variability Guide

Category	Requirements Variability
Erratic	25–50% or more
Fluctuating	15–25%
Routine	5–15%
Stable	<5%

The exploration factor's technology dimension also has four categories: bleeding edge, leading edge, familiar, and well known. "Bleeding edge" would involve a technology so new that very few people have experience with it. With bleeding-edge technology, learning by trying is the only strategy because no one else knows how to use it, either. Leading-edge technology is relatively new, but there are pockets of expertise to turn to—although the cost and availability of these experts might be an issue. Projects employing bleeding- or leading-edge technology have much higher risk profiles than those using familiar or well known technologies. Development teams should carefully evaluate in what parts of the product technology risk is justified, because even within a single product, not all components should be bleeding or leading edge.

Combining these elements, we might find that an erratic requirements, bleeding-edge technology problem space receives an exploration factor of 10, whereas a stable requirements, well known technology project receives a factor of 1. A project with fluctuating requirements and leading-edge technology receives a factor of 7. By calculating the exploration factor, teams can now discuss projects from the perspective of the overall "uncertainty" of the problem space. An 8, 9, or 10 project will require an agile approach because the uncertainty and risk are high. Short iterations, story-driven planning, frequent reviews with customers, and recognition that plans are very speculative are imperative for solving problems in this domain. In contrast, projects with a 1, 2, or 3 rating will be relatively stable and low risk. Plans for them may be more deterministic, iterations could be somewhat longer, and additional up-front requirements gathering and design time might be cost effective.

> *Without the recognition of different problem domains, one-size-fits-all project processes and practices seem justified. With such a recognition, customization and tailoring to specific problems will help teams to be successful.*

Project Community

A key project community vision can be summed up in four words: Get the Right People. Author Andrew Hill (2001) once asked legendary basketball coach John Wooden who he thought were the best coaches he faced. Without hesitation Wooden replied, "The ones with the best players." Hill continued, "So many top-level managers feel they can make do with mediocre employees. What I learned from Coach is that you must have top-notch talent to succeed."

In product development, as in most endeavors, getting the right people involved is the critical success factor. "Right" consists of both having the appropriate technical ability (or domain expertise) and exhibiting the right self-disciplined behavior. Getting the right people doesn't necessarily mean getting the most talented and experienced people, just the most appropriate people for the job.

That said, there are reasons for getting overqualified people, especially in product development projects in which effectiveness and speed are so important. In his classic book *Software Engineering Economics*, Barry Boehm (1981) offers his Principle of Top Talent: "Use better and fewer people." As Boehm summarizes, "The top 20% of people produce about 50% of the output." If you plan to take on difficult, demanding projects, you need the best talent. If you take on less demanding projects, you'll still do better with better-than-average talent. People sometimes counter this argument by saying, "But you have to understand that half the people are below average." My response is twofold: "One, that might be true, but it doesn't have to be true for my company or my project. Second, nearly everyone has the potential to be above average at something. It's a manager's job to help them find that something."

Author Jim Collins (2001) is adamant not only about getting the right people "on the bus," but also that getting those people is even more important than figuring out where the bus should go. He declares, "The 'who' question comes before 'what' questions—before vision, before strategy, before tactics, before organizational structure, before technology." Everyone understands the notion that casting is critical in theatre or the movies. As authors Rob Austin and Lee Devin (2003) observe, "It is also clear that no matter how good you get at repeating a play, you can't replace Dustin Hoffman or Sigourney Weaver with a less-experienced beginner and expect to maintain quality."

Two factors determine whether or not a team has the "right" people: capability and self-discipline. There was much ado during the last decade about how having the right process could make up for having the wrong people (after all, the reasoning went, we can plug just about anyone into a well-defined process). In reality, having a reasonable process can help the right people work together effectively, but it can't make up for having the wrong people.[4]

Jim Collins (2001) aptly expresses this point with his analogy of getting the right people on the bus: "Most companies build their bureaucratic rules to manage the small percentage of wrong people on the bus, which in turn drives away the right people on the bus, which then increases the need for more bureaucracy to compensate for incompetence and lack of discipline, which then further drives the right people away, and so forth." This observation fits right into the delivery-compliance dichotomy—the right people focus on delivery, while the wrong people generate extra compliance work.

Collins's ideas are intended for organizations as a whole, but many of his ideas apply at the project level. Part of getting the right people involved, from a capability perspective, is having some idea of the project and the required skill set to carry it off. A group's capability should influence what products or projects are appropriate to pursue. Most people are coming to the understanding that *process isn't a substitute for skill*. Process may be an enabler, it may prevent reinventing the wheel, but it is not a substitute for skill. Process may assist a group of skilled people in working together more

---

[4] Larson and LaFasto (1989) articulated these ideas before Collins. Their research indicated that "it was imperative to select the right people." Secondly, they defined the right people as those with the necessary technical skills and personal characteristics (working well within a team).

effectively, but the fundamental capabilities, the fundamental skills, must be present in the team.

Several years ago I participated in a project retrospective with a software development team. The project was an outsourced Web project, and the customer ended the project unhappy with the technical architecture because the application was slow and difficult to change. The team admittedly did not have sufficient capability in the new Web technology; however, to mitigate the risk, it had established an architectural review process. Unfortunately, none of the reviewers had any experience in the technology either—they had instituted a process without sufficient capability.

The second aspect of getting the right people involves finding (and developing) those with self-disciplined behavior. Rigorous self-discipline differs from ruthless imposed discipline. One is generated from internal motivations, the other from authoritarian admonitions, usually playing on fear.

Getting the right people extends to the product team as well. I often get asked questions like, "What if we don't get the right customer involvement or customer voice on our project?" The answer is easy—don't do the project—although implementing it in most organizations is not. Not doing a project when the fundamental reality is that the team doesn't have the right customers or the right staff is part of the rigorous discipline required to succeed. Undisciplined organizations go ahead; they ignore reality or convince themselves through bravado that they can succeed in the face of information that indicates otherwise.

There is a difference between getting the right person and getting the perfect person. Your team may need an expert geophysicist but not be able to obtain one with the exact skills and experience desired. If you find one with the right self-disciplined attitude and sufficient technical skills, she will figure out how to obtain the right information. If, on the other hand, you find a pharmacologist and expect him to make the jump, that would be wishful thinking. The right person is the one who has the required capability or enough capability to grow—with coaching by the project leader and the team's technical specialists—into what is needed for the project. Similarly, the right person from a self-discipline perspective will have enough motivation to learn the behaviors that create a well functioning team.

Participant Identification

Early in project planning all the potential participants need to be identified so they all understand their and other's roles, so everyone understands the decision-making structure, and so expectations can be understood and managed.

Project participants comprise any individuals or groups that are part of the project community: from customers of the product, who can influence the project and determine requirements; to executives who provide funding and assume some managerial oversight of the project; to the core team members who work to deliver the product.

There are three broad categories of participants: customers (which could include end users, their managers, product specialists, the product manager, and the executive sponsor), development team members, and stakeholders. In this book, the term "stakeholder" will be used for internal participants, such as managers who are not direct customers of the product, and external participants such as vendors.

From a broad-brush perspective, customers provide requirements, team members build the product, and stakeholders contribute oversight and constraints. Customers are those participants who use the product to create value for themselves or their organizations. Team members are the developers and managers who are actively involved in delivering the product. Stakeholders provide oversight, constraints, compliance requirements, and resources (vendors). For example, the audit staff dictates certain process and control compliance requirements, whereas the financial department may require certain reports from the team. External regulatory agencies may impose product testing constraints.

Figure 6-9 shows the product team–customer interface. The interface differs between a product development effort that has external customers and a project (as in many IT organizations) that serves internal customers (or clients as some prefer). Looking at the diagram from left to right, some representative of the final end user or customer should be included in a feedback loop to the team, even if that person is not part of the product team. For example, a software company may involve key customers in reviewing development releases of products to get early and continuous feedback. In an IT project the End User/Customer circle and the Product

Team circle may overlap significantly, whereas in a software company project they may not overlap as much. In the case that few product team members are actual customers (where the circles overlap little or none) they must remember that they represent the customer but they are not the customer.

> *Big problems can occur when product team members who are not*
> *actual customers forget that they only represent the actual customers.*

Figure 6-9
The Product Team-
Customer Interface

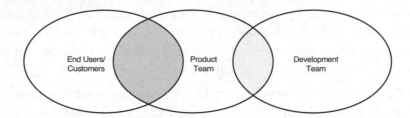

As the diagram shows, sometimes the customers will actually be a part of the product team—especially with internal projects in which customer representatives work part time (or full time) on the product team. Even then, other end users are often drawn into the project to provide domain expertise or to participate in iteration focus groups. The product team itself may include the product manager, business analysts or product specialists, subject matter experts (usually part time), and QA staff who would assist with developing automated acceptance tests. QA staff, and others such as user interface designers, may have roles to play on the product team. Finding the right mix of individuals to serve on the product team, and getting enough of their time, can be a very difficult transition in many organizations because the commitments required to participate in an agile team are usually more than would be required on a traditional team.

Author Rob Thomsett proposes three levels of participants (whom he calls "stakeholders"), each with a different potential degree of impact on a project:

- *Critical*: These are the participants who can prevent your project from achieving success before or after implementation; in other words, the showstoppers.
- *Essential*: These participants can delay your project from achieving success before or after implementation. In other words, you can work around them.

- *Nonessential:* These participants are interested parties. They have no direct impact on your project, but if they are not included in your communication, they can change their status to critical or essential (Thomsett 2002).

Identifying a project's participants is a project leadership task that is very easy to talk about and often most difficult to do well. Project team after project team has been blindsided by unidentified participants coming forth to bury the project with unforeseen political agendas.

But identifying and managing participants has another subtle, but important justification—it helps improve teamwork. According to Carl Larson and Frank LaFasto (1989), "external support and recognition" of the team by the organization contributes to success, or more precisely, lack of that support is a cause of failure. A development project doesn't operate in a vacuum; it operates within a larger organizational environment. When that wider organization withholds recognition, resources, or support, development teams will feel isolated and abandoned.

A list of project participants might include

- *Executive sponsor:* The person (or group of people) who champions the product and makes key decisions about the product's goals and constraints
- *Project leader:* The leader charged with delivering project results, and focuses on stakeholders external to the project and release issues more than iteration issues
- *Product manager:* The person who leads the team responsible for determining what results to deliver
- *Product specialist:* The person(s) who work on the product team as subject matter experts and analysts and support the product manager
- *Iteration manager:* The person who leads the development team and focuses on iteration activities and team dynamics
- *Lead engineer (developer, architect):* The person who guides the technical aspects of the team's delivery
- *Management:* A potentially wide range of individuals who can be in charge of participant organizations; may have budget or technical decision-making authority or influence over the project outcomes

- *Product team*: The individuals, both full- and part-time, who are charged with determining features that need to be built, prioritizing them, and accepting the results
- *Project team*: Members of the product and development teams, both full- and part-time, who are accountable for delivering a releasable product
- *Development team*: Individuals whose primary responsibility is developing and testing the product (engineering)
- *Suppliers*: External companies or individuals who provide services or product components
- *Government*: Regulatory agencies that require information, reports, certifications, and more

The more complex the participant group, the more time project leaders must spend managing expectations, getting critical project decisions made, and keeping the project from being pulled in too many directions. Identification is the first step in integrating various participants into the project community.[5]

Product Team–Development Team Interaction

A significant number of project failures are caused by poorly defined product team–development team interfaces. Although product specialists and developers are in the same community, they are in separate sub-groups, each having definitive roles. When this interface—which is defined by information flows, accountabilities, and responsibilities—is ill defined, project failure looms close by.

---

[5] Identifying the right project participants in product development efforts, and getting them involved at the right time, is critical. For example, software licensing decisions can impact design, so waiting until the later stages of a software project to include the legal department can cause delays at the end. A great reference on this topic for software product developers is *Beyond Software Architecture: Creating and Sustaining Winning Solutions* by Luke Hohmann.

Figure 6-10 shows a general outline of role responsibility on a project. Within any project there should be a development team and a product team. The development group should be headed by a project leader and the product group by a product manager (in Scrum these are called product owners). Arrows on the diagram indicate the major interactions between development and product teams and therein the responsibilities of each. At one level the responsibilities of the product team and development team are simple—the first is responsible for "what to build" and the second for "how to build it." In practice, each role, each person, has input and influence on the entire project—both the what and the how.

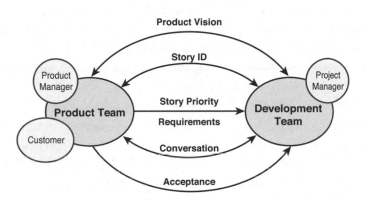

Figure 6-10
Defining Product Team-Development Team Interactions

Without a strong product manager, the worst situation arises—prioritization fails, and the development team, to keep the project from bogging down, begins making the priority decisions itself. This degenerates into a no-win situation, as the customers can always fault the decisions and then use that failure as an excuse to reduce their involvement further. When a project loses its partnership relationships and parties abdicate their responsibilities, that project is in big trouble. This problem sometimes occurs in companies because product managers tend to have both a marketing and a product definition role. The marketing role takes up so much time that they have little left over for working with development. Even product companies are rarely staffed with sufficient product team members to fulfill their agile roles. Many have had to add product specialists to fulfill the internal role while product managers focus externally on customers.

One of the key reasons internal IT projects fail, or underperform, is misunderstanding the nature of these two roles. Product companies often do a decent job of differentiating these roles, but IT projects often miss the product manager role. In many IT projects the role of product manager, by default, tends to fall to someone in IT, which usually leads to disaster. The rule for IT projects should be: No customer-supplied product manager, no project.

> *One of the key reasons internal IT projects fail, or underperform, is misunderstanding the project leader and product manager roles. The product manager must come from outside the IT department.*

For a small project, the product manager could also be the primary customer. For an IT project for which there are ten customer departments, spread across six cities, with 150 users providing requirements input, a product manager should be appointed to coordinate the customer information flow and decision making. For a product development organization, the product manager coordinates the gathering of information from thousands or even millions of retail customers, condenses them into a usable form, and then coordinates the project decision-making process.

This brings up another wider issue. Roles are not static descriptions we slavishly follow; roles are instantiated by individuals, and every person who fills a role plays it differently. Just as every actor playing Macbeth brings his own talents, interpretation, and experience to the play, every person who fills a product or project leader role (or any other role) plays it differently. One product manager may have extensive technical experience, another less. To tell the first person that she shouldn't have any input to the technical decisions would be throwing away a valuable resource. Telling a product domain–experienced project leader or developer that he will have no input to the product vision or specifications would be an equal waste of talent.

Project management books and company job descriptions often contain specific role narratives that include decision-making authority. Although role boundaries are important, in practice a role should be flexible, adapting to the specific person who fills it. At best, a role takes a page of description. Roles are finite. People are infinite. Role descriptions are merely a starting point for actual product and project leaders to build relationships that will quickly transcend static roles. How each individual interprets his or her role and how he or she interacts with others who are interpreting their own roles results in a richness of relationship that transcends our feeble attempts at role descriptions. Trying to force people into a fixed role description is not only ultimately impossible, it is counter to agile principles.

> *People are not only more important than process, they are more important than roles.*

Although any decisions made without interaction and debate between the customer and development groups will be poor ones, ultimately the "what" decisions are made by the customer team and the "how" decisions are made by the development team. Good development groups have a wealth of knowledge about the product domain and should have significant input into the "what" decision. Product managers and other customer group members often have significant input into "how" a product might be designed. In the end, however, each group has its own primary responsibility.

The responsibilities of each group and the interactions between the two groups are key to success. In a project's early Envision stage, both groups are involved in creating a product vision, but the product manager makes the final decisions. During the Speculate and Explore phases, the groups interact to analyze requirements, to identify features (or stories), and then to prioritize those features. Customers define feature requirements and help the team make day-to-day refinements. Larger projects may have many customers, who often have conflicting needs and priorities. No single person may have knowledge of all the feature requirements. For these larger projects, or for projects with wide-ranging needs for customer information, it is important to consolidate multiple voices into a consistent "customer voice," a task that is ultimately the product manager's responsibility.

The last interaction shown in Figure 6-10 is acceptance. It is the product team's job to accept the product by verifying that it meets product release goals. This acceptance should be done through a combination of automated testing and customer focus group reviews. A technical quality assurance group may assist the product team in this effort, but ultimately the responsibility for acceptance lies with the product team.

As with many other practices, defining the customer-developer interface presents different challenges when you are using it with a team of 10, or 100, or 1,000. Trying to corral 100 customers from disparate business departments is much more difficult than working with a single one. Similarly, working with a group of 100 engineers creates more challenges than working with 2. However, the basic interactions shown in the customer-developer interface diagram and the responsibilities of the roles as described here don't change with size.

Delivery Approach

One of the characteristics that defines high-performance teams is their approach to doing their work. Approach rivals vision and objectives in importance because it determines how a team will execute, how it will deliver, and how team members will work together (Katzenbach 1993). Because APM stresses execution, the team's approach to that execution becomes vital. Part of the self-discipline required of a team is that it agrees on an approach and then actually uses it. Either failure to agree or failure to execute indicates lack of self-discipline.

Process and practice tailoring defines the approach that the team will use to deliver a product. Teams starting with the organization's standard framework and practices, and then tailors the framework and practices to their needs. For example, a company might use the APM delivery framework with organizationally mandated checkpoints (approvals) at each phase. Within this framework, the company would identify a set of standard practices and deliverables (a streamlined set) such as those in Figure 5-4. The team then tailors the required practices and adds additional ones the team deems necessary.

Self-organization strategy concentrates on how people work together, how they collaborate, and the mechanisms for that collaboration. Processes and individual practices concentrate on what people actually do. Although the strategy and process seem to overlap, they are actually complementary. For example, the practice of daily stand-up meetings describes the concepts and mechanics for conducting short daily meetings to coordinate team activities. But if there are multiple feature teams, the project needs a strategy for using these meetings effectively in larger groups.

Finally, processes and practices evolve. In the Envision phase the team may develop a general plan for its use that will undoubtedly be revised as the release plan details are developed in the Speculation phase. Then, as each iteration reaches completion, the processes and practices will be adapted to the feedback from the project itself. Teams are encouraged to adapt everything except the bare essential policies and process framework to the reality of the actual situation as it unfolds.

Self-Organization Strategy

The term "self-organization strategy" sounds like an oxymoron, because self-organization implies that "stuff happens" without planning and forethought. Some consultants and practitioners have interpreted the ideas of complex adaptive systems to mean that self-organization happens magically within groups of people. All groups self-organize, but if we want *effective* self-organization, we have to think carefully about how to grow this type of environment.

Project managers often perpetuate a hierarchical, command-control management philosophy in their project organizations by focusing on organizational charts, detailed process and activity identification, and documentation requirements. Thinking about a self-organizing strategy attempts to break this mindset by having the team focus first on interactions—how everyone associated with the project will play together. The strategy establishes the team's approach to communications, coordination, collaboration, decision making, and other individual-to-individual and team-to-team interactions. Teams need to ask questions such as those posed in Figure 6-11. After we design how people are going to collaborate, then, and only then, should we figure out the processes and practices that will support that collaboration.

Self-organizing Strategy Questions

- How will we collaborate with customers?
- How will members from different feature teams collaborate with each other?
- How will the team in Atlanta collaborate with the team in Seattle or Bombay?
- What does empowerment mean to our team?
- Who needs to talk to whom when?
- How are these people who talk to each other going to make decisions?
- Who is accountable for what?
- What practices are they going to use to facilitate the above?

Figure 6-11
Self-organizing
Strategy Questions

Most project management approaches include a communications plan. The Project Management Institute's *A Guide to the Project Management Body of Knowledge* (Project Management Institute 2001) includes communications management as one of its key knowledge areas. However, communication is not enough. Communication is basically asynchronous—I send you information (even if you send some back). Collaboration is much more than communication; it involves interaction to produce some "joint" result. Collaboration integrates your ideas and mine into a whole. We communicate status reports to management. We collaborate among team members using practices such as whiteboard brainstorming sessions to create a design. Throughout the product development world, in industry after industry, the rising tide of cross-functional teams speaks to the need to collaborate.

Process Framework Tailoring

Even in an agile project, the broad process framework is shaped by the organization. For example, product development organizations often employ some type of phased lifecycle framework that products must follow (see Chapter 12, "Governing Agile Projects"). At each phase certain information, features, or artifacts must be available and approved. To balance structure and flexibility, this common framework should be as streamlined as possible, enabling a degree of consistency from a senior executive perspective with flexibility at the team level.

The process framework should strive to identify the barely sufficient (or minimum acceptable) standards for an organization for the project, although "minimum" may be different for large projects than for small ones. The greater the "weight" of this framework—number of process elements, number of required artifacts, number of decision gates, greater documentation formality—the less agile the team can be.

Practice Selection and Tailoring

Agile development and project management are built on an underlying premise that individual capability is the cornerstone of success, and furthermore, that individuals are unique contributors. It follows from these premises that rather than molding people to a set of common processes and practices, processes and practices should be molded to the team itself. Although an organization might insist that project teams follow a guiding framework, there should be flexibility as to what individual practices are used to meet the needs of each phase. The team should discuss what practices are going to be used or not used. Just because a practice is a good one doesn't mean it needs to be used in every project. With individual practices, each team will tailor them in different ways according to the capabilities of the team members, the size of the project, the number of customers, and many other factors.

The team should ask itself four fundamental questions about the practices they select and tailor for a particular project:

- What practices are required?
- What supplementary practices do we need?
- What modifications do we need to make to the selected practices?
- What level of formality or ceremony should be used for documentation, approvals, changes?

In addition to a barely sufficient process framework, organizations may also specify a set of barely sufficient practices for each project phase. For example, developing a story-based release plan is a requirement, not an option, for a company applying APM, although the practice can be tailored for characteristics such as iteration length.

The practices of APM focus on value delivery activities, but as previously noted, every organization also has compliance activities and deliverables that need to be added to the set of required delivery practices. Although project leaders can attempt to reduce these as much as possible, at some point the team just has to accept some level of compliance work and add those practices to the required set.

The best trigger for implementing supplementary practices is to note when something isn't working through an iteration or two. If problems or risks are getting lost, for example, an issues recording and monitoring practice may need to be instituted—maybe putting them on a sticky note on a flip chart page would be sufficient. Team members and project leaders need to fight the tendency to add supplementary practices early—they need to wait until a specific and significant need arises.

"Significant need" is an important qualifier. Too often, reasonable mistakes (after all, innovation requires both successes and mistakes) are followed by knee-jerk reactions to add controls or new reports or new restrictions on the development team. For a large number of these "mistakes," much more time and energy goes into processes and procedures to prevent them from occurring again than would be spent on a "fix on occurrence" strategy.

As with adding supplementary practices, teams should usually wait to modify practices until after they've tried them for an iteration or two. If the practice itself has been defined using the barely sufficient principle, it will usually provide enough guidance to get the team started. In large projects, the team may determine early that a practice isn't sufficient and enhance it.

The implementation of documentation and approvals is often what separates bare sufficiency from bureaucracy. The breadth of things that are documented, the formality or ceremony of that documentation, and the review and approval processes for the documents can determine whether a practice, or process, is streamlined or not. For example, a change control practice (which in traditional projects often becomes a change resistance practice) can be a simple activity of discussing changes and documenting them minimally, or it can be an elaborate process of documentation, analysis, and review that eats up both time and paper. Author Michael Kennedy (2003) relates the view of documentation in the Toyota product development system: "At Toyota, specifications are the documentation of the results, not a recipe of the plan."

When tailoring their documentation practices, teams should consider distinguishing between permanent documentation (which is consistently updated because a budget has been established) and working papers (which don't need to be updated). They should also contemplate the level of ceremony they need—rough notes work fine for many, many documents. To use key engineering staff effectively, project leaders should offload nearly all compliance documentation to administrative staff. The issue isn't zero or burdensome documentation, it's first what documentation contributes to delivery (today and in the future) and second what documentation is required for external compliance (regulations, for example). Colleague Lynne Nix has a great mantra for documentation: "A little documentation goes a long way if it's the right documentation."

> *The issue is not documentation; the issue is understanding.*

Final Thoughts

Envisioning goes beyond project initiation. Initiation conjures an image of administration, of budgets and detailed schedules. And though these artifacts may be necessary, they need to flow from a well-articulated, discussed, and agreed-on vision. The four components of vision were expressed as questions early in this chapter:

- What is the product vision?
- What are the project objectives and its constraints?
- Who will be included in the project community?
- How will the team deliver the product?

For some projects this Envision phase can be accomplished in a day, or several days. For others, particularly those that haven't gone through a feasibility study of some kind, it may take longer—not necessarily in effort, but in the calendar time it takes for the vision to jell within the project community.

Envisioning doesn't stop after the Envisioning phase. At the beginning of each iteration (or milestone), as the team meets to speculate about the next iteration, team members need to revisit the vision. This revisiting can be for the purpose of modifying the vision or to remind the team, amid the hectic daily grind, of the purpose of their endeavors.

Chapter 7

The Speculate Phase

Plans are guides, not straightjackets. Agile teams plan, but they recognize that reality always intrudes. Plans in this context serve as a vehicle for embracing change, not blocking it. Plans have to adapt because the customers' understanding of their requirements changes, because estimates of work effort vary, because people arrive or depart from the team, and for a variety of other reasons. Plans are both conjectures about the future—our best guess at what will occur given the information we have—and guides to the future—determining what we want to occur and making it happen. Development generates new information that in turn creates the need to replan.

Planning is an important activity, but speculating is a more appropriate term as uncertainty increases. Speculating establishes a target and a direction, but at the same time, it indicates that we expect much to change over the life of a project. As mentioned in Chapter 5, speculating isn't wild risk-taking but "conjecturing something based on incomplete facts or information." Plans are always conjectures about the future. When we "plan," we expect the actual project result to conform to that plan, and then deviations become team mistakes or a sign of the team's failure to work hard enough. When we "speculate," we take the opposite perspective—it's the plan we suspect was wrong. The plan, or speculation, is a piece of information, but it is only one piece that we will examine to determine our course of action in the next iteration.

The Speculate phase spotlights product and project—creating and understanding the product structure, the backlog of capabilities and stories, and the release plan.

Speculating on Product and Project

The product of the Speculate phase is a release plan based on capabilities or stories to be delivered rather than activities (as in traditional project plans). This book doesn't specialize in business or product analysis or defining requirements, but some basics of both need to be described because capabilities, features, and stories are the building blocks of project plans. The release plan utilizes information about the product's specification, platform architecture, resources, risk analysis, business constraints, and target schedules.

There are two crucial components of an iterative planning and development approach—short iterative timeboxes and features. For software projects, iterations are generally two to four weeks in length. Hardware projects will have longer iterations and greater variation—electronic devices will generally have shorter timeboxes than, say, automobiles. Short iterations act to accelerate projects. When they keep timeframes short, teams have to figure out faster ways of accomplishing every aspect of development. For example, in serial software development, major quality assurance activities are performed once toward the end of the project. In iterative development, QA activities are completed every iteration. The QA staff has to figure out how to be more effective and efficient because they perform these activities six, ten, or forty times during a project rather than once.

Feature-based development is not a software-only technique. Many hardware product development efforts are driven first by the creation of a product structure and then an extensive list of the features. In addition, because more and more products include embedded software, hardware and software features are both candidates for this feature-driven approach.

The first goal of feature-based planning and development is to make the process visible, and understandable, to the customer team. All too often product development planning has concentrated on making the technical work understandable to the engineering team. Customers and product managers have to wade through lists of technical activities, many of which made little sense to them. A software development task such as "create a normalized data schema design" means little to most customer teams. However, a hardware feature such as "Develop a DVD feature that will play sections of movies" resonates with customers. Customers understand products, components of products, and features of those components. They also understand how they use the products. Product teams can attach significance (value) to these and therefore can make priority decisions about them. The engineering staff can then translate from a customer-facing view to a technical view to design and build the product.

Features act as the interface between development engineers and product teams—a medium for shared understanding. This shared space takes the form of story cards, each written on an individual index card, that break features down into chunks that can be implemented. The front of this index card contains requirements information for planning purposes, whereas the back of the card contains technical task information that enables the team to estimate effort and manage its work (often the technical tasks are listed on a flip chart, the "virtual" back of the index card).

Using this style of planning, product managers control which features are included in the product. Development engineers control how features are designed and implemented. Product managers wouldn't have the authority to say, "We're running behind; let's cut testing time." Instead, they could only say, "We're running behind, let's cut features 34 and 68." Similarly, the development team couldn't arbitrarily add a feature because "it would be way cool." Obviously this delegation of responsibilities undergoes discussion and debate, as product managers may have suggestions about (but not final authority over) how products get built, and development engineers may make suggestions (but not final decisions) about potential features.

Agile project speculating helps the project team

- Determine how the product and its features will evolve in the current release
- Balance anticipation with adaptation as the project unfolds
- Focus on the highest-value features early in the project
- Think about the business goals, project objectives, and customer expectations
- Provide necessary cost and schedule information to management
- Establish priorities for tradeoff decisions
- Coordinate interrelated activities and features across teams
- Consider alternatives and adaptive actions
- Provide a baseline for analyzing events that occur during the project

Everyone accepts the premise that our business world constantly changes. However, we still shrink from the implications of those changes. We still anticipate that plans won't change, at least not very much. We still view change as something to be controlled, as if we have some power over the world outside our projects. We still believe the way to reduce the cost of change is to anticipate everything at the beginning of the project so nothing has to change.

The only problem is that this approach doesn't work. If we constantly measure people's performance against the plan, then adaptability will suffer. If we want adaptability, flexibility, innovation, and responsiveness to customers as they learn new information, then we need to reward the team's responsiveness to these changes, not admonish team members for not "making plan."

Through their actions, performance measurements, and vision, agile leaders constantly need to encourage teams to learn and adapt as projects evolve. Evolutionary projects are difficult—full of ambiguity, change, and uncertainty—but the rewards for adapting to deliver business value are great.

Before going on with this product and project plan discussion, we need to examine the objectives of this chapter and the next—Advanced Release Planning. Just as titles indicate, this chapter covers the basics of creating a product backlog and developing a release plan, and the next chapter goes into advanced topics. For example, this chapter assumes the project is small and relatively short and can be planned at a single level—stories can be identified and then put into a release plan. The next chapter looks at multi-level planning, capabilities and stories, and how to plan bigger projects using capabilities for long-range planning and stories for the short range. The next chapter also introduces new topics such as planning themes and value points.

Product Backlog

The objective of creating a product backlog is to expand the product vision, through an evolutionary requirements definition process, into a product feature list, or backlog.

The Speculate phase product backlog expands and refines the one developed in the Envision phase—identifying and listing the features and stories from feasibility or marketing studies, requirements-gathering efforts, and product visioning. For existing products, customers, developers, product managers, and customer support staff constantly make suggestions about product enhancements that add to the backlog. This backlog list, is maintained by the product manager and is the major inputs for release, wave, and iteration planning.

Feature details evolve over the development phases. In the Envision phase the team creates a preliminary feature or product breakdown structure in which features are identified (as shown in Chapter 6, Figures 6-5 and 6-6). In the Speculate phase, the team expands this list, and for each feature creates one or more "story" cards that contain basic descriptive and estimating information. During the Explore phase, in the specific iteration in which a story is planned for implementation, the requirements are determined in detail, and the story is built and tested.

There are tremendous differences between developing an automobile, an electronic instrument, a software application, or an airplane, and so the specifics of analyzing and specifying requirements and features vary widely. Some products require more early requirements specification than others based on the cost of altering designs during development. Because software is more malleable than nearly any other product, an evolutionary specification process will usually serve it best. However, as mentioned before, even the most sophisticated industrial products are undergoing evolutionary development via the use of simulations and modeling.

> *Software is the most malleable product. Companies need to use this characteristic to their competitive advantage, and sticking to traditional waterfall development negates this advantage.*

The results of the requirements specification process, whatever the engineering discipline involved, should be documented as a hierarchy such as product, platform, group, and component. For business software applications, these categories could be application, business area, capability, feature, and story. Small software products might use only the story level, whereas large industrial products may use the entire hierarchy.

For a growing number of computer, instrumentation, and electronic products, a feature hierarchy includes both hardware and software features. Part of the design process involves determining whether low-level features will be implemented in hardware or software. Products that were once considered "hardware" products with rudimentary embedded software now have such a large set of software features that they could be considered software products with supporting hardware. In just a few years, for example, cell phones have progressed from hardware with minimal software to hundreds of thousands of lines of software code that drive (or "support," depending on whether you are a hardware or a software engineer) all aspects of the hardware.

From the list of potential stories, the product team and the engineering team need to discuss prioritization and scheduling issues during the assignment of stories to iterations within the release plan. One characteristic of agile projects is the volatility of the stories on the backlog. During the planning for each iteration, the list of stories to be included in that iteration can change from the original release plan.

What Is a Feature, a Story?

So what is a feature or story, anyway? In general, a feature or story is defined as a piece of a product that delivers some useful and valuable functionality to a customer. Features for a software product (the ability to check a customer's credit rating) or an airplane (a comfortable seat for the passenger) are very different, but they both focus on delivering value to the customer. The basic difference in a story and a feature is that a story is a small piece that delivers useful functionality, but may not deliver a complete function. Using the customer credit check feature, for example, the complete checking "feature" may take several weeks of effort, whereas a "story" should be on the order of 2–10 days of effort for effective iteration planning. So in this case, several stories would be needed to deliver the complete feature, as illustrated in Figure 7-1. That said, capabilities, features, and stories are primarily used as a hierarchical structure to manage increasing product size.

Figure 7-1
Feature-Story
Example

> ## Feature-Story Example
>
> Feature: As a credit analyst I need the ability to check a customer's credit rating.
> - Story 1: As a credit analyst I need the ability to check the prior payment history with this customer.
> - Story 2: As a credit analyst I need the ability to check this customer's credit bureau status.
> - Story 3: As a credit analyst I need the ability to calculate our internal credit rating based on history and credit report.

The first edition of this book used features as the smallest development "chunk." I have switched to using story as the smallest chunk for two reasons. First, the term "story" has become the norm for a wide range of agile practitioners. Second, and more important, because agile development is evolutionary in nature, we should use terminology whenever possible that connotes "evolutionary" rather than fixed. Stories evolve over time; they don't represent a set of "fixed" requirements. The goal should be to deliver something of high customer value, not a set of fixed requirements. The term "story" engenders that evolutionary feeling better than other terms.

The Focus of Stories

Defining stories can be very difficult for individuals who are experienced with a technical task approach to development. In software development, for example, teams may be used to tasks such as: "develop the user interface" or "implement a data base schema." These tasks are not user oriented like "the ability to check customer credit rating." Figure 7-2 illustrates these two perspectives: customer and technical. The figure shows a typical technical layered architecture of user interface, business objects (business rules), middleware, and database. Traditional project plans focus on these technical task areas. Stories, on the other hand, are customer oriented.

Figure 7-2
The Focus of Stories

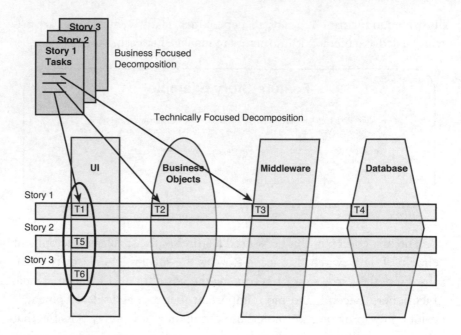

For release planning, allocating work to iterations in a release plan, we use stories because we want to involve the product team in the process and they don't relate to technical tasks. For detailed iteration planning, stories are broken down into technical tasks, which the development team then uses. These technical tasks are small because they implement only what is needed for a story.

At one client site, several software developers were complaining about this breakdown because they viewed the small technical tasks as inefficient. For example, they mentioned that coding small pieces of a user interface screen would be less productive than doing a whole one. To which the product manager in the room said, "Yes, but remember on the last project. We were nine months into it before I saw any results, and they were wrong." Not having demonstrable customer-understood stories causes projects to get off track quickly, and furthermore, by combining tasks from several stories during an iteration, most perceived inefficiencies can be eliminated.

Some stories will invariably take longer, or appear to take longer, than one iteration to complete. Usually when teams are pressed to decompose a "big" story into bite-sized stories, they figure out a way. Inability to break things down in this manner is usually an issue of lack of experience rather than a un-decomposable story.

In planning a product, however, some items that need to be delivered may not sound—at least to customers or product managers—as though they provide direct benefit. An interface component deep in the bowels of an electronic instrument may have minimal interest for an end customer but be a necessary "technology domain" feature. For project planning and delivery purposes, teams need to include these technology stories in the plan. However, the danger in building technical features before customer ones is "dark holes." The longer the technical team "stays dark"—building techie stuff— the further off track the project can get before receiving feedback from the customer team.

Story Cards

The purpose of story cards is to provide a simple medium for gathering basic information about stories, recording high-level requirements, developing work estimates, and defining acceptance tests. Story-based development is intended to be customer-facing development. Story cards[1] are intended to identify, but not to define in detail. Story cards act as agreements between customers and team members to discuss (and document, to the extent necessary) detail requirements during an iteration. Discussion is critical to understanding, which in turn is critical to estimating.

Story cards, as illustrated in Figures 7-3 (structured) and 7-4 (casual) are index cards on which the project and customer team members record the information gathered in their discussions, such as a brief description of the story written in the form of "<persona> has the ability to perform <some function>". The critical piece is the discussion. As in other agile practices, the entire team interacts to produce story cards. The project leader facilitates the discussion and monitors action items, but agile planning is a team sport.

---

[1] The term "story" comes from Extreme Programming. Other agile software development methods may use similar, but not identical, terms—components, features, use cases, backlog items.

Figure 7-3
A Story Card

Story Card		Planned Iteration:	3
Story ID: 25		Story Type:	Cust
Story Name: Establishment Sales Territorities			
Story Description:			
As as Sales Manager, the ability to create U. S. sales territories based upon			
states and standard metropolitan areas.			
Est. Value Points:	13		
Est. Story Points:	8		
Requirements Uncertainty (E, F, R, S):	R (routine)		
Dependencies with other Stories:	None		
Acceptance Tests:			

Figure 7-4
Cards Can Be
Very Informal

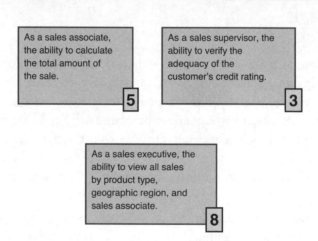

As a sales associate, the ability to calculate the total amount of the sale. **5**

As a sales supervisor, the ability to verify the adequacy of the customer's credit rating. **3**

As a sales executive, the ability to view all sales by product type, geographic region, and sales associate. **8**

The cards themselves are important. They provide a mobile, tactile medium that team members can write on, shuffle about on the table, and have conversations around. After data gets entered into a formal medium people are less likely to change it. The information on the cards becomes the product of the team's collaborative effort and a focal point for mutual understanding of the product at a detail level. A few key items of information should be recorded on story cards and supplementary documents for details. Typical information on story cards is shown in Figure 7-5.[2]

[2] Acceptance test criteria could be implemented in specific test cases or included in a customer focus group review. Figuring out acceptance criteria compels the customer team to define what "done" means. Detailed acceptance tests and the use of tools such as FIT can essentially automate detailed requirements.

Figure 7-5
Story Card
Information

Story Card Information

- Story identifier and name
- Story description: A sentence or two that describes the feature in customer terms
- Story type (C=customer domain, T=technology domain)
- Estimated work effort: The estimated work effort needed to deliver the story, including time for requirements gathering, design, coding, testing, and documentation
- Estimated Value Points (described in Chapter 8)
- Requirements uncertainty (erratic, fluctuating, routine, stable): An "exploration factor" for a specific story
- Story dependencies: Dependencies that could influence implementation sequencing
- Acceptance tests: Criteria the customer team will use to accept or reject the story

Customer-recognizable stories and technical activities provide orthogonal views of the same problem space. In planning the next iteration for a project, the team first turns the story cards over and lists the technical activities required to specify, design, build, test, and document the story. To progress from a customer-recognizable unit of work to a recognizable technical unit of work, there is likely to be a reaggregation of that work. Technical activities from several customer stories may be aggregated into a single technical work package.

The development team also uses the task breakdown to estimate the work to implement the story. Mike Cohn suggests using "planning poker" for such an exercise (Cohn 2006). In planning poker each team member jots down an estimate for the story and then they all reveal their estimates to each other. This process can be quick, but it is valuable: The estimate differences reveal any misunderstandings about the story requirements or the story development tasks.

For larger projects—those with 1,000 stories, for example—the story cards will probably require some form of automation for sharing among feature teams. Although each individual team may use cards for its own planning sessions, sharing across multiple teams could prove difficult. Distributed teams and teams working under formal contracts may need to automate the cards—or more correctly, the information on the cards—even for smaller projects. As with other agile practices, the team should let the need dictate formality of the documentation.

The level of requirements uncertainty and the technology risk factors influence not only story scheduling, but also the team's approach to implementing a story. Generally, high-risk stories (erratic or fluctuating) will be scheduled in early iterations so the team can determine first whether the story can be implemented at all, and second whether it will take more time or money than anticipated. If the requirements are difficult to gather or pin down, a series of discovery prototypes may be required. If the best design option isn't clear, a series of design experiments (simulations, quick throwaway implementations) may need to be conducted. Highly uncertain features may require additional research work before they can be planned at all. Even within a product there will be technology areas or features that run the gamut from low to high risk. Treating each with an approach geared to the level of risk improves both effectiveness and productivity.

Creating a Backlog

A backlog is a list of capabilities, features, and stories that the product team has identified. A backlog generally has limited information—such identifier, name, brief description, priority, exploration factor, estimate—about backlog item. This backlog data is used for both release and iteration planning (although the two plans may be done at different levels of detail). There are two key parts to this topic: who does this work and practices for identifying and defining backlog items.

Who does the work raises issues that have been floating around the agile community—one being the specialist versus generalist argument. For example, one group maintains that the traditional role of business analyst just puts another person between the developers and the customer. Others think that a business analyst, or similar role in a product management organization (product specialist), is needed to do tasks such as analyzing business processes, identifying areas for automation, and defining requirements.

In product development, lack of or poor customer involvement in the process has been a recurring problem. However, the root of the traditional problem wasn't as much specialist intervention as poor collaboration between the product and development teams. In a waterfall environment, business analysts interact with customers and create documents that are passed on to development teams. Development teams have little contact with customers or analysts. In a well-functioning agile team, collaboration among customers, product specialists, and developers supersedes documentation in importance and improves the entire requirements understanding process.

Agile teams tend to be staffed with more generalists than specialists, but eliminating those remaining specialists is not the key to success. Collaboration, not eliminating specialty roles—like business or product specialists—is the key to success. Agile teams tend to grow members' "general" skills because the team works closely on so many aspects of development. Improved learning—of both technical and domain knowledge—is one of the benefits of collaborative agile teams.

There are many approaches to business/product analysis and story definition. Many organizations utilize Use Cases, some in concert with business process analysis techniques. Whatever the technique, and at whatever level of analysis, three things are key to understanding: the people involved (that is, identifying the roles or personas that exist in the customer's environment), identifying the functions performed by these personas, and breaking that functionality down into implementable chunks—stories. Roles can be derived from personas (a profile of a type of user—for example, Harriett the order processing administrator). Functionality can be broken down in a hierarchy of product area, product capability, feature, story (hierarchies are addressed further in the next chapter).[3]

How teams create backlog items is important and too many agile teams are paving cow paths. In software development, paving cow paths means automating business processes as is, without thinking too much about whether or not the business processes are effective or efficient. Effective business process automation initiatives involve figuring out ways of doing those processes in entirely new ways that were impossible prior to automation (for example, work flow automation and digital image processing).

[3] For an in-depth look at developing stories, the relationship between Use Cases and stories, and estimating stories, see Mike Cohn's book, *Agile Estimating and Planning*.

Some agile teams seem to be forgetting important history lessons from "traditional" development and blithely aide customers in paving more cow paths. Although the agile principle of early delivery of working software has created enormous benefits for many companies, there is an underlying assumption in many agile methods (Dynamic Systems Development Method [DSDM] being a significant exception) that customers have done their homework, that they 1) understand their business processes, 2) have done the necessary business process analysis and rationalization, and 3) understand how automation might change processes themselves.

The danger in this assumption is further increased by requirements definition approaches that begin at the micro level—individual stories or features. Team members examine the details and assume the customer has the big picture. Agile teams sometimes become developer-centric and leave out the critical business process analysis role (and therefore miss the need for a product specialist). When developers who don't understand business processes interact with users who understand only the current business processes, and the "methodology" for requirements investigation doesn't look at business context, business process flow, and business information needs within a wider framework, teams miss a tremendous opportunity to increase delivery of extra customer value.

Release Planning

A release plan presents a roadmap of how the team intends to achieve the product vision within the project objectives and constraints identified in the project data sheet.

Agile lifecycles are both iterative and story-driven—a significant change from traditional plans that are waterfall- and task-driven. The story-driven aspect changes the primary focus of planning and executing from tasks to product features. Most traditional project management plans utilize tasks to construct work breakdown structures (WBSs) to organize work. Although experienced project leaders concentrate first on deliverables and then on the tasks necessary to create those deliverables, work- or task-driven plans often degenerate into very detailed, prescriptive plans. Any product has a set of features that customers use for some purpose. The more quickly we can link those customers to the features they have requested and get feedback on them, the more likely the product development effort will be successful.

Seasoned project leaders understand that how they break the project down into work breakdown structures can have a significant impact on how that project is managed and implemented. Each possible WBS has advantages and disadvantages. A feature breakdown structure (FBS) may strike some project leaders as being more difficult to administer,[4] but it offers the significant advantage of increasing interaction between the team and customers. Furthermore, phase-based WBSs (requirements, design, build, test, etc.) may be easier to administer, but they don't match how engineers actually work.

Agile development focuses the team on delivering the product features rather than intermediate documentation artifacts. This doesn't minimize the importance of "reasonable and barely sufficient" documentation; no one would consider building, say, an airplane or an automobile without documentation. The problem is not documentation per se, but that teams often get lost producing intermediate artifacts that have little bearing on the team's real progress toward a final product.

Iterations produce running, tested, accepted stories. The agile goal is to have a product that could be deployed at the end of any iteration—that is, the stories, tests, documentation, and other product deliverables could be packaged and deployed. Actual deployment of the iterative results— referred to as incremental delivery—depends on a variety of factors.

A development team uses an iteration to concentrate on small increments of work. In software development, an iteration might be two to four weeks or slightly longer for some projects.[5] If you're building an airplane, the iterations will surely be longer (although early prototype analysis might use short iterations). Features developed within a team (usually fewer than ten people who work on a group of features) should be integrated and tested by the end of the iteration.

---

[4] With a task-based WBS, tasks are relatively permanent. With a feature-based WBS, features can be added or deleted during each iteration. This adding and deleting of features can cause resource plan management and reporting difficulties when using traditional project management tools.

[5] Iteration length will vary considerably across product types. Even within a single product, iterations for the hardware and embedded software features may be of different lengths, but they must synchronize at milestones.

Waves, or milestones, are intermediate points, usually from one month to three months apart. Waves can have both a project management and a technical function. From a project management perspective, they provide a chance to review progress and make adjustments. Additional details on levels of planning, including releases and waves, will be covered in the next chapter.

> *Two primary factors drive release plans—customer value and risk.*

The primary task in release planning is assigning stories to iterations, chiefly on the basis of value and risk.

A story may deliver high value but not be risky, or it may employ risky new technology that is invisible to the end customer. Normally the first priority in assigning stories to iterations is delivering customer value as defined by the product team, and the second priority is to schedule stories that reduce risk early in the project. Sometimes a technical risk takes top priority. For example, if an airplane has a performance criterion that it must fly 10,000 miles without fueling and the technology to do this is as yet unknown, then there is no point in having the customers prioritize features until the technical team has some degree of confidence that it can meet the performance requirement. All other scheduling considerations—resource availability, dependencies, and others—are subordinate to those of value and risk.

Release planning should be a collaborative team effort—product team, development team, and executives. Although executives may not participate in the entire planning process, the team needs to get executive input at the beginning of the process and discuss the plan with them toward the end. Often an executive perspective can help the team overcome what they considered to be significant barriers.

Scope Evolution

APM approaches scope management realistically. Scope creep isn't the problem, even though many observers lament the problems with escalating requirements. Reality is more complex than an admonition to "avoid scope creep" can handle. Some scope changes are inexpensive but valuable. Some scope changes are extensive and expensive but crucial to delivering customer value. Of course, scope changes can be detrimental to a project if they are arbitrary and ill thought out. But in general, scope changes that are incorporated to meet evolving customer requirements and undertaken with an understanding, and approval, of their impact on the project increase the probability of project success.

At the XP2002 software development conference in Italy, Jim Johnson of the Standish Group presented some interesting information related to scope. First, Johnson discussed two federally mandated state child welfare projects—one in Florida and the other in Minnesota. The Florida project was begun in 1990 with an original budget of $32 million, a staff of 100, and a delivery date of 1998. As of the last review, the project was estimated at $170 million and expected to be completed in 2005. The Minnesota system, with the same basic goals, began in 1999 and finished in 2000 with a staff of 8 who expended $1.1 million. Admittedly, many factors could be responsible for the differences, but a significant portion of the difference was attributed to "gold plating" requirements.

Gold plating is a type of scope creep that can be a significant problem, as the Standish and other studies (Jones 2008) show. Agile development encourages change that arises from evolving knowledge, while at the same time it discourages the gold plating and requirements bloat that often occur in traditional up-front requirements gathering. Johnson reported on two other Standish studies (one done for DuPont and another general study). In the first, Dupont estimated that only 25% of the features implemented in its software applications were actually needed. The Standish study estimated that 45% of software features were never used, and only 20% were used often or always. This points out another reason why partial deployment can be instrumental in ROI generation—it may keep you from building costly but unused features!

Given these numbers, it's ironic that many traditional requirements-gathering practices decry the dreaded "scope creep" as a major problem in development. I would contend that it's faster and cheaper to let features evolve over the life of the project than to hallucinate about what the requirements are in the beginning and then build them without constant customer involvement. A strategy of building minimum features and a capability to easily and reasonably adapt to change can be very profitable.

Agile development is about focus and balance—focusing on the project's key vision and goals and forcing hard tradeoff decisions that bring balance to the product. Agile development plans by story, in customer terminology, thereby concentrating the planning process on something the customer can relate to and prioritize easily. Because plans are adjusted each iteration based on actual development experience, not someone's guesses or wishes, nice-to-have stories are pushed into later iterations and are often eliminated completely.

A product's scope should be driven by customer value, technical feasibility, cost, and critical business schedule needs. It should not be held hostage to a plan developed when product and project knowledge was still in its infancy.

> *Simplicity—the art of maximizing the amount of work not done—is essential (The Agile Manifesto).*

The short iterations in agile development, combined with end-of-iteration customer reviews, make the entire team—developers, customers, and managers—face reality. We can take a requirements document and "estimate" how long it will take to develop and test the code, or we can build a small set of stories and measure how long it actually took to develop them. "Yes, we estimated that we could implement 25 stories this iteration, but in reality, we only delivered 15. Now what?" We now have to drop stories, add staff, and/or extend the project time. Note that we do this early in a project when there is still time to compensate. Traditional approaches delay these difficult decisions until the point at which adaptive action is nearly impossible. Short-cycle reality checks keep "featuritis" from getting out of hand. Reducing the total work effort by either eliminating stories or reducing the story depth can have a major impact on productivity.

> *When schedule problems occur, waterfall approaches cut tasks— typically testing—whereas agile approaches cut stories. The first reduces quality, the latter scope.*

Short iterations also keep developers focused. With a deadline approaching every few weeks, the tendency to "enhance" stories diminishes. The prioritization previously discussed emphasizes reducing the number of stories undertaken, and short iterations then act to limit their size. Agile practices incorporate change into the development process, while at the same time reducing project size by constant and intense concentration on essentials.

Iteration 0

Some people think agile development gives developers license to dive in and build (or code, in the software arena). They condemn agile methods, saying that such methods spend little or no time on early requirements definition or architectural issues. On the other hand, there has been an equally negative reaction to projects in which months and months of planning, requirements specification, and architectural philosophizing occur before any customer value is delivered. Iteration 0 is an attempt to find some middle ground. The "0" implies that nothing useful to the customer—stories, in other words—gets delivered in this time period. However, the work is useful to the team. Recognizing that iteration 0 doesn't deliver customer value pressures the team to keep it short.

> *Iteration 0 helps teams balance anticipation with adaptation.*

The following are a couple of examples of work done in iteration 0. A project to develop a large business software application, one that must be integrated with other business applications, may require some data architecture work to adequately define the interfaces with those other applications. In the case of an electronic instrument, the team might find it useful to create a preliminary component architecture. Teams utilizing unfamiliar technology may need time for training prior to a project's launch and time to establish a development environment. A customer may demand some requirements documentation prior to signing a contract. All these examples indicate a need for some time expenditure prior to launching into iterative story development. For each of these tasks in iteration 0 a card (which will usually specify an artifact—a skeleton architecture diagram, for example) should be created and placed in iteration 0. The need for an iteration 0 is usually obvious before the project gets underway and may be included as part of the Envision phase.

Although the relevant issues may vary, the outcome is the same—some projects require more initialization work than others. The key to effectively utilizing iteration 0 is to balance the possible advantages of further planning with the growing disadvantage of lack of customer-deliverable stories. There are always tradeoffs to balance. The timeframe of an iteration 0 for a next-generation jumbo jetliner will be much different than that for a portable CD player.

Iterations 1-N

For most projects, the team needs to create a plan that assigns stories to iterations for the duration of the project to get a feel for the overall plan and determine completion dates, staffing, costs, and other project planning information. The development and product teams, including the product manager, do release planning. The activities involved in laying out the plan include

- Determining how identified risks will influence iteration planning
- Identifying the schedule target (the "desired" schedule from a product management perspective, without respect to achievability)
- Developing a theme for each iteration
- Assigning story cards to each iteration, balancing value, risks, resources, and dependencies as necessary
- Summarizing the release plan in some combination of story card layout (Figure 7-6) (usually on a wall), a complete release plan (Figure 7-7), or a project parking lot (Figure 7-8)[6]
- Adjusting the completed plan as necessary, using the tradeoff matrix as a guide

Figure 7-6
Release Plan
(small project)

[6] The parking lot diagram was developed by Jeff DeLuca, one of the authors of *Feature-driven Development*.

	Iteration 0	Iteration 1	Iteration 2	Iteration 3
	Task...	Story 1 — 3	Story 6 — 5	Story 4 — 4
	Task...	Story 2 — 4	Story 8 — 4	Story 14 — 4
	Task...	Story 12 — 5	Story 11 — 2	Story 3 — 4
	Task...			
Plan		12	11	12
Capacity		12	12	12

Figure 7-7
A Partial Release Plan

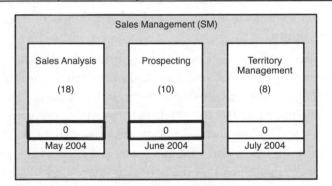

Figure 7-8
Release Plan Parking Lot Diagram

Sales Management (SM)

Sales Analysis	Prospecting	Territory Management
(18)	(10)	(8)
0	0	0
May 2004	June 2004	July 2004

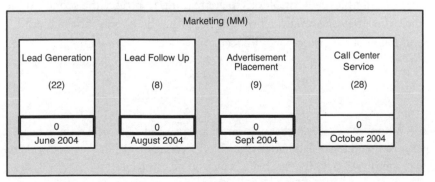

Marketing (MM)

Lead Generation	Lead Follow Up	Advertisement Placement	Call Center Service
(22)	(8)	(9)	(28)
0	0	0	0
June 2004	August 2004	Sept 2004	October 2004

As previously discussed, customer value and risk are the primary drivers for story scheduling. For example, in a project with an erratic requirements risk (the team realizes that requirements will be difficult to determine and volatile), the decisions on what stories to implement early may be different than for a project with high technical risk (the team has never used the technology combination before). There may be times when high-value stories, which would normally be implemented first, will have to be deferred in favor of high-risk stories, which need to be implemented early to reduce the risk. A risk list should be reviewed to determine what impact risk mitigation might have on the release plan, specifically the sequencing of stories and the incorporation of high-risk items.

Every project has some target delivery date selected by marketing, management, or a customer. A target establishes what someone outside the project team desires because of an understanding of the business. Although the rationale behind these dates can vary from a thoughtful analysis of the market to an off-the-cuff guess, these dates are important. Whether off-the-cuff or thoughtful, they represent the stakeholders' expectation. Every project also has a planned date, which the engineering team develops as part of the release planning process. Both these dates will be used in the negotiation process, but the team needs to understand the stakeholders' expectation, even if it is outlandish.

In many cases the target date becomes a constraint on the project. Let's say the best planning and negotiation still yield a date that the product manager, with executive concurrence, deems two months too long. The earlier date can be designated as the constraint date, provided everyone understands its purpose. Because there are many unknowns about the project, everyone—the development and customer teams and executives—works to resolve those unknowns such that the project is completed by the earlier date. For example, everyone looks to cut features to reduce the scope. At the earliest time that information indicates the earlier date cannot be achieved, a reevaluation of the project would occur.[7]

[7] This process of negotiating between target and planned dates works only when all parties are working collaboratively to achieve a common goal. It does not work in a situation in which parties are being arbitrary and capricious.

For each iteration the team should develop a guiding theme. This is critical for focusing and ensuring that the team balances between breadth and depth of features. Theme development often evolves from the process of assigning stories to iterations, but they can also be predetermined. These themes (e.g., "Demonstrate the basic instrument data acquisition capability"), help focus the team in ways that a list of individual stories may not. Themes can also reflect risk abatement strategies (e.g., "Prove that our high-risk valve design is viable"). For large projects in which many stories are being built each iteration, themes are particularly important. (Themes are covered in detail in Chapter 8, "Advanced Release Planning").

Agile teams continue to use index cards as a primary release planning tool. They are effective because they are tactile, visual, and can be easily shuffled during planning sessions. For small projects the team may lay cards out on a table, whereas for larger ones cards may be stuck to whiteboards. A summary spreadsheet can show a snapshot of the entire project and maintain resource summaries. Although cards should identify stories that are as independent from each other as possible, dependencies will occur and influence the order of implementation.

Other techniques can ensure a more reliable plan. The first is to add time to each iteration for changes that are identified during an iteration review. One story card titled "Rework and Contingency" is placed in each iteration. I've often seen plans with inspection or review tasks but without any time allotted for the changes that arose from those reviews! At the end of each iteration, an agile project goes through several quick reviews, both customer and technical. Including a rework and contingency "story" in each iteration (e.g., 10%+ of the effort scheduled for the iteration) provides time for changes that are inevitable, even though the details aren't known. These rework and contingency cards should be scheduled just as with any other story.

> *Rework and contingency stories of 10% of each iteration's total effort help build a more accurate release plan.*

A second technique for increasing the reliability of the schedule, particularly with high exploration–factor projects, is to set aside one or more "empty" iterations at the end of the project. These buffers can be used to accommodate changes, fix defects, or refactor. In addition, stories assigned to the last iteration or two should be those with lower priority in case they need to be dropped.

Despite superficial appearances, release planning is *not* prescriptive planning. Even though a full release plan with stories assigned to each iteration may *look* prescriptive, the plan is subject to review and revision at the end of each iteration. Agile release plans are used to *adapt successfully to inevitable change*, not to *follow a plan with minimal changes*.

First Feasible Deployment

Because there are significant benefits to early product deployment, a product team should determine a first feasible deployment (FFD) strategy; that is, the first iteration in which the product could potentially be deployed. For example, a company might be able to deploy early versions to key customers who have been asking for such a product. The customers understand that the product has only certain features, but they are willing to work with that limited functionality. Early deployment might bring in revenue, help with concept validation, and generate feedback. Early deployment has certain benefits but also potential cost such as deployment costs that could offset benefits.

> *This issue of deployable versus deployed has been confused by many aspiring agilists. Iterative development creates done-done, deployable pieces of a product. Those deployable pieces may or may not be actually implemented (deployed) incrementally depending on circumstances. Actual deployment is preferred, but not required.*

Teams contemplating an early deployment strategy need to think about it during initial release planning because story scheduling may be impacted. For example, an early deployment strategy might suggest scheduling all the features in a particular capability early so that the product would be rich enough in that one area to deploy. Early deployment and beta test strategies also need to be considered together.

In some types of software development—Web-based systems, for one—each iteration result might be deployed. Other products are difficult to partially deploy. For example, if a competitor has a product on the market with a certain capability, it may not be feasible to deploy your product until it has comparable capability.[8] And needless to say, it would be inadvisable to deploy a partial airplane.

Estimating

In nearly every presentation or workshop, I get the question, "How do you estimate an agile project?" The basic answer is "Using the same techniques you already employ." However, there are subtleties underlying the "how to estimate" question:

- Estimating the unknown
- Estimating by stories rather than tasks
- Estimating progressively
- Estimating can be a huge time waster
- Estimating versus sizing
- Using story points versus staff hours

Because agile methods are often used for high exploration–factor projects, the critical estimating question becomes "How do you estimate the unknown?" and the answer is "You can't." When there are unknowns, you are guessing, not estimating—and it's the best we can do. This is one reason why time and cost are often best viewed as constraints, not estimates, in agile projects. Agile organizations learn to live with uncertainty rather than trying to demand certainty in a fast-changing world.

Agile projects are planned by capabilities and stories, whereas many project leaders may be more familiar with task-based estimating. These leaders have to learn to apply their experience in estimating tasks to stories. For

[8] On the other hand, Ken Delcol notes that "Waiting for a full-featured product can be a mistake. Partial deployment forces you to identify which of the features are most important to your customers. Most software products have way too many features that the customer rarely uses. Partial deployment when the competition has a complete product may allow you to learn something about the customer that you and the competition do not know."

example, rather than estimate requirements-gathering for an entire project, they will be estimating it on a story-by-story basis. Team members who have spent several days identifying stories and assigning them to iterations usually have a much better understanding of the product than those who have relied on task-based planning. So in most cases, story-based planning provides better estimates.

Reducing waste, a lean thinking principle, involves looking at activities and eliminating or reducing those that don't directly generate customer value. Estimating can be one of those time-wasting activities. Detailed estimating of items too early in the project lifecycle wastes time because the items may be dropped anyway. Estimating items over and over again while they are in the backlog can also be wasteful. Many small maintenance items can be completed nearly as fast as they can be estimated. So estimating, particularly the level of detail and frequency, should be tied to the benefits of that estimating. Some Kanban (a newer practice described in Chapter 8) software teams have eliminated estimating completely.

One approach that can ease the estimating burden is differentiating between estimating and sizing. On a 12-month project with 125 capabilities, most agile teams attempt to set boundaries—not produce exact estimates. What they are after is enough sizing information to feel comfortable that the release plan is feasible. Sizing attempts to answer strategic questions about the team's ability to deliver a releasable, quality product within the project's constraints.

Many agile software teams estimate story points rather than staff hours. Story points are an attempt to define a unit of work size rather than work effort, much as a painter uses square feet of wall space to then estimate effort (hours per square foot). In software development, historical attempts to provide this metric were lines-of-code and function points—both of which have problems, the greatest of which is that for early estimating too much work is required. Story points are a "relative" measure (e.g., this story looks about three times larger than that story). Experienced teams can usually do this relative sizing much faster than teams trying to estimate hours. Conversely, at some point management usually needs a total effort estimate or a total cost estimate and so story points have to be converted. Some organizations use hours for release planning and story points for iteration planning.[9]

[9] For an in-depth analysis of estimating with story points versus hours, see Mike Cohn's *Agile Estimating and Planning* (Cohn 2006).

As good project leaders using task-based planning know, accumulating a project estimate from detailed estimates of either tasks or stories can result in overestimating the entire project. Multiple techniques—bottom-up and top-down, comparisons to similar projects, using estimating tools—can help teams arrive at better overall project estimates, but they can't make up for uncertainty. Although multiple techniques provide a better estimate for the entire project, team member estimates should be used for iteration plans. It is important for team development and cohesion that team members be responsible, and accountable, for iteration plans. As projects progress, the team members should get better at estimating for the next iteration, which should also improve the estimates for the rest of the release.

As projects increase in size, estimation requires more than team members estimating stories. Although teams may have a reasonable idea of how long it will take them to develop stories (at least for iterations early in the project), they will usually underestimate the workload involved in coordinating with other teams. As team size increases, productivity decreases, sometimes dramatically. For example, in software development a single small team with good tools might achieve a productivity rate of 50 function points (a sizing measure) per staff month, whereas a 100-person team would be highly unlikely to achieve even one-half of that. Understanding industry norms and using software tools in estimating can provide teams with sanity checks on team estimates. Even the best team is unlikely to deliver a product in one-half the time that anyone has ever done it before.

Just like every other artifact in agile development, estimates and sizes evolve over time. Teams need to limit time revisiting estimates, in part by understanding the difference between sizing a capability to develop an initial release plan and estimating a task for a two-week iteration plan.

Other Card Types

Although user story cards will dominate release planning, all other work needs to be accounted for in some way. Plans go awry because work is left out and then at the end the team wonders why they didn't achieve their planned story completions. Other types of planning cards include performance (work done to plan and to perform stress, performance, and load testing), task (work that must be done that doesn't directly produce user stories), technical (non user-facing story), and buffer (time allocated to anticipated changes). Several of these other story types are covered in Chapter 8.

Final Thoughts

Product development hinges on managing information and how that information evolves over the course of a project as learning takes place. This progression of information requires a framework, or model, that assists in getting the right information to the right people at the right time, guiding project participants, and monitoring real progress.

Three key activities need to be completed prior to beginning story development—articulating a product vision, defining the project's objectives and constraints, and creating an iterative, story-based release plan. The release plan is constructed from the product feature/story backlog that evolves during the Envision and Speculate phases. After the release plan has been completed, other common project management planning artifacts—such as expenditure budgets—can be finalized. The fact is, when you get the backlog and release plan done, the rest is relatively easy!

While a Speculate phase may sound a little, well, speculative, in reality the practices presented in this chapter have proven highly reliable in creating useful planning information early in development. Feature-based planning forces the engineering and product teams to understand the product in ways that task-based planning rarely does. With the replanning that occurs at the end of iterations and waves, plans and the product evolve as information is gained through experimentation and constant feedback.

Chapter 8

Advanced Release Planning

Over the past five years since the first edition of this book was published, significant new ideas about release planning and backlog development have emerged. The last chapter contained the basics on these topics that were, with some updates, contained in the first edition. This chapter is new to the second edition of APM and contains a set of advanced topics that have proved useful in a number of organizations. These topics include the value of release planning, capacity-based planning, value point analysis, planning themes, dealing with uncertainty, and work-in-process versus throughput.

Release (Project) Planning

Lack of good release planning is endemic in parts of the agile community. Teams seem caught up in iteration-at-a-time development plus backlog building and not planning out an entire release or project. Even those who create initial release plans often fail to keep them current. Of course this view enables teams to resist management's request for "spurious" information such as "how much is this project going to cost?" Or, "when will we have a releasable product?" Or, "how long is this project going to take?"

This lack of response to legitimate business questions leaves managers and executives frustrated with agile teams. Many development teams seem to view agile methods as a way to combat the historically dysfunctional approaches to projects in which schedules were forced on teams. So some teams have tried to go from forced schedules to no schedules.

Management approves a project because they want a business problem solved. They want to know how the problem will be solved, how much it will cost, how long it will take, and how much risk they are incurring. When an agile team, or any other team for that matter, doesn't respond to this request, they are viewed as lacking commitment. The issue is one of flexibility versus stability—"How do we commit to something with a reasonable assurance of delivery and at the same time leave room for change, learning, and surprises?" "How can we be innovative with a fixed deadline?" The best teams are ones who can solve this seeming paradox.

Neither forced schedules nor no schedules is the right answer. Being agile and adaptive means that the entire project community—managers, development teams, project leaders, etc.—must have some idea of where they are going, and also a mindset that adjustments to that plan (adaptation) are normal. In more traditional planning, unfortunately, "the plan" was cast in concrete and became a deterministic goal. Adhering to plans became a test of wills between development teams and managers.

So how are we better off if we abandon traditional plans? There is still a test of wills, but it's between managers who want (and really need for business reasons), a reasonable idea of what value will be delivered by what date and development teams who say "You can't ask us that because we are agile." My contention is that we are no better off, and in fact are worse off.

Going from fixed plans to no plans is not the answer and it will hinder wider acceptance of agile approaches. Getting everyone to look at plans as adaptable guidelines won't be easy, nor quick, but in the long run utilizing this approach will demonstrate to management that development teams understand the constraints of running a business, and it will demonstrate to development teams that managers understand that projects evolve and fixed plans are unworkable. To solve this plan/no-plan dilemma, all parties must understand the purpose of an agile release plan is to

- Foster a better understanding of project viability and feasibility
- Outline assessment and mitigation of risk
- Enhance a team's ability to prioritize capabilities and stories
- Give the team a "feel" for the entire project

- Enable answers to management questions about value, schedule, and cost
- Create a comfort level about the project with both team members and management
- Create a plan for partial deployment

Wish-based Planning (Balancing Capacity and Demand)

Many companies do a lousy job of capacity planning, that is, balancing the demands for work to be done with the actual capacity of the organization. All too often the planning is wish-based, not capacity-based. Tales of extraordinary project successes in industry articles lead managers into thinking that if they just push their teams hard enough they will all be extraordinary. More often than not, this motivational gimmick leads to dysfunctional teams, not high-performance ones. My experience across a range of companies is that some managers don't understand the difference between stretching limits and being completely unreasonable. Over time, stretched project plans become irrational wish-based plans.

Balancing capacity and demand is complex because it involves quantitative issues such as estimation, and qualitative issues such as escalating customer demands and staff motivation. The quantitative issues revolve around estimating and planning skills, or the lack thereof, with the added nuance of trying to estimate and plan when risk and uncertainty are high. Organizations succumb to wish-based rather than capacity-based planning—product managers wish they could deliver 50 features in the next release because that's what the market demands, even though developers know 30 features are realistic. Many managers use pressure as a motivational technique and loading people up with work seems to be one of the most widespread techniques.

The tremendous pressures that companies face today contribute to wish-based planning. The marketplace demands more, and product managers want to respond to competitive pressures. It's a product manager's job to push the envelope, but when "must have because I say so" replaces realistic planning, problems ensue. Wish-based planning creates a dangerous dynamic. First, plans are created in which demands greatly exceed capacity, and development groups are pressured into accepting those demands (but they don't actually buy into the demands). Second, schedules and features are inevitably missed as always happens when plans are unrealistic. However, the failure to deliver is considered a "performance" problem rather than a planning problem, creating a lack of confidence in the development organization's ability to either plan or deliver. In a renewed triumph of wishing over reality, marketing or management dismisses input from development (no credibility), and proceeds with the next round of wishing. Mistrust is generated on all sides, which makes the next round of planning even more contentious.

Inevitably organizations try to fix the problem by solving the wrong problem. The preferred solution is almost always to improve estimating and planning skills because wish-based planning and motivational beliefs are part of the management culture and difficult to change. Many organizations have put millions of dollars into improving estimating and planning skills to no avail because they lack the will to address these other issues.

> *In a wish-based culture, impeccable estimates will always be overridden by wishes, so the accuracy of the estimates makes little difference.*

Development organizations are not without fault in this scenario. They often have poor estimating practices and skills, even though it's hard to differentiate poor skills from forced unrealism. Many development organizations have "cried wolf" so many times that their low credibility rating is justly deserved. They also put themselves in a poor position by constantly saying "no." This negativism isn't, however, always their fault. If someone constantly asks you to do something that is impossible and you constantly say "no," you may be tagged as negative, but they must wear the tag of unrealistic expectations.

One other skill area development organizations often lack is good negotiation skills. Steve McConnell (*Software Project Survival Guide* and other books) provided this nugget in a talk several years ago. Many individuals in management and marketing have well-honed negotiating skills. Development teams try to negotiate project schedules with these skilled negotiators and almost always come out on the short end of agreements. Engineers tend to be optimistic, and enthusiastic, about what they can accomplish, and plans based on comments like, "I don't know if we can do that or not, but we will try," get locked in concrete. All people remember are the dates and dollars, not that the plan was considered a stretch to begin with.

Another huge problem with plans (demands) is that they are often used as the basis for "motivating" teams. With a reasonable plan schedule of nine months, based on good estimating techniques, someone may say, "let's give them six months to motivate them." This causes problems with single projects, but those problems multiply when multiple projects in the portfolio are affected and cooperation between teams disappears. The best motivation is internally imposed, not externally imposed. Imposing unrealistic schedules is more apt to act as a de-motivator.

All these factors cause software teams to eliminate stories late in releases as reality catches up with wishes. This cause huge inefficiencies as teams try to "back-out" poorly implemented or tested stories, which can cause huge problems in the code base. Pressure also usually translates to poor testing, which further complicates problems towards the end of a release. And finally, as people begin to face the reality that release plans were really fantasy, the wrong people are rewarded and punished. The teams who signed on to unrealistic plans without complaint, and didn't make their plans, are often rewarded for all their hard work at the end. Teams who tried to push back on the unrealistic plans at the beginning are considered to be "obstructionists," and not team players. Rewarding the wrong behaviors then leads to the next round in which performance and delivery suffer further. The capacity versus demand imbalance creates spiraling dynamics that push organizations deeper and deeper into dysfunctional behaviors.

Multi-Level Planning

For medium to large projects, the story-level planning described in Chapter 7 is too fine grained. In automotive development, for example, a parts explosion for an entire car contains thousands of small parts. Similarly, a large software application may contain thousands of stories. Although the development team needs to plan and deliver at a detail level, plans longer than 3 months are more effective at a higher level of granularity. Because plans change over time, constructing a story-level plan in two-week iterations for an 8 month plan (17 iterations) would be a waste of time. The plan needs to be granular enough to answer key questions, but detail plans offer only a false sense of certainty.

Figure 8-1 shows two product hierarchies, one for software and one for hardware. The number of levels used will depend on the size of the project (huge projects might need another level). A small, 3-month project could be planned entirely at the story level. However, a 200-person, 18-month project would need to be planned at several levels (business area, capability, and story, for example). In a customer relationship management (CRM) application project, the hierarchy might be business area (Sales), capability (a sales manager needs the ability to conduct Sales Profitability Analysis), and story (a sales manager needs the ability to generate a Territory Sales by Product Report). For an automobile project, the hierarchy might be platform (SUV Truck Body), group (Drivetrain), component (Transmission), and feature (Shift Lever).

Figure 8-1
Examples of Product Hierarchies

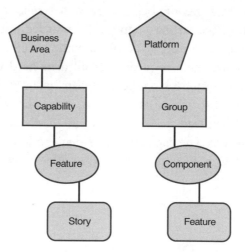

Multi-level planning helps address a critical dilemma: the conflicting needs for predictability and flexibility. Executives and managers need some degree of predictability for things like financial and marketing planning, while at the same time they want to be able to adapt to new situations and information. They also have a fiduciary responsibility to their organizations to monitor projects via status reporting. One partial solution to this problem (unfortunately under conditions of uncertainty there isn't an infallible solution) is to think of the capability level as reasonably fixed and the story level as flexible. The team, for example, would lay out a plan and make reasonable commitments to deliver the capabilities planned. However, the team would retain flexibility at the story level as to just which stories would implement the capability (narrower or wider functionality) and the depth within each story.

A Complete Product Planning Structure

There are four layers to a complete product planning structure, as shown in Figure 8-2: a product roadmap, a release plan, a wave (or milestone) plan, and finally, an iteration plan. Table 8-1 summarizes the characteristics of the last three of these levels.

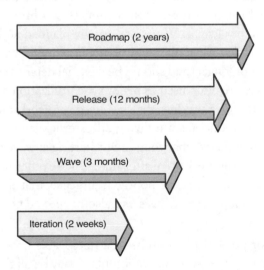

Figure 8-2
A Complete Product Planning Structure (timeframes vary)

Table 8-1
Product Planning Structure

Characteristic	Release	Wave	Iteration
Timeframe	Long-range	Medium-range	Short-range
	(6+ months)	(3 months)	(1–4 weeks)
Level of Detail	Capability	Story	Story/task
Commitment Type	Project feasibility	Capability commitment	Story commitment
Deployment	Final release to customer	Possible interim release to customer	Customer review process

An iteration plan, as introduced in the previous chapter, is a day-to-day work plan for a development team. For software projects iteration lengths vary from 1–4 weeks, but experience in agile projects over the last few years has driven most teams to shorter lengths of 1 or 2 weeks. Iteration plans are developed jointly by the development team and the product/customer team. Iteration plans utilize stories and break those stories down into tasks. They are the most detailed–level plans.

A wave (or milestone) plan spans several iterations and for software projects a typical length is three months, unless synchronization requirements dictate another length. Waves are usually planned at the story level, but not down to tasks. Wave plans are particularly useful with longer projects (nine months or longer) and should be a partial deployment release if at all possible. Waves are often used as major synchronization and integration points, particularly for a product that has hardware and software components. A software product team utilizing an external vendor for a component might plan to integrate that component starting at wave two (6 months into the project) and at every wave after that. On the other hand, if less frequent synchronizations are going poorly, it indicates that the synchronization should occur more often. Waves can also be viewed as "intermediate" planning horizons.

A release (or project) plan results in a deployable product. For short projects, 3–6 months release and iteration plans may be all that are needed. For longer projects, wave plans may be necessary. Except for very short projects, release plans are normally done at the capability or feature level.

Release plans try to answer the question, "Is it feasible for this project to deliver a quality releasable product within the identified constraints of scope, schedule, and cost"? A release plan is constructed by the development and product teams, often with the collaborative help of managers and sponsors. Bringing an executive perspective to release planning can help the team better understand strategic issues and the key release criteria of importance to management.

A Product Roadmap lays out a multi-release map for a product's evolution. It could be several years in its timeframe and consists of summary-level (capability) functionality. The product team constructs the roadmap by envisioning how the product might evolve over time. A roadmap is more about possibility than feasibility, and utilizes gross sizing more than estimating. A roadmap includes technical components also.

A large financial products software company client used all four of these levels. Their product management group had a 2–3 year roadmap of business areas and capabilities to be implemented. We worked out an 18-month feasible release plan of some 300 capabilities for several teams that totaled about 75 people. Then each of the teams developed a 3-month story-level wave plan and then developed detailed story- and task-level iteration plans. As the development effort moved forward, each of the plans was updated periodically.

Although every product and business is different, a general guide would be to keep each cycle as short as possible. Two-week iterations are generally preferable to 4-week ones. Frequent releases should be pursued rigorously but also be matched to the business needs. Replacing an existing product has a different release strategy than that for ongoing enhancement releases of a product. Replacement products usually require that a significant percentage of the old product's functionality be completed prior to release. These types of projects often take 18+ months, so an overall release plan with 3-month wave plans would be appropriate. While releasable features should be in near-final form each wave, actual deployment to customers would be near the end of the project. The danger in this approach is the potential lack of real customer feedback until late in the project, although this risk can be mitigated with periodic customer reviews of product capabilities

In contrast, some software applications can be released every 3 months, and might need a only a product roadmap and a 3-month release plan. Even more interesting are products that proceed from wave plan to wave plan, but have much more frequent releases—even weekly. The teams plan in waves, but release each iteration. One financial services company, with a huge credit card processing application, deployed new releases with an average of 100 new features every month.

As a company's ability to release new versions quickly increases, their horizon for detail planning can shrink, greatly increasing their ability to respond to customer needs.

Capabilities

A capability describes a high-level business or product function that is complete and valuable, whereas a story delivers a piece of useful and valuable functionality to a customer. (Some people use the synonym *epic* rather than *capability* to indicate an epic tale made up of many stories.) Differentiating between capability and story is difficult, because there is always ambiguity about what is a complete or partial function. However, large projects are best planned with a hierarchy of functionality, and the best way to differentiate between levels can be just size. A story should be around 2–10 days of work; a capability should be somewhere in the range of 20–100 days of work. Another guideline is that each level by 3 times the lower one. Features would be 6-30 days and capabilities would be 18-90 days.

In Chapter 7, Figure 7-8 showed a hierarchy for a Customer Relationship Management (CRM) system, in the form of a parking lot diagram that includes two business subject areas (Sales Management and Marketing) and seven capabilities, each represented as a box within each of those subject areas (e.g., Sales Analysis, Prospecting, and Territory Management under Sales Management). The numbers in parentheses under the capability names indicate the number of stories identified for that activity (e.g., 18 for Sales Analysis), and the date at the bottom of the box indicates the month and year when that activity is planned for completion. Large applications, like those for CRM, might have 200 to 500 capabilities, several thousand stories, and 20–30 business areas. With a multi-level approach to planning, the customer and development teams could develop a roadmap at the capability level of granularity, a wave plan at the story level, and iteration plans at the story and task level.

Capability Cases

Another avenue to defining a capability comes from the book, *Capability Cases: A Solution Envisioning Approach*, by Irene Polikoff, Robert Coyne, and Ralph Hodgson (Polikoff 2005). The authors position capability cases as a bridge between the wants and needs of the business and what the system does for the business users. The name "capability case" plays on the more common term "use case" and includes both a business want or need and a range of possible technology solutions. A capability case could be thought of as a "big" use case. With the myriad of technologies available today to solve almost any problem, proposed solution alternatives at the capability level may be warranted.

The U.S. and Canadian military departments have been early adopters of what they label "capability-based planning." In this approach to procurement of weapons systems, they define the capabilities they want—speed, distance, armament delivered, etc.—and the contractors develop the detail specifications to deliver those capabilities. If we think of capability cases as high-level business needs with defined solution options, then teams can estimate them within some range. Teams can "commit" to delivering a set of capabilities, while leaving the detailed requirements and specifics about implementation (stories) to the project team. Working in this way does require that both management and the project team understand the process and have appropriate expectations.

> *Companies need predictability and flexibility. Using a capability-story approach can provide both predictability at the capability level and flexibility in exactly how those capabilities are delivered at the story level.*

Creating a Product Backlog and Roadmap

A product backlog is a list of items to be developed that will include all product structure levels. Many product management groups use spreadsheets to manage these lists, but there are open source and commercial software tools that both manage backlog items and assist in release and iteration planning. A product backlog grows over time as more detailed breakdowns occur (capability to story for example) and new items are added. The information about each backlog item improves as existing data is refined (better description, better estimate). As this information is gathered over the development process, a just-in-time philosophy should be applied—that is, don't gather too much detail until it is really necessary because things will change and the time will be wasted.

A product backlog, particularly for a legacy application, can also contain system change requests (SCRs). Although these items—maintenance requests, persistent defects, small enhancements, technical debt reduction—may be managed by a separate SCR application, they are part of the backlog of work for a product.

Although backlog items may come from a variety of sources, the product team has the responsibility for managing the backlog (this may not be the case for SCRs). Figure 8-3 shows a product's lifecycle, starting with a product conceptualization phase in which the product team begins developing a high-level roadmap and populating it with capabilities. Someone from the development team, likely a senior developer or architect, may be involved at this point, mainly commenting on technical feasibility and providing gross sizing estimates.

Toward the end of the conceptualization phase, a project chartering session that includes the entire product and development teams meets for several days to go through the product vision, project scope and boundaries, and release planning activities. Depending on the size of the project this joint effort might generate release, first-wave, and first-iteration plans. During the chartering session, as new stories were identified, the backlog list would be updated.

In developing a product backlog and roadmap, a team needs to have techniques for analyzing who uses the product (personas and roles), the product domain, and product components. There are a number of good

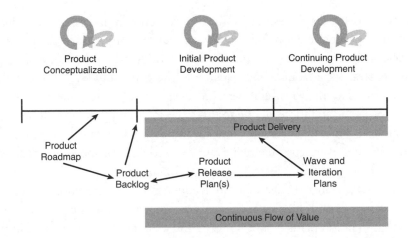

Figure 8-3
Product Lifecycle

books and sources of requirements analysis techniques, but the secret is to use them in an agile way—and most importantly to keep it simple because some of these techniques arose to support serial development. For example, UML modeling can be valuable as a documenting technique, but it also has caused many organizations to go diagram crazy. So temper modeling efforts by referencing work such as Scott Ambler's *Agile Modeling* (Ambler 2002).

An Optimum Planning Structure

There are so many different types and sizes of projects that it's almost presumptuous to recommend an optimum planning structure. Furthermore, a planning structure that works for an immature agile organization won't be optimal for a mature one. That said, from my experience with a number of companies, I'll offer two suggestions for optimal planning structures oriented to mature agile organizations. The two scenarios are 1) a product development effort in which the product is continuously evolving over a multi-year period, and, 2) a major product development or re-development effort in which the minimum releasable (to the market) functionality takes 12 or more months to deliver. The first scenario is more typical than the second.

Many software companies typify the first scenario—they have a product that is updated and a new version is released every 1–2 years (hardware tends to be longer cycles than software). When companies with products that fit this scenario adopt agile methods, they learn to shorten their release cycles. As these organizations mature, they tend to adopt this optimal structure: A strategic roadmap and backlog at the capability level that extends from three months to several years; a release plan of three months at the story level, and iterations of one to three weeks. The roadmap will be more detailed in the early timeframe, and the capability estimates will be rough. Although not every customer will want or need to implement every release, the product is actually released to some set of customers every three months. Even if the product is released more frequently—every iteration, for example—a three-month plan gives the team a reasonable intermediate perspective that iteration plans do not. Going from an annual release to a quarterly (or more frequent) one requires changes not just in the product company, but in how they interact with their customer base.

The second scenario arises in IT organizations and in product companies where products undergo a major development or redevelopment effort. In these situations, a significant amount of functionality has to be developed before an initial release can be made. I've worked with a number of software companies whose products were undergoing a transformation from one technical infrastructure to another. Their customers' minimum acceptable functionality threshold was most of what the old product offered[1]. These are usually stressful projects with major investment commitments and typically long efforts, in the 12–24-month range (or longer). Combining financial and market pressure stress with longer projects increases the emphasis on questions like, "Are we going to meet our release date?"

In the first scenario the train station analogy works: Every three months there is a release (a train arrives at the station), and stories that are ready get on—ones that aren't ready get slipped until the next train (release). In the second scenario the train takes a long time to arrive and managers are very concerned about what capabilities and features get on since they can't get on again for a long time.

So the planning for this second case (let's assume the first release is in 18 months) includes the following: A 3-year product roadmap at the capability

---

[1] Sometimes these thresholds are not as high as companies think, and they need to be pushed to re-examine the minimal acceptable functionality for a releasable product to shorten the initial release period.

level; a release plan, at the capability level, for the 18-month project; a wave plan for the first 3-month wave, and iteration plans. Although everyone realizes the 18-month release plan will change, maybe even substantially, laying it out (which may only take a couple of days after the capabilities are defined by the product team) will help everyone answer the key question, "Is this project feasible?" Projects like this will usually require a Concept phase before the release plan is developed (see Chapter 12, "Governing Agile Projects" for an explanation of the Concept phase).

Value Point Analysis

"Value over Constraints" was the theme of Chapter 2. Focusing on value has a high priority in agile methods, but specific practices that tell teams how to capture, or even evaluate, value are sparse. The product team usually determines the relative value of stories or capabilities, but quantifying value is difficult, especially at the capability or story level, so we tend to move on. In *Software by Numbers*, Denne and Cleland-Huang (Denne 2004) addressed this issue, but missed the mark in two key ways: not keeping the calculations simple, and not providing mechanisms for assigning revenue to small chunks (stories, features, etc.).[2] However, their book raised the issue and pushed people into thinking about the "value" side of the equation in a quantitative way.

Stories, as you have seen, are small chunks of user functionality. They can be estimated in either relative (story points) or absolute terms (hours). However, for a product that has 1,500 story points total at the end of the project, what does that total represent? Although many organizations show

---

[2] Cost allocation in companies can be difficult. For example, how should you allocate accounting expenses to a car's cost in the auto industry? But there is a thriving cost accounting discipline dedicated to figuring out appropriate allocation bases. Allocating revenue is more difficult because appropriate bases are harder, if not impossible, to determine.

burn-up charts of story points (a measure of delivery performance as illustrated in Chapter 10, Figure 10-3) to indicate progress (and indirectly indicating that the burn-up chart represents value delivered), the total story points really represent the total cost of the project. So if the project cost $600,000, then each story point represented $400 in cost. Why not think of value in a similar way and create something called value points to represent relative or monetary value?

A few issues make value points more difficult to implement than story points, but in concept, if value is really important, shouldn't we spend as much time trying to get a decent estimate of value as we do of cost? Understanding the value and cost, even if they are relative numbers, of stories and capabilities would improve the team's ability to deliver the highest-value stories early. However, as you will see later in this section, value and priority need to be separate considerations, so the highest-value stories are not always the highest-priority stories.

But what is the bottom line here? Why go to the trouble of another series of calculations? Aren't story points good enough? The answer is multi-faceted. As Chapter 13 goes into in detail, if we want to build agile organizations rather than settle for agile development teams, one of the critical factors in making that transition is changing performance measures. If we are tied to the age-old, traditional project management measures of scope, schedule, and cost—and conforming to plans in all those dimensions—then our quest to grow an agile organization will be difficult. If we believe in the agile triangle of value, quality, and constraints, then we must show executives and managers something concrete and measurable—even if the measurements are a little fuzzy. Better appropriate fuzzy metrics than inappropriate precision metrics.

Value points are a way of showing that we are serious about value.

In summary, value points are beneficial for four reasons:

- Their use indicates to executive management a serious, quantitative approach to value.
- They can assist teams in making priority decisions during release, wave, and iteration planning.
- They can assist teams in negotiating depth of story functionality. (Is a 3-value-point story worth 21 story points?)

- They can help increase ROI by pushing the planning of high-value capabilities and stories earlier.

Although the value points discussed in this section are quantitative, it must be stressed again and again that they are either relative or allocated values. Spending $56.75 for a widget is both quantitative and definitive. Adding up all such costs provides total project expenditures. Value numbers are fuzzier, but as the use of story points for planning has shown, fuzzy numbers about something important are much more useful than definitive numbers about something unimportant.

Value Point Determination: Roles and Timing

There are two key questions in determining value points: who does it and when is it done. The question of who is straightforward: the product team headed by the product manager does the value point estimating. The potential problem facing many teams with this task is that often customer teams are small, or even a single individual, and calculating the value points takes time. However, just as the product manager participates in the team discussion about story points (but doesn't have the final decision-making authority), the entire team, including developers, may be involved in the value point discussion. Having the team participate in the value point discussion is important because it helps create a shared vision of relative importance in a way that story point discussions help the team members understand relative effort.

> Cost and value should equally emphasized. If the team doesn't have time to estimate value points it doesn't have time to estimate costs.

Although a team needs to estimate effort at some level (story, capability) to develop a full release plan, in general value point estimating can be just-in-time (JIT). For wave or iteration planning, this would involve estimating value points for stories that are being considered for that next wave or iteration. For a release plan, this would involve assigning capability or feature-level value points only.

Calculating Relative Value Points

Value points can be calculated at multiple levels, but this discussion will illustrate capability and story levels. Story points, the cost side of the cost/benefit equation, can be calculated from the bottom up—define the stories, estimate their point value, summarize the points. There isn't an upper limit on story points in a project. Value points are different. One potential difficulty with value points is that there is not a feedback mechanism that corrects bad estimates as there is with story points. If a team estimates a story at 35 story points and development only takes 25, adaptive action is indicated. If product owners get carried away and assign high value points to all stories, there isn't a similar feedback to correct erroneous assignments. For example, if different teams are working on two capabilities, there needs to be a way to prevent one team from artificially inflating their value points.

So value points need to be an allocation of a total value calculation. There are two methods to help keep value points relevant and useful and not let teams get carried away with them. First, value points for individual stories should be limited to a short series of possible numbers (1, 2, 3, 5, 8, 13). Second, total value points should be allocated on a percentage basis to capabilities, thereby capping the total number of value points in a set of stories. Capabilities should be assigned a capability point value (1, 2, 3, 5), and then a percentage of total capability points should be calculated for each capability. For example, if a project had 5 capabilities, with capability points of 2, 3, 3, 5, 1, then the capability percentages would be 14%, 21%, 21%, 36%, and 8%.[3] As value points are assigned to stories, the totals have to approach these percentages. Following up on the previous example, percentage limits help keep teams from artificially inflating value points. However, in the final analysis, teams that can't resist the "everything is a 13-value-point story" will lose most of the benefits of this practice.

The allocation algorithm offered here is somewhat arbitrary, but any allocation scheme is somewhat arbitrary. This algorithm should be adjusted for individual organizations (you may want to use 1 through 21 as possible

---

[3] These allocation percentages may need to be recalculated from time to time as capabilities are added or removed; however capabilities are relatively stable during most projects so this should not take much time.

values, for example), but as long as the scheme seems reasonable it will be useful. Resist the urge to make the algorithm more complicated (in the hope of making it more accurate), because we are mainly interested in comparing relative values to improve planning and decision making. Spending extra time and effort developing complicated algorithms will yield marginal, if any, improvements in the allocation and almost no improvement in decision making.

It should be noted that story-level value points and capability-level value points are independent from each other—that is, they indicate relative priorities of story to story and capability to capability only. Remember that value points represent an "allocation" of the total revenue stream. In the absence of an actual total revenue figure to be allocated, the capability value percentages act to keep story-level value point assignments from ballooning and becoming meaningless.

One critical caveat to using relative value points: They cannot be directly compared with story points on status reports because they represent different units. The only time they can be somewhat compared, as mentioned in the opening list of benefits of value points, is when negotiating story functionality. For example, in looking at story cards with both value points and story points as shown in Figure 8-4, if during iteration planning low–value point stories had generally high story points, then a mismatch (21 story points and 2 value points), might trigger a discussion along the lines of "Is this low-value story really worth this much work?"

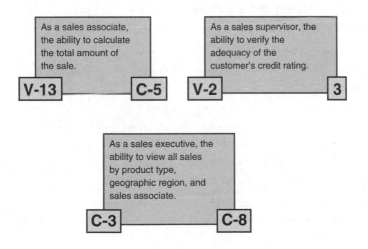

Figure 8-4
Story Cards with Value Points

Calculating Monetary Value Points

Many organizations do not want to go through the step of converting relative value points to monetary value points. However, if your organization does a business case analysis for projects and has overall benefit and cost numbers, allocating those figures to capabilities can be easy and straightforward. Doing good business case analysis and determining ROI is hard; allocating after they are done is easy—and can be beneficial. One benefit is that monetary value points and monetary story points *can* be used together to provide value-earned versus cost progress reports.

First, monetary capability value points are calculated by allocating the net present value (NPV) of the revenue stream used in the business case to capabilities based on the percentages already calculated. Looking at the previous example, if the revenue NPV was determined to be $2,500,000, then capability 1 would be worth $350,000 (14% of $2,500,000). Then, when the iteration plan for capability 1 was underway, the $350,000 would be divided by the total number of value points calculated for all the stories—let's assume 125—to give a monetary value point of $2,800. An individual story that was estimated at 15 value points would then be allocated a value of $42,000.

Although an allocation of revenue or NPV is appropriate for value points, actual costs expended should be used on the cost side (because it is more easily available) and a running value delivered versus cost expended chart could be developed for management, as shown in Figure 8-5.

Figure 8-5
Value and Cost Delivered

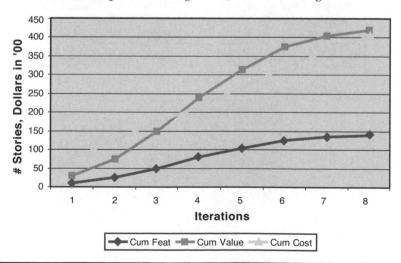

ADVANCED RELEASE PLANNING

Non-Customer-Facing Stories

What about the stories that aren't directly customer facing, such as technical debt reduction stories, technical stories, or refactoring stories? Should they carry a zero value? As you will see later, these stories may be handled differently in the priority setting and planning process. My recommendation is to assign a relatively small set of values to these types of stories, say 0, 1, 2, or 3, depending on the situation (0 possibly for some small story). Technical stories may support customer-facing ones, but developing complex calculations to allow for these dependencies seems counterproductive. This method of just assigning a set of smaller values follows the "simple is better" mantra.[4]

Value and Priority

As teams approach their release and iteration planning activities, they need to recognize the difference between value and priority. The planning themes section in this chapter outlines a number of factors that go into scheduling capabilities and stories into plans—from business process flows to risk mitigation. For example, an upcoming trade show might drive a wave plan toward a certain set of capabilities that weren't necessarily the mostly highly valued ones in the long term. The product manager would be substituting short-term value (trade show dazzle) for some reduction in ROI.

Although value remains the greatest determinant of priority, other factors discussed—themes, risk reduction, dependencies, politics (yes, politics)—will also be part of the capability and story allocation to plans. The importance of different factors will also change over the life of the project; for example, risk mitigation is extremely important early in a project.

---

[4] Colleague Israel Gat cautions that the use of non-customer-facing stories could be dangerous for immature agile teams. If these types of stories exceed about 20% of the total a red flag should go up.

Priority setting becomes a thorny issue when dealing with non-customer-facing stories. The first controversy is who makes these priority decisions. Although product teams understand user functionality, they don't understand technical debt reduction, maintenance items, and technical infrastructure stories. A contingent within the agile community recommend that the product team be responsible for all priority setting. I don't think this is very practical.

For example, assume that the team is working on a new release of a legacy product that has been around a while and management has agreed that reducing technical debt within the product is an important goal. The best way for this goal to be implemented is to assign an investment percentage to the technical debt reduction effort—say 15% of the project cost. If the team's velocity has been 100 story points per iteration, then we would expect, over several iterations on average, that 15 story points per iteration would be applied to technical debt reduction stories (refactoring code or data, improved automated testing).

Reducing existing technical debt in a product is an investment decision in making a product more adaptable and therefore more responsive to customers and reduces the risk to the brand with commercial products. Although the product and development teams would have been part of the decision to invest in technical debt reduction, new stories will always tend to take precedence at the point where wave or iteration planning is done. Only by a percent investment commitment can organizations ensure that this work will be done.

However, there is always the countervailing problem that too little of the prioritization work will be left for the product team, so the maximum percentage of stories to be prioritized by this percentage investment approach (the refactoring stories would be prioritized by the development team) would be in the 20 +/- % range.

Release Planning Topics

The following half dozen or so release planning topics have arisen during various client engagements over the past five years. They have generally, but not always, come from larger projects or from clients who have experienced initial agile projects and have discovered problems or come up with good ideas for better ways to accomplish release planning.

Planning Themes and Priorities

In the rush to deliver in short iterations (weeks), teams often sub-optimize their pursuit of business value. Although a particular feature may have greater business value than another, some combination of lower-valued individual features may be the best to implement first. To bring an appropriate focus to business value, projects need both an overall "vision" and shorter-term "themes" that implement that vision. Themes can be useful for iterations, and in larger projects for waves. Several different types of themes might be used either individually or in combination: business function, business function breadth or depth, business process flow, risk mitigation, deployment plan.

A business function can be a grouping of capabilities, features, or stories that fulfill some identifiable business purpose. In breaking requirements into small stories we sometimes loose track of the business purpose we are trying to implement. When we say, "Capability xyz has the greatest priority for this iteration (or wave)," we provide the team with a higher-level organizing or focusing theme for story implementation.

In implementing business functions we can also opt for breadth or depth first, depending on an analysis of business value and risk. In some situations it may be advantageous to implement a particular business function in great depth first, whereas in others it would be better to implement a wider range of functions in a skeletal fashion and then flesh out the skeletons in subsequent iterations.

Business process flow is the sequence of business functions that produces some final result. There are certain standard types of business process flows in organizations such as order-to-shipment, or bill-to-payment, and many specialized flows. In terms of having shippable software at the end of an iteration or wave, it might be better to complete a particular business process flow than to have pieces of multiple flows.

Early in projects, focusing on risk mitigation may be more important than focusing on business value (in a way it does address value). For example, there may be a technical hurdle that needs to be overcome or the entire project will fail. Implementing extensive business functionality prior to mitigating the technical hurdle could be a complete waste of money. Risk mitigation themes, particularly for those risks that are show stoppers, should be considered early in projects.

Finally, partial deployment plans may impact feature/story implementation priorities and create wave themes. For example, let's postulate a nine-month project with partial deployments scheduled at three- and six-month waves. This deployment schedule might dictate that basic install capabilities be implemented in the first three months (and upgraded at six months) even though they weren't the highest business value.

As mentioned earlier, use of these themes will often overlap. Using a partial deployment as a theme may mean using business process flow as a sub-theme. When practicing iteration-at-a-time planning, these higher-level themes often get lost. Completing full release plans, and using themes even at a cursory level, can have a big impact on delivering the highest business value early and often during a project.

> *The key question a team should ask itself at the end of each iteration is, "What is keeping us from shipping a product right now?"*

The team should be thinking about what would be shippable if the project funding was cut. Any project can be cut or deferred. A colleague worked with a client team whose project was ranked high in priority out of a hundred or so projects. At one point every project except the highest two priority projects were cut—leaving the team with two weeks to wrap up their project. Enough of the project was shippable that the customer received useful value even though only 20% of the project capabilities were complete. Teams shouldn't get in the position in which pieces of multiple capabilities are finished, but nothing is usable to the customer.

Increasing Productivity

There are two ways to improve productivity: Do better, or do less. Doing better, improving the flow of output per input, can clearly be accomplished by agile methods as indicated by Micheal Mah's metrics studies outlined in Chapter 1, "The Agile Revolution". The second way to improve productivity is harder to measure, but very significant: Identify features we either don't do or do less of. One study showed that over 64% of software functionality is rarely or never used, whereas just 20% was often or always used.[5] But how do we measure the productivity of things not done? The answer goes back to value: Are we delivering the customer's expected value, but doing so with less work? One of the reasons for projects becoming larger and larger is the absence of immediate feedback on efforts to accomplish individual features, so "featuritis" sets in.

Paul Young, Vice President Business Capabilities and Integrations MDS Sciex, talked about this type of productivity: "A user requirements list usually has somewhere between 50 and 200 items. Do you need all of them? Fine, we'll give you all 200. No problems, no arguments. Which three do you want first? And they say: What do you mean? We say: We're going to give them all to you, but they're going to come out one at a time. Which three do you want first? The most interesting thing I learned—I was totally shocked by this—was by the time you get to number 20, nobody is interested in the remaining 80 any more. They would say: Forget about that stuff. We didn't know what we were talking about when we wrote that. If you had hired a service provider to build all those requirements to a contract, that would just be putting money in the middle of the room and setting it on fire."[6]

Agile projects can improve productivity by doing less in two dimensions—breadth and depth. Paul Young's comments are mostly about breadth—lists of user requirements of which some number are eliminated. The depth dimension involves implementing a requirement or story, but

[5] Jim Johnson, Standish Study reported at XP2002 Conference.

[6] Paul Young, "Risk Management & Solution Acceptance Using Agile IT Project Methods," Information Management Forum, September 19-20, 2005.

altering the depth of functionality. This usually happens when teams are doing iteration planning. When the product team faces capacity constraints (e.g., we have only 30 story points available this iteration), they may opt for leaner stories (the 5 rather than the 13 story point version) to get more stories done.

Risk Analysis and Mitigation

Because APM was designed to handle high-risk, uncertain product development projects, a separate risk analysis may seem redundant, but it is crucial that risk analysis and mitigation become an integral part of every APM phase and process.

Until a final product emerges, the product development process is fundamentally one of gathering information and collaborating. A product's design evolves from understanding requirements and constraints and the underlying science or engineering. "Will this specialized chip do everything we specified? Will this titanium piece pass our stress tests?" Product development consists of answering hundreds, or even thousands, of such questions. Each answered question, each new piece of information, reduces the risk of project failure. Planning doesn't eliminate project risks; constant gathering of information systematically reduces them over the life of the project. Gathering information costs money, so we want to constantly ask what information has the highest value. The strategies we employ to gather information should be guided in part by our risk analysis—it's an integral part of the product development process and a critical component of release planning.

Rather than summarize what has been well documented by others about risk management, I will use existing material to discuss how APM addresses different categories of risk. In *Waltzing with Bears*, their book on software risk management, Tom DeMarco and Tim Lister identify five core risks that dominate software projects:

1. Inherent schedule flaws
2. Requirements inflation (creep)
3. Employee turnover

4. Specification breakdown
5. Poor productivity (DeMarco and Lister 2003)

First, as these authors point out, "The best bang-per-buck risk mitigation strategy we know is incremental delivery." Inherent schedule flaws occur when the size of the product to be developed is either grossly misestimated or the engineering team is given a date based on fantasy rather than reality. For a highly uncertain product, failing to meet a schedule plan may not be a flaw but merely the impossibility of scheduling the unknown. In these cases, executives and product marketing (and the engineering team) have to understand what the process of exploration involves—and what are reasonable and unreasonable expectations. Although APM addresses the issue of schedule flaws in a number of material ways, no process—agile or otherwise—can make up for an organization fixed on the politics of fantasy.

APM techniques that address schedule risk are

- Team involvement in planning and estimating
- Early feedback on delivery velocity
- Constant pressure to balance the number and depth of features with capacity constraints
- Close interactions between engineering and customer teams
- Early error detection/correction to keep a clean working product

Requirements creep must be differentiated from requirements evolution. Requirements evolution is inevitable in exploration projects; in fact it is desirable, because the cost of change remains low in agile projects, and therefore requirements evolution remains cost effective. Requirements evolution is a rational process in which the development and customer teams are constantly evolving the requirements of the product while considering other constraints. Requirements evolution is a joint effort in which all parties participate in deciding on features. Requirements creep occurs when there isn't a joint effort, when customers or developers add features indiscriminately. Requirements creep has acquired a negative connotation because of the high cost of change in many development efforts. Eliminate or greatly reduce that barrier, and evolving requirements become a virtue, not a vice.

Employee turnover, particularly losing a key person, remains a risk factor for any product development effort. The impact of turnover can be reduced by cross training (which rarely happens) and documentation (which coveys very little of the tacit knowledge that is so critical to success). Agile projects have built-in turnover mitigation because of the emphasis on collaboration. In software development, for example, the use of pair programming has demonstrated better knowledge sharing within the team, which reduces the impact of turnover (Williams and Kessler 2003). Employee morale generally improves in an agile environment because of the emphasis on self-organization and the excitement of frequent iteration delivery of working products.

Specification breakdown occurs when the customers or product managers fail to agree on specifications. For example, when an internal IT project has 10 customer departments and they can't decide on business process or business rules issues, the specification process breaks down. Unfortunately, in many serial projects the project continues under the false assumption that the decisions will be made sometime later. The result of indecision—conflicting specifications or multiple near-duplicate features—can have devastating results for the project. APM lessens this risk by insisting on a product manager role. The product manager, aided by the executive sponsor, is charged with either stopping specification breakdown or halting the project until the specification process can be fixed. Creating a viable specification decision-making process is the responsibility of the product manager and team.

DeMarco and Lister's final risk of poor productivity arises from three sources: having the wrong people on the team, having a team that doesn't work well together, and poor morale. The APM practices of getting the right people on the team, coaching and team development, and forcing reality on the project help offset these risks. Similarly, using short iterations to focus on features, feature depth, and feature value often reduces the total amount of work on a product, which contributes to ROI, if not directly to productivity.

Understanding the project and how much risk can be safely assumed requires experience. Mountain climbers who get into the most trouble are those who don't understand the risks. Experienced mountaineers know their limits; they have a sixth sense about when to continue on—because getting to the top of major peaks requires pushing oneself and one's team to the edge, but not over the edge—and when to turn back. Teams and managers need to be visionary and positive, and at the same time, brutally honest about the risks. For teams operating at the edge on highly risky projects, there are no formulaic answers to managing risk.

Risk management is a tricky proposition for project leaders. On one hand, they must be realistic about the dangers facing the project—denial leads to surprise, which leads to last-minute scrambling and firefighting. On the other hand, constantly harping on risks can demoralize a team. There are so many difficult questions about product development: "Will it sell? What exactly do the customers want? What are our competitors doing? Can we deliver it on time? Can we build it for the target cost? Will the new electronic control system be ready in time?" And on and on. The project leader needs to project confidence in the positive outcome of the project without glossing over the dangers. Like most other aspects of leadership, risk management is a delicate balancing act.

Selection of an agile approach, particularly the use of iterative development in and of itself, reduces some risks and increases others. For example, APM projects advocate less up-front planning, architecture, and requirements-gathering because information is gathered for these as the project unfolds. Short planning and delivery iterations reduce the risks of losing customer involvement, wasting up-front work as project changes occur, encountering analysis paralysis, and delaying returns. On the flip side, too little initial planning increases the risks of major rework due to oversights and scope oscillation due to hurried customer interaction, plus the increased cost of frequent changes.

"A totally predictable process will generate no information," writes Donald Reinertsen (1997), an expert in industrial product design. Reinertsen believes that the design process is about producing economically useful information. With a product design, until the final manufacturing engineering plans are in place, no one knows for sure whether the product can be made to the specifications that customers demand. However, as a product gets closer and closer to the "release to manufacturing" stage, the more confident the development team should be. Product development is first and foremost about generating and processing information, not predictability. If a process is predictable, if all variations are accounted for, if the process is repeatable in a statistical quality control sense of the word, then it won't generate any new information. The ideal of statistical repeatability sought by "heavy" process proponents flies in the face of product development reality.

Planning and Scanning

Agile methods are geared to managing uncertainty—uncertainty related to "ends" (customer objectives and requirements), and uncertainty related to "means" (technology and people). One way in which agile methods deal with uncertainty is frequent re-planning based on progress to date and new information gathered during development iterations. The idea of uncertainty and an exploration factor to measure that uncertainty was introduced in Chapter 6 and illustrated in Table 6-2. The positive aspect of agile methods is that they encourage dealing with the uncertainty early in a project and focus on working software (or products) rather than documentation to ensure that the information gathered is very realistic.

> *Agile teams can place too much emphasis on adaptation or evolution and too little on anticipation (in planning, architecture, design, requirements definition). Failure to take advantage of knowable information leads to sloppy planning, reactive thinking, excessive rework, and delay. Remember: Agility is the art of balancing.*

Unfortunately, these very aspects of agile can also have potential negative outcomes: sloppy planning and reactive thinking. All agile projects combine aspects of anticipation (early planning) and adaptation (revisions based on reflections). Too great an emphasis on adaptation (we can always fix or refactor it later) means that we don't take advantage of information we already know (or should know with minimal effort). For example, spending a week at the beginning of a project defining customer requirements and constructing a skeleton data model may significantly improve the quality of a plan and the speed of development.

Second, although developing adaptation skills is critical to agile methods, too much emphasis on adapting can cause excessive rework and time delay. A simple example would be ignoring a well known software design pattern and thinking that a series of programming and refactoring sessions would create the best solution. The agile mantra, "We have more confidence in our ability to adapt than in our ability to predict the future," can be taken too far and lead to short-sightedness—a common theme of agile critics.

One solution to this potential problem of placing too much emphasis on adapting over anticipating is to expand our practices to include both planning (working with what we know), and scanning (looking ahead to learn the unknown as quickly as possible).

Scanning can take several forms: experimenting, managing risks, monitoring assumptions, and anticipating decisions. Scanning is basically about reducing uncertainty through the systematic, proactive, and early gathering of information or identifying the information that needs to be gathered at a future point.

When teams discover an unknown, say not knowing whether a design will work or not, then they can perform short experiments on multiple options (spikes) to see whether one or more of the options works to their satisfaction. In software development, experiments may take the form of (potentially) throw-away code. In hardware development, experiments may take the form of engineering breadboards or simulations.

Managing risks is another form of scanning. Because risks are defined as probabilities of something happening, they essentially identify potential future information states. A risk that a key resource person has a 50% chance of being pulled off the project identifies a potential future information state—not having the person. The team can try to mitigate the risk early or it can figure out potential future responses. These are all "alternative" project plans.

Managing assumptions is a third type of scanning. Although risks identify potential information states, assumptions define an information state that the team will use until it is proven to be false. For example, the customer may not know early in the project whether the volume of Web site hits will be 50,000 or 100,000 per day. To make some early skeleton architecture decisions, the team will "assume" a level of 75,000. The team is assuming a piece of information to proceed. However, the team needs to constantly "scan" the list of assumptions and compare them to current information to alert the team when a key assumption may become invalid.

Finally, teams need to maintain a list of key future decisions to be made. For example, a team may identify that for the project to continue on schedule, a key architectural decision must be made within two months. As each key decision is listed, the team can begin accumulating information related to the decision. In the previous example of assuming Web hit rates, the team can identify this as a key assumption that needs to be validated one month prior to making the final architectural decisions.

Proactive scanning keeps teams from falling into the trap that "adaptation" (or refactoring) will solve any mistakes that are made. Although adapting is indeed a major part of agile development, it shouldn't be used as an excuse for sloppy project management. Good project leaders know that waiting until something happens can have terrible consequences for a project. Combining good planning and scanning with an ability to adapt when necessary provides a powerful project management combination.

Timeboxed Sizing

Agile development has always included the practice of timeboxing—setting a fixed time limit to overall development efforts and letting other characteristics such as scope vary. However, timeboxing can also be used in another interesting way: timeboxing capabilities and features.

Working with a client that was in an early stage of development of a large (over 40 people), lengthy (over 2 years) project, we used the idea of timeboxing capabilities during release planning. We were planning at the capability level, but some of the capabilities were reasonably well defined and others were still ambiguous. There were, in fact, a significant number of capabilities for which the potential scope was wide (in one case estimates ranged from 50–600 days of work). Furthermore, some of these capabilities were tentatively scheduled late in the project. Rather than spend significant time scoping and estimating capabilities that were subject to change anyway, we approached sizing by constraining (timeboxing) rather than estimating.

Constraining approaches the problem of sizing by looking at business value rather than requirements. The question becomes, "How many hours or story points do you think we can spend on this capability given its value relative to other capabilities?" On the capability whose range of possibilities was between 50 and 600 days, it was actually fairly easy for the product manager to say, "I think we should timebox this capability to 75 days." The 600 day estimate was way out of line with the relative value of this capability. The "timeboxed size" of 75 days seemed a reasonable cost given the overall product objectives.

Remember, this was a release planning exercise (that was actually more of a road map with additional estimating) for a large project with a two-year overall effort, and the objective of the planning session was to establish the feasibility of the project and lay out a early plan. Constraining size rather than estimating size was much faster than trying to discuss and agree on the scope. Constraining capabilities allowed the team to rapidly reduce the project's uncertainty. It also let the team, product, and executive management understand that for the project objectives to be met, certain capabilities would have to be bounded.

In many projects, the fuzziness of scope allows two groups to have very different expectations about what will be delivered. One group, usually product management, envisions a gold-plated capability while the development team envisions a bare-bones one. Timeboxed sizing can help bring these expectations into line early in the project. It is easy to misinterpret a scope description to meet one's own expectations (no matter how much time is spent defining that scope). It is harder to misinterpret a sizing number—75 days.

Early sizing in project release planning is inexact regardless of method used. Attempts at defining scope and estimating often end up wrong as projects unfold and teams learn more about the requirements. Similarly, sizing by constraining can give a false sense of correctness, particularly if little thought is given to the "reasonability" of whether adequate functionality can be delivered within the capability timebox. For early release planning efforts, both types of sizing should be used. Scoping and estimating is preferred for some capabilities, timeboxing for others. They can even be used together—timeboxing to get into a ballpark, then scoping and estimating within that ballpark. It is necessary, however, to keep track of which capabilities are sized with each method.

For timeboxed sizing to work, all parties—the development team and product and executive management—need to understand the benefits, and the limitations, of such an approach. Timeboxing size rather than estimating size can be another useful technique in the agile team's toolbox.

Other Story Types

Although 80–90% of the stories in a release plan should be customer-facing ones, the other 10%–20% cannot be forgotten. Some of these are non-customer-facing stories that can be both dangerous and necessary. They are dangerous from the perspective that immature agile teams will use them to fall back into non-agile habits. Too many technical stories or too many task-like stories indicate that the team doesn't understand the "chunk of customer valuable functionality" definition of a story. Conversely, not including non-customer-facing stories leads to underestimation of the total workload, but even more importantly, leads to ignoring critical work. Although an agile team needs to heed the lean value stream principles (every task seeks to deliver customer value), teams ignore other stories or tasks at their peril. It's true that much of this work can be identified as tasks within stories, but having a few other options can lead to better plans.

> *The overriding concept should be that all work should be accounted for in release and iteration planning.*

Maintenance Stories

Although the optimum agile strategy calls for full-time staffing, reality in many organizations requires some level of multitasking on activities such as maintenance work for legacy systems. This maintenance or enhancement work should be identified, placed on a backlog (System Change Request backlog), and prioritized along with other stories.

The question, "Does agile work for maintenance?" comes up frequently. The answer, of course: Maintenance and enhancements requests (SCRs) can be mapped into stories (a story can be a collection of SCRs) and then planned into iterations just like new development; the only thing that changes is the nature of the backlog items. However, there is another factor. Although new development agile teams work in collaborative groups, "maintenance" work is often done by individuals. Maintenance work should be done in small collaborative groups just as it is with new development.

Task Cards

Two concepts separate agile from traditional planning—story versus task and short iterations. Some people get the short iterations, but then plan short iterations by technical task. However, just because story planning takes precedence over task planning doesn't mean that tasks are completely eliminated. Tasks show up, of course, in iteration planning when stories are broken down into tasks. But there are circumstances in which several days of work cannot realistically be included on a story card. Research efforts are one example. One or more team members might spend 40 hours over a few-week period researching some new technology before making a final decision. That decision might impact many stories, and although the time could be accounted for by allocating 4 hours from each of 10 stories, convenience indicates consolidating the effort into a task card.

Change Cards

Product demos or customer focus groups (Chapter 10) are conducted at the end of each iteration. The feedback from customers or product managers usually takes the form of change requests. Allocating time to resolve these requests makes the work explicit and indicates to customers that the team is serious about dealing with their requests. Another reason for making changes explicit is that they can be better monitored and prioritized. High levels of change requests may also indicate problems with another part of the process, such as breakdown of the requirements conversations.

Inter-team Commitment Story Cards

ICS (Inter-team Commitment Story) cards are used on large projects (with multiple teams) to capture the work required when one team commits to do work for another within the project team. This concept is covered in detail in Chapter 11, "Scaling Agile Projects."

Decision Milestones

Decision milestones, as represented by the diamond box in Figure 8-6, indicate critical junctures in projects where decisions are required. These decision milestones don't represent work effort by decision events. Many projects run into schedule problems because they fail to anticipate dependencies, especially decision dependencies. One of the principles behind agile and lean methods is to put off decisions until the last possible point (when the best information will be available), but not too long. Automated testing and refactoring, for example, enable teams to practice evolutionary design in which design decisions can evolve over time as new information becomes available, rather than needing to be made too early in a project.

Figure 8-6
A Complete Release
Plan

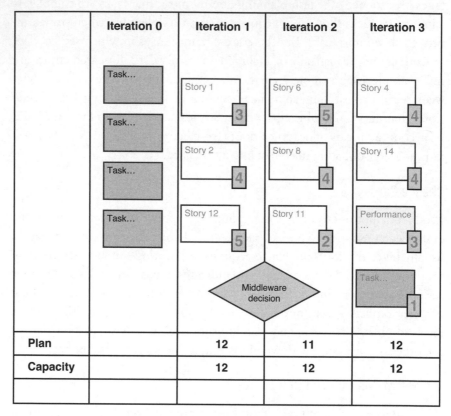

Although any project, agile on not, needs to monitor decision points, the criticality of doing this increases on agile projects because of postponing decisions. Keeping track of those decision deadlines creates a focal point so teams and managers don't let these critical points creep up on them and cause schedule delays.

Performance Cards

Performance requirements cards document the key operations and performance requirements of the product. They are important because performance considerations drive design decisions and because team members must spend time developing and conducting performance tests. Although some performance requirements can be covered as acceptance tests on a story card, in many situations a distinct, and very visible, definition of performance and operational requirements is necessary. For example, myriad design decisions—in fact the major design decisions—in aircraft design revolve around weight. Weight isn't a function of a single feature, whether it is avionics or engines, but a property of the entire plane. Similarly, the expected load on an Internet site is a function of all capabilities, not an individual story or capability. In these cases it would be inappropriate to have the performance requirement be an acceptance test for an individual story, although in the case of aircraft design, each subsystem team is given a weight target. If subsystems are too heavy, teams must coordinate by trading weight credits and negotiating other performance criteria.

Performance cards contain the name, description, and quantitative performance goals of the product, as shown in Figure 8-7. A card might be labeled, say, "Database Size" or "Aircraft Weight Limit" or "Training Time." Teams should focus on those performance attributes that will drive the design process. For example, weight, payload, range, and speed are critical aircraft design parameters; each would have a performance card (obviously backed up by more extensive documentation). Performance cards should also contain acceptance tests—how the team will demonstrate to the customer team that the product meets the performance criteria. These tests are essential when the performance criteria to be met involve critical real-world risks (e.g., planes falling out of the sky). Because some tests are very difficult to run until the product is fully built, creating interim tests (using simulations, prototypes, models, or historical calculations) should be considered.

Some performance attributes can be derived from the guiding principles established during the Envision phase. Others are well known by engineers who work with specific products. In any case, although feature specifications tell the engineering team what to build, performance requirements often have great relevance to the design process itself: They force design tradeoffs and often must be dealt with early in the project. They are a vital part of the information a product development team has to gather and analyze as it plans and implements features.

Figure 8-7
A Performance Card

Performance Card	Demonstrated Iteration: 6
Performance ID:	PC-12
Performance Name:	Flight Avionics Package Weight
Performance Description:	The weight allocated to the flight avionics package is 275 pounds, not including the display screens in the cockpit, which are included in the cockpit display package.
Difficulty in Achieving (H,M,L):	M (moderately difficult)
Acceptance Tests:	Weight of all components beginning in iteration 3, followed by completed instrument package weighing in iteration 6.

Work-in-Process versus Throughput

Work-in-process versus throughput issues first arose in manufacturing. Companies that don't focus on throughput initiate far too many concurrent projects, and this concurrency introduces significant delay times in their projects. The conceptual background for this work-in-process versus throughput issue comes from the Critical Chain Project Management approach of Eliyahu Goldratt (*Critical Chain*, 1997; *The Goal*, 1984). Goldratt's work had tremendous impact on manufacturing during the 1980s and 1990s when he showed that traditional accounting numbers led manufacturing plants into less throughput and more work-in-progress.[7] Similar problems occur in software development when too many projects force people into severe multitasking—lots of work is being done, but few products

[7] For a software-oriented view of this issue, see David Anderson, *Agile Management for Software Engineering*, 2004.

are actually being delivered (and those that are tend to be in large chunks). Reducing the number of projects, having staff dedicated to projects as much as possible (as agile methods recommend), and adequately staffing projects (rather than having too many projects, each with below-par staffing) can have a huge impact on throughput.

"Capacity" problems in organizations, as opposed to projects, arise from ignoring throughput issues. The problem that everyone agrees with, but few deal with, is working on too many projects at the same time—increasing work-in-progress and reducing throughput to a trickle as engineers work a little bit on many projects. Agile teams combat this trend because of the agile emphasis on full-time team participation, but the problem persists. Capacity planning based on wishes rather than facts and this sub-optimal utilization of staff are both issues caused by a basic failure to prioritize.

Here is an illustrative example. Take three projects, each with ten two-day tasks—three analysis tasks, four design tasks, and three programming tasks—and one of each resource. There are two basic strategies for completing the project—having each resource multi-task work between projects (i.e. the analyst works on project 1 for two days, project 2 for two days, etc.) or having each resource work on projects one at a time until they are finished (the analyst works on project 1 for six days, then moves to project 2.) Figures 8-8 and 8-9 illustrate that using the multitasking strategy (and not calculating any time for task switching), project 1 is completed in 48 days (the analysis, design, and programming tasks are sequential), project 2 is completed in 50 days, and project 3 in 52 days. Using the non-multitasking strategy, project 1 is completed in 20 days, project 2 in 28 days, and project 3 in 36 days. Multitasking introduces inevitable wait time into the work. Furthermore, task switching time introduces even more delays in projects.

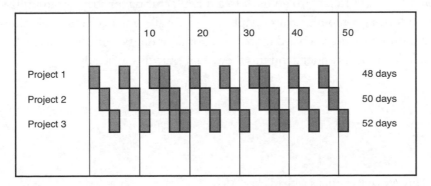

Figure 8-8
multitasking Strategy (try to keep everyone happy)

Figure 8-9
Concentrate Resource
Strategy (emphasize
throughput)

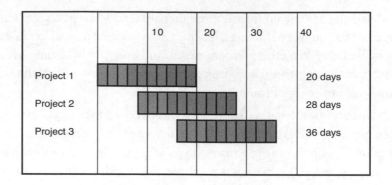

Many companies find it very difficult to focus on throughput because they must sell customers on delayed start times for projects. Politically, it's easier to tell upper management or product management that "We're working on that," even when "working" means a few hours a week. The problem is that management interprets "working on" in a very different way.

Referring back to Chapter 1 and Michael Mah's metrics table shown in Table 1-2, BMC Software reduced their project's schedule versus industry average by 58%, in part by doubling staff. Because of their effective agile testing practices (and others) the team was also able to keep defects low. Mah has also discussed how, for a given size project, low staffing levels can greatly lengthen schedule.[8] These metrics add more evidence to the conclusion that throughput can be greatly increased by minimizing multitasking.

This seems to be an issue that everyone can agree with, but one that's very difficult to take on. Setting priorities, delaying projects, and dedicating resources is very difficult for most companies because the effects of runaway multitasking are hard to see. Everyone looks very busy, so that must be good—right? In fact, to go back to a manufacturing analogy, when utilization levels get too high, throughput suffers. Agile practices guide development organizations toward more throughput and less work-in-process, but unless managers understand this they can negate this agile advantage.

[8] Private conversations with Michael Mah.

Emerging Practices

In addition to the topics already covered, a set of emerging industry practices are worth mentioning. The information in this section is intended as introductory, and additional details can found in the references. These types of practices help answer the question, "Where do we (the agile movement) go from here?" The implementation of these ideas will differ from a small ISV to a large IT organization, but they help in driving the strategic initiative of building agile organizations and potentially changing entire business models.

Kanban

The term Kanban came from the Japanese process for continuous improvement and the name has been applied to an approach to software development. A previous section discussed the issue that growing work-in-process (WIP) reduces throughput and productivity as staff multitasking increases. Kanban systems begin to solve the high WIP problem and are increasing in popularity in the software arena. Kanban, as it is being practiced in a growing number of software organizations, has grown out of a combination of the lean development movement and Goldratt's theory of constraints (Goldratt 1999), and is being popularized by David Anderson (Anderson 2004 and 2009) and others.

Kanban introduces a signaling system into the scheduling process in which a limit is set on WIP (depending on resources), and new work (stories or other work items) is introduced as in-process work completes. Work is "pulled" through the system (as an item is completed it pulls the next item off the backlog). Kanban isn't for everyone because some of its premises can be controversial in organizations—it does away with fixed-length iterations, may eliminate estimation, and minimizes planning (Anderson 2009). In a Kanban system, stories progress through a series of phases (In Requirements, In Engineering, In Development, In Test) in which work in each stage is also "pulled" from completed work in the prior stage. Stories can be of variable length and remain in the "system" for varying lengths of time. Although Kanban systems have periodic releasable timeframes, they don't use strict iteration lengths in which all stories are completed.

Because of the lack of fixed iteration lengths, somewhat waterfall-looking phases (although these are very short), and some staff specialization (in each phase), some don't consider Kanban to be agile—I'm not one of those people. The fundamentals of Kanban are agile—value orientation, self-organizing teams, reflections, short iterations (although not fixed), and adaptability (Kanban systems may even be more adaptable than other agile planning methods)—so I consider Kanban to be very much a part of the agile movement. Kanban deserves serious consideration as an agile organization matures and looks for additional performance improvements.

Consolidated Development

I've often wondered about the split between new development, enhancement, and maintenance in an agile world. Independent software vendors (ISVs) and IT organizations handle these stages of development differently, but the common issue revolves around staffing these categories of development. IT organizations tend to be divided into new development and maintenance, whereas ISVs tend to put new development, maintenance, and enhancement into a single group, but then break out customization for particular clients into a separate group. However, as quality deteriorates, ISVs then tend to break out separate maintenance groups for quick fixes, as these tend to overwhelm the development group that is working hard on the next release of the product. The bottom line is that multiple groups and multiple sites often use the same code base, but each has a different agenda.

Having multiple groups working like this has arisen for seemingly good reasons, the best being management of conflicting priorities among new development, customization, and maintenance work. New development teams seem to get bogged down in maintenance work and key customers want their customization work done quickly and to a committed schedule. Rather than deal with conflicting priorities directly, most organizations deal with them by creating separate teams. When organizations are using a large-chunk development approach (i.e., a waterfall approach) and code quality is wanting, this multi-organization approach is almost a necessity.

However, having multiple organizations working off the same code base causes many problems, the worst being splintering of domain and technical expertise and creating multiple code streams, all of which cause confusion and severely impact QA, thereby causing further degradation of quality. Having three groups working on the same code base causes multiple other problems.

The ideas for solving this problem and creating a truly integrated development team came from Jeff Sutherland.[9] This solution isn't for the faint of heart and it should be attempted only by mature agile teams, but the practice can significantly enhance effectiveness. In Jeff's approach, a single organization (implemented at his company PatientKeeper, a healthcare software company) works on all facets of delivery (new functionality, enhancements, SCRs) and is 1) governed by a strategic prioritization system, and 2) allocated to one of three simultaneous, overlapping iterations (Sprints in Scrum terminology).

Three iteration lengths are running simultaneously—weekly, monthly, and quarterly. The weekly iterations target maintenance or minor enhancements; the monthly iterations target specific enhancements; and the quarterly release targets major new functionality. This approach enabled PatientKeeper to deliver 45 releases of their product in 2004. There are numerous ramifications of this model, both to the development organization and to its customers, most of which are very positive.

The first question most would ask about such an approach would be, "How would you balance the priorities between the types of work?" The answer demonstrates why only the truly committed and experienced should apply this approach. Prioritization is a strategic organizational process—involving not only the product manager, but the CEO and other key executives at Jeff's company. Only at this level can priority decisions such as, "Does customer x's enhancements take precedence over new feature y" be made. In other companies, one of the portfolio management decisions required would be identifying the responsible prioritization executive (CTO, VP Product Management, Chief Operating Officer, etc.) for different product lines.

There are significant barriers to succeeding with this advanced model of agile development—both technical and organizational. For example, it works only where agile delivery has been proven and management is comfortable and satisfied with the process. It works only where continuous inte-

---

[9] Jeff Sutherland, "Future of Scrum: Parallel Pipelining of Sprints in Complex Projects," Agile 2005 conference.

gration and automated testing is ingrained in the development process. It works only with well functioning and integrated product management, development, and QA. These are prerequisites to implementing this advanced model.

Hyper-development and Release

What would be the business ramifications of ultra- or hyper-fast development, distribution, and deployment? The previous section on consolidated development focused on integrating multiple story types and on different iteration lengths into a faster development environment. Israel Gat, former VP at BMC Software, Inc. goes an additional step—from high-speed development to high-speed distribution and deployment.[10] Gat introduces the use of virtual appliance technologies to speed up distribution (quickly packaging releases into multiple deployment environments) and deployment at a client's site. Using hyper-fast development and deployment, Gat goes on to postulate that these two practices, operating together, make it possible to customize software packages for high-end customers at affordable cost.

At this point, consolidated fast development combined with fast distribution and deployment offer a range of possibilities for changing business models. If you are an ISV with a traditional 12–18 month new release cycle, key customers might have to wait many months, or even years for business-critical software updates. What if you could offer your top-tier customers a 3-month turnaround on significant feature updates? Gat concludes that this ability greatly enhances customer intimacy and thereby strengthens strategic relationships.

[10] Israel Gat. "To Release No More or To 'Release' Always." Cutter Agile Product & Project Management Advisory Service, Executive Updates, Vol. 9, No. 21, 22, 23 (November & December 2008).

Final Thoughts

Release planning is one of the most important and sometimes the most ignored of agile project management practices. Effective release planning can be done at different levels of detail, depending on the timeframe (e.g., the end of an 18-month project should be planned in less detail than the beginning) and different timeframes. Release planning gives the team a game plan that compensates for the often short iteration focus of agile projects and gives product marketing a context within which to make key priority decisions about capabilities and stories. Finally, release planning gives management and executives a baseline against which to determine the feasibility of delivering a high-quality, releasable product within the identified constraints.

Chapter 9

The Explore Phase

The Explore phase delivers running, tested, accepted stories. But rather than concentrate on the technical details of how to accomplish this goal, APM focuses on the agile leaders' tasks of creating self-organizing, self-disciplined teams that can deliver a releasable product. Exploration covers three of the four agile development methodology levels introduced in Chapter 5—project management, iteration management, and technical practices. As described before, iteration management covers planning and management during short iterations and leading feature teams, whereas project management covers longer timeframe release management and working with external stakeholders. For small projects one person usually fulfills both project leader and iteration manager roles, whereas for large projects the roles may be split out to separate individuals. Even if these roles are filled by different people, both project leaders and iteration managers help in building the project community.

Agile leaders—project, product, iteration—must function in a wider organization. They need to manage up (making sure functional managers and executives understand the benefits and differences of agile methods), manage out (making sure customers understand their key role and responsibilities in an agile projects), and manage the team (encouraging them to embrace and fully understand agile principles and practices).

The transition from the Envision phase to the Explore phase is shown in Figure 9-1. It shows that the release planning done in the Envision cycle connects to iteration planning in the Explore cycle. Major Explore activities are:

- Iteration Planning and Monitoring
  - Iteration planning
  - Workload management
  - Monitoring iteration progress
- Technical Practices
  - Technical debt
  - Simple design
  - Continuous integration
  - Ruthless automated testing
  - Opportunistic refactoring
- Project Community
  - Coaching and team development
  - Participatory decision making
  - Collaboration and coordination

Figure 9-1
The APM Envision
and Explore Cycles

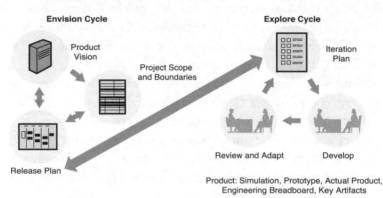

A complex adaptive system (CAS) is a collection of agents who explore to achieve a goal (fitness in a biological sense) by interacting with each other according to a set of rules. A CAS experiments with alternatives, selects and executes viable ones, compares the results against its fitness goals (the system's objectives), and adapts as necessary. Extending this metaphor to a team, the project leader's job takes on new dimensions—to constantly help the team articulate and understand the goal and the constraints, to help the team interact effectively, to facilitate the decision-making process, to encourage the team to take risks, to ensure appropriate feedback is being gathered and incorporated into the next iteration, and to keep score and deal with reality when things go off track, as every project does.

Agile Project Leadership

The core of this chapter is about agile leadership. Even when discussing technical practices such as refactoring, the focus is on what leaders need to know to manage refactoring, not what developers need to know to do refactoring.

Agile project leaders focus on adding value to a project. Unfortunately, many development engineers consider project management to be a roadblock—a hindrance, not a help. Project managers are viewed as administrators who put together detailed task schedules, create colorful resource profiles, bug team members about micro-task completions, and write reams of status reports for upper management, but don't serve as direct contributors to delivering value to customers. Teams often view project management as overhead. As Michael Kennedy (2003), author of *Product Development for the Lean Enterprise* writes, "Our product development philosophy is based more upon administration excellence than technical excellence, and it's getting worse."

"Buy pizza and stay out of the way" expresses too many product engineering teams' view of "good" project management. Rather than overhead, project management should be seen as offering inspirational leadership focused on delivering customer value. We have missed this point because many project management practices and project managers are focused on compliance activities, not delivering value. These managers are project administrators, not project leaders. Customers pay for value; everything else is overhead—necessary overhead in some respects, but overhead nonetheless. Team activities or deliverables that help comply with government regulations are necessary, but they rarely add customer value. Documentation that conforms to legal requirements may be necessary, but it may not add value—at least not directly. Status reports assist managers in meeting their fiduciary responsibilities, but they don't add value. Endless approvals may delude management into thinking they are in control, but they don't add value.

Finally, neither the best project leader nor the best team performance can trump organizational politics. Nor can any methodology make up for outrageous fantasies or dictatorial edicts. These traits make for what Ed Yourdon (1999) calls "death march" projects—projects that have failed before they begin and go downhill sharply from there. Agile project management can't deliver on fantasies, and its management style is at the opposite end of the spectrum from dictatorial edicts. Agile methods won't help on death march projects.

Iteration Planning and Monitoring

Iteration planning and monitoring consists of three main activities: iteration planning, workload management, and monitoring iteration progress. The primary responsibility for managing this work lies with the iteration manager. The iteration manager may also facilitate meetings such as retrospectives held at the end of each iteration (covered in Chapter 10, "The Adapt and Close Phases").

Iteration Planning

After the overall release plan has been established for the project, the team turns to developing a detail plan for the next (or the first, if it's the beginning of the project) iteration. The team takes each story card from the release plan and identifies a list of the technical and other tasks required to implement the story and records those tasks. The team then re-estimates the work effort and adjusts the stories planned for the iteration if necessary. Figure 9-2 shows stories as they have been assigned to an iteration. Story tasks are often listed on a flip-chart, as in Figure 9-3, or in a progression sequence, as shown

Figure 9-2
Story-Level Iteration Plan

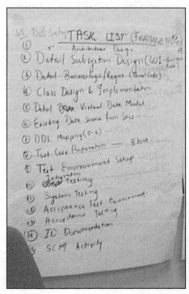

Figure 9-3
Task List Breakdown for a Story

Figure 9-4
Story Progression
During an Iteration

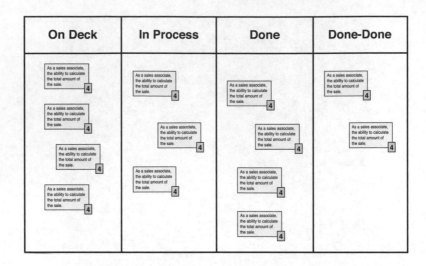

On Deck	In Process	Done	Done-Done

in Figure 9-4. The progression in this last figure can be used for either stories or tasks, depending upon the situation.

The entire project team—product manager, product specialists, customers, developers, testers, iteration manager, project leader—should participate in the iteration planning session as it provides everyone with the context for work to be accomplished during the iteration. Functional manager participation can help the team better understand strategic priority issues and demonstrates commitment to and support of the project.

Iteration planning sessions will vary in time required, depending on the type of project and length of the iteration, but 1–2 hours per week of iteration would be a reasonable guide. So for a three-week iteration, 3–6 hours of iteration planning might be needed. If a team was taking two days to plan a three-week iteration, it would be an indicator that something was amiss. Teams should work hard to reduce iteration planning time to the "just barely enough" level.

During a release or wave plan the team may have developed iteration "themes" (discussed in Chapter 8, "Advanced Release Planning"). If so, the themes should be revisited and adjusted if necessary. Iteration themes provide a focus for an iteration so the team does not get bogged down in detail tasks. Themes for iterations can be both customer oriented, such as "complete the credit validation capability," and technical, such as "complete the database refactoring defined in the last technical review."

One problem that can arise with agile methods (or any method) is lack of team commitment to outcomes. Because the principle behind agility is flexibility, then how can teams commit to an outcome? But agile methods should not be an excuse for lack of commitment, and that commitment should start at the iteration level. Teams are heavily involved in planning, estimating, and executing the iteration plan, and team members need to recognize that with involvement comes accountability—they need to commit to achieve what they have planned. If they plan to deliver six stories during the iteration, then there should be a commitment on every team member's part to deliver on those stories.[1]

Estimating and Task Size

The objective in agile planning is to match capacity with plans and not engage in wish-based planning. Many agile teams use story or story-point velocity (number of stories or story points delivered per iteration) as a capacity number, but if the number of stories is small then velocity can vary widely. Some teams use a velocity as an initial measure of capacity for the iteration, but then adjust that capacity because the team thinks they can do more (or less) through looking at the tasks and task estimates. In any case, the objective is to match capacity with plans and try to increase the capacity through productivity improvements during the project's life.[2, 3]

Teams also struggle with determining the right "size" for tasks. Guidelines are that stories generally should take 2–10 days of effort and tasks less than 8 hours. However, in a mature, high-performance, self-organizing agile

---

[1] Israel Gat, private email, "We used the 'fist of 5' for team members to express their confidence and commitment to a plan when it is developed. Worked amazingly well." (Fist of five: 1 finger=don't support the plan, 3 fingers=moderate support for the plan, 5 fingers=full support of the plan).

[2] For more on estimating, see Mike Cohn, *Agile Estimating and Planning*, 2006.

[3] Israel Gat, private correspondence. "You might want to add a word of caution about betting on linear learning curve effects for Agile. After successful delivery of three releases of our product, I assumed capacity would improve in a linear fashion. By so doing our next release was messed up big time. For one reason or another our productivity between the last two releases did not improve, but it did spike later. Hence, I work to improve productivity but do not count on it anymore in my planning."

team, shouldn't task breakdown and size be determined by the team members? One team might want a detailed breakdown, whereas another might be comfortable with scribbling high-level tasks.

> *As long as teams are delivering on their commitments, they should decide the level of task detail.*

Iteration Length

There seems to be a mantra among agilists that the shorter the iteration, the more agile the team. Although short iterations are usually preferable, sometimes the "shorter is better" mantra gets in the way of progress. It may also be a symptom of a process being too developer-centric.

Three criteria should be looked at when setting iteration length: delivering chunks (stories) of user valued functionality, building and testing the stories (working software), and product team acceptance of the stories. Additional factors are release timeframe, exploration factor, overhead, and learning needs.

When stories begin failing the "user-valued functionality" test (i.e., the stories don't have much meaning to the customer team because they seem to be technical stories), then the iteration length may be too short—stories have a tendency to be technical (and task-like) rather than user oriented. A four-hour story is almost always a task in disguise.

Another determinant of iteration length is the time it takes for unit testing, integration, and QA testing. Iteration length isn't just about developers completing their job, it's about the team completing all the necessary work. If development is on two-week iterations and it's taking QA a week into the next iteration to complete testing, the team is really using three-week iterations. Similarly, product teams often spend a few days prior to the iteration identifying stories and doing some preliminary requirements definition, but if the product team always spends the entire week prior to the official iteration start doing these tasks, then how long is the real iteration?

One thing that can severely impact QA's ability to complete software testing within a short iteration is a legacy code base. Turning around a large legacy code base to enable the team to complete testing in two weeks may take time, an investment in automated testing tools, and considerable refactoring. A slightly longer iteration length may prove useful in this situation. Even then, because of difficulties in testing the code base, some testing may have to be done after the iteration. In this case, the goal would be to refactor the product into good enough shape that testing after the iteration would no longer be necessary.

Other factors to consider in setting iteration lengths are release time-frame, exploration factor, preparation and review time, and learning needs. Generally, the longer-release timeframes accommodate longer iteration lengths, so, for example, a twelve-month project might utilize four-week iterations, whereas a three-month project might utilize two-week iterations. Working with a tool vendor in the early 1990's, we used one-week iterations on four-week "demo" projects. As exploration factors (uncertainty) increase, iteration lengths should decrease. High exploration factor projects are risky, and therefore team members need to learn as quickly as possible using short-cycle build-review cycles.

Preparation and review time also impacts iteration length. Preparation includes requirements definition, iteration planning, and some aspects of backlog management. Review includes times to complete customer focus groups, retrospectives, and technical reviews. If these activities were taking three days, a one-week iteration length would be very inefficient. Conversely, a small, highly efficient and mature team that could accomplish iteration planning in two hours and all review activities in three hours might effectively use a one-week iteration.

One key reason for short iterations, especially when a team is in an agile learning mode, is that repetition breeds fast learning. Having to do things frequently improves learning, plus high frequency forces teams into learning how to do things quickly. For example, it a team is forced into going from daily to hourly builds, they will find ways to automate the process that they may not have been forced into otherwise. So for immature agile teams, try shorter iterations in the beginning to force learning. Novice teams often want longer iterations because they are nervous about delivering in such short timeframes. What they are nervous about is climbing their learning curve—which, somewhat counterintuitively, happens more quickly with shorter iterations.

Also, iteration lengths should be constant, not two weeks one iteration and three the next. With different-length iterations, teams can't get into a good rhythm and velocity estimating becomes very difficult.

All that said, shorter iterations (two weeks seems to be a growing standard in many organizations) are generally good, but not universally good.

Each of the factors—good user-oriented stories, completion of all work, legacy code, and acceptance testing—should be evaluated in determining the optimal iteration length for any project. One week may be fine for developers, but very difficult for QA or product management. The entire team needs to be considered in determining iteration length.

Workload Management

The objective of workload management is to have team members themselves manage assignment of the day-to-day tasks required to deliver stories at the end of each iteration. To the greatest extent possible, teams should manage their own workload. Each individual and the team as a whole are accountable to deliver the stories to which they committed in the iteration plan. How they accomplish that goal (within the process and practice framework the team designed) and which team members take on which tasks should be left to team members collectively to decide. As with many of the agile practices, individuals and teams that exercise self-discipline can carry this off effectively—others can't.

In developing an iteration plan, team members determine the tasks required to deliver planned stories and sign up for those tasks themselves—project or iteration leads don't assign tasks. However, the question becomes *when* members need to sign up for tasks. Some would recommend this happen during the iteration planning session, but then what about changes during the iteration? Some recommend signing up just in time, but then team members might not be able to plan their work a few days ahead. So again, my recommendation is to try different approaches and find one that works for your team—and let team members decide.

Workload management also involves team members monitoring their own progress during an iteration (in part during daily stand-up meetings) and making necessary adjustments. This does not mean that the project leader abdicates her management responsibilities. When the team consistently meets its commitments, few interventions by the leader are required. However, when the team is implementing a new practice or technology, when new or less-experienced members join the team, leader intervention—often in the form of coaching—may be necessary.

The project leader needs to monitor without micro-managing, primarily by establishing and monitoring performance goals (stories, quality targets, required practices) rather than tasks. Micro-managers attempt to specify detailed tasks and then constantly monitor whether or not those tasks are completed on time. At their core, most of these managers view nonattainment of micro-tasks as a motivational problem. They believe that employees aren't working hard enough or fast enough. Agile leaders follow the principles articulated in Chapter 3, "Teams over Tasks." Agile leaders leave management of tasks to individual team members.

Agile leaders understand that there will be motivational problems with only a small percentage of employees (they have tried to get the right people, after all). They approach performance as a capability issue and first assume that staff members who aren't performing don't have the information, tools, or experience for the task at hand. They see their role not as the hallway monitor, but as the teacher who helps with resources, information, or technical coaching.

> *A coaching leader's attitude is reflected in the question, "How can I help you deliver results?" The micro-manager's attitude is reflected in the question, "Why isn't task 412 done yet?"*

The project leader possesses particular skills, abilities, and experience, and it would be a waste of those capabilities for her to stand aside and let the team flounder. Leaders (project or iteration) are expected to guide and coach to further develop the team's capability. Agile project leaders steer rather than control; they nudge rather than bludgeon. Continued intervention by the leader is an indicator of failure.

Monitoring Iteration Progress

By working side by side with the team on a day-to-day basis and participating in daily stand-up meetings, iteration managers should have a good feel for iteration progress. Progression charts like that in Figure 9-4, or story/task check-off charts like that in Figure 9-5, are maintained by the team and can be helpful. In Figure 9-5 the check marks for stories are "in progress," "development complete," and "accepted." For tasks the check boxes indicate "in progress," and "complete". The simpler the better (low overhead) for iteration management.

Figure 9-5
Story/Task
Progress Chart

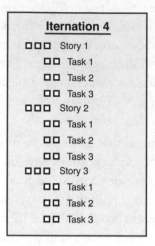

Many agile practitioners use a task burndown chart, which shows the number of tasks completed each day of the iteration, similar to the one in Figure 9-6 to monitor progress. I think task burndown charts can hinder self-organization when used by project leaders or iteration managers. If a leader is monitoring tasks daily, it takes away from the team's self management, although a team might want to use a burndown chart for its own internal use. In any case, if a burndown chart is used, I recommend a unitary task burndown chart, one that shows whole tasks completed, rather than the burndown of total iteration hours that many use. When iterations are three or four weeks long, using burndown charts may be justifiable, but keeping track of burndown hours on a one- to two-week iteration seems to be "heavy" management rather than "self-organizing" management.

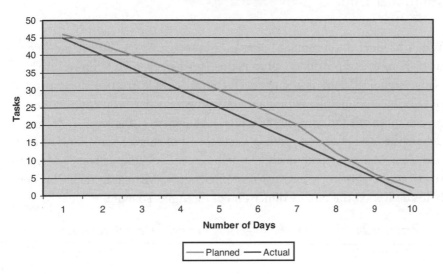

Task Burndown Chart

Figure 9-6
A Task Burndown
Chart

Technical Practices

Most technical practices are specific to the product's engineering domain. However, several practices can be applied generically to many types of products—both hardware and software. These generic technical practices are driven by the desire to keep quality high and the cost of change low. The four technical practices discussed in this section—simple design, continuous integration, ruthless automated testing, and opportunistic refactoring—also work in concert with each other. Although there are many other technical practices, these four are critical to adaptability.[4]

But first, let's consider the phenomenon that makes these practices necessary: technical debt. High technical debt reduces the speed of current development and adversely impacts the ability to deliver in the future.

---

[4] This is not a book on engineering—software, electronic, mechanical, or otherwise—so it doesn't include specific technical practices. However, foundational skills in the various disciplines are critical to success. Software products don't get built without good, fundamental software engineering skills. Electronic instruments don't get built without good, fundamental electronic engineering skills. Project leaders and team leaders need to understand their teams' technical capabilities.

Technical Debt

When product development teams give lip service to technical excellence, when project and product managers push teams beyond quickness into hurrying, technical debt is incurred. Technical debt can arise during initial development, ongoing maintenance (keeping a product at its original state), or enhancement (adding functionality). As shown in Figure 9-7, technical debt is the gap between a product's actual cost of change (CoC) and its optimal CoC. Managing technical debt helps ensure reliable delivery *today* and ready adaptation to *tomorrow's* customer needs. Managing technical debt helps deliver on the quality dimension of the Agile Triangle.

> *Rising technical debt is the single largest impediment to continuing product viability.*

Figure 9-7
Technical Debt

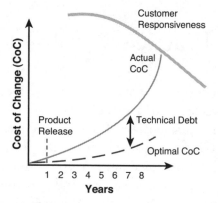

For software products in particular, the actual CoC curve rises slowly at first and then accelerates rapidly after a few years. With software that has been around 10 years or more, developers are loath to touch the now "fragile" code. Constant pressure to cut the time and cost of enhancements, no allowance for periodic refactoring, and poorly maintained automated test data all contribute to fragility and the increased CoC—which is exemplified by companies with 10- to 15-year-old products whose QA cycles extend for a year or more. Every product, software or otherwise, has a curve such as the one in Figure 9-7, but they will have different shapes and business implications.

The bottom line is that increasing technical debt directly reduces responsiveness to customers. Customers and product managers, internal and external, don't understand why a seemingly simple enhancement takes months and months to implement. Yet their relentless pushing for features, features, features, faster, faster, faster is often the root cause of the problem. Without a firm dedication to long-term technical debt management, development groups are pressured into the increasing technical debt trap. As the debt gets worse, the delays become greater. As the delays lengthen, the pressure increases, usually leading to another hurried implementation, which increases the technical debt yet again.

Exiting this downward spiral is very difficult, because the longer the technical debt cycle goes on, the more expensive it is to fix. And fixing it is a political nightmare, because after spending significant time and money, the product's functionality won't be any greater than before (although defects will be reduced). The bigger the debt, the more expensive it is to fix, the more difficult it is to justify, and therefore the death spiral continues.

Conversely, there doesn't seem to be much incentive for narrowing the technical debt early in a product's lifecycle (when doing so is inexpensive), because the development delays are still short. Nevertheless, the secret to long-term technical debt reduction lies in doing it early and often while the cost is low. The smaller the debt, the less expensive it is to fix, the less difficult it is to justify, and this virtuous cycle reinforces itself. Reducing technical debt, keeping the cost of change low, has to become a ingrained technical strategy—part of an organization's dedication to technical excellence.

It must be noted that managing technical debt doesn't keep products from becoming obsolete. A technical debt strategy doesn't attempt to stave off eventual obsolescence but to keep the cost of change low so that customer responsiveness remains as high as possible during a product's life.

The historical approach to this issue was to get it right the first time and then hold on tight. Hold on tight, that is, to the original design or architecture, and resist meaningful change. When the pace of change was slower, this strategy may have worked, but in most product situations today, clinging to the past and resisting change don't work. Holding the cost of change down by not changing only means that when change has to happen, neither the product nor the people will be ready for it.

"Okay," you may think. "This sounds good, but I'll never get my customers or management to invest the time or money in early technical debt reduction." I have a couple of answers to this. First, the alternative will be to lose customers to competitors who are more responsive, especially new entrants into a market who are not burdened by old products. New companies have different economics: They don't have technical debt—yet. Second, a well-functioning agile team will work faster and at lower cost when practicing technical excellence.

Simple Design

The objective of simple design is to keep the engineering team grounded in what is known rather than anticipating the unknown. There are two fundamental approaches to managing change—anticipation and adaptation—and good design strategies encompass aspects of both. Anticipation involves planning for the future and predicting what kinds of change are probable. Adaptation means waiting until requirements or design issues arise and then building them into the product.

Building a tax-rate parameter into a software payroll system *anticipates* future changes in federal withholding rates. Componentizing electronic instruments *anticipates* using the instruments in configurations not currently foreseen. If there is a high probability that something will change, we should design the system to easily incorporate that change, if it is a *known* type of future change. In hardware design a lot of effort is spent defining interfaces; hence subsystems act as black boxes and can be swapped in and out provided the interface does not change. A good design leaves some unused bandwidth for future opportunities; for example, a backplane that contains a few unused signal and data lines. Other examples include using recognized standards and protocols, which allows greater flexibility, and using chip mounts that allow easy upgrading of CPUs/memory to the next generation. Because the cost of change is higher for hardware, adaptability often requires a modicum of anticipatory design.

Conversely, there are changes to the business design and environment that are very difficult to anticipate. For example, IT organizations immersed in developing client/server systems in the mid-1990s had little inkling of the Internet boom that would rapidly overtake those efforts. Companies that spent hundreds of millions of dollars on enterprise resource planning systems during this same time were concerned with internal integration of applications, whereas a few years later integration across companies became critical. Today, anticipating changes in the biotechnology industry explosion would be impossible. Dealing with these unanticipated, and often unforeseeable, changes requires adaptation.

Simple design means valuing adaptation over anticipation. This means designing for what we know today and then responding to what we learn in the future. If our objective is an adaptable product, we should be able to demonstrate its adaptability during development by responding to new information. However, the extent to which this approach is useful depends on the malleability of the medium in which we are working; software is very malleable (with good design), whereas hardware is less so. The more malleable the medium, the lower the cost of change and the easier it will be to tip the balance of anticipation versus adaptation toward the latter.

So malleability creates low-cost iteration, but some components, even in software systems, are not very malleable. Therefore the balance of anticipation and adaptation must swing back toward anticipation. Platform (and product line) architectural decisions, for example, are often expensive and time consuming to change, and thus they should be approached from an anticipation perspective.

But even with less-malleable hardware systems, the advent of highly sophisticated simulation and modeling technology provides hardware designers with nearly as malleable an environment as software designers— the design of the Boeing 777 being a good example. Of course changes immediately became more expensive when the 777 transitioned from design to construction, but until that point Boeing employed simple design practices (to a certain degree) through their creative and extensive use of simulation.

The effectiveness of simple design and refactoring indicates to a product team how adaptable its development process can be. Barriers to these practices are barriers to reducing the cost of change. The key question isn't "How much does it cost to implement these practices?" but "Can you afford not to implement them?" Note that simple design doesn't mean simplistic design. Often coming up with understandable, adaptable, simple designs takes additional time. Doing less, by eschewing nonessentials and focusing on customer value, can free up the time required to do better— simple design.

Continuous Integration

The objective of continuous integration is to ensure that product features fit together into an integrated whole early and often during development to reduce both the high cost of late misalignment and the burden of testing. No matter what the product—from software to automobiles to industrial control systems—the less frequent the integration, the more susceptible the development effort will be to major problems late in the process and the more difficult, and expensive, it will be to find and fix them.

Consider some common problems with embedded software in industrial products. Hardware and software components never seem to be complete at the same time. Software engineers complain that hardware isn't available, whereas hardware engineers have the same complaint about the software. Although software simulations and hardware prototypes can ease the situation for some products, they can both be expensive and oversimplify real-world situations. One company that was developing the embedded software for a cell phone ran into frustrating problems with hardware test equipment from a major vendor, slowing their testing efforts. An oilfield service firm found that simulations couldn't replicate all the variations of the real world, but "live" testing was prohibitively expensive. Operating system and computer hardware developers seem to be constantly out of phase during development. At some level, integrating hardware and software will always be challenging, and the problems only partially solvable. However, development teams need to strive for frequent integration to mitigate the problems.

Ken Delcol used this approach in developing mass spectrometers. "We have just gone through this process. Our firmware group delivered firmware to the hardware group in iterations based on its testing schedule. Once sufficient functionality was confirmed, then the software group was brought in to add applications. With this approach we didn't need a fully populated digital board to begin firmware and hardware integration testing. We achieved a number of things (the best we have ever achieved): Integration testing started sooner, hence issues were resolved more quickly (better schedule and cost); integration was continuous once minimal hardware was in place, hence no peak in resources; and communication was improved because all groups participated in the integration."

Changing to an agile development model can improve the flexibility of products containing both hardware and software. An agile approach, rather than attempting to limit (freeze) requirements, takes advantage of software's flexibility by overlapping the concept development and implementation activities and thereby extends any "software freeze" until much later in the product development process. This allows the distinct possibility that late-discovered hardware flaws (or new requirements) can be implemented in software. Furthermore, the flexibility of software features, and often inexpensive throwaway features, can be used to advantage in the testing of key hardware components.

Marco Iansiti (1998) provides an example of how frequently hardware problems were solved by software solutions during a Silicon Graphics workstation development project. When hardware problems were found, software workarounds were used 70% of the time, the problems became "features" 10% of the time, a combination of hardware and software changed 10% of the time, and pure hardware changes were involved only 10% of the time.

In serial models, "a distinct separation exists between concept development and implementation," says Iansiti. "This model works well when technology, product features, and competitive requirements are predictable." In an agile approach (which Iansiti calls a flexible approach), "the key to the process is in the ability to gather and rapidly respond to new knowledge about technology and application context as a project evolves. Technology integration capability is central to meeting the challenges of such unpredictable change" (Iansiti 1998).

In an agile approach, control occurs not by conformance to concept-driven plans, but by constant integration and testing of feature sets as they emerge during the product development process. Having a product architecture is important, but having good technology integration is vital to success. For this reason, architects need to be heavily involved in product integration.

Ruthless Automated Testing

The objective of ruthless testing is to ensure that product quality remains high throughout the development process.[5] The closer a team comes to running, tested features (RTF) every iteration, the more effective it will be. Michael Mah's metrics, presented in Chapter 1, support the contention that higher-performance agile teams are those that embrace ruthless testing (Mah 2008).

> *Experience has shown that the biggest difference between mature and immature agile teams lies in their commitment to ruthless automated testing.*

The old adage that quality can't be added on but must be built into the development process remains true. Extensive test instrumentation assists development of everything from cell-phone chips to automobile engines. Ruthless testing contributes to the goal of creating adaptable products because finding faults early, when there is still time to correct them, reduces the cost of change. When product developers wait until late into the lifecycle to test, the testing process itself becomes cumbersome. Furthermore, the lack of constant testing removes a necessary feedback loop into the development process. Wait too long, and designs solidify. Then when tests are finally run, the team is unwilling to make design changes. Constant ruthless testing, including acceptance testing, challenges the development team—no matter what the product—to face the reality of how its design actually works.

In software development, ruthless testing includes software engineers performing constant unit testing, integrating quality assurance testing into each development iteration, and having a full range of those tests automated. Many development teams are also practicing test-driven development (TDD) by writing test code prior to executable code. They consider TDD and automated testing to be significant development accelerators.

---

[5] The term "ruthless testing" comes from *Sustainable Software Development* by colleague Kevin Tate (Tate 2006). While a growing number of software developers use "test-first development," ruthless testing is a better generic term that is widely applicable to all types of products.

Automated acceptance testing, using tools such as FIT, also enables teams to use the test scripts as automated detail requirements. The ultimate goal is to produce a shippable product at the end of each iteration.

Opportunistic Refactoring

The objective of opportunistic refactoring is to constantly and continuously improve the product design—make it more adaptable—to enable it to meet the twin goals of delivering features today and in the future.

A client was considering a multiyear, multimillion-dollar product redevelopment project for an existing software product—20+ years in its evolution—which contained several million lines of code. Although the product had been instrumental to business success, it was also viewed as an anchor to future progress. Their technical debt was high, maintenance and enhancements were taking longer and longer to implement, and the costs of integration and regression testing had increased substantially. At the same time, the company's customers were increasingly asking for shorter response times. Replacement was seen as the solution to the problems of a creaky old system. My caution to them was that the new product would face similar problems within five years if they didn't include a systematic product-level refactoring discipline into their development process.

> *One of the greatest competitive benefits of software is its malleability. High technical debt caused by a lack of a refactoring discipline destroys that advantage.*

Refactoring involves updating a product's internal components (improving the design), without changing externally visible functionality to make the product more reliable and adaptable. One unfortunate legacy of serial development is the idea that reducing the cost of change depends on getting correct architectural and design decisions in the beginning. Given the constancy of change and our inability to predict those changes with any accuracy, designs should instead be based upon what we know today and a willingness to engage in redesign in the future—an evolutionary design process. Because it is inevitable that product enhancements are sometimes "bolted on" without proper design considerations, a refactoring discipline encourages teams to revisit these decisions periodically and correct them. In software, refactoring applies to test code (often forgotten) as well as executable code.

Another client who implemented agile methods had a software product they developed to coincide with another company's major platform announcement. Although they utilized refactoring and ruthless testing, the immutable delivery date caused them to "hurry" a little more than they would have liked. So upon the first release, rather than diving right back into the new feature enhancements marketing was clamoring for, they spent six weeks refactoring and getting their automated tests in shape. Only then, with a technically solid product in hand, did they resume developing features for the next release. I asked the product development manager if they would have taken that six weeks prior to implementing agile development, and his answer was "no." Living with the pain of another legacy product for which the "technical debt" had gotten away from them was something team members were determined would not happen on this new product.

But refactoring should not be used as an excuse for sloppy design. The objective isn't refactoring; the objective is to maintain a viable, adaptable design. This requires good design practices at every step.

> *Old axiom: Get it right the first time.*
>
> *New axiom: No matter how good it is the first time, it's going to change, so keep the cost of change low.*

Decisions about refactoring are difficult, because on the surface they appear to be technical decisions. But in fact they are product management and executive decisions, and they therefore need to be examined, and funded, from that perspective. Without the support of product managers, digging one's way out of a degraded product design will be nearly impossible. On the upside, however, product managers are usually amenable to investing in refactoring after they understand the consequences of high technical debt. With customers clamoring for enhancements and development cycles lengthening because of technical debt, their current situations are often untenable.

To refactor, two factors are paramount: automated testing and persistence. One barrier to redesign and refactoring is the risk of breaking something that is already working. We reduce that risk by thoroughly integrating testing into the development process and by automating tests to the greatest extent possible. Having automated tests reduces the fear of breaking something that already works.

This brings up the second factor—persistence. For software teams, it means considering doing a little code refactoring with every code change—always trying to leave the code slightly better than before. It means thinking about redesign during every development iteration and allocating time to implement redesigns. It means planning some level of refactoring into every new product release. It means slowly, but surely, building up automated tests and integrating testing into the development process. For hardware, persistence means applying these practices to development as fully as possible, particularly for those parts of the development process that are accomplished by software simulations.

Every investment requires an adequate return. Refactoring itself takes time and money. It can degenerate into endless technical arguments about "right" designs. But many product companies understand that the status quo isn't working any more. From product managers who lament the unresponsiveness to customer requests, to developers who struggle to understand code that no one wants to touch, to QA departments who are viewed as bottlenecks because their activities take months and months, to executives who watch their products slip in the marketplace, the incentives to rethink this topic are real. Persistence involves a constant—release after release, iteration after iteration—investment in refactoring, redesign, and testing to maintain a product that responds to marketplace demands.

Coaching and Team Development

Many individuals, even some in the agile community, think agile project management equates to less management. In my experience, agile management may be different, but it is certainly not less time consuming. The people management aspects—empowering, coaching, facilitating, working with customers and stakeholders—are a significant load on the project leader's time. These activities are key to building teams rather than managing tasks. As authors Marcus Buckingham and Curt Coffman (1999) write, based on extensive research (interviews with over 80,000 managers during the last 25 years), "The manager role is to reach inside each employee and release his unique talents into performance."

The project leader, in her role as coach and team builder, contributes in six key ways to project success:

1. Focusing the team on vision, objectives, and delivering results
2. Molding a group of individuals into a team
3. Developing each individual's capabilities
4. Providing the team with required resources and removing roadblocks
5. Coaching the customers
6. Orchestrating the team's rhythm

The essence of an agile project leader's role is not creating Gantt charts or status reports (although doing that remains a part of her work); it is growing a high-performance team from a group of individuals. Exploration and experimentation, the foundations of new product development, involve the risk of making mistakes—of failing—and then learning from those mistakes. Managers must respond by making risk taking, well, less risky. As authors Rob Austin and Lee Devin (2003) note, "Artful managers must also do their part; they must create conditions in which makers can work at risk. Willingness to work at risk is vital in ..., in part because exploration is uncomfortable." Whereas team members themselves must participate in these activities, the project leader's role is to make sure they happen. It is a difficult, never-ending, and ultimately rewarding role.

Dee Hock (1999) has a unique perspective on the responsibilities of a manager. The first is to manage self, which he defines as: "One's own integrity, character, ethics, knowledge, wisdom, temperament, words, and acts." The second is to manage the people who have authority over you—managers, supervisors, executives, regulators, and others. The third is to manage peers, "those over whom we have no authority and who have no authority over us—associates, competitors, suppliers, customers."

The response to this list of managerial responsibilities, Hock reports, can often be paraphrased as, "If we do all that, we won't have time to manage subordinates." To which Hock says, "Exactly!" The more teams manage themselves, the less the project leader has to intervene. And the more time the project leader can spend managing upward and outward—that is, managing the participants outside the team—the more effective she is.

Focusing the Team

Every team member gets mired in details and forgets the goal—at least periodically. Good project and iteration leaders remind the team about the goals from time to time by revisiting the key constraints and by reinvigorating the group with the ultimate vision and objectives of the project. This is part of encouraging exploration, which might be considered a leader's cheerleader role, but it's a role that must be based in reality rather than fantasy. Team members want a boost every now and then, but they don't want meaningless rah-rah speeches. Team members want the facts, even negative ones, so they can help figure out how to deal with the situation.

> *"Define the right outcomes and then let each person find his own route towards those outcomes" (Marcus Buckingham and Curt Coffman 1999).*

One of the key motivators for individuals is understanding what is expected of them—but in terms of outcomes, not steps. Great leaders manage outcomes, not activities. If you have the right people, they want to know *what* needs to be accomplished and their role, but they want to figure out *how* to deliver the results. They want to understand why what they do is important, and they want to work with a team that is committed to delivering quality work.[6] Individuals assume accountability for delivering stories or completing tasks, whereas the team as a whole assumes accountability for delivering all the stories planned for an iteration. The project leader holds both individuals and the team as a whole to their commitments. Leaders manage outcomes and interactions, not tasks.

On large projects it is difficult to keep the end goal in sight without giving in to the worry "I don't know how we're ever going to finish this." Part of the value of an iterative approach, is that it breaks large development efforts into manageable chunks. Although facing a two-year development effort seems daunting, trying to deliver a handful of stories in the next few weeks doesn't. The project leader needs to help the team balance—understanding the end goal but working hard in the present iteration. She begins

---

[6] According to Buckingham and Coffman (1999), these are two of the twelve core elements needed to attract, focus, and keep key employees.

each iteration by reminding the team of the overall vision, objectives, and constraints of the project by reiterating the vision box and project data sheet information. The vision provides a context for day-to-day decisions about current work. She radiates confidence. She then rapidly focuses on the next iteration and, in particular, the theme of the iteration. This may appear to be an easy task, but with the high rate of change and the pressure to deliver quickly, the task is a difficult—and constant—one.

Molding a Group of Individuals into a Team

Tom DeMarco and Tim Lister (1999) use the term "jelled team" to define when individuals make the transition from a group to a well-functioning team. But getting a team to jell isn't easy (few teams actually make the transition) because it involves four things that are difficult to achieve in any group of people: trust, interaction, satisfactory conflict resolution, and participatory decision making. Teams with little trust interact on only a superficial level. Lack of interaction fosters a focus on individual rather than team goals. Unsatisfactory conflict resolution reduces trust. Win-lose decision making undermines people's commitment to the team.

Trust is an easy word to bandy around, but it is a difficult thing to achieve. "Trust is the confidence among team members that their peers' intentions are good, and that there is no reason to be protective or careful around the group," says Patrick Lencioni (2002). Trust enables team members to share half-baked ideas without the fear of ridicule. Trust and respect are also closely tied together—it's difficult to respect those we don't trust, and vice versa—which is one reason that getting the wrong people on the team can have such a detrimental effect. Respect comes from understanding other people's roles on a project. Engineers need to understand how product marketing contributes to project success, and product marketing likewise needs to acknowledge engineering's contribution. Frequent interactions help generate understanding, which in turn can lead to respect and trust.

> Great managers "know that if, fundamentally, you don't trust people, then there is no line, no point in time, beyond which people suddenly become trustworthy" (Buckingham and Coffman 1999).

Leaders have to trust their teams. Those who fundamentally don't trust people will jump at the first failure to impose strict controls: "See, I told you we can't operate without rigorous controls." Conversely, leaders who do trust people know some failures will occur because of human nature and systemic problems. For the few truly untrustworthy individuals, the great leaders have a solution—get rid of them, rather than abuse the entire organization with burdensome controls.

Jelled teams often have fierce debates and conflict over issues. Part of the project leader's role is to channel the debate so that it builds trust and respect rather than undermines them. The leader can facilitate this by focusing the discussion on the issues and not on individuals. Managing the "mood" of the team (mostly by managing one's own mood) is one of those "soft" leader skills that are so hard to do well. Although self-discipline comes from within each team member, a leader can help the team build its discipline of debate, conflict, and decision making to further "jell" the team.

Interaction drives innovation. One of the tenets of adaptive organizations is that innovation emerges from the interaction of diverse individuals, each with ideas, who bring information and insight to the development process. Product development projects usually involve teams whose members possess a complex mix of information and talents. Engineers, product specialists, and scientists from diverse domains must consolidate their expertise into a consistent, high-quality product design. To accomplish this goal, individuals balance time alone to develop their particular piece of the product puzzle with face-to-face time with others to fit the pieces together. When team members don't interact, there is no synergy of ideas, and innovation suffers. Interaction can take many forms (brainstorming sessions, hallway chats, technical design reviews, online group discussions, and pair programming), but the objectives are the same: to share information, to co-create a product feature or development artifact, or to make a joint decision about an issue. Project leaders must encourage this peer-to-peer interaction, particularly as pressure mounts and individuals have a tendency to "go dark" (they stop communicating because they are hard at work on their own tasks).

Although making mistakes enhances learning, it does so only if those mistakes are identified. One of the most difficult tasks of working well within a team is confronting team members who violate behavioral or performance standards, but if they aren't confronted, the mistake isn't identified, and no learning occurs. Failure to address these issues head-on is one of the greatest complaints against project leaders (Larson and LaFasto 1989).

There is more to successful interactions than talking. From time to time in any team's development there are "crucial conversations," characterized by varying opinions, high stakes, and emotional intensity. These are the make-or-break conversations, the ones in which the character of the team is forged. Do these conversations degenerate into personal attacks and finger pointing, or do these conflicts help jell the team? There are a couple of things that determine whether the team has the self-discipline and character to have successful crucial conversations. First, each and every member must take the initiative to confront others when they are not performing, or behaving, according to team rules. This includes the administrative assistant calling the project leader on her actions when the situation dictates. No one should be exempt. Ignoring the problem, letting it fester, isn't acceptable behavior. The second critical thing is that the conversation be directed toward getting all the relevant information out on the table. Without this, crucial conversations cannot be effective. The process described in the section on participatory decision making is intended to do just this—extract relevant information that is devoid, for a while at least, of individual biases.[7]

Several years ago I was working with a team that was under enormous stress—tight delivery deadlines, constantly changing requirements, and high pressure because of the revenue implications of the project's outcome. The team leaders and many staff members thought the ambiguity and anxiety within the project should somehow be mitigated, that the environment should be less chaotic and more stable. I pointed out that this kind of project was always be borderline chaotic and, furthermore, that attempting to stabilize it—although it might make everyone feel better—was unlikely to lead to successful completion.

What ultimately helped the situation was showing the team leaders how they were making the situation worse by reflecting, rather than absorbing, the team's frustration. Each time a team member would come to a team leader and say something like, "Wow, things are really screwed up," the lead would counter with, "They sure are, and I wish someone would fix it." This

---

[7] The research information in this paragraph comes from several sources, but the best is *Crucial Conversations: Tools for Talking When Stakes Are High* (Patterson, 2002).

exchange magnified the frustrations. Although the team leaders needed to acknowledge the reality of the situation, they also needed to respond positively, to defuse the situation by remaining calm themselves. Just telling the team leaders that a degree of ambiguity and frustration was a natural part of this type of project helped reduce their anxiety and kept the emotion and frustration level below a "constant crisis" level. They were then able to convey this new mood to team members.

Management research shows that mood or "emotional intelligence" in leaders has a much larger impact on performance than we may have imagined. "The leader's mood and behaviors drive the moods and behaviors of everyone else. A cranky and ruthless boss creates a toxic organization filled with negative underachievers who ignore opportunities," say Daniel Goleman, Richard Boyatzis, and Annie McKee (2001). These authors describe how a leader's emotional intelligence is contagious, racing through an organization like electricity through wires. Researchers at the University of Michigan found that in 70 work teams in diverse industries, team members picked up the same moods within a couple of hours.

Teams are groups of people, who respond to emotions and whose emotions may experience wide swings—from despair to euphoria—over the life of a project. Encouraging appropriate moods and discouraging others can help create group interactions conducive to generating emergent results.

Finally, managers should assist the team in developing a set of "rules of engagement," ground rules for how team members are expected to treat each other. The team should participate in developing, enforcing, and adapting these rules over time—it is a part of being self-disciplined.

Rules of engagement are not meant to reduce conflict and contention but to direct them in positive ways. Great teams froth with tension, contention, and diverse ideas directed at delivering a high-quality result. Poor teams froth with tension, contention, and diverse ideas directed at each other. Rules of engagement, sometimes called working agreements, serve three primary purposes as the bases for: relationship building, practice definition, and decision making. A relationship building rule of engagement would be: Encourage open and honest communication. A practice definition rule would be: Iteration length will be 3 weeks. A decision making criteria rule would be: No cutting corners (a quality oriented rule).

An example of team rules of engagement is shown in Figure 9-8. The team should decide on the list of rules, post it prominently (especially during team meetings), and add to it freely during the project (another example of rules of engagement between two teams is shown in Figure 11-5).

Figure 9-8
Team Rules of
Engagement

> ### Team Rules of Engagement
>
> - Everyone has an equal voice.
> - Everyone's contribution is valuable.
> - Attack issues, not people.
> - Keep privacy within the team.
> - Respect each other and your differences.
> - Everyone participates.

Developing the Individual's Capabilities

Buckingham and Coffman have a nice little mantra that reflects the beliefs of great managers:

> *People don't change that much.*
> *Don't waste time trying to put in what was left out.*
> *Try to draw out what was left in.*
> *That is hard enough (Buckingham and Coffman 1999).*

Great project leaders encourage individual development. They try to understand people's inherent talents and build on those rather than trying to put in something that was left out. Developmental coaching comes in three flavors: technical, domain expertise, and behavioral. Project or iteration leaders may not do the technical or domain coaching, but they facilitate its happening—often by pairing less experienced team members with more experienced ones or pairing people with different technical skills to broaden each person's technical capability. The leader also coaches individuals in how to help the team jell. They may help some overbearing team member lighten up, while encouraging reticent ones to participate more fully.

Individuals contribute by applying their technical skills and engaging in self-organizing behavior, which includes

- Accepting accountability for results (no excuses)
- Confronting reality through rigorous thinking
- Engaging in intense interaction and debate

- Working within a self-organizing framework
- Respecting colleagues

Not all these behaviors come easily, particularly for engineers. However, developing the self-discipline to do these things is critical to creating jelled teams. Helping individuals learn these skills can be one of the highest-leverage activities a project leader can engage in.

Moving Rocks, Hauling Water

Project leaders contribute directly to delivering results by removing impediments (moving rocks) and providing resources (hauling water). When individuals are waiting for resources, they lose productivity, but more importantly they lose time. Examples of resources include computers, lab equipment, and staff assistance. Moving rocks can also include ensuring that critical dependencies between feature teams or with outside sources are well managed. Rather than doing the work, the project leader ensures that everyone has the resources to do his or her work. This style of project management is one of providing services to the team—an approach Robert Greenleaf called "servant leadership" (Frick and Spears 1996)—rather than having the team "work for" the manager.

Leaders also remove roadblocks that impede the team from working efficiently. For example, project and iteration leaders need to quickly and effectively resolve impediments that are voiced in daily team stand-up meetings. Roadblocks can be things such as resources (the team doesn't have them), information (the team can't get it from a customer), or decisions (a stakeholder manager hasn't made them in a timely fashion).

Coaching the Customers

Another critical coaching job—that of coaching the product team—goes to the product manager. Many internal IT projects have crashed on the shoals of poor customer involvement—for the last 30–40 years! The problem is simple, the solution complex. The fundamental problem is poor customer-developer partnership, caused by one of any number of factors:

- Development's lack of credibility in the eyes of customers
- Lack of customer involvement
- Poor accountability on the customer's side for making decisions and accepting the consequences
- Long development schedules, exacerbated by delivery of meaningless (to the customer) intermediate artifacts
- Unrealistic project schedules based on poorly articulated requirements
- Lack of acceptance criteria and testing by customers

Individually, any one of these factors can doom a project. Collectively, they almost always lead to project failure.

Just as the development team needs coaching in both technical and behavioral skills to meet their responsibilities, so does the product team. Product team members may not know how to write acceptance tests or participate in requirements specification sessions or take part in the decision-making process of setting priorities. Just as the project leader facilitates the smooth running of the engineering team, the product manager must facilitate the smooth running of the product team.

Consider an IT project that is building a business software application for multiple customer departments, each of which can identify requirements for the application. These requirements are gathered and documented, usually by a business analyst (product specialist) in IT. The analyst often inherits, because no one else wants it, the task of reconciling differences between multiple customer departments and trying to determine feature priorities. This approach leads to requirements bloat because the analyst has little power to say no to feature requests, and customer departments feel no obligation to make difficult priority decisions.

With a product manager appointed from the customer ranks, these problems are reduced because the customers, through the product manager, must accept accountability for identifying, defining, prioritizing, and accepting features. One of the product manager's jobs is to coach the customer team through this process. For industrial or consumer product development projects, the product manager has to work with (coach) internal "proxy" customers—marketing, executives, product specialists—as well as gain information about the actual customer base through periodic customer involvement, beta testing, and other means.

Orchestrating Team Rhythm

At times, the project leader's job mirrors that of a maestro, keeping the players in rhythm while bringing each into the music at the right time. At other times the team operates more like a jazz band, with each player improvising around a common structure. Working with the rhythms of agile projects can be a difficult transition for many individuals. People are used to linearity, at least in the way projects are usually planned. Execution is never linear, which is one reason people constantly complain that how they actually work never matches the plan.

Agile projects are rhythmic. Furthermore, there are rhythms within rhythms, which makes describing agile projects difficult to those who are used to experiencing linear projects. There are the rhythms of iterations, which alternate between intensity and reflection as teams work to deliver features and then pause to reflect on the results. There is the rhythm of daily stand-up meetings and interactions with customers on story details. There is the rhythm of releases, waves, and iterations. There is the rhythm of constantly thinking, designing, building, testing, and reflecting on small increments of work. There is the rhythm of anxiety and euphoria as people try to solve, and then succeed in solving, seemingly intractable problems.

Project leaders orchestrate the beat. They help team members learn to slow down to reflect after high-pressure delivery work, they help them find the right rhythm of working alone and working collaboratively, and they help team them deal with anxiety and ambiguity. Creating task lists and checking completion boxes characterizes one kind of project management—orchestrating rhythms characterizes another.

Participatory Decision Making

The objective of participatory decision making is to provide the project community with specific practices to frame, analyze, and make the myriad decisions that arise during a project. The lack of adequate decision-making processes in organizations is evident in a couple of quotes from clients I've worked with over the years.

"That one decision-gradient diagram [Figure 9-9] was the most important piece of the two-day consulting session," said a product development VP client recently stated. The gradient kept them from focusing in too early on binary yes-no decisions and led to better discussions.

"It's difficult to speed up development when management takes weeks to make key decisions," laments an Irish development manager whose company executives are in Silicon Valley.

"Our project managers are like a herd of deer standing on the highway with a tractor-trailer truck bearing down on them," says one team member. "They can't figure out which way to jump, but if they don't decide soon, we're going to get run over."

As I trek around the world of product development and project management I'm continually amazed at how little organizations think about their decision-making processes. Many of them put time and energy into processes such as time recording and virtually ignore decision making. However, in a fast-paced agile project, decision making—like other activities—must be done quickly and effectively. Slow decision making, revisiting decisions again and again, over-analyzing decisions, and poor participation in the decision-making process will doom a project, as poor decisions cascade into a flood of additional decisions.

However, decision making can improve, and it can be participatory, as the GE jet engine plant in Durham, North Carolina, proves. "At GE/Durham, every decision is either an A decision, or a B decision, or a C decision," writes Charles Fishman (1999) in an article in *Fast Company*. "An A decision is one that the plant manager makes herself, without consulting anyone. B decisions are also made by the plant manager, but with input from the people affected. C decisions—which make up the most common type—are made by consensus, by the people directly involved, with plenty of discussion."

Using this system, the plant manager only makes 10–12 "A" decisions in a year and spends significant time explaining those to the staff.

The article goes on to address the very crucial issue that arises in discussing self-organizing teams:

> *What is the role of a plant manager in a place that manages itself? If the plant needs a manager like Sims to make just 10 decisions a year, what does she do with the bulk of her time?*
>
> *She does the kinds of things that most managers talk about a lot but that they actually spend very little time on. At the operational level, her job is to keep everyone's attention focused on the goals of the plant: Make perfect engines, quickly, cheaply, safely. Strategically, the plant manager's job is to make sure that the plant as a whole is making smart decisions about talent, about time, and about opportunities for growth (Fishman 1999).*

These management roles are analogous to the coaching and team development practices discussed earlier in this chapter. Oh, and the GE/Durham plant is a model of effectiveness and efficiency.

Even authors Carl Larson and Frank LaFasto (1989), who at least recognize the importance of decision making, don't delve into how to actually improve the process. They do, however, observe, "The third set of leadership principles, and we believe the most important, clearly focus attention on the creation of a supportive decision-making climate." They also point out that achieving a goal requires change, that change requires decisions be made, and that making decisions involves risk. Without a safe environment in which team members can take risks, effective decision making will be stymied.

At its core, collaboration is about decision making. We can talk, share ideas, and debate issues, but in the final analysis decisions must be made—about design, about features, about tradeoffs, about a host of issues. Collaboration isn't talking, it's delivering, and delivering means making decisions. A participatory decision-making process can be useful for larger groups or for two individuals—the process and the issues are the same. Furthermore, although the steps of the decision-making process may proceed less formally between two individuals than they would in a group, the emphasis on sustainable, win-win decisions based on debate and full participation remains key.

> *The biggest complaint from people isn't that they lack a vote in decisions; it's that they don't even get heard on decisions that affect them.*

One definitional point is critical: Participatory decision making (everyone participates) is different from consensus decision making (everyone votes in favor). The latter is too slow and isn't appropriate in many project situations where the divergence of ideas and opinions would limit the effectiveness of the decision-making process. The critical element isn't consensus but sustainability: Will the team consistently implement decisions that are made? Participation leads to sustainability efficiently and effectively. In consensus decision making everyone votes on the decision, and no decision can be implemented without a unanimous vote. In participatory decision making, team members participate in the decision process, and the decision is made by a preponderance of the vote.

No doubt decision making is hard, but it is made harder than necessary by poor practices, and there are practices that can assist teams in making better, implementable decisions. Three elements compose a decision process: decision framing, decision making, and decision retrospection. Framing establishes "who" gets involved in the process, whereas decision making establishes "how" the "whos" go about making a decision. Retrospection provides feedback into the decision-making process. As with other APM practices, decision-making practices must be implemented with the Simplify principle in mind; otherwise the team will end up with just another unwieldy set of procedures and forms.

Decision Framing

The often overused term "empowerment" means to delegate decision-making authority to lower levels of organizations by changing who *makes* decisions. Decision framing focuses on who gets *involved* in the decision process. Managers who make decisions without input from subordinates and peers make poor decisions. Engineers who make decisions without input from managers and peers make poor decisions. Who makes the decision is less important than getting the right people involved in the decision process.

However, framing involves more than "who"; it also means considering the values and principles that participants share. Without shared values and principles, teams will have difficulty reaching sustainable decisions. The agile values and principles articulated in earlier chapters, whether adopted verbatim or adapted for a specific organization, are vital to decision making. There is a hierarchy of decision-making criteria—values and principles, product vision, project objectives, and tradeoff matrix, as well as detailed criteria such as design parameters (e.g., usability). Teams that fail to agree on principles—explicitly—will have problems making sustainable decisions as projects progress.

The first task in framing decisions involves identifying types of decisions that need to be made. For example, in an agile project, re-planning occurs at the end of each iteration or wave. Re-planning often involves making trade-off decisions—schedule versus cost versus stories. Projects should include a decision framework for asking the basic question, "Can we release this product now?"

For each decision type, typical framing questions are

- Who is impacted by the decision?
- Who needs to provide input to the decision?
- Who should be involved in the discussions about the decision?
- Who should make the decision (the product manager, the project leader, the team, the project leader with the team, etc.)?
- What decision criteria should be used?
- How and to whom should the decision results be communicated?
- Who should review the decision?

The answers to these questions will involve several overlapping groups of individuals. For example, a wide group of people may be impacted by the decision, but only selected individuals from those groups may be contacted for input. Everyone who provides input to a decision may not be involved in the discussions about those decisions. Many decisions bore team members, and thus they don't want to be involved, whereas they do want to be heard on other decisions. Sorting out the various involvements should be the result of careful thinking by the team members and the project and product leaders.

Team members often feel isolated from decision processes, not knowing when, why, or how decisions get made. Making decisions is only part of implementing them. Rapid, effective implementation requires a participatory process that involves the right people, with the relevant information, gathered together at the right time.

Many companies and project leaders spend far more time on development processes than decision making, which brings to mind a race car engine running on increasingly viscous sludge. Both will grind to a halt. Framing is the first step in getting the sludge out of your decision-making process.

Decision Making

In many organizations, decision making is viewed as a win-lose proposition. Participants in the process have a preconceived view of the right answer, and their approach is to argue as loudly as possible until the opposition gives up. Collaborative decision making focuses on win-win—or "both/and" rather than "either/or." Win-win decision making focuses on mutual understanding rather than loud posturing. This shouldn't imply a lack of heated discussion, but a discussion focused on trying to understand the underlying issues rather than debating preordained positions. Participatory decision making can be contentious but civil, based on mutual trust and respect. It moves teams beyond compromise to reconceiving. Participatory decision making is a process of reconceiving a solution to a problem based on information from all team members. Compromise implies giving up one idea for another (and often results in inferior decisions); reconceiving implies a joining of ideas.

Collaboration is hard. In seemingly interminable meetings, team members often flounder in the "groan zone," author Sam Kaner's (1996) wonderful term for the time period in which meeting participants struggle to understand each other. Although many people have heard of the famous team progression process "forming, storming, norming, performing" (or, more aptly at times, forming, storming, thrashing, crashing), Kaner's model consists of the divergent zone, the groan zone, and finally the converging zone.

Any decision-making process must be judged against two objectives. First, does the process result in the best choice given the circumstances in which the decision was made? Second, was the decision implemented? As many project leaders have found out the hard way, making and implementing decisions are two different things. How many times have you encountered decisions made within the confines of a conference room that fall completely apart when the participants walk out the door? Anyone can make a decision, but effective managers grasp that implementation requires people to understand and support the decision.

A participatory decision-making process has three components: principles, framework, and practices. The fundamental principles have just been alluded to: viewing the process as a win-win process and treating all participants with respect. All collaborative practices are based on trust and respect, or perhaps more precisely, on building trust and respect.[8] Kaner's diverge-groan-converge model provides a framework for building these positive relationship qualities. In the diverge-groan-converge framework, the transition from the divergent zone to the convergent zone explains how team members move from having individual opinions to having a unified position. At first, people's ideas diverge. Even though each person wants to contribute to success and to making a quick decision, each wants to voice his or her own opinion. Everyone has a different perspective or a different experience, which brings needed diversity to the decision process but not much agreement. This groaning period takes time—time for people to speak and hear, time for them to build trust. A little extra time (it's not really extra, but it seems as if it is) taken on decision making in the early stages of a project will significantly reduce time as the project continues.

Convergence occurs as the individual ideas are integrated into a whole solution. Convergence, done correctly, does not necessarily mean that everyone is in complete agreement, but that everyone has participated and will support the final decision. The goal is not merely agreement but "sustainable agreement"—a unified position.

[8] The idea of building trust may seem counter to the earlier statement that managers either trust or don't trust. However, a manager can believe in trusting team members but also understand that the level of trust must be maintained through actions. People are predisposed to trust or not trust, but they still want proof in support of that predisposition.

The transition period between divergence and convergence, the groan zone, is the time during which team members groan and complain. In the divergent zone, most group members voice their opinions to make sure the group hears their ideas. Much of this time initially could be considered presentation, during which members are primarily trying to sell their own ideas. Participants then begin to groan because they are trying to understand one another, and understanding requires thought. It is relatively easy to take a position and argue for it. It is much more difficult to attempt to understand why other participants hold their opinions. Participants want to ask questions, they want to be heard, they want to—participate. The groan zone provides a perfect description of what happens in most teams; it is a turbulent zone where innovative, creative results are generated.

One of the best tools for testing how the decision-making process is proceeding, and for arriving at the decision itself, is a decision gradient that replaces the familiar yes-no voting. A decision gradient, as shown in Figure 9-9, gives participants more options: in favor; OK, but with reservations; mixed feelings; disagree and commit (to implement the decision); veto. When all participants plot their responses on a line with these gradations, the entire team gets to view its collective opinion. The team can then address issues like trying to understand the person who vetoed the decision or trying to understand why so many people are clustered around "mixed feelings." Voting—or actually, the discussions about why the voting went one way or another—leads to a deeper understanding of the issues and eventually to another vote. Decision gradients make for better discussion and more effective, sustainable decisions.[9]

When some person (manager, technical lead) is designated as the decision maker, a preponderance of agreement among participating team members is helpful but not essential. But when a team as a whole is the decision maker, what actions craft a sustainable decision? In many people's minds, consensus has come to mean "unanimous," the connotation used earlier in this section. But consensus has another definition that corresponds to the idea of a preponderance of agreement among participants. Intel is one company known for its attention to decision making. Intel emphasizes decision-making training for employees, and the company focuses on decision

[9] See Kaner (1996) for more information on decision gradients.

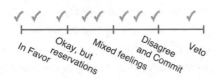

Figure 9-9
Decision Gradients
Tell a Story

framing and making on a regular basis. Intel has an engrained decision-making culture in which the phrase "disagree and commit" is often used. It means that someone might disagree with a decision, but he will commit himself to its implementation.

This non-unanimous type of consensus is built on the following premises:

- Everyone has had an opportunity to have his or her ideas heard and discussed.
- Consensus does not imply unanimous agreement, but it does mean that people understand the decision rationale.
- No one has been silenced due to fear or intimidation.
- The preponderance of the group votes in favor of the decision (or in favor with some reservations).
- No one vetoes the decision (instead, they disagree and commit).

Decisions thus reached are sustainable in ways that lead to team cohesion and positive outcomes. Arbitrary and capricious decisions, those imposed by force of will or organizational power, have the opposite effect.

An additional benefit to a participatory process such as the one just described is that as mutual understanding of the context (including the decision criteria) increases, the time required to make similar decisions decreases rapidly. For example, a defect triage team that develops a shared understanding of the relevant quality factors involved in reaching decisions will speed up its decisions over time. Conversely, teams that do not take additional time in the beginning to fully understand each other's perspective on some issue (e.g., quality) will constantly argue the same points meeting after meeting, wasting irreplaceable project time.

Different kinds of decisions require different decision criteria. Coin flipping works for what time to go to lunch. The tradeoff matrix steers constraint decisions, just as performance criteria might steer technical decisions. Release decisions might use agile triangle quality criteria. For each kind of decision, one of the discussion topics should be the criteria to be used in making that type of decision. You may even need to go through a decision-making process to arrive at the criteria for making a decision.

Decision Retrospection

End-of-iteration, wave, and project retrospectives should include time to review decisions as part of reviewing the team's performance (discussed in the next chapter). However, if project retrospectives are difficult to do in general, then decision retrospectives are even more so, because finding whom to blame often seems more important than learning. But how do we get better at decisions unless we understand which ones worked out well and which ones didn't?

Still, few organizations want to examine decisions in any depth, which probably corresponds to the general lack of interest in decision making. Was an error-prone product released? Why? What were the decisions that led up to the release decision? Maybe the decision was actually a "good" one from a market perspective. If so, then the development staff needs to understand the nature of the decision, why it was made, and who was involved in the decision. Maybe the decision was based on market timing information, but the decision makers didn't listen to the developers, and the actual release was a disaster. If the disaster isn't analyzed, if the decision tradeoff of product stability versus market need analysis isn't revisited, then nothing will be learned and similar mistakes will be made in the future. On the other hand, a decision may be perceived as incorrect, but further analysis shows that it was actually the correct one given the circumstances. In this case, lack of analysis might keep us from making the same "correct" decision in the future.

Participatory decision making may spell the difference between success and failure on agile projects. Framing decisions, developing a collaborative decision-making process, and conducting decision retrospectives to learn from both success and failure are components of this practice.

Leadership and Decision Making

A good project leader has to be a visionary, a teacher, a motivator, a facilitator, and other things, but she must also be a decision maker. The same is true of lead engineers for technical issues. So the question becomes, at what point does a manager's decision making damage self-organization? First, when the team loses respect for the leader. But what causes loss of respect? The answer: when the manager begins making unilateral or arbitrary decisions. The more unilateral decisions, the less participation from the team, and the less likely the decisions are to be effectively implemented.

Every team and situation are different, so there isn't a quantitative answer to the question of how many unilateral decisions are too many. However, even though presenting absolute numbers risks misinterpretation, I think the following guidelines may help define appropriate "levels" of management decision making that will continue to foster self-organization. For both project leaders and lead engineers, this rough guide is one unilateral decision every month or two, three to four decisions per month with team involvement, and then delegate the hundreds of other decisions to the team. In practice, few good managers make completely unilateral decisions—they normally talk issues over with at least key members of their team. But occasionally there is a need to get things moving by making a unilateral decision. In that same vein, it is appropriate for project leaders and lead engineers to make certain decisions with team participation, but if they are making more than three or four of these decisions per month, even with team involvement, they are probably too absorbed in the details.

> *Leaders at any level—executive, functional manager, project leader, iteration manager, technical lead—who are making more than three or four unilateral decisions a month are adversely impacting their team's ability to self-organize.*

Another issue related to management decision making is the leader's job of absorbing ambiguity. In fast-moving product development efforts in which key decisions must be made quickly, consensus (unanimous) decision making fails, but even participatory decision making can get mired in discussion and debate. Many product development issues, both technical and administrative, may be fuzzy and ambiguous. In these cases, after participation has evolved to a certain point, managers have to be willing to make final decisions. "Well, the information available to us isn't crystal clear, but to move forward with the project, we'll go in this direction."

Good leaders have earned the credibility to make these decisions. The technical staff respect the leader's judgment (based on previous actions taken), participate in the analysis and debate process, and willingly accept the decision to move on. The leader has absorbed the ambiguity of the situation, whereas leaving the decision to consensus would have bogged the project down in interminable debate. Good leaders know when to step in and take charge and when to encourage the team to take charge. They also know when to dig into why team decision making isn't working as it should.

Set- and Delay-Based Decision Making

If we want to build adaptive teams and products, not only do we need a participatory decision-making process, but we also need to look at criteria for decision making that encourage experimentation. Point-based engineering dominates current product development. Point-based engineering views design as a series of decisions in which each decision narrows the options for further decisions, and the product progresses in a steady fashion from a gleam in the marketer's eye to a final product.[10]

Toyota upset this apple cart, at least as it pertains to the automotive industry's design process. Toyota's approach, set-based concurrent engineering (SBCE), provides a new insight into product design. SBCE operates on two fundamental concepts: postpone design decisions as late as possible and maintain "sets" of design solutions throughout the majority of the design process.

"SBCE assumes that reasoning and communicating about sets of ideas leads to more robust, optimized systems and greater overall efficiency than working with one idea at a time, even though the individual steps may look

---

[10] Using Real Options is another practice making headway in the agile toolbox. See, for example, "Real Options Underlie Agile Practices," Chris Matts and Olav Maassen (www.infoq.com).

inefficient," write Durward K. Sobek, Allen C. Ward, and Jeffrey K. Liker (1999). Rather than converge on a design "answer," Toyota's engineers maintain sets of designs. For a particular car project, they might maintain six alternative solutions that include prototypes and mock-ups for the exhaust system design.

Unlike point requirements, set-based requirements focus on ranges or minimum constraints. So the body design group would impose a criteria "range" on the exhaust system, keeping the tolerances as broad as possible in the beginning and narrowing them over time as the car approaches manufacturing. As the body design and exhaust system designs evolve, engineers are more likely to balance subsystem optimization with overall vehicle optimization. In a point-based approach, each subsystem team has a tendency to quickly create optimized designs for its particular subsystem that are often at odds with overall system design effectiveness.

Toyota's slow narrowing of options extends even to die making. Rather than specify precise part fit, designers specify wider tolerances. The die makers themselves create the parts, see how they actually fit together, and then send the precise measurements back to the design groups to finalize the detail CAD drawings.

Engineers, whether of automobiles or computers, tend toward point-based solutions—they analyze the problem, review the constraints, and then design "the" solution. But there are always multiple design options, and the larger the product or product family, the more likely that early design decisions will lock the team into suboptimal solutions. Maintaining multiple sets of solutions and delaying final design decisions, even though it may appear to be inefficient, may in fact be faster and more efficient in the long run. As Sobek and his coauthors observe, "Toyota considers a broader range of possible designs and delays certain decisions longer than other automotive companies do, yet has what may be the fastest and most efficient vehicle development cycles in the industry" (Sobek 1999).

Collaboration and Coordination

There are several agile practices for encouraging collaboration and coordination: daily stand-up meetings, daily interaction with the product team, and stakeholder coordination.

Daily Stand-Up Meetings

Daily team stand-up meetings help team member coordinate activities on a daily basis. One of the first agile practice implemented is usually the daily stand-up meeting.[11] These daily get-togethers (referred to as scrum meetings in the Scrum methodology) focus on one objective: peer-to-peer coordination through information exchange (Schwaber and Beedle 2002). "Daily software builds are used to raise the visibility of development work and ensure that code modules integrate. Daily scrum meetings serve the same purpose for people—raising the visibility of each person's work (to facilitate knowledge sharing and reduce overlapping tasks) and ensuring that their work is integrated. If daily builds are good for code, then daily 'builds' should be even better for people" (Highsmith 2002).

The daily meeting enables the team members to coordinate their work by monitoring status, focusing on the work to be done, and raising problems and issues. The meetings should follow guidelines such as those outlined in Figure 9-10.

To the extent possible, the daily meetings should be held at the same time and place every day. Attendance may vary from day to day, but that is preferable to the hassle of constantly trying to reschedule. Meetings can be held in a break room, in the corner of a work area, in a conference room—teams are very creative about finding meeting space. Most team members find these short meetings to be efficient and effective. They eliminate the need for other meetings and help the right people to team up to resolve issues.

---

[11] The term "stand-up meeting" is an indication of the brief nature of the meeting, so brief in fact, that no one needs to sit down for the meeting.

Figure 9-10
Stand-Up Meeting
Guide

Stand Up Meeting Guidelines

- The meetings are held at the same time and place every day.
- The meetings last less than 15 minutes.
- All core team members attend the meetings.
- Product and project leaders attend as peer participants (not to gather status).
- Other managers usually do not attend these meetings, and if they do, they are observers, not participants.
- A team member, iteration, or project leader facilitates the meetings.
- The meetings are used to raise issues and obstacles but not to pursue solutions.
- Each participant is encouraged to address three questions:
  - ➤ What did you do yesterday?
  - ➤ What are you planning to do today?
  - ➤ What impediments are in the way?

Time duration is critical to meeting success. When daily meetings begin to slide past 20–25 minutes, people gradually stop coming. Even worse, lengthening time frames are a sure indication that the wrong things are being discussed.

> *Daily stand-up meetings should not be used to solve problems, only to identify them. When problems are identified, the team members involved get together after the stand-up meeting to solve them.*

The project or iteration leader's participation is another delicate factor in successful stand-up meetings. The objective of these meetings is coordination, not status review. When managers begin asking questions like "Why didn't that task get finished as planned?" team members feel pressure, sometimes subtle, sometimes not so subtle, to conform to the plan rather than discuss coordination issues. The astute leader rephrases the question to uncover impediments to progress and find out what team members need from him to get back on track. Performance pressure in these integration meetings should come from peers, not from managers.

The meeting facilitator's role, which can be rotated from day to day, is to smooth the progress of the meeting itself. The facilitator might nudge the team, "That's a great point, but let's take the further discussion offline from this meeting."

Responses to the question "What impediments are in the way of your work?" become action items for the technical lead, iteration manager, or project leader. Impediments may be organizational—"We can't get a response from the marketing department"—or resource related—"We're having trouble getting an electronic circuit board we need"—or have some other cause. Leaders—team, iteration, project—need to remove the impediment as quickly as possible.

Daily stand-up meetings are a tool for self-organization; they assist the team members in coordinating their own work and solving their own problems. As such, the leader's role should be as unobtrusive as possible. He should use other forums for gathering status, coaching, or working with the team on performance issues.

As with any other practice, the characteristics of the daily meeting (meeting time, frequency, and attendees) will need to evolve for different situations. One such adaptation might be for the core delivery team members to meet daily, whereas members from specialty areas join in weekly. Other adaptations can be made for projects with multiple feature teams.

Finally, and most importantly, the team should constantly ask questions (especially at milestone reviews) like: "Are these daily stand-up meetings adding value to the project?" and "How could we improve them?" The objective of these sessions is coordination, not having daily meetings or answering the three questions (accomplished, planned, impediments) for their own sake. Those activities merely facilitate achieving the objective.

Daily Interaction with the Product Team

Daily interaction with the product team helps ensure that the development efforts stay on track to meet the needs and expectations of the customer. One of the key tenets of APM is close development team interaction with product managers, product specialists, and customers. When dealing with uncertainty, risk, fluid requirements changes, and technological frontiers, product managers need to be fully involved in identifying stories, specifying requirements, determining priorities, making key tradeoff decisions (cost, schedule, etc.), developing acceptance criteria and tests, and more. Being the "customer" for an agile project is not an insignificant job, but it may not need to be full time. The key to keeping the project moving is frequent, if not daily, interaction in which the team receives a constant flow of information and decisions from the product manager.[12] While interaction with the product team may be important to other types of projects, it is absolutely essential with high exploration-factor projects.

Stakeholder Coordination

Project leaders are responsible for stakeholder coordination. Project leaders must secure resources and ensure ongoing support for the team. One team may need a component from another or from an external supplier. The accounting department may need periodic information. Executives may need to be briefed on the progress of the project. Project leaders who don't identify each stakeholder and initiate a coordination plan to ensure that each one gets the service he or she needs from the team run the risk of getting blindsided by a disgruntled stakeholder. Some stakeholders contribute to the project's success, and others can be serious impediments—but they all have to be managed. Although members of the team can assist, managing up and out is generally the responsibility of the project leader, who must shelter the team from the sometimes crazy politics of stakeholder coordination.[13]

Final Thoughts

Exploring is how agile teams execute. Rather than stepping through a prescriptive plan, agile teams execute through a series of planned experiments,

---

[12] Although, strictly speaking, daily interaction may not be necessary or even possible, titling this practice "frequent" interaction leaves too much room for misinterpretation. A more explicit title such as "regular, high-frequency interaction" would be more specific, but not enough to overcome the verbosity of the phrase. In the long run, I choose to stick with "daily" since it better conveys the sense of this practice.

[13] For some specific tools for managing stakeholder relationships, see *Radical Project Management* by Thomsett.

a series of story deliveries, a series of attempts to create a concrete formulation of the product vision within the boundaries of a business model.

Exploring is accomplished by competent, self-disciplined teams led by competent leaders who create self-organized environments. Team members work in a semi-autonomous fashion, striving to meet iteration plans that they themselves have had a hand in constructing, managing their own workload, collaborating to generate innovative ideas, and applying specific technical practices aimed at building adaptable products that in turn facilitate the very exploration process that they are employing.

Project leaders and product managers are direct contributors to the team's exploration process. They encourage rather than motivate; they are demanding, but not arbitrary; they empower the team, but make certain decisions themselves; they coach rather than criticize; and they facilitate rather than command. Effective agile project leaders work hard to unleash the talent and abilities of their teams by focusing their efforts, molding individuals into jelled teams, developing each individual's capabilities, providing resources to the team, working with customers and stakeholders, and facilitating a participatory decision-making process.

Anyone who still believes that the project leader's role is to buy pizza and get out of the way ignores the abundant research on successful projects. Conversely, anyone who believes that project management is mainly about prescriptive tasks, schedules, resource charts, and preordained plans will have a rude awakening trying to apply these ideas to volatile product development projects. Agile leadership, executing on project plans, favors those who can lead teams over those who manage tasks.

Chapter 10

The Adapt
and Close Phases

If plans are speculations or hypotheses about the future, then teams need to test those hypotheses with frequent and effective feedback. Agile projects are exploration projects, and as such, success depends upon reality-based feedback. Adaptation depends upon understanding a wide range of information, including an assessment of the project's progress, technical risks, the requirements evolution, and ongoing competitive market analysis. APM has the potential to save money through the early termination of projects, but only if the team and executives are willing to face reality early. Iterative projects are also prone to oscillation—going back and forth without making progress. Two things counteract this potential risk: a good vision and continual feedback. Every team needs to constantly evaluate and make appropriate adaptations in the following four areas:

1. Product value
2. Product quality
3. Team performance
4. Project status

Adaptations can take many forms. A team that rushes to deliver features but creates defects—hurrying rather than being quick—needs to adapt its behavior. A creeping design degeneration gives rise to additional "refactoring" activity in the next iteration. Cost overruns are highlighted by the project status review, and appropriate action can be taken.

The common project management term for responding to deviations from plan is "corrective action," a phrase that implies that the team has made an error or underperformed. The "conformance to plan" mentality runs deep in project managers' psyches. The *Project Management*

Body of Knowledge defines corrective action as "anything done to bring expected future performance in line with the project plan" (Project Management Institute 2000). The term *corrective action* is based on the assumption that the plan is correct and the actual performance lacking. Because plans are speculations in the first place, APM abandons the term *corrective action* in favor of *adaptive action*—reacting to events rather than to a predictive plan.

Adapt

As presented in Chapter 4, a traditional project manager focuses on *following the plan with minimal changes*, whereas an agile leader focuses on *adapting successfully to inevitable changes*. Adapting to events is more difficult than correcting to a plan, because the team has to answer four critical questions:

1. Is value, in the form of a releasable product, being delivered?
2. Is the quality goal of building a reliable, adaptable product being met?
3. Is the project progressing satisfactorily within acceptable constraints?
4. Is the team adapting effectively to changes imposed by management, customers, or technology?

Correcting to a plan means comparing the plan to actual performance and developing corrective actions. Adapting to the inevitable changes to plans means first evaluating the plan to see whether it's still valid—and then potentially adapting to both plan changes and actual performance. To measure success in this fluid environment, the team, and management, must continually connect performance to vision and value.

"Is value, in the form of a releasable product, being delivered?" The highest-level value question in a project is always, "Are we progressing toward a releasable product?" Although scope issues such as the number of capabilities or stories delivered indicates such progress, the product team must constantly evaluate the overall question of releaseability. Because there are always more backlog items than capacity to implement them, the question of "must have" capabilities to release should always be part of the prioritization decision. One of the reasons for focusing on wave and release plans, rather than iteration plans, is that this question of releaseability cannot be answered without reference to these longer-range views.

Because of changes over the course of an agile project, teams need to continually review stories and their value. The customers and product manager make frequent adjustments in the story priorities based on their interpretation of value. Measuring value can be difficult, more difficult than measuring cost or schedule against plan, but without a constant attention to determining value—whether a product team's allocation of value points or an explicit monetary calculation—guiding an agile project will prove difficult. The product manager needs to assess whether the value generated during an iteration was worth the cost of development.

"Is the quality goal of building a reliable, adaptable product being met?" Another way of asking this question would be, "Does the product work according to requirements?" and "Can the product be easily maintained over time?" Answers to these questions come from an analysis of defects and an evaluation of technical debt—code quality (for software), design, and architecture.

"Is the project progressing satisfactorily within acceptable constraints?" This question is also more difficult to answer than whether the project is conforming to plan. Conformance to plan is one aspect of satisfactory progression, but only one. Members of the team must ask themselves the question, "Given the circumstances during the last iteration, did we make sufficient progress, and what additional information did we learn?" Most organizations have systems established for measuring cost and schedule progress. The team tries to evaluate progress not just against plan, but against their own standard of doing the best job possible.

"Is the team adapting effectively to changes imposed by management, customers, or technology?" As requirements evolve, staff changes take place, component delays occur, and a multitude of other things impact a project, team members need to assess how they are adapting to those changes. Also, if managers and executives want teams that can be flexible and adapt to change, then they must give teams appropriate credit for that flexibility. When a team deviates from the original plan but effectively responds to a surprise product release from a competitor, that team should be evaluated against the situation and their response, not the outdated plan.

The Adapt phase contains product, project, and team reviews and adaptive action. Most of the practices within this Adapt phase should be scheduled at the end of each iteration (e.g., product evaluations). Part of the team review should include evaluating the time periods between these various reviews. In APM, nothing should happen by default; the team should always be evaluating the relevance and contribution of every practice. For example, team reviews may need to be more frequent in the beginning of a project and less frequent toward the middle and end.

Product, Project, and Team Review and Adaptive Action

The objective of the review and adaptive action practices is to ensure that frequent feedback and high levels of learning occur in multiple project dimensions. There are two main reasons for conducting review and adaptive action sessions at the end of an iteration. The first reason is obvious: to reflect, learn, and adapt. The second is more subtle: to change pace. Short iterations give a sense of urgency to a project because a lot has to happen in a few weeks. Team members work at a quick pace, not hurrying, but working quickly at a high level of intensity. The end-of-iteration review period should be more relaxed, a brief time (normally a half-day or so) in which the team reflects on the last iteration and plans ahead for the next. Most teams need this break in intensity periodically to gather their energy for the next iteration. During this reflection period, four types of reviews are useful: product functionality from the customer team's perspective, product technical quality from the engineering team's perspective, team performance checkpoints, and a review of overall project status.

Customer Focus Groups

Customer focus group (CFG) sessions demonstrate ongoing versions of the final product to the product team to get periodic feedback on how well the product meets customer requirements.[1] Although CFGs are conducted at the end of iterations and waves, they should be scheduled early to ensure the right participants are available.

Acceptance testing for a product should include CFGs (in addition to automated testing). Individuals from the product team, together with developers, meet in a facilitated session in which the product stories are demonstrated to the product team. The sessions follow scenarios that demonstrate the product's use (capabilities and stories) by customers. As the "demonstration" proceeds, change requests are generated and recorded.

---

[1] Some agilists call these sessions demos, but experience has shown that the extra participation and structure of focus groups engender better customer feedback.

*Customer or product team acceptance through the use of customer
focus groups in which the actual product is demonstrated remains one
of the most crucial and beneficial agile practices.*

Whereas customer team representatives work with the engineering team
throughout a development iteration, a CFG brings a wider audience into the
evaluation process. For example, whereas one or two individual customers
from manufacturing might be involved in the day-to-day work with a team
on a manufacturing software application, six to eight might be involved in a
CFG. This wider audience participation helps ensure that features don't get
overlooked, the product encompasses more than the viewpoint of a few people, confidence in the product's progress increases over time, and customers
begin to become familiar with the product before actual deployment. These
review sessions typically take two to four hours, but this timeframe is highly
dependent on the type of product and the iteration length. CFG reviews are
wonderful vehicles for building product team–development team partner-
ships.[2]

In a shoe development process, for example, designers work with ideas,
sketches, and then more formal CAD drawings. At several points in the
process, the designers take their ideas over to the "lab," where technicians
build mock-ups of the shoe. These mock-ups are wearable, usable shoes
built in very small quantities. At some point, the shoes can be shown to the
marketing staff for their feedback or even to a selected group of target customers.

The definition of acceptance testing varies by industry, but in general
CFG reviews provide a wider focus than acceptance testing. Acceptance
testing concentrates on system behavior related to critical engineering
design parameters, whereas CFGs focus on how the customers use the product. CFG reviews gather feedback on look and feel, general operation of the
product, and the use of the product in business, consumer, or operational
scenarios. For example, a specific acceptance test could measure the heat
dissipation of an electronic instrument, or a software acceptance test case
might ensure a business rule is properly calculated. Running exhaustive
engine, electronic, and hydraulic tests to check predetermined values would
be part of an airplane's acceptance testing. Actual flight testing—testing the
product under conditions of actual use—would be similar to a CFG.

---

[2] Who participates in CFG sessions depends on whether the product is for internal or
external customers. In the case of external customers, product marketing has to determine when, and if, external customers will be brought in to review the product. Considerations that impact these decisions include confidentiality, beta testing strategies,
and early sales potentials.

The intent of a CFG session is to stimulate discussion about the product to generate customer and product team feedback. The sessions are designed to encourage participation, questions, and change requests from the product team. As change requests are made, they are recorded, but the resolution (whether or not to accept the change or modify it) is left until after the session. Finally, although every change request is recorded, the act of recording isn't a commitment to make the change. After the CFG session, the team meets to discuss and resolve change requests.

CFG review sessions

- Should be facilitated
- Should be limited to eight to ten customers and product team members (Development team members are present but are primarily observers)
- Review the product itself, not documents
- Focus on discovering and recording desired changes, but not on gathering detailed requirements (if, for example, new features are identified)

CFGs are particularly useful in distributed development scenarios in which daily contact between development and product teams is difficult. When teams have less-than-optimal contact with customers during iterations, end-of-iteration focus groups can keep the team from wandering too far off track.

Customer change requests are recorded for review by the team *after* the focus group session. It's best to wait until after the CFG to do this because analysis of these requests often leads to technical discussions that aren't relevant to many of the participants. Furthermore, the engineering team's initial response to changes tends to be defensive—"That will be difficult (or expensive)"—which customers may interpret as a negative response to their suggestions. This environment discourages further suggestions, and sessions lose their effectiveness. The better approach is for the technical team to evaluate the requests the next day and then discuss options with the product manager. Normally, 80% or more of the requests can be handled with little effort, whereas the others may require additional study or fall outside the project's scope. Accumulated small changes are handled within the time allocated to the change cards described in Chapter 8. Significant changes and new stories are recorded on story cards that will serve as input to the next iteration planning session.

Technical Reviews

One of the key principles of exploratory, agile projects is to keep the cost of iteration low so the product can adapt to changing customer needs. Keeping the cost of iteration low and adaptability high depends on unceasing attention to technical excellence. Poorly designed, poor-quality, defect-prone products increase technical debt, reducing customer responsiveness.

Periodic technical reviews, both informal and regularly scheduled, provide the team with feedback on technical problems, design issues, and architectural flaws. These reviews should also address the key technical practices of simple design, continuous integration, ruthless testing, and refactoring to ensure that they are being effectively implemented. As always, these reviews should be conducted in the spirit of agile development—simple, barely sufficient, minimal documentation, short sessions, lots of interaction.

Technical reviews, informal ones at least, occur continuously during the delivery cycle. However, at periodic intervals—and at least once per iteration—a scheduled technical review should be conducted. It should not take more than a couple of hours, except in special situations. Technical review sessions are facilitated, are generally limited to two to six individuals who are competent to evaluate the technical material, and review the product, selected documents, and statistics, such as defect levels. (The technical team should take time to reflect on the overall technical quality of the product and make recommendations about refactoring, additional testing, more frequent integration, or other technical adaptations.)

Team Performance Evaluations

A fundamental tenet of APM is that projects are different and people are different (and thus teams are different). Therefore, no team should be shoehorned into exactly the same set of processes and practices as another. Project teams should work within an overall framework and guidelines (such as this APM framework and its associated guiding principles), but they should be able to adapt practices to meet their unique needs. Self-organizing principles dictate that the working framework should grant the team as much flexibility and authority to make decisions as possible. Self-disciplinary principles dictate that after the framework has been agreed upon, team members work within that framework. Assessments of team performance should touch on both of these factors.

Many project management methodologies recommend doing retrospectives at the end of a project. This may be fine for passing learning on to other teams, but it doesn't help improve performance during a project. Iteration retrospectives give teams an opportunity to reflect on what is working and what isn't. In coming up with this assessment, the team will want to examine many aspects of the project, asking questions like, "What went well?" "What didn't go as well?" and "How do we improve next iteration?" The team might also ask Norm Kerth's interesting question, "What don't we understand?"

The information shown in Figure 10-1 can be used as a starting point for evaluating team performance. The team evaluates itself in two dimensions—delivery performance and behavior—on a three-point scale: below standard, at standard, or above standard. On delivery performance, the team members are asking themselves the fundamental question, "Did we do the best job we could do in the last iteration?" Notice that the question isn't related to plans but to the team's assessment of its own performance. Whether teams conform to plan or not depends on both performance and the accuracy of the plan (so one piece of this evaluation might be for the team members to assess how well they planned the iteration). A team could meet the plan and still not be performing at an optimal level. In a well-functioning team, members tend to be open and honest about their performance. The team discussion, not the assessment chart itself, is the important aspect of this exercise.

Figure 10-1
Team Self-assessment Graph (The points on the graph identify from each iteration)

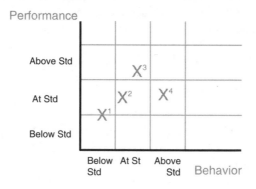

THE ADAPT AND CLOSE PHASES

---

[3] A good reference book on conducting retrospectives is *Project Retrospectives* (Kerth 2001).

The second aspect of the evaluation is team behavior, in which the team, again, assesses its own performance. This evaluation involves answering the questions, "How well are we fulfilling our responsibilities?" and "How well is the organization fulfilling its responsibilities?" Answering these two questions could generate a raft of other questions, such as

- Are all team members participating in discussions?
- Is someone regularly absent from daily meetings?
- Are team members accountable for their commitments?
- Is the project manager micro-managing?
- Does the team understand how and why key decisions were made during the last iteration?

The team members assess their overall behavior and develop ideas for improvement. For teams that are new to using agile practices, a questionnaire to help them measure their "agility rating" could also be useful.

Finally, the team should evaluate processes and practices so they better fit the team. For example, although a team wouldn't decide to eliminate requirements gathering, it might alter the level of ceremony and detail of the requirements documentation. The team might determine that daily stand-up meetings between feature teams be changed to twice-weekly meetings attended by two members from each feature team. The team might decide that two-week iterations are causing too much overhead. They could switch to three-week iterations and evaluate the impact.

There are a myriad of ways in which teams could adjust their processes and practices. The crucial thing is that they view processes and practices as adjustable and that they not feel the need to continue activities that are not contributing to the goals of the project.

Project Status Reports

Project status reports should have value to the project leader, the product manager, executives, other key stakeholders, and the project team itself. The reporting of information should drive activities aimed at maintaining control of the project and enhancing team performance. Developing the reports should help the project, and product leaders reflect on the overall progress of the project—to separate the forest from their daily battle with the trees. The number and frequency of reports and the information in the reports need to match the size, duration, and importance of the project.

Part of the project leader's job involves managing stakeholders, particularly those in upper management, by providing appropriate information to them. What stakeholders ask for may be different from what is needed to manage the project, but the project leader neglects this other information, and periodic interactions with those stakeholders, at her peril. Managing the expectations of various stakeholders can be a delicate balancing act.

Attending status meetings, giving management presentations, gathering accounting information, and a raft of similar activities can drain valuable time from delivering product. At the same time, management and customers are spending money for a product, and they aren't receptive to being told, "Just wait six months until we are finished." Executives and managers have a fiduciary responsibility, and they need periodic information to fulfill that duty. Customers, product managers, and sponsors need information to make project tradeoff decisions. Status reports must provide information to assist in answering questions such as, "Is the prognosis for the product such that it is still economically feasible?" and "Should features be eliminated to ensure we make the product release schedule?"

Most status reporting needs to address the Agile Triangle dimensions of value, quality, and constraints (scope, schedule, and cost). The team needs to examine not only stories delivered versus stories planned, but also the value of those stories delivered. Also, because uncertainty and risk drive many agile projects, the team should monitor whether risk and uncertainty are being systematically reduced.

Value and Scope Status

A "parking lot" diagram provides the development team, the customer team, and management with a useful overview of value and scope status. Whereas the typical Gantt charts emphasize schedule and tasks, a parking lot diagram emphasizes capability and story progress first and foremost. In Chapter 7, Figure 7-8 showed a parking lot diagram used for project planning. A similar diagram, Figure 10-2, can be used as the basis for status reporting. In the figures, the bar just above each scheduled delivery date indicates the percentage of the stories that have been completed (partially completed stories are excluded). Colors enable a quick analysis of the project's progress, especially as the project continues and the colors change from month to month. A white box indicates that no work has begun on the activity, whereas a blue box indicates that work has begun on some stories. A green box indicates that the stories have been completed, and a red box indicates that at least one scheduled story has not been delivered in its planned iteration. Figure 10-2 shows project progress by business activity area and capability.

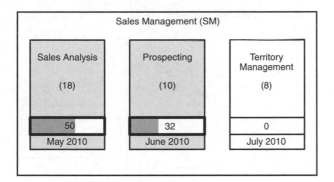

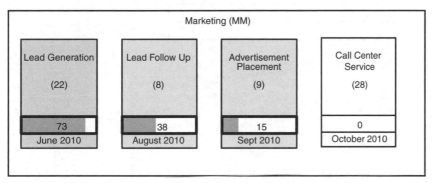

In an agile project, value can be indicated (rather than measured) by scope performance, such as measuring stories completed versus plan, by iteration, as shown in Figure 10-3. (This chart can be used as supplementary to the parking lot report.) In general, because stories can be added or deleted by the customer team over the life of a project, development teams should be evaluated based on the number of stories delivered rather than the specific ones delivered. If the team delivers 170 of 175 planned stories, then its performance is very good, even if 50 of those stories are different from those in the original plan. Scope tells us the raw volume of capabilities and stories delivered, but not how valuable they are.

Parking lot charts imply customer value, but organizations may want to go further than measuring relative value to measuring explicit value and ROI, as introduced in Chapter 8, "Advanced Release Planning".

Because the objective of agile development is to deliver high-value features early, in some cases to achieve early ROI, then a beneficial report would be the "stories and cost delivered" report shown in Chapter 8, Figure 8-5. For this report, the product team needs to apportion the product's value to individual stories or capabilities.

Figure 10-3
Delivery Performance
(Burn-Up Chart)

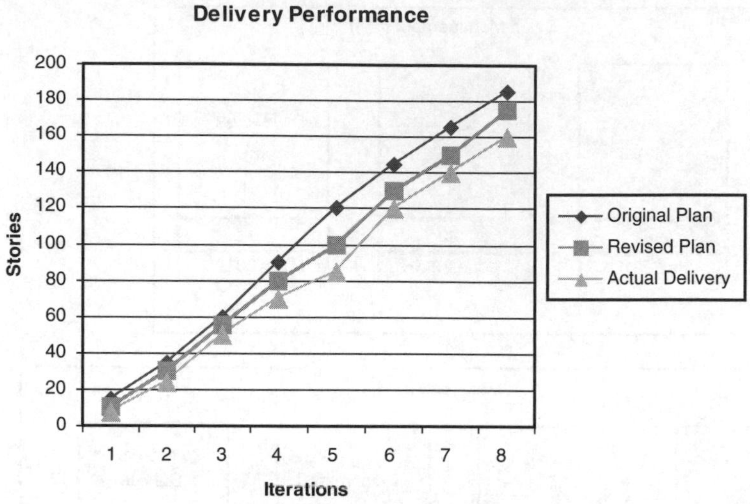

Quality Status

As with other project measurements, there are a wide range of quality metrics, many of which are product dependent. One important aspect of quality is a team's assessment of its work, as shown in Figure 10-4. Given the results of technical reviews, defect reports (e.g., find and fix rates), and the team's sense of the project's "feel" or "smell,"[4] this chart plots the level of technical quality—as assessed by the team—each iteration. Another example of a quality measure in software development is the growth of test code compared to executable code—both should be growing proportionally, as shown in Figure 10-5.

---

[4] In Extreme Programming, aspects of quality are evaluated by "smell," a term that conveys an intangible, but at the same time a very real, evaluation.

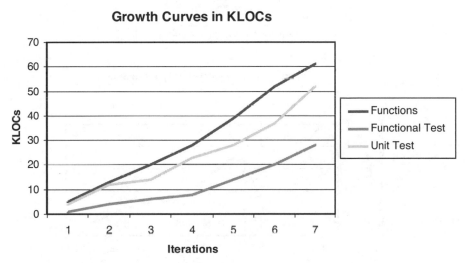

Figure 10-4
Product and Technical
Quality Assessment

Figure 10-5
Growth of Functional
and Test Code

Quality reports should also be geared to provide feedback on progress toward the quality objectives identified on the project data sheet.

Schedule and Risk Status

Schedule reports can take a variety of shapes, depending on the organization's standard practices. Figure 10-6 is an example that shows projected end dates (in elapsed weeks) for a project. During the replanning for each iteration, the team estimates, based on progress and story changes, the projected number of weeks for the entire project. Notice that the range of these esti-mates is wider at the beginning of the project (greater uncertainty) and nar-rower at the end (greater certainty). A range that isn't narrowing indicates that uncertainty and risk are not being reduced adequately and the project may be in danger. Accordingly, Figure 10-7 shows a qualitative assessment of risk, which should decrease over the life of the project, particularly in earlier iterations.

Figure 10-6
Projected Schedule

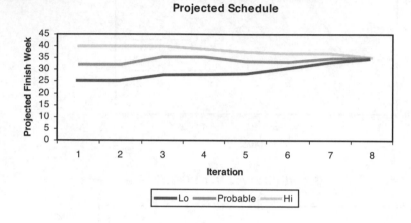

Figure 10-7
Technical Risk and
Uncertainty
Assessment

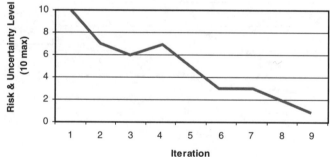

Agility

Agility measurements can also be useful. At a story level, the team can track and report on changes each iteration—original stories planned, original sto-ries deleted or deferred, and new stories added. The team can also track the change requests from the customer focus groups and report changes requested, implemented, deleted, or deferred. These reports showing the

THE ADAPT AND CLOSE PHASES

team's response to requested changes can assist in explaining variances in schedule or costs.

Cost Status

Cost reports can also take a variety of shapes, depending on an organization's practices. Although accounting reports are outside the scope of this book, one key number that many managers watch is expected cost to complete.

Project Team Information

It's not just executives and product managers that need project status information—team members do also. Agile projects are open projects, meaning that project information is widely shared among all team members and with customers and stakeholders. Project teams need to have key information readily available and communally shared. It needs to be visual and prominently posted—either on walls or a whiteboard for collocated teams, or on a common virtual whiteboard for distributed teams. Alistair Cockburn (2006) calls these displays "information radiators."

> *"An information radiator displays information in a place where passersby can see it. With information radiators, the passersby don't need to ask questions; the information simply hits them as they pass." (Alistair Cockburn 2006)*

Visual displays of project information need to concentrate on vision, objective, progress, issues, risks, and other items the team deems important. Figure 10-8 shows a variety of these "visual controls" in use by one team. Teams often get so caught up in details that the big picture gets lost. Arguments over details can frequently be resolved by a review of the product vision information or the guiding principles. Risk and issue lists are used to jog team members' consciousness so they are periodically thinking about solutions.

Figure 10-8
Visual Controls

Adaptive Action

As mentioned earlier, the term "adaptive action" conveys a sense of responding rather than correcting. To evaluate the value, quality, progress, and adaptation dimensions posed in the beginning of this chapter, three questions need to be asked about each dimension: "Where are we?" "Where did we plan to be?" "Where should we be?" Adaptive actions run the gamut, from minor tweaks to the next iteration's planned stories, to adding resources, to altering the planned schedule (with appropriate story adjustments). Adaptive adjustments can impact technical activities (e.g., allocating more time for refactoring) or modify delivery processes to make them more effective. Any of the four review types—product, technical, team, project status—can result in adaptive actions.

Close

A project close is both a phase and a practice. Organizations have a tendency to spend too much time initiating projects and too little time closing them. During one client engagement, I encountered the "failure to close" problem again. The customers of an IT project considered IT delivery to be less than stellar, partially because customers *thought* the project had been underway for years. In reality, the application in question had been installed for several years, but the initial production and ongoing enhancement releases were not differentiated from each other. So from the client's perspective, the "project" just went on and on.

Because resources are always scarce, people are moved on to the next project quickly, often without anyone taking time to close up the last project and give credit for its completion. Several activities are involved in closing a project, most of which don't take much time but do pay off. First and foremost is a celebration. A celebration serves two primary purposes. One, it shows an appreciation for all those who worked hard on the project. Including key clients in the celebration helps declare that this project is over, done, finalized, thus providing a sense of closure. Projects that go on and on without closure (or a series of projects couched as one) are terrible for morale.

Another less-glamorous closing activity is to clean up open items, finalize documentation and production or manufacturing support material, and prepare required end-of-project administrative reports, release notes, and financial reports.[5]

The most important closing activity is conducting a project retrospective. Teams using APM have done mini-retrospectives each iteration. These minis help the team learn about its own processes and team dynamics as the project progresses and as such are *intra*-team learning activities. The retrospective at the end is for *inter*-team learning, for one team to pass along to others in the organization what went well and what went bump in the night.[6]

Companies often confuse products and projects. Products are ongoing, whereas projects have a finite lifespan (at least the good ones do!). Differentiating between projects and products—ending projects and getting recognition and closure—is an important but often overlooked aspect of good project management, agile or otherwise.

[5] Mike Cohn recommends another activity for software developers: "One other thing I traditionally do when closing a project is to make sure we archive the development environment. I've seen too many projects where people thought they were covered because they had the code in a configuration management system. But the system was buildable only from inside something like Visual C++, or it required specific versions of software files to build. I always burn CDs of all that stuff at the end."

[6] Resources for retrospectives are *Agile Retrospectives: Making Good Teams Great* by Esther Derby and Diana Larsen (2006) and *Project Retrospectives: A Handbook for Team Reviews* by Norm Kerth (2001).

Final Thoughts

Monitoring and adapting (traditionally referred to as monitoring and control) are part of any good project management method. Although agile teams utilize some common project management practices, their attitudes toward monitoring and adapting are unique. For example, rather than corrective action, agile teams prefer adaptive action. Although corrective actions are necessary from time to time, the predominant attitude of agile teams is to adapt and move forward rather than to blame and write exception reports.

Frequent iterations that deliver working features allow agile teams to make frequent adjustments based on verifiable results rather than documentation artifacts. This can create an uncomfortable situation for managers and customers who don't want to deal constantly with either reality or the need to make tradeoff decisions.

Finally, the Adapt phase provides a short respite from the intensity of short-cycle iterative development. In a serial project, in which a working product may be months or even years in the future, it is very difficult to maintain high levels of work intensity—there is always tomorrow. Agile projects sometimes have the opposite problem—they can be overly intense. The brief review, adapt, and replan activities of the Adapt phase give team members time to catch their breath, and their mental faculties, before rushing off to the next delivery iteration.

Chapter 11

Scaling Agile Projects

The best way to approach large, uncertain, complex projects is to reduce the project's size, use small teams and increase staff only as absolutely necessary, hire only highly talented and experienced people, collocate the team, and use agile methods. Unfortunately, these recommendations often conflict with today's organizational and business realities. So, for those who aren't able, for a variety of reasons, to follow these recommendations, the concepts and practices in this chapter should help deliver successfully when not all of these conditions are met.

There exists a scaling myth that goes something like this: "Agile development works well for smaller projects, but doesn't scale to larger ones." Whether because early agile projects were small or the Extreme Programming focus (in early years) was on smaller projects, the myth has stuck even as agile project teams of 50, 100, and 500[1] have been successful. In looking at this myth we need to ask a couple of questions: "At what size does delivering value to customers fail to be important?" "At what size does the core value of creating self-organizing teams diminish?" "Can large organizations afford to be inflexible, rigid, and unresponsive?" When viewed in the light of these questions, it becomes obvious that applying agile methods to large projects is essential. The real question is "How?"

Large agile projects may "look" like large traditional projects, but they should "feel" like agile projects. "Look like" means there may be additional structure—organization, architecture, documentation, process—but that structure will have an agile feel—easier change processes, iterative with shippable product features (code for software products) at the end, collaborative (with good tools), barely sufficient documentation, self-organizing

---

[1] I have personally worked with teams of these sizes.

teams at all levels. Increasing uncertainty in projects requires agile practices, no matter the size of the project. Likewise, increasing project complexity (size, distribution, etc.) requires additional structure. Large agile projects require increasing structure while at the same time maintaining core agile values and practices.

As would be expected, success rates on small (<10 people), short (3–6 months) projects are very high. Conversely, success rates on very large (1,000+ people), long (> 18 months) projects are much, much lower. Problems with large projects include increased bureaucracy, excessive paperwork, unmanageable communications networks, and inflexibility. Applying agile principles as projects scale up actually help overcome these scaling problems.

The Scaling Challenge

Agility is a mindset, a way of thinking, not a set of practices or processes. The lifecycle framework and practices outlined in this book encourage agile behavior; they reinforce the principles, but they don't define APM—the core values and guiding principles do—and they are key to scaling. In an agile project management forum, Glen Alleman described the practices he used on a moderately sized project for the US Department of Energy. Because it was a government contract, a number of specific practices and documents were required. As he described the team's practices, the list appeared to define a heavyweight, not an agile, process. However, the team applied agile principles to the practices they used, trying to keep them as simple as possible given the nature of the agency and contracting requirements. They utilized short iterations and feature-based planning. They used a customized version of earned value analysis. They adjusted based on feedback each iteration. This was an agile team, even though it was using what might appear on the surface to be non-agile practices. Alleman's team illustrates the point that agile is more about attitude than practices, or more precisely, that agile teams use their guiding principles to shape the processes and practices to the job at hand.

Many of the misconceptions about scaling to larger projects come from managers who focus first on organizational structure (matrix, hierarchy), process (phases, tasks, artifacts), and development practices. They tend to build scaling mechanisms based on hierarchy, control, documents, and ceremony—which eventually cause compliance activities to dominate delivery activities as each hierarchical level justifies its existence.

> *"Management expertise has become the creation and control of constants, uniformity, and efficiency, while the need has become the understanding and coordination of variability, complexity, and effectiveness"* (Dee Hock 1999)

Agile teams balance flexibility and structure. So as project size increases, structure—of necessity—increases also. But they don't have to revert to an authoritarian, hierarchical structure. Large organizations can be adaptive, flexible, and exploratory—they just have to expand their structures in concert with agile principles, not abandon them. This chapter focuses on how to think about scaling these structures (such as organizational design or multi-level product structures) and practices (such as decision making or multi-level release planning) in an agile way, in a way that increases structure but retains the essence of flexibility and semi-autonomy at the individual and feature team level.

Scaling Factors

To illustrate scaling factors, think about two teams, one a six-person collocated team and the other a 100-person team divided into eight feature teams. Furthermore, focus on a particular task—setting up and maintaining the process and tools for build, integration, and testing (BIT). By examining how these two teams might handle this task we get insight into scaling issues.

First, how would the small team handle the BIT tasks? The entire team would probably discuss the problems and solutions, a couple of team members might do some research, the entire team would make the key decisions about process and tools, then a couple of team members might do the initial setup. Team members would discuss how to use the tools, and key information might be put on a flip chart (and/or recorded in a team wiki). The task would be handled collaboratively with the entire team making the decisions, and knowledge sharing would be informal and interactive. Team members would rotate BIT maintenance activities on an informal basis.

Obviously, using this scenario for a 100-person team would be extremely time consuming and expensive, so a reasonable scenario might be as follows. First, a part-time BIT team of 3–5 individuals would be organized. Members would be drawn from feature team members who had expertise or interest in BIT. These BIT team members would discuss issues, do any necessary research, and propose the process and tools. The proposal draft would be discussed with feature teams and team members would make comments back to the BIT team. The BIT team would make the final decisions, work to set up the BIT environment, and document the process in the team's wiki. BIT team members would be available to discuss their process and tools, or possibly make a presentation. Support of BIT on an ongoing basis would be done by a rotating team (members from feature teams would work part-time on the BIT team for some period of time).

Four key organizational factors come into play in these two scenarios: organizational design, decision-making design, collaboration/coordination design, and agile culture. These four could be labeled organizational-type scaling factors.

With a small, 6-person team there isn't much organizational design—everyone contributes based on skills and interests. As the overall team size grows to 100, design options range from hierarchical and functional to networked and cross-functional, with agile teams tending towards the latter.

Notice from the scenarios that in the small team everyone on the team was part of the BIT decision making, whereas in the larger team scenario the BIT team made the decisions with input from others—but they made the final decisions. As team size grows, the design of who makes what decisions is critical. Having 6 people involved in all team decisions is one thing, having 100 people involved in quite another.

Which brings us to one crux of scaling from an organizational perspective—collaboration versus coordination. Because agile development is highly collaborative, agilists tend to be indiscriminant about labeling person-to-person interactions—everything tends to be called collaboration. However, collaboration can be defined as working together to jointly produce a deliverable or make a decision. Coordination is sharing information. Collaboration is more involved and more expensive, and not always required. So in the second scenario, the BIT team made *collaborative* decisions and then *coordinated* those decisions with the feature teams (or communicated decisions to them). Matching communications modalities to tasks (most effective for least cost) is critical to project scaling.

How to apply agile culture or principles as projects scale is the final factor. One might argue that agile self-organizing principles dictate that all 100 people in the large team should be involved in the BIT decision, whereas another interpretation might be that decisions should be made at the network nodes (feature team or BIT team) to the greatest extent possible. There are agile principles, and then there are interpretations of agile principles, and individuals need to understand the principles well enough to apply them. As projects get larger, appropriate interpretation and application of those principles become both more difficult and more critical to success.

> *A 100-person team will never feel like a 6-person team, but each can definitely be agile. The key is appropriately applying agile principles to organizational design, decision making, and collaboration/coordination design.*

The second set of scaling factors are product related (the first four were organizational)—multi-level release planning, multi-team backlog management, processes and tools to ensure releasable product components, and planning and collaboration tools. These factors are covered in the last part of this chapter. Another type of scaling, which is beyond the scope of this book, is scaling to other parts of the organization—marketing, sales, product support, and more. Some far-thinking organizations have begun this last category of scaling.

Up and Out

> *"At scale, all agile development is distributed development"*
> *(Leffingwell 2007).*

Although the myth of "agile is only good for small projects," is being proved wrong every day, a number of issues still need to be addressed to scale agile—in two dimensions, up and out. The "up" dimension means scaling agile to larger projects—basically more people—and the "out" dimension pertains to distributing agile projects across multiple locations (buildings, cities, countries, continents). Many of the practices required for up and out are the same. For example, studies show that collaboration begins to break down at distances exceeding 50 feet. If that's true, then collaboration and communications practices (beyond those for collocated teams) will be needed whether a big team is located on three floors of a building or a smaller team is geographically dispersed.

Uncertainty and Complexity

Scaling is influenced by two critical issues—the size or complexity of the project and its uncertainty or risk. A very big, low-uncertainty project is very different from a very big, high-uncertainty one. These issues can be analyzed using a project profile model like the one developed by Todd Little and others at Landmark Graphics, Inc. (Pixton 2009). This profile has two dimensions—uncertainty and complexity—that can be shown in a 2×2 matrix. Uncertainty comes from issues such as market uncertainty, technical uncertainty (these first two are reflected in the exploration factor described in Chapter 6, "The Envision Phase"), number of customers, and project duration. Complexity comes from factors such as team size, team location, dependencies, and domain knowledge gaps. Scaling up or out brings several of these factors into play.

Two key questions can be addressed by evaluating projects with this profile: "Should this project be agile?" and, "How should we adapt agile practices for this type of project?" Both these questions help focus on the best way to address the risks introduced by a project's uncertainty and complexity. A cultural compatibility factor would also be required to answer the first question, but the profile provides a great starting place for looking at scaling issues. Managing increasing uncertainty is best accomplished by agile, flexible practices, whereas managing complexity requires more structure. The most difficult projects are those that require both flexibility and structure. A highly complex project, by its very nature, requires more structural elements, but for projects that are also highly uncertain, agile and structured practices must be balanced carefully.

An Agile Scaling Model

Figure 11-1 shows the major components of a scaling model: business goals, agile values, organization, product (product backlog), and process. Organization, product backlog, and process are shown at three levels (the actual number of levels in practice depends on overall team size)—levels that are needed to manage larger projects. This model illustrates that agile development reflects a product lifecycle approach (continuous delivery of value), rather than a project approach (begin-end). While an individual release of a product can be managed as a project, an agile approach views a release as a single stage in a product's ongoing evolution. Whether you are working on a commercial software product or an IT application, the software has a much longer life than individual projects. When we look at the agile principle of delivering continuous value, now and in the future, delivering a releasable product is important, but equally important is delivering a product that is high quality and can therefore be enhanced easily over time (adaptability).

The product backlog structure in the figure consists of three levels—capability, feature, and story. The process/practice structure consists of product roadmap, release plan, and iteration plan. The product backlog results from practices such as product visioning, architectural planning, and defining product requirements. The implication from the figure is that the

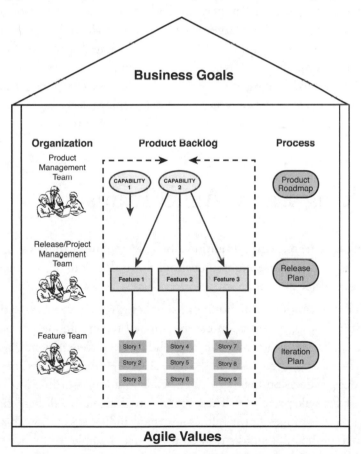

Figure 11-1
An Agile Scaling Model

product management team generally works at the capability level to address longer cycle and higher level (product) issues such as a product roadmap. The release/project management team generally works at the feature level on mid-range plans such as a 3–6 month release plan, while feature teams work at the story level on tasks such as creating an iteration plan and then developing and testing those planned stories. Because the teams are cross-linked (members of the release team are part of the product management team and vice a versa), lower level teams always have exposure to the broader product context. For a small project, a single team would perform the practices from several levels, for example, the same team would do release and iteration planning.

The remainder of this chapter expands on each of the components of this model, beginning with organizational scaling. Building large agile teams, not product backlogs or process, is the core of successful scaling. The Agile Manifesto value—"Individuals and interactions over process and tools"—is just as valid for large projects as for small. Building large agile teams requires a concerted look at organizational design, collaboration design, decision-making design, and determining how to build large self-organizing teams. Scaling the product and process components address product architecture, developing multi-level backlogs, large scale road mapping and release planning, and maintaining releasable products.

Building Large Agile Teams

Building large teams, either traditional or agile, requires careful design. Bigger teams involve more communication, more decisions, more meetings, more documents, and, of course, more politics.

Agile principles of collaboration, simplicity, responsiveness, and minimally sufficient documentation can be applied to building larger teams—but the application is far from simple. Building effective, efficient large agile teams takes a concerted effort in the four areas mentioned earlier: organizational design, decision-making design, collaboration/coordination design, and applying agile principles. These factors are designated "design" because there are a wide range of possibilities and many influences on how to accomplish each of them. Some distributed teams may be able to do face-to-face release planning (preferable), but others may not because of cost, so they have to pick another mechanism for release planning. By understanding each of these organizational design areas and understanding the uniqueness of each situation, hopefully you can come up with an adequate design for your large team. And oh, remember to adapt that design as the project proceeds.

Although collaboration, coordination, and knowledge sharing are critical to large projects, the downside of too much communications can be endless meetings and wading through tons of documentation and emails. Too little or poor communications, however, means no one understands the project nor their part in it. So whether we are doing organizational design or collaboration/coordination design, agile teams always balance on the side of "just a little bit less than just enough."

Organizational Design

If we are to foster the core values of an adaptive workplace, then the organizational structure of the team needs to reflect those values—and hierarchical structures fail this test. Hierarchical structures foster many problems, as colleague Bill Ulrich relates:

> *The political agenda was furthered by the hierarchy chart, which had little to do with dynamic, highly functional information management teams. Hierarchical IT infrastructures established an atmosphere where politics flourished and collaboration floundered. Hierarchies also led to an embedded culture that fostered adversity and encouraged the consolidation of individual power bases, as opposed to delivering quality information to the enterprise. As power bases enlarged, struggles ensued and adversity grew. You soon had an environment where 80% of workers' time was dedicated to working around the system, and only 20% was focused on doing their job. Hierarchical management structures are also a classic way to punish those that refuse to play the game and to reward those who know how to manipulate the political machinery (Ulrich 2000).*

A network model for project organizations, as shown in Figure 11-2, reflects aspects of both hierarchical and network structures. Each node represents a team (specialty or feature) within the larger project organization. As the figure

Figure 11-2
A Network
Organization
Structure

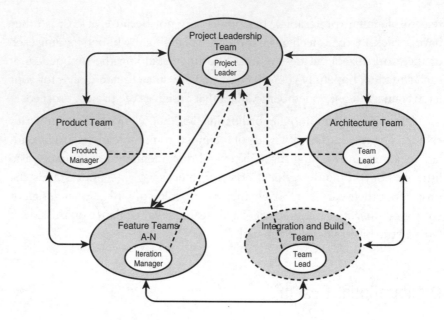

indicates, there may be several feature teams, a product team, an architecture team, and even an agile center of excellence team (not shown). Teams may be real, virtual (part-time members), or a combination. As discussed in the introduction, the build, integration, and test team, which has a specific role and meets periodically, could be a virtual team, made up of selected part-time members of the other teams. The architecture team might have a combination of full-time and part-time members. Teams such as the BIT and architecture teams can be thought of as "specialty" teams versus feature teams.[2]

In general, as projects escalate from large to very large the number of specialty teams will increase and a few members of the specialty teams will be full-time members. In addition, as size increases, feature teams will be organized into a structure—product area team, capability team, feature team—based on the product's component architecture. Whereas in a traditional large-team hierarchy the teams might be functional (requirements analysts, developers, testers), large agile teams maintain their cross-functional and

[2] I use the term "specialty" rather than "staff" because these teams have either direct delivery responsibilities or directly support other feature teams. When discussing both specialty and feature teams in the chapter, "feature" team will sometimes be used to indicate both to keep the wording simpler and shorter.

product orientation (e.g., the capability team would be cross-functional and all its subordinate feature teams would support that capability). Where very close coordination is required between feature teams (or between certain feature and specialty teams) cross-linking should be used in which one person from each team sits in on key meetings of the other. Another design criteria is that a large agile team maintain the flattest structure possible (more nodes, less hierarchy).[3]

The project leadership team (which might consist of the project leaders, product managers, iteration managers, and technical leads from feature teams) provides leadership and coordination and facilitates project decision making. This team, supplemented with key developers and product specialists, might also develop the capability-level roadmap or release plan and then allocate capabilities to feature teams. This organizational structure focuses on the collaboration and coordination between autonomous but linked groups. As the team size increases to encompass several feature and specialty teams, there is a critical combination of *team* self-organization and self-discipline required. Individuals have responsibilities within a team structure, and teams have responsibilities within an overall project structure.

This network structure isn't a hierarchically controlled one, but neither is it a pure network structure in which all control is delegated to the nodes. The structure might be labeled a "modified network" structure in which a significant amount (but not all) of the power and decision making are distributed to the feature teams.

Collaboration/Coordination Design

In *Agile Software Development*, Alistair Cockburn (Cockburn 2006) discusses various communications modalities and indicates each one's relative effectiveness. For example, a two-way face-to-face discussion at a white board is more effective than sending a document to someone. However, for large and especially distributed teams, the enemy of effectiveness remains cost. Although it may be very effective to have a face-to-face design discussion at a white board, the cost of doing it when the individuals are located

[3] An interesting approach to implementing large self-organizing teams can be found at www.holacracy.org.

5,000 miles apart may be prohibitive, although new Web 2.0 collaboration and project management tools are continually reducing these costs.

So the real question is not just effectiveness, but cost-effectiveness for the particular job at hand. What makes communications design so difficult is that it rests on a foundation of relationships—of trust, respect, appreciated cultural differences, and shared context. A team that is "in sync" can get away with lower effectiveness communications modalities because they have a good relationship context for sharing information. Another team—distributed across countries—in which there is little respect, trust, or multicultural understanding will need higher effectiveness communications modalities. This also means that the collaboration/coordination design will probably change as projects progress and relationships become better established. Communication modalities that might not work early in a project may work fine toward the middle and end.

Two factors in designing collaboration/communications practices and tools for a team are relative effectiveness of the modalities and the foundation of trust, respect, and understanding of different cultural norms. The third factor is contained in the title to this section: understanding the difference between collaboration and coordination. As briefly described earlier, collaboration can be defined as working together to jointly produce a deliverable (think pair programming as an example) or make a decision, whereas coordination is sharing information. A team that meets to develop a release plan has to collectively make a series of decisions about product vision, project objectives and boundaries, backlog item priority, estimates to complete, and assignment of capabilities to iterations—specific tasks done in a collaborative way. On the other hand, teams use daily stand-up meetings to coordinate work and keep abreast of what each other are doing. One can easily visualize that having a daily stand-up meeting over the telephone, or even instant messaging, could be effective, whereas trying to conduct a release planning session over the phone (without other tools) might not be.

A final factor to consider in this design process would be the coupling or integration inherent in the product being developed. For example, if one feature team is working on a capability that is very loosely coupled to others (an independent piece of the product), then the need for highly collaborative sessions with other teams may be low. With another feature team, say the foundation (common services) team, their work would be highly coupled to other teams' work and they would therefore have need for higher effectiveness interactions.

Looking at these factors for a large team may appear to be a daunting and time consuming task, but the design process should be based on a risk assessment and some standard guidelines. From the preceding discussion, the higher risk areas would be product components that have high degrees of coupling or integration (and even higher risk if teams are distributed), teams that need a higher level of relationship building (cultural or trust issues are apparent), and activities in which either critical and or many decisions must be made (release planning, for example).

A simple set of collaboration guidelines:

- Use a wide variety of interaction modes
- Match interaction needs with collaboration practices
- Use lower-cost modes to the extent possible
- Use higher effectiveness modes on critical, higher-risk activities

If you were designing for a team that had four distributed feature teams—each in a different country; who had not worked together before (low relationship quotient); and were working on a highly integrated product and using a common daily build, integration, and test environment—then skimping on communications costs would be disastrous.

In one very large IT organization, several people lamented the lack of communication—a common complaint. However, another individual saw it differently: "We have too much communication. Just look at my email inbox each morning." He was right. What this organization lacked was not "communication," but a culture of collaboration, of jointly working on issues rather than slinging emails and documents at each other. Teams need to figure out new and creative ways to collaborate. For example, teams can use the concept of traveling pairs from software development. As I've recommended elsewhere, "Every other iteration, a pair from one feature team could travel to the second site where they then pair with developers from the second team. Traveling pairs transfer knowledge about the team's features at a working level. No matter how good the architectural decomposition of a product, two distributed teams working on the same product need a certain amount of working-level conversation and collaboration" (Highsmith 2002).

Exchanging people will be much more effective than exchanging paperwork.

From the design factors described it can be seen that project coordination meetings should also be carefully designed and adjusted as needed. Having a hierarchical structure of daily stand-up meetings (1–2 people from lower-level meetings attend higher-level ones) may not be the best design—just as the organization has a network structure, so should coordination meetings. The meeting topics should be specific also. For example, while feature team meetings should focus on work completed the past day, impediments, and work scheduled next day; higher-level meetings should focus on major work items completed/planned (summary), decisions made or needing to be made that affect the group, cross-team or external dependencies, and information in general that has a cross-team impact.

Furthermore, although feature teams may have daily stand-ups, specialty teams may need to meet only 1–2 times per week. Specialty team member attendance at feature team meetings (when they are not full-time members of the feature team) must be reasonable. I once had a senior manager lament, "My UI designers are attending 42 stand-up meetings a week because each is supporting several teams. Furthermore, the teams are telling them that if they don't attend they aren't being agile!" These kinds of issues arise when scaling, and project leaders must be smart, and practical, about how they handle them.

Finally, in terms of a network of stand-up meetings, participants should feel their participation is worthwhile, that they are not just attending to be attending. If people aren't getting benefit from the meetings, then the design is probably wrong. Fifteen-minute meetings are still the rule, even for upper-level stand-ups.

Decision-Making Design

In the decision-making section of Chapter 9, framing was the first task in decision making and it is the primary task in decision-making design. The key framing questions listed in Chapter 9 are modified somewhat for decision design:

- What tasks are being accomplished by each feature and specialty team and what key decisions need to be made to complete these tasks?

- What other teams are impacted by the decision?[4]
- Do any of the impacted teams need to provide input to the decision?
- Do any of the impacted teams need to be involved in the discussions about the decision?
- Who should make the decision (the feature/specialty team, the iteration manager, the product manager, the project leader, the project leader with the team, etc.)?
- How and to whom should the decision results be communicated?
- Who, if anyone, should review the decision?

Examining several examples may be the easiest way to visualize using these questions in design. Figure 11-3 shows the answers to these questions for the architecture specialty team and their task to develop an overall application data model. Similarly, the guideline for feature team decision making is show in the box. These decision making guidelines are an integral part of rules of engagement between teams much like the internal rules of engagement that feature teams develop, as introduced in Chapter 9.

> *Feature team guideline: If in implementing a story the team abides by guidelines established (architectural decisions made by the preceding process, for example) and that implementation does not appear to impact any other team, then the feature team is delegated the right to make all decisions relevant to their story.*

Designing a decision-making framework doesn't require the team to look at all decisions, but a relevant sample. This can be done during the Envision phase and updated as needed—decision design evolves over the project. Just as architecture teams don't try to anticipate everything they will need three months hence, neither should the leadership team anticipate all the types of decisions to be made. The entire team needs to understand that the way decisions are made isn't an afterthought, but something carefully considered. Decision-making design should be part of the working agreement that all agile teams develop.

---

[4] Teams should not make unilateral decisions on items that impact another team without engaging that team in the decision process (a rule of engagement). So, for example, a team could not change an interface design without coordinating it with other teams that use that interface.

Figure 11-3
Decision Making
Summary

> **Team: Architecture**
> **Task: Develop an Application Data Model**
>
> - Teams impacted: All feature teams and several specialty teams.
> - Teams to provide input: Foundation team. Selected feature teams.
> - Discussions involvement: Foundation team has 2 part-time members of the architecture team. 1 senior designer from feature team N.
> - Decision Maker: Architecture team.
> - Decision results communication: Team wiki (data model, key decision rationale), email to all team leads, John Jones point person from architectural team for questions.
> - Decision review: None.

As projects get larger, more specialty teams arise: architecture, UI design, BIT, high-level release planning, and others. Each of these teams, and even other feature teams (especially, for example, the foundation team) assumes some of the decision-making responsibility on tasks that a small six-person team would take on itself. So, one can readily ask, "How is a large agile team different from a large traditional team from an organizational perspective?" The answers to this question may be subtle, but that doesn't undercut its importance:

- First, a large agile team has a flatter, less hierarchical structure—fewer layers of managers.
- Second, to the greatest extent possible, decisions are pushed out to the feature teams or specialty teams.
- Third, feature team members participate in specialty teams to ensure their input is heard and to take part in the decisions.
- Fourth, team decision making, whether project or technical decisions are being made, are accomplished in a participatory fashion.
- Fifth, specialty teams are encouraged to issue guidelines, not fiats, and furthermore—like managers—they are encouraged to make as few decisions as possible.
- Sixth, peer-to-peer (feature team to feature team) interactions and dependency management are encouraged. For example, rather than having a project leader manage inter-team dependencies, the teams themselves manage them through mechanisms such as the ICS cards defined later in this chapter.
- Seventh, the team embraces agile principles.

Although a 100-person agile team won't quite feel like a 6-person one, it should feel a lot different from a 100-person traditional team.

Knowledge Sharing and Documentation

I recently had an MRI on my knee. The medical report was full of words like joint effusion, medial patellar plica, acute medullary bone contusions, and medial femoral condyle. Although my doctor could easily read and interpret the report for me, my attempts to understand the report were doomed.

> *The primary problem with documentation is the difference between context and content. Documentation can provide content, but understanding the context requires domain expertise.*

Documentation and knowledge sharing are two important issues in scaling agile projects. A 6-person team needs different documentation practices than a 100-person team does. Agile critics always bring up the "no" documentation issue, that is, they say agilists don't believe in documentation. But the issue is *not* documentation, the issue *is* understanding. Do the developers *understand* what the customers want? Do the customers *understand* what the developers are building? Do testers *understand* what the developers intended to build? Do software maintainers *understand* what the developers built? Do the users *understand* what the system does for them? Understanding takes a combination of content and context, and documentation is a poor conveyor of context.

The Agile Manifesto states, *"Working products over comprehensive documentation."* Large, front-loaded projects that spend months, and even years, gathering requirements, proposing architectures, and designing products are prone to massive failures. Why? Because teams proceed in a linear fashion with little reliable feedback—they have good ideas, but they don't test them in the cauldron of reality. Working products don't preclude the need for documentation. Documents support communication and collaboration, enhance knowledge transfer, preserve historical information, assist ongoing product enhancement, and fulfill regulatory and legal requirements. They are not unimportant, just less important than working versions of the product.

Understanding comes from a combination of documentation and interaction, or conversation—the conversations among people who have domain knowledge. Furthermore, as the complexity of the knowledge to be transferred increases, the ability of documentation alone to convey that knowledge decreases and the need for interaction with knowledgeable people increases dramatically. Documentation provides *content* (partially), but conversations are necessary to provide the necessary *context*.

> *Documentation is not a substitute for interaction. In a complex situation, documentation by itself can provide only 15–25% of the understanding required.*

When a customer and a developer interact to jointly develop specifications and produce some form of permanent record (documents, notes, sketches, story cards, drawings), the documentation is a by-product of the interaction. When the customer sits down with a business analyst and they write a requirements document that gets *sent* to a development group, then the document has become a substitute for interaction. In the first scenario, the documentation may be valuable to the development team. In the second, it has become a barricade to progress. Little knowledge is either gained or transferred. Furthermore, as interaction decreases, the volume of documentation increases in a fruitless attempt to compensate.

Recently a manager of a development group asked me about a requirements workshop. When I asked why he wanted the workshop he replied, "We want to document our requirements to a sufficient level of detail and correctness that we can ship them offshore for coding." As I questioned him, he also stated that when this company hired local contract help, it took them six months to become knowledgeable enough about the company's product domain (a complex engineering product) to become productive. My comment to the manager was that they didn't have a requirements or documentation problem but a knowledge transfer problem. Not only did they need to convey requirements, but the engineering context that made those requirements understandable. His outsourcing plans were doomed to failure.

Let me postulate a simple test. If you had a choice, which project would you prefer to manage (and be accountable for)? On project 1 you would be provided 1,000 pages of detailed specifications, but no access to the client or users. On project 2 you would be provided with a 50-page outline specification, but constant access to the client. I've never had anyone pick the first project. Understanding comes from a combination of documentation and interaction—or information and conversation—with the interaction being by far the more important. This is not to say documentation is unnecessary. I would not have written four books if I felt documentation was useless, but documentation is not enough.

A little research into the field of knowledge management shows that early efforts to document best practices (software development, engineering, or otherwise)—filling reams and reams of web pages with details—has generated marginal benefit. In thinking about knowledge transfer, one must distinguish between transferring explicit knowledge (written down) and tacit knowledge (in someone's head). "Tacit knowledge cannot be transferred by getting it out of people's heads and onto paper," writes Nancy Dixon in her book *Common Knowledge* (2000). "Tacit knowledge can be transferred by moving the people who have the knowledge around. The reason is that tacit knowledge is not only the facts but the relationships among the facts—that is, how people might combine certain facts to deal with a specific situation." A briefly outlined best practice combined with a mechanism for the transferee and the transferor to have face-to-face conversations has proven much more effective at tacit knowledge transfer than sending off documentation.

I vividly recall a statement from a project postmortem several years ago, "The specifications for our project were great; we just interpreted them in radically different ways." So the issue between agile and document-centric (or model-centric) methodologies is not one of extensive documentation or no documentation, but rather the correct mix of documentation and interaction to convey understanding. Agilists lean toward interaction, whereas traditional methodologists lean toward documentation. Neither extreme works for other than the most extreme situations.

The Agile Manifesto "working software" principle has two critical components. First, it says that working software is critical to measuring real success, but it does not say that documentation is unimportant. Second, the word "comprehensive" denotes "heavyweight" rather than lean documentation. It's not documentation per se that Agilists downplay, but the reams and reams of traditional documentation that either 1) people say they need but never have time to develop (but think they should), or 2) they develop initially but never update so it becomes useless.

> *Compliance documentation, whether it is for the FDA, SOX, or internal control, is a cost of doing business. Compliance documentation should not be viewed as having value in communicating information within the development team—it is basically overhead.*

Excluding compliance documentation, Figure 11-4 lists guidelines for agile documentation. Documentation can be valuable or a waste of time. A document that was invaluable for our 100-person team may be a complete waste of time for the 6-person one. These guidelines can help each size team determine what is valuable for them.

In summary, documentation should be designed in a lean, barely sufficient manner, both formal (for retention) and informal (temporary), highly visual and visible, viewed as support for collaboration and coordination, and vary considerably by project size and type (regulated environments for example). Ultimately the issue isn't documentation but understanding.

Figure 11-4
Agile Documentation
Guidelines

Agile Documentation Guidelines

- The fundamental issue is knowledge transfer—understanding, not documentation.
- Knowledge transfer requires person-to-person interaction, particularly as the complexity of the knowledge increases.
- Documentation should be barely sufficient, but not insufficient: Use overviews rather than try to document all the details.
- High-quality readable code and test cases, particularly when the test cases are automated, may be adequate for detailed requirements documentation.
- Models are a form of documentation. Keep them light and barely sufficient also. Develop only those models that are useful to the development team, and develop them "with" the team.
- Documentation should be as informal as possible—white boards, flip charts, digital pictures, wikis, etc.
- Interactive, dynamic documentation is important in agile projects: Wiki, Web 2.0.
- Working software is one goal of development, enabling the ongoing enhancement of that software is a second. Think about the barely sufficient documentation to support both.
- Documentation requirements vary by industry, company, and project.
- Permanent documentation is that which an organization is willing to spend the money, and time, to maintain. Working papers are documents that are used during a project (and may be very informal) but are not maintained. Don't confuse these two types.
- User documentation should be identified as a story and prioritized by the customer team just as software stories.

Self-Organizing Teams of Teams

An agile team consists of individuals—quasi-independent agents—who interact within a structure of self-organized and self-disciplined rules of engagement. Individuals have a degree of autonomy within this loose structure, and they, in turn, exercise self-discipline to be accountable for results and behave as responsible and thoughtful members of the team. Larger agile teams, those consisting of multiple feature and specialty teams, operate the same way—individuals are the agents in teams, whereas feature teams are the agents in a larger project. In building large agile teams, a network replaces the common hierarchical structure, decision making and collaboration must be carefully designed, and discipline reflects rules of engagement across teams.

The basics of self-organizing teams from Chapters 3 and 9 apply to larger teams, but there are extensions to those ideas. Creating a self-organizing framework for a larger team entails

- Getting the right leaders
- Articulating the work breakdown and integration strategies
- Encouraging the interaction and information flow across teams

The organization, through the project leader, is responsible for staffing the project with the right people. At the team level, getting the right people means finding those with appropriate technical and behavioral skills. At the project level, the project leader and project leadership team work to ensure the right leaders are assigned to each feature and speciality team.

The project leadership team has the responsibility to ensure everyone understands the product vision and his or her feature team's assignment within that overall vision. The envisioning process described in Chapter 6—vision, objectives and constraints, architecture skeleton, release plan—needs to be conducted for the entire project. Then, each feature team goes through its own envisioning exercise—vision box, etc.—for their individual piece of the product. An architectural overview, component descriptions, and interface definitions can help each feature team understand both the big picture and its piece of the product.

One important inter-team task is managing dependencies, a task frequently relegated to the project leader. All too often dependency management falls into the same trap that serial development does—management by documentation rather than conversation. Within a feature team, the members themselves manage dependencies between stories. They identify dependencies in planning meetings and note them on story cards, suggesting alternative scheduling when they anticipate problems. They also identify dependencies during daily team stand up meetings. These discussions not only identify the dependency, but also the exact nature of that dependency and how to assign work to allow for it.

The same discussions occur at the inter-team level during high-level release planning. Project leaders may know about dependencies, but the team members have the detail information required to figure out how to work with them.

Although there are practices that create team-to-team interaction (e.g., stand-up meetings), there is no small set of practices that cover all the situations encountered in larger projects. Each project is unique, and the leadership team will need to experiment with interaction practices just as it does with technical ones. That said, several key practices can help create the right kinds of relationships and interactions among various teams. One practice is the inter-team commitment stories (ICS) described later in this chapter. Another such practice is to establish inter-team rules of engagement and accountability.

> *The project leader's role should be to facilitate the interactions between the teams, not the specific activities each team uses to produce deliverables.*

An example would be the rules of engagement between architecture and feature teams within a project as shown in Figure 11-5. These rules of engagement, which evolve over time, guide the integration of teams within a project. Rules of engagement place a context around overall collaborative efforts and specific documents. Without rules of engagement, teams will be constantly dragging the project leader into decisions that they should work out among themselves. As defined in Chapter 9 (for rules of engagement within teams), the three categories of inter-team rules are the same: relationship building, practice definition, and decision making.

Figure 11-5
Example Rules of
Engagement

Feature Teams
- Feature teams shall have input to, and participate in (the number of participating teams may be limited) architectural decision that impacts their work.
- Teams shall have the right to assess the impact of any architectural change and adjust estimates and schedules accordingly.
- Teams shall have the right to request that the project leader review any architectural decision in which the team's objection is overridden.

Architecture Team
- The team shall receive prompt information about and feedback on proposed architectural plans.
- The team shall expect prompt notification of problems that feature teams encounter in implementing architectural decisions.

Team Self-Discipline

Just as individuals have responsibilities to their teams, teams themselves have to be self-disciplined to work within a larger self-organizing framework. The behaviors required of teams closely parallel those for individuals:

- Accept accountability for project results.
- Engage collaboratively with other feature teams.
- Work within the project self-organizing framework.
- Balance project goals and team goals.

A team that is unwilling to work within the established framework disrupts the work of the larger project in the same way that individuals who are unwilling to work within the team framework do.

Teams have to align their own goals with those of the project. There will always be too much to do and too little time, and the tendency will be to work on one's team goals rather than on project goals.

Just as individuals have a responsibility to fully participate in their feature team's activities, teams have a similar responsibility to participate within the larger project. For example, when a team estimates how many stories it can deliver in an iteration, its members must factor in time to coordinate with other teams because team members will undoubtedly serve on specialty teams (e.g., the architecture or BIT teams). Feature teams will have to interact not only with their product team, but also with other feature teams. For instance, a team may utilize a component or information from another feature team, or it may supply a component or information to another feature team. The same trust and respect that form a foundation for individual interaction also apply to feature team interaction.

Process Discipline

> *Don't always fix things that are broken.*

We all know the saying "Don't fix things that aren't broken." For larger teams, we need to give this advice a twist: "Don't always fix things that *are* broken." Although smaller teams are not immune to excessive process, this tendency becomes more prevalent as teams get bigger. Let's say that at the end of a wave the integration of several modules causes a couple days of extra work. The immediate reaction, particularly by the people who had to clean up the mess, might be to fix the problem by instituting additional coordination meetings. Unfortunately, two things may happen. First, the meetings themselves may take more time than fixing the problem did. Second, unanticipated consequences always arise. Just as agile teams don't try to anticipate future requirements or design, choosing instead to let them emerge over time, they shouldn't attempt to anticipate every problem and put processes or practices in place to prevent them. It's often cheaper and faster to fix an actual failure than to spend excessive time anticipating failures that may never occur.

Scaling Up—Agile Practices

There are a number product related scaling factors for agile projects including project architecture, product roadmaps and backlogs, multi-level release plans, maintaining a releasable product, inter-team commitment stories, and tools.[5]

[5] For another look at scaling practices, see *Scaling Software Agility*, by Dean Leffingwell (2007).

Product Architecture

As product size increases, architecture work increases in importance—even for an agile project. Product architecture guides both the technical work and the organization of people who carry out the technical work. Architecture serves several objectives: It provides the structure for implementing product requirements, lowers the cost of development, improves adaptability, and guides organizational design.

A product's architecture, together with the overall size of the project, has significant implications for project and product success. For example, the organization of components and modules may impact decisions about outsourcing or distributed development and how to configure distributed groups. Similarly, if a team is building a complex product with both hardware and software components, the interface specifications may have a major impact on the change management process.

One of the agile balancing acts is how much up-front architecture work to do before beginning development iterations. Although the months-long architectural (and requirements definition) work done on waterfall projects wasn't effective, neither is starting coding with a 100-person development staff on day one. The most effective approach is to put a small, cross-functional team in place, with a higher ratio of product specialists and architects than for normal feature teams, and have this group develop the initial architecture, product road map, and capability/feature backlog. This information can then be used at the next level of planning, organizational design, and allocation of work to feature and specialty teams.

To improve allocation of work to teams, architecture should focus on coupling, cohesion, and interfaces. As introduced in previous sections of this chapter, highly cohesive components that are loosely coupled with well specified interfaces can be assigned to distributed teams where the collaboration costs need to be kept lower. Conversely, highly coupled components with undefined interfaces should be allocated to either collocated feature teams or ones with a proven track record of working together. If this allocation isn't feasible for some reason, then managers need to recognize the higher risk and design highly effective collaboration/coordination practices.

Roadmaps and Backlogs

The basics of roadmaps and backlogs were covered in Chapters 7 and 8 on release planning and the hierarchy for planning and executing large projects is shown in Figure 11-1. When looking at practices for large projects there isn't "a" solution because large is a relative term. The practices used for a 100-, 500-, or 1,000-person projects will be similar, but their implementation will be adjusted for project size. So, for example, different size teams would use roadmaps, backlogs, and release plans—but one team might use two levels of product breakdown (capability, story), and another four levels (business area, capability, feature, story). One might use a single backlog, another multiple coordinated backlogs. Because there are so many possible variations, I'll use a case study approach (assembled from several client engagements) for a company called Select Software, Inc. to illustrate one usable structure for medium-sized projects.

Select Software had product suite of eight ERP-like products and a development staff of 75 people organized into five feature teams and two specialty teams with a total of three product managers and five product specialists. The product structure was product, capability, and story. The company had developed a three-year roadmap that included some significant component replacements and re-architecture work. They wanted verification that the first significant release could be accomplished in 18 months with the staff on hand. A single backlog was developed that had about 350 sized capabilities.[6] Using this backlog, an 18-month release plan was developed. There is always a lot of consternation from development teams trying to plan at this level—they don't want to "commit" to high-level plans. But commitment isn't the goal; the goal is determining overall feasibility. In this case, the capability-level release plan indicated questionable feasibility for the "must have" functionality and an additional feature team was added.

In this case study, the high-level roadmap and release plans were done by part-time teams made up of feature and specialty team members and several development and product managers. About 15-20 feature and specialty team members were involved in this high-level planning, enough to ensure that each team was well represented.

[6] Many of these capabilities were "timeboxed sized," a technique introduced in Chapter 8.

Because all these teams were located in the same building and the over-all team size wasn't too large, a single product backlog was utilized. From the release plan, capabilities were assigned to feature teams. In some instances, just as with stories, capabilities were split to make feature team assignments. Each feature team then did a three-month wave plan, breaking capabilities down into stories (but not tasks) and assigning stories to one of the six iterations (a seventh, one-week iteration was used for cleanup, refac-toring, additional testing, and planning the next wave). As each team broke capabilities into stories they maintained them in a common backlog. Each feature team then developed iteration plans for their next two-week iteration.

In the Select Software case, the roadmap was updated about every six months (or more frequently if significant changes occurred), the release plan was updated every month, and the wave plans were updated every iteration.

Multi-level Release Plans

In the Select Software case were four planning timeframes: roadmap, release, wave, and iteration. Assuming on average about 10 stories per capa-bility, developing a release plan with 3,500 stories would not be easy, nor effective—it would be elaborating details much too early in the project. So the release plan was developed at the capability level, still a significant effort with 350 capabilities, but reasonable for a project of this size. Figure 11-6 shows an example of these levels. The product team worked on defining and

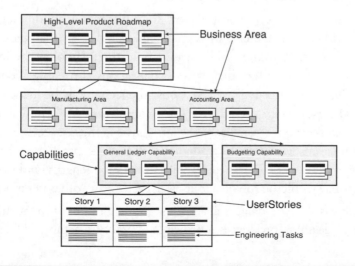

Figure 11-6
Multi-level Planning
Components

general prioritizing of capabilities prior to the release planning session. One of the outputs of the release plan was an allocation of capabilities to feature teams. The backlog was maintained in an Excel spreadsheet.

Each feature team then constructed its own wave plan based on the capabilities assigned to it by the release plan. These wave plans, only done for the next three-month period, were constructed at the story level. The product teams associated with feature teams and a few key development leads worked prior to the wave planning sessions to begin breaking capabilities into stories (these were only drafts and were modified during the planning sessions). Finally, each feature team developed detailed iterations plans, to the task level, for their next two-week iteration.

Select Software did a partial deployment to select customers every wave (three months). They operated on a "release train" system in which the release dates were fixed and stories either were complete, in the "train station," and got on, or if not ready, were delayed until the next train.

Maintaining Releasable Products

Maintaining a small releasable product is relatively easy. Doing the same with a multi-product suite of products with significant legacy code across a widely distributed team is quite another. Although the technical challenges of these two situations are vastly different, the principle is the same—maintain a releasable product. But, be practical.

It is both principled, and practical, to implement a build, integration, and test (BIT) environment for a small, collocated team that allows team members to run 30-minute BIT cycles. Could the technology be made to work for a 50-person team spread over two locations? Probably. Would it be practical and cost effective? Maybe. Could the technology be made to work for a 500-person team spread over three continents? Maybe. Would it be practical and cost effective? Probably not. Maybe in the last scenario individual feature teams would work on 30-minute BIT cycles, product teams would work on a two-week cycle to correspond to iteration lengths, and the entire product suite would be run on a four-week cycle (every other iteration).

Agility is always a balancing act—just enough, but not too much. Maintaining a releasable product is a principle of agility. Keeping BIT cycles as short as possible should be a goal, but practicality should balance "short as possible" with cost. However, particularly in the early stages of a project, push hard to unlock opportunities. Don't let comments like "It's too expensive to build, integrate, and test our product every week" become an obstacle to opportunity. Agile project leaders must constantly be searching for the right balance between obstacle and opportunity.

Inter-team Commitment Stories

"Organizational responsiveness comes from giving individuals and groups the freedom to behave in ad hoc ways to respond to unforeseen circumstances. For this reason, organizational roles are defined in terms of accountability for commitments to particular outcomes, rather than in terms of activities" (Stephan Haeckel, former director of strategic studies at IBM's Advanced Business Institute, 1999).

If we are going to build a network organizational structure and manage outcomes rather than activities, then there needs to be a mechanism for feature and specialty teams within the project structure to manage their commitments to each other. Rather than have the project leader keep up with and manage all inter-team dependencies, the teams need to accept that responsibility themselves, just as development teams commit to product teams on features. However, as project size increases, a slight increase in formality and documentation is necessary to help teams handle these dependencies. An Inter-team Commitment Story (ICS), which is based on Haeckel's (1999) commitment management protocol, can assist with this task.

The ICS addresses two key issues in managing large teams: "How do we manage commitments between teams?" and "How do we manage the work itself?" We can think back to the small project model for clues. First, the executive sponsor, with the advice and consent of the project and product leaders, agrees to the overall project plan. Second, the development team and the product team make iteration-to-iteration commitments to each other. The product manager can add, modify, or cancel stories without going up the management chain for approval, as long as the project stays within its agreed-upon boundaries. The developers and customers agree on stories—a commitment for the iteration—and then the customers put the stories through acceptance testing at the end of the iteration. Because there is only one team, an ICS is not needed.

As project size increases we need similar mechanisms to allow feature teams to work together with minimal management involvement. This mechanism is the Inter-team Commitment Story, a brief written agreement between feature teams. Rather than having work assignments flow from the project leader down, the teams themselves decide on how they are going to work together (although the project leader does facilitate and influence the agreements). The objective of the ICS is to enable groups to manage their work for each other with the least management involvement. It assists in overall project management by clarifying inter-team dependencies.

An ICS identifies a contract-like relationship between two feature teams. Rather than have a project leader say, "Do this by this date," the teams contract with each other and document their commitment on an ICS card, as shown in Figure 11-7. For example, in the development of an electronic instrument, an ICS card might state that the circuit board team agrees to deliver a prototype board to the instrument design team by a certain date. Or the product line architecture team might have an agreement to deliver platform architectural requirements to the instrument design team by a specified date.

The outcome is negotiated between two teams in the same way that a feature card would be negotiated between a development team and the product team (although an ICS card may be for a larger chunk of work than a user

Figure 11-7
Inter-Team Commitment Story

ICS Card			
Outcome ID:	C42		
Outcome Name:	Acquisition System Diagnostics		
Supplier Team:	Embedded Software Team		
Consumer Team(s):	Electronics Design Team		
Description:	Preliminary software to do all the diagnostic		
	testing of the data acquisition component.		
Intermediate Deliverables:	N/A		
Acceptance Criteria:	All instrument diagnostic tests completed		
	successfully.		
Est. Work Effort:	25 hours for the coordination		

story). And just as a story card acknowledges a relationship between customer and developer and defines a set of obligations and responsibilities on each party's part, an ICS card acknowledges a relationship and a set of partnership responsibilities between two (or more) feature teams. As in contracts with outside suppliers, the "customer" side in an ICS agreement has the right to accept or reject the work based on documented acceptance criteria.

ICS cards get scheduled just like story cards. They state explicitly the cost of team-to-team coordination, and most importantly, they engage the teams with each other in ways that a project leader–drawn dependency arrow on a network diagram cannot. Although the project leader should participate (so that he understands what the teams are doing and can provide information they might not have) with the teams in establishing these dependencies and developing the ICS, the fundamental agreement is between teams.

However, someone has to champion inter-team commitments and the most logical person for that is the iteration manager. Product managers want new stories and teams are often caught up in delivering them and the priority of work for other teams gets downgraded. Although iteration managers focus on their teams, they also should have an overall project perspective. Because ICS stories often deal with important dependencies, the iteration managers are usually the best at knowing when to schedule them.

As a team develops commitments with other teams, the members have to keep track of what they can realistically commit to, and scheduling the ICS cards as part of an iteration's workload helps. As is the case with stories, when an iteration is full, it's full. At that point, adding additional commitments to other teams requires dropping some other block of work.

A practice such as an ICS has several advantages:

- It makes coordination work visible so teams can actually see why they are less productive than when they work independently.
- It helps teams with workload management.
- It helps build cooperative relationships between feature teams.
- It pushes the coordination load to the people who have the detail information.
- It raises the feature teams' sense of accountability because they decide on the commitment.

Although some might argue that ICS cards are too structured and time consuming (and they *may* become burdensome if they are created for minor items), in practice they reduce overall coordination time and effort. Not using some form of inter-team commitment-accountability agreement would be analogous to eliminating story cards. Story cards create a minimal structure within which product and development team members can execute flexibly and efficiently. ICS cards create a minimal structure within which feature teams can interact in this same way.

Tools

For larger projects, particularly those with far-flung feature teams, supporting tools will also be necessary. These tools fall into general categories: collaboration, development environment, information sharing, and project management. Collaboration tools attempt to bring people together as if they were in the same room—an impossible goal, but one that technology gets better at each year. Collaboration tools include email, discussion groups, teleconferences, instant messaging, and that old standby, the telephone. Newer, Web 2.0 tools for collaboration and project management are built around people and their interactions and have the potential to improve teamwork. Information sharing technology ranges widely—from complex product data management systems for industrial products such as automobiles and electronics to wikis. Agile development has also sparked improvement in software build and integration, testing, and modeling tools. Project management tools, both open source and commercial, have been effective for large, distributed teams.

Assembling the right tool infrastructure for large projects can be a significant task and one that should be started as early as possible—in iteration 0 if not before.

Scaling Out—Distributed Projects

Larger projects require scaling "up" practices and organization, whereas distributed projects require scaling "out" practices and organization. Luckily, many of the techniques used to scale up and out are the same, particularly because larger projects by their very size are usually distributed. First, we should differentiate between distributed projects and outsourced ones. Distributed projects basically have multiple development sites that can span buildings, cities, or countries. Outsourced projects involve multiple legal entities, therefore contracting, contract administration, and dealing with different development infrastructures are added to the team's workload. Obviously projects can be both distributed and outsourced.

But first let's address the fundamental question that everyone asks: "Do agile methods work for distributed projects?" According to a 2008 research study (2,319 completed surveys from 80 countries) conducted by Version One, 57% of all agile projects are distributed, which indicates that a large number of people think the answer to the question is "yes."[7]

> *The fundamental difference between collocated and distributed projects is the difficulty in building relationships.*

Today's collaboration and communications tools are very powerful, such that teams with solid relationships can function very effectively. Those same tools are less effective in building good relationships, although they can help. Some of the factors that complicate building relationships in distributed and outsourced teams include time zone, language, company culture, and country cultural differences. However, these factors are at play in non-agile projects also.

I've worked with a large 600-person development team, located primarily in a single, two-story building in which the collaboration and communication was poor. I've worked with another company, with a 100-person team distributed over five international locations in which there was very effective collaboration and communication. Poor organizational and communications design characterized the first, good design the second. Furthermore, the management of the second company realized that team distribution required spending additional money on face-to-face meetings to build the required relationships.

Many of the practices and tools agilists prescribe for distributed agile projects are the same ones prescribed by non-agilists for traditional projects. So what enables agile approaches to outperform traditional approaches on distributed projects? I think there are two factors that answer this question:

[7] 3rd Annual Survey: 2008, "The State of Agile Development." VersionOne Corporation, 2008.

- The short iterations in agile development force continuous close collaboration and coordination.
- Control of distributed agile projects is better because a releasable product is built each iteration.

Traditional distributed projects get off track because of the overreliance on documentation ("just ship the specifications off to India or China and get someone to code it") and therefore less emphasis on collaboration and coordination. Agile projects emphasize and force tighter collaboration and coordination and therefore help overcome this problem with traditional approaches to distributed development. Secondly, the frequent feedback from running-tested-features (RTF) provides much better project control than traditional projects in which proof that software is working comes near the end of a project. Figure 11-8 shows a summary of distributed agile guidelines.

Figure 11-8
Distributed Agile
Guidelines

Distributed Agile Guidelines

- Agile methods not only work on distributed projects, they produce better results than traditional methods.
- The problems with distributed teams are similar no matter what methods are used. Relationship building, especially when time zones, languages, infrastructures, and cultures are different is difficult.
- The principles, practices, and tools used for distributed projects are the nearly the same as those for large projects. The primary difference is that organizational design (organization, decision making, collaboration/ coordination) have additional cost issues (e.g. face-to-face meetings are more expensive).
- Distributed projects tend to have additional testing cycles.
- Don't attribute the general difficulties with distributed projects as being agile issues. Many difficulties apply equally regardless of methodology.

Final Thoughts

Although this chapter has a number of organizational and product practices for scaling agile methods to larger projects, the fundamental question remains—do agile principles apply to large or distributed projects? For large/distributed projects, is it more important to deliver value or to meet constraints? For large/distributed projects, is it more important to lead teams or to manage tasks? For large/distributed projects, is adapting to change more important than conforming to plans? To me, the unequivocal answer to all three questions is "yes." The question is not, "Can agile methods work with large/distributed projects?" but, "How do we adapt agile methods to work on large/distributed projects?"

All the enhanced practices and tools in this chapter can be accommodated within the APM framework. Agile principles still apply. The need for self-organizing, self-disciplined teams still applies. Short, story-based iterative development still applies, as does the need for frequent, comprehensive feedback and adaptive adjustments. Scaling to larger projects requires additional thought, and practices, for both people and product. ICS cards provide one mechanism for scaling the self-organizing practices of single teams to teams of teams. Capability-level planning and reporting (using a parking lot graphic) provide a mechanism for scaling story-based planning to larger projects. Project leaders will bring other practices to bear on larger projects, some taken from traditional approaches.

Large agile teams will not be as nimble as small ones, but then they probably don't need to be. They just need to fulfill the fundamental purposes of APM—delivering valuable products to customers and creating satisfying work environments.

Chapter 12

Governing Agile Projects

Agile development began its evolution at the team level, first appealing to software developers, and as successful projects emerged from these teams, managers and executives began to notice. Since then the agile movement has expanded, and the growing visibility of agile methods has created a new set of challenges—or opportunities depending on your viewpoint. The main challenge: How do we move from agile projects to agile organizations? This challenge generates questions from senior executives ranging from how to measure success to how iterative development can be managed alongside traditional life cycle projects. Executives want to know how agile methods impact them directly and which implementation details that they need to worry about.

The concepts and practices behind agile methods are not limited to development teams, so executives need to understand how agile development impacts their organizations, project portfolios, and overall project governance. Referring to the Agile Enterprise Framework (Chapter 5, Figure 5-1) this chapter will concentrate on Portfolio Governance—how executives monitor projects within the context of their entire project portfolio. The top level in this framework might be called Portfolio Management, but the entirety of that subject is outside the scope of this book. The discussion in this chapter covers three portfolio management topics: Portfolio Governance (the primary topic), methodological "fit" for projects, and "chunking" at a portfolio level.

Portfolio Governance

As agile methods (for both hardware and software products) become widespread in organizations, the debate over serial, waterfall life cycles versus iterative life cycles is moving from an engineering-level to an executive-level discussion.

> *In terms of project governance, executives are interested in two things—investment and risk.*

Fundamentally, governance is about making investment decisions in an environment of uncertainty. Executives have to make investment decisions, defined in terms of return on investment (ROI), and assess the probability attaining that ROI. ROI includes three components—value produced (inflows of money), costs expended (outflows of money), and time (timing of inflows and outflows). Executives have to answer two basic questions: What is the projected value or return on investment? What is the probability that this return can be achieved? Investment decisions are linear: Spend some money, receive some results, decide on the next investment increment. Dollars and time are not iterative: When they are spent, they are gone.

Operational delivery is about defining the best methods of delivering project results. Engineering, whatever the product, is inherently iterative—think a little, try an experiment, observe the results, revise. Sometimes the iterations are long, sometimes short, but engineers have never really operated on a linear, waterfall model—unless forced to by an organization process. When development was sequential, the need to differentiate between governance and operations was masked. However, as organizations began to implement iterative methods, the disconnect between governance and operations began to cause a friction between executives and project teams.

> *The critical issues for organizations, then, is bridging this seeming gap between linear investment decisions and iterative/agile product development. The solution is separating governance from operations and then loosely coupling them—abandoning the tight coupling that led to the trouble in the first place.*

Governance is, or should be, separate from operations—although they are definitely linked. Operational delivery is about assembling the best set of methodologies, processes, practices, and people to deliver results. Although the governance framework should be common to all projects within an organization, the operational delivery approach should be matched to project type. It is important to note that executives play a vital role in both the operational delivery of products and in governance. Separating governance from operations doesn't negate the executive role in each.

Investment and Risk

Product development balances opportunity and risk—the opportunity to generate significant ROI, balanced with the probability that something will intervene to undermine the opportunity. That a huge percentage of new product development (NPD) projects fail speaks to its difficulty. Executives use various information to make project funding decisions. Some known information can be assembled into planning documents, but the crux of product development rests on discovering the unknowns, the solutions to problems that have yet to be identified.

There are two fundamentally different types of projects (although there are many variations)—production and exploration. Production projects are characterized by a known problem and a known solution. For production projects, because the solution is known, careful planning can reduce much of the project's risk. Exploration projects are very different. They are characterized by unknowns—there is a known problem and an unknown solution, a unknown problem and a known solution, or an unknown problem and an unknown solution. Both ends (the objective or problem) and the means (solution) can have significant uncertainties associated with them (as encompassed in the exploration factor discussion in Chapter 6, "The Envision Phase"). For example, just because we can specify the problem doesn't mean we can design a solution. As an extreme example, imagine that plans for a new spacecraft specifies a top speed of 195,000 miles/sec. Because this specification exceeds the speed of light, coming up with a solution may be tricky. We might be reluctant to commit $14 billion to this project, no matter how high the projected returns, until we found a way to overcome this design problem.

> *For exploration projects, specifying detailed requirements won't reduce serious risks. Only exploration into the problem space reduces these risks. Exploration may take the form of simulations, models, prototypes, engineering breadboards, feature builds (for software), or in some cases scientific or engineering investigations. For these types of risks, months of planning and product specifying contribute mightily to cost, but little to reducing risk.*

As another example, postulate that product management in an electronics company decided that the next version of their product needed to be 50% smaller in size. Further assume that the 50% size reduction was both a critical requirement for the new product and that the engineers were concerned about meeting the size constraint with a cost that had acceptable gross margins. Solving the design issue would be critical to the continued viability of the project. A significant amount of engineering and prototyping would be needed to answer the design question. Action, not planning, produces information when problems are known but solutions aren't. So the decision might be to conduct a proof-of-concept phase for the project in which the engineers would try to solve the design problem by building prototypes or doing simulations. Other parts of the project would be delayed until this key question had been answered.

For such a project, executives might authorize a $100,000 expenditure for a concept phase to gather enough information to reduce the risk of making a five million dollar full product development decision. Executive decision making follows this scenario through the various phases—define an information gathering strategy based on key risks areas, then decide which activities to fund based on mitigating those risks as early and with as little expenditure as possible. From an executive perspective, this model is serial—spend money and time, obtain information, decide on continuing the project.

However, from an engineering perspective, a linear model doesn't serve well. In the electronics example, a serial model would have focused initially on specifying the requirements for the entire product in detail. At the end of this requirements phase (at which point possibly 20–25% of the cost would be expended), the executives would have relatively complete (in theory) information on the product's requirements, but no information on the critical size design issue. After expending $900,000, they wouldn't have reduced the key risk. The team that actually did some design work, constructed a prototype, and tested it might find the key problem was in testing—electrical interference from a component that they hadn't suspected. In a serial project, the team might not have discovered this critical issue until 80% or 90% of the project had been completed and would probably cause significant delays. By developing an iterative prototype, the problem was uncovered 10% of the way through the project for $100,000 and did not cause a project delay.

The funding model for projects should focus on what executives need to carry out their oversight and fiduciary responsibilities. They need a systematic way to view information gathered at key intervals to make the best investment decisions based on their understanding of the risks involved. These intervals are defined by phases (the period when work occurs) and gates (when decisions are made). For each gate the key decisions, decision makers, and information required to make the decisions are defined. Gate reviews aren't about deliverable check-offs; they are about providing executives and managers with relevant information to make decisions about continued funding and acceptable risk.

Executive-Level Information Requirements

Figure 12-1 shows a desirable progression in information gathering across a project of three phases. (The first set of figures on the graph is pre-project and we won't bother to name the phases at this point because they are irrelevant.)[1] Let's first look at the progression from an executive perspective. Prior to the project, the risk factor is high at 100 (on a relative scale), whereas the investment, architecture, and features delivered are at 0%. This makes sense because prior to the project no risks have been mitigated, no planning has been done, no costs have been incurred, nothing has been built. The customers may have some ideas about target features and desired schedule, but that is all pure speculation at this point.

---

[1] Even though the progression in this example is desirable, every project has a different profile. For certain projects a significant amount of money might be spent before the risk can be significantly reduced.

Figure 12-1
Managing Product
Life Cycle Investment
and Risk

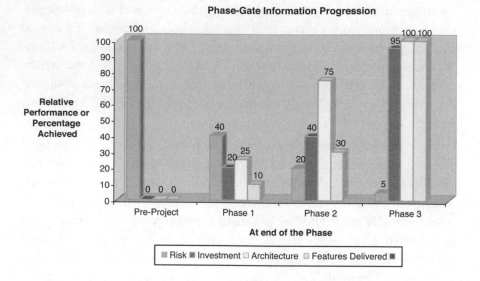

Phase-Gate Information Progression

Relative Performance or Percentage Achieved

At end of the Phase

■ Risk ■ Investment □ Architecture □ Features Delivered ■

So what would executives like out of a first phase? Basically, they would like to spend as little money as possible to reduce the risks (not just identify them but actually reduce them) and gain a better understanding of the project's feasibility. The results of Phase 1 in Figure 12-1 indicate that this executive goal was achieved. The project risk has been reduced from 100 to 40 (for example, three critical high-risk items have been mitigated by building engineering breadboards and actual development of the software features required for the breadboard), 20% of the cost has been expended, 25% of the architecture (a skeleton architecture) has been defined, and 10% of the actual product features have been built, tested, and reviewed with the customer. Of all these accomplishments, the fact that high-risk elements have been mitigated by building and reviewing actual product features is a critically important component of the information gathered.

During Phase 2, even more progress was made. For expending 40% of the cost, the risk factor has been reduced to 20 (some of the lower impact risks are still left), 75% of the architecture is in place, and 30% of the product has actually been built. Although some executives might be concerned that for 40% of the cost only 30% of the product has actually been built, the key is that the risk and uncertainty have been driven down to a point that the remaining expenditure has an extremely high probability of delivering a releasable product on time, plus much of the architecture work was completed.

During Phase 3, the product was completed, but some small amount of risk, uncertainty, and cost remain for final product deployment. During Phase 3 the bulk of the work was reasonably well understood—no critical design problems were deferred to this phase. The risk of Phase 3 failing was very small, and yet 60% of the cost was incurred during this phase—a very appealing prospect to executives.

This three-phase example could be construed as an incremental funding model, but in reality, every project has incremental funding. Even in a waterfall project, executives retain the ability to cancel the project at the end of any phase. The difference in the agile approach is that it produces incremental product, not just documents from activities (planning, architectural definition, requirements definition, etc.). The focus of agile development is on systematically delivering high-value product features and reducing risks—exactly what executives are looking for.

As a final example, a client was building an application to support a well understood accounting process. However, the entire architecture of the application was changing from a Cobol, DB2, mainframe-based system to a multi-tiered web architecture, C#, SQL Server environment. This project had a relatively stable and knowable set of business requirements, but a risky technology implementation because it was new to the staff. In a waterfall approach, the team might spend 20% of the cost to gather and document the requirements. However, this would have little impact on reducing the risk and uncertainty of the project. This client's approach was to take a couple of small business features and go through all the activities to implement them across the entire architecture. The team was able to do this for 5% of the cost, learn the ins and outs of the technology, and thereby significantly reduce the risk factors.

Engineering-Level Information Generation

As you saw in Figure 12-1, managing projects might be simply defined as buying information. The critical success factor is buying the right information for the right price. As you have also seen, spending lots of money for planning and requirements documents, in contrast to spending money for working products or software, is rarely investment/risk–efficient.

Figure 12-2 shows the traditional waterfall phase-gate process. Using this model, the governance and operational models are the same—both linear. The phases are broken down into activities and the entire process takes on a very linear character.

> *A waterfall approach assumes (implicitly) that completing the requirements phase reduces the most risk—an unlikely scenario for most projects.*

Figure 12-2
Traditional Waterfall
Phase-Gate Model

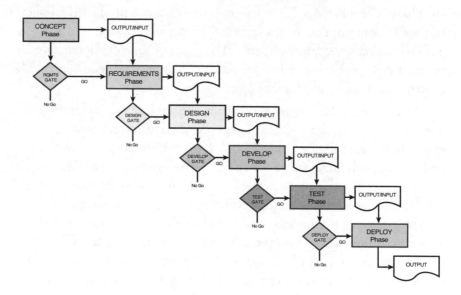

Figure 12-3 shows another phase-gate progression in which the governance and operational models are separated—an executive perspective at the top and an engineering perspective at the bottom. The executive perspective is a series of linear phases, in which work is accomplished, and decision gates, at which continuation decisions are made. The development perspective is a series of iterative planning (Envision) and iterative delivery (Explore) cycles. Figure 12-4 shows how planning, development, review, and even deployment operational iterations can be used in every governance phase.

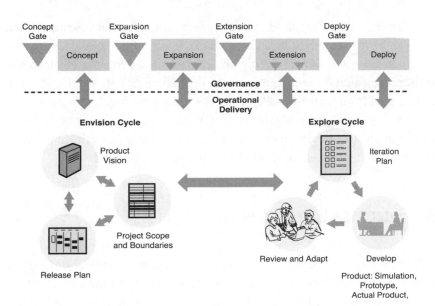

Figure 12-3
Connecting a Linear Governance Model with an Iterative Development Model

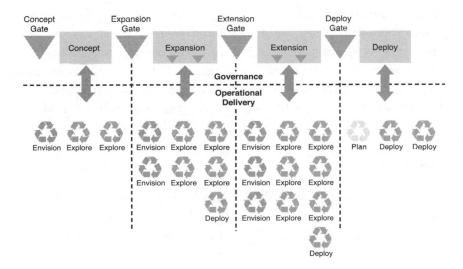

Figure 12-4
Multiple Iterations within Each Phase

The software development community uses the term "loose coupling" in design to indicate that two modules operate together, but that they are independent and therefore can be easily modified independently—linked, but not integrated. Project governance and operational delivery should be viewed in the same fashion—linked, but independent.

Phase-gate funding models can promote the idea that investment and risk can be managed best by a linear model, while at the same time promoting an iterative model for operational delivery. Agile projects, which consist of iterative Envision and Explore cycles, produce exactly what executives are looking for to make funding decisions. By separating, but linking, a linear funding model with an agile development model, the needs of engineers for an innovative development process and executives for critical information to make investment and risk decisions are both fulfilled.

An Enterprise-Level Governance Model

In the last section a generic phase-gate life cycle was shown, but for most companies a little more definition than Phase 1-2-3 is required. If we are going to decouple a linear funding model from an iterative development model, then we should use phase names that do not reflect activities (requirements, design, construction), but investment and risk mitigation phases. Figures 12-3 and 12-4 show a four-phase life cycle that can serve as a high-level governance model that will work with multiple operational-level delivery methods. The four phases are Concept, Expansion, Extension, and Deployment (which is somewhat activity based).[2, 3] The objectives of each of these phases should follow the information progression outlined in Figure 12-1.

Concept Phase

No projects, even agile ones, should start instantly, but they should start quickly. The Concept phase has two overriding objectives—to create and confirm the vision for the product and to identify and mitigate risk. The

[2] The Rational Unified Process uses a similar phase progression—Inception, Elaboration, Construction, and Transition. However, the phases are not defined in the same investment/risk language, the "Construction" phase title detracts from the underlying iterative nature of RUP, and the Inception phase doesn't emphasize risk mitigation but is more focused on risk identification.

[3] For long projects, the Expansion and Extension phases could be further broken down into 3–6 month sub-phases.

vision may contain product, marketing, financial, and team components. Risk areas include marketing (can we sell it?), technical (can we build it?), and financial (can we make money with it?). The Concept phase can be considered a proof-of-concept endeavor, not just a feasibility study or risk identification activity.

> *Experience with clients convinces me that often an iteration 0 isn't enough and that in fact many projects, especially those characterized by large size, high risk, and uncertainty, need a Concept phase.*

The Concept phase includes work identified earlier in iteration 0 such as capability-level requirements, development environment preparation, and architectural sketching. The Concept phase consists of an iteration 0 (no actual stories delivered), and a few short development iterations (stories delivered). Helping a client launch several complex medical instrument projects (hardware and software) in which high-risk research ideas were crossing from the lab into engineering convinced me of the need for a Concept phase.

The goal of the Concept phase is to identify—AND mitigate—enough high-risk and uncertain items to make it possible to realistically plan the rest of the project. Often a full release plan can't be done until the Concept Phase is completed—there are just too many unknowns.

The Concept phase is far more than a traditional feasibility phase—it should demonstrate proof of the concept, not merely analyze finances as in most feasibility documents. Many methodologies use a concept-like phase to identify risks, but what I learned from the hardware developers is *to use this phase for actual risk reduction, not just identification*. On these projects there were so many unknowns and uncertainties, many of which were design issues, there was no way to do an overall project plan in the beginning (for some of these hardware projects the Concept phase was six months or more because they were bringing ideas out of the research lab and trying to determine whether they really could productize them). The Concept phase is a mini-project—a planning cycle of visioning–scoping–release planning (for a few iterations) and a delivery cycle of iteration planning–developing features–adapting. It is a mini-project to gather enough information about the full project to determine whether or not to proceed.

An example of using a Concept phase was for a software company project, a 12-month effort that incorporated a new product architecture (early 1990's era architecture and language to Java, n-tier web architecture), a new development environment, and a new agile methodology. There were so many unknowns the team had little basis on which to create a release plan for the entire project. The Concept phase (shown in Figure 12-5) was one month. Iteration 0 was a two-week period for developing the architecture, getting the development environment set up, doing several technology and customer investigations, and delving into the old system to extract complex business logic, and so on. In the second two-week iteration, the team developed several "stories" front to back to exercise the entire architecture, as well as to define requirements for another part of the system (at a high level so the team could create story cards and estimate the work). At the end of the Concept phase the team had enough additional information and experience in actually building a piece of the application that they could create a reasonable Release Plan for the rest of the project. This Concept phase was short—one month—but the results were appreciated by both management and the development team.

Figure 12-5
An Example of a Concept Phase of Two Two-Week Iterations

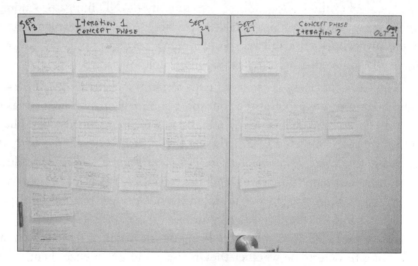

Starting a project requires more than planning and paperwork; it should include enough actual development work to reduce the areas of highest risk and uncertainty.

Expansion Phase

Expansion means just that—expanding on the work done in the Concept phase, specifically expanding to areas of lesser risk than those covered in the first phase. For example, if the highest risk item was proving that all the technology worked together and that it was adequately addressed in the Concept phase, then the Expansion phase might focus on broad capability implementation to confirm that the project's scope was well understood. The objectives of the Expansion phase should be to drive out remaining risk items from the project and build high-value features.

By the end of the Expansion phase executive management should expect the completion of the project with few surprises. There will always be projects in which there remains final integration and use risks, but teams should make every effort to drive out absolutely as much risk as possible before transitioning to the Extension phase.

Extension Phase

The objective of the Extension phase should be to do more of what we already know how to do. There should not be many, if any, surprises in this phase, even though up to a half of the total budget might be expended in this phase.

Deployment Phase

As with nearly every life cycle process model, the Deployment phase is where the product is deployed into actual use. The Deployment phase could be the "final" deployment as many agile/iterative projects deploy incremental pieces of the product.

Gates

> *Most organizations spend far too much time defining phases and processes when the time would be much better spent thinking about decision gates and the information needed to pass those gates.*

Although most development life cycle approaches concentrate on phases, focusing on gates is more effective. Gates are critical decision points in a project when the team reports information and the executive review team considers whether or not to invest in the next phase. At any phase the decision may be to pass the project into the next phase, revisit the prior phase to gather more information or further reduce risk, or to terminate the project. For example, at the Extension gate (transitioning from the Expansion to Extension phases) the types of questions that the executives should be asking are

- Have all the significant risk items (marketing, technology, financial) been mitigated through the delivery of working features and other investigations?
- Has the product architecture stabilized?

At the Expansion gate the questions might include

- To what extent have the highest risk items (marketing, technology, financial) been mitigated through the development of architectural spikes, delivery of working features, and other investigations?
- Has the work on a skeleton architecture and any development spikes convinced us that the project is technically feasible and will operate within required performance specifications?
- Can the Expansion phase be estimated with a reasonable degree of confidence in having a releasable, quality product?
- Are the estimates for the entire project still within its constraints?

Using the Agile Governance Model

Organizations have three options in using the Agile Governance Model: 1) Don't use it, 2) Use the Concept phase, 3) Use the entire model. For many organizations, especially those with smaller projects or limited product lines, not using any of the phase-gate model may be the appropriate course of action. In these organizations, probably those on the smaller end of the size scale, in which all teams are using the same agile methods, using an iteration 0 and the standard project control reports may be completely adequate.

However, even if your organization doesn't need the entire model, using a concept phase, even for small projects, can be very beneficial. There are cases, like the one illustrated in Figure 12-5, where the technical or requirements uncertainty (or both) is high enough that developing a release plan is just not feasible. In many of these cases, a one- or two-month concept phase can significantly reduce uncertainty and provide greater confidence in the release plan when it is prepared.

Finally, in large organizations, particularly those with large projects, projects being developed with a variety of methodologies, and those that use stricter financial controls on project portfolios, using the full agile phase-gate model can be beneficial. However, as mentioned earlier, implementing such a model should be done with the agile principle of simplicity in mind—don't introduce unnecessary bureaucracy into the organization.

Portfolio Management Topics

Although the majority of this chapter focused on portfolio governance, two additional portfolio topics are introduced here. However, as discussed in the introduction, these are only two of the many topics required for a complete look at agile portfolio management.

Designing an Agile Portfolio

The biggest potential change to portfolio management mirrors the change to project management—small chunks and short iterations. If we look at agile project management, the benefits over a serial approach are

- *Demonstrable results*—Every couple of weeks stories are developed, implemented, tested, and accepted.
- *Customer feedback*—At each iteration customers and product managers review stories and provide feedback.
- *Better release planning*—Planning, both release and iteration, is more realistic because it is based on continuously evaluated actual results.

- *Flexibility*—Projects can be steered toward changing business goals and higher-value stories because changes are easy to incorporate at the end of each iteration.
- *Productivity*—There is a hidden productivity improvement with agile methods from the work not done. Through constant negotiation at every level, features are both eliminated and pared down.

When applying agile practices at the portfolio level, similar benefits accrue:

- *Demonstrable results*—Every quarter or so products, or at least deployable pieces of products, are developed, implemented, tested, and accepted. Short projects deliver chunks of functionality incrementally.
- *Customer feedback*—Each quarter product managers review results and provide feedback, and executives can view progress in terms of working products.
- *Better portfolio planning*—Portfolio planning is more realistic because it is based on deployed whole or partial products.
- *Flexibility*—Portfolios can be steered toward changing business goals and higher-value projects because changes are easy to incorporate at the end of each quarter. Because projects produce working products, partial value is captured rather than being lost completely as usually happens with serial projects that are terminated early.
- *Productivity*—There is a hidden productivity improvement with agile methods from the work not done. Through constant negotiation, small projects are both eliminated and pared down.

With this portfolio planning approach, large multi-month projects can be developed in 3–6 month "waves" in which each wave delivers a usable portion of the application. Flexibility, earlier ROI, increased productivity, and better customer response can be generated by these improvements in portfolio management just as they are in agile project management.

> *"Simply put, Project Chunking involves taking larger projects and breaking them down into smaller bundles that reduce risk, realize benefits sooner, and increase flexibility by providing more choice points." Chunking helps 'respond to uncertainty and velocity by building choice points an delivering value more quickly.' Cathleen Benko and Warren McFarlan (Benko 2003).*

Agile Methodology "Fit"

In a large organization, not every project will be agile. Determining what projects do fit an agile profile, and how agile practices should be adapted for different types of projects, is an important portfolio management topic. There are a number of models for selecting a methodology or set of practices to match a specific project. In his Crystal series of methodologies, Alistair Cockburn (2006) identifies a range of methodologies—clear, yellow, orange —that are determined by size, criticality, and other factors. In *Effective Project Management*, Bob Wysocki (2003) identifies uncertainty as the key factor in determining whether a traditional, adaptive, or extreme project management model fits best. Todd Little (Pixton, Little, Nickolaisen and McDonald 2009) from Landmark Graphics uses a quadrant analysis (in which the axes are uncertainty and complexity) to match project type with approach. Frameworks that included organizational culture were presented in Highsmith (2002) and Boehm and Turner (2004).

In examining all these approaches, there are three critical elements in determining methodology fit:

- Project factors (complexity and uncertainty)
- Cultural factors
- Governance and compliance factors.

For project factors, which should dominate methodology selection, I like Todd Little's model (introduced in Chapter 11, "Scaling Agile Products"). In this model, complexity factors include team size, team distribution, mission criticality, and domain knowledge gaps, whereas uncertainty factors include market uncertainty, technical uncertainty, and project duration. Each factor has a 1–10 value, and then all factors are combined and used to plot projects to a quadrant.

> *Managing increasing uncertainty is best accomplished by agile, flexible practices, whereas managing complexity requires additional structure. The most difficult projects are those that have high uncertainty, requiring greater agility, and high complexity that requires additional structure. Finding project leaders who can handle both agility and structure is a challenge.*

The second aspect of methodology fit has to do with culture.[4] Highly uncertain projects are best handled by organizations with agile, flexible, collaborative cultures. Organizations with very structured, conformance-to-plan cultures will have difficulties with highly uncertain projects. Similarly, a very low formality, flexible, ad hoc culture may have difficulty with highly complex projects.

As organizations look at their project portfolios, they first need to look at project type and determine the best approach based on the requirements of the project. They then need to assess their culture to see whether it fits. Unfortunately, many companies are unwilling to face this second aspect of fit: They try to impose a single methodology on a multitude of project types and cultures. Splitting project governance from operational delivery will help organizations address this issue by enabling them to create a single governance model fed by multiple operational models.

The third aspect of methodology selection is governance and compliance factors. The biggest mistake organizations make is letting governance and compliance factors drive the development process rather than figuring out the best development process and then adding practices for compliance. For example, several years ago a company that produced medical software felt that FDA compliance dictated a waterfall lifecycle. After some discussion, they figured out how an iterative lifecycle was both best for their development and could satisfy the compliance requirements.[5]

Governance and compliance factors are part of the cost of doing business today. They are important and necessary (at least some of them are), but they should not drive the engineering processes. Engineering practices are

---

[4] More details on cultural fit can be found in Chapter 24 of Highsmith, *Agile Software Development Ecosystems* (2002).

[5] I've worked with AgileTek, a Chicago consulting firm that specializes in agile development projects with FDA-regulated medical and pharmaceutical companies.

the ones that deliver customer value. Compliance and governance processes add cost—a necessary cost of doing business, but a cost nonetheless. Focusing on engineering practices, streamlining them as much as possible, and freeing them from compliance work should be the winning strategy. Offloading as much compliance and governance work from the team as possible helps deliver value and meet compliance demands in the most efficient and effective way.

These "methodology" fit factors should be used as a guide in determining what type of method to use on a project, but they may also have a greater use in developing hybrid methodologies to use on multiple types of projects. If we look at all the levels—project governance, project management, iteration management, and technical practices—and different sizes and distribution of projects, then the range of useful practices—both agile and traditional—is very wide. The factors discussed in this section can help managers and teams adapt practices to their project at hand.

Final Thoughts

Project leaders and customers, and even middle managers, look primarily at project results based on the agile triangle—value, quality, and constraints. Executives who are reviewing projects tend to look at investment and risk profiles. This isn't to imply that customers don't look at risk or that executives don't look at quality, but each tends to have a primary focus. Managing a project on a weekly and monthly basis is different than managing a portfolio of projects on a quarterly basis.

This chapter explores two key points. First, the operational delivery approach to projects needs to be separated from the governance approach. Second, the governance approach should focus on investment and risk information, not delivery activities. Separating these layers enables organizations to better integrate agile projects into their wide portfolio of projects, some of which may not use agile methods.

Chapter 13

Beyond Scope, Schedule, and Cost: Measuring Agile Performance

Chapter 13 is for the agile executive and manager. Over the decade of 2000–2009 there have been thousands of very successful agile projects. There have been far, far fewer successful agile organizations. Although agile project success has become nearly routine, these agile teams are often at odds with other parts of their organizations. An agile organizational transformation requires work in six areas: organization, process, performance measurement, alignment (business and technical), governance, and culture. Of these six, performance measurement is key because it becomes the feedback mechanism for the others.

Agile organizations must adhere to the same values as agile teams:

- Delivering value over meeting constraints
- Leading the team over managing tasks
- Adapting to change over conforming to plans

Executives and managers need to lead their organizations in living these values and taking actions based on them—and one of the critical areas on which they need to take action is measuring performance in ways that encourage their organizations to embrace agility.

Chapter 1 introduced the Agile Triangle (see Figure 13-1) as a replacement for the traditional Iron Triangle of project management. If an agile leader focuses on *adapting successfully to inevitable changes* rather than following *the plan with minimal changes*, then measuring success by strictly adhering to a scope, schedule, and cost plan will be dysfunctional. Agile teams and agile organizations need a new triangle, the Agile Triangle, whose dimensions are, as previously stated,

- *Value goal*: Build a releasable product
- *Quality goal*: Build a reliable, adaptable product
- *Constraints goal*: Achieve value and quality within acceptable constraints

Figure 13-1
The Agile Triangle

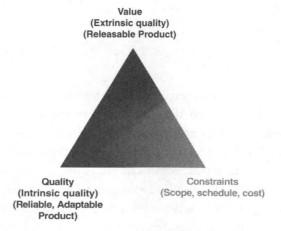

Value
(Extrinsic quality)
(Releasable Product)

Quality
(Intrinsic quality)
(Reliable, Adaptable
Product)

Constraints
(Scope, schedule, cost)

If agile values are key to success, then we need to find measurement systems that support these values, and current constraint-oriented measurement systems don't. To illustrate how current performance measurements don't guide organizations in the right direction, Bjarte Bogsnes, in *Implementing Beyond Budgeting* (Bognes 2009) asks a simple question, "What is the best performance (if high is good): delivering 100 against a target of 100, or delivering 105 against a target of 110?" Most people would agree that 105 is better than 100, however most performance measurement systems would call 105 against a 110 target a failure—a failure to achieve plan. Bogsnes also highlights the boxed quote from Aristotle that illuminates this problem with how success is measured.

> *Our problem is not that we aim too high and miss, but that we aim too low and hit. —Aristotle*

This chapter builds the rationale for a new way of measuring success—an Adaptive Performance Management System—by looking at problems with current measures, agile alternatives, and begins with a discussion of the nature of quality.

What Is Quality?

Customer quality (which is extrinsic or external) delivers value in the short term. Technical quality (which is intrinsic or internal) enables continuous delivery of value over time. Poor quality work results in unreliable products, but more critically, it results in products that are far less responsive to future customer needs. There are software companies beginning to build new business models (see the Hyper-development and Release section in Chapter 8, "Advanced Release Planning") around truly understanding extrinsic and intrinsic quality.

> *How many people go to work each Monday morning determined to perform poor quality work?*

This boxed question seems silly for those who pride themselves on delivering a high-quality product, but although most people voice a belief and conviction about quality, they often spend far too little time discussing what quality means to them within their team.

Robert Pirsig delved into the quixotic nature of quality in the 1970's: "Quality is the continuing stimulus which causes us to create the world in which we live." "Quality...you know what it is, yet you don't know what it is." One philosophical definition, one practical. Or even more insightful, "You take your analytic knife, put the point directly on the term Quality and just tap, not hard, gently, and the whole world splits, cleaves, right in two—hip and square, classic and romantic, technological and humanistic—and the split is clean" (Robert Pirsig, *Zen and the Art of Motorcycle Maintenance*, 1974).

The fundamental dichotomy, and definitional dilemma, articulated by Pirsig is whether quality is intrinsic or extrinsic. Years ago I used a workshop exercise in which teams were given a set of requirements and asked to build a house of cards. Teams got points for height, surface area, ability to hold an object without collapsing, schedule, and so on. Finally, the instructor (me) awarded points for esthetics. Every team complained about the esthetics scores! They felt that they were arbitrary and capricious—and they were. But it emphasized the point that part of quality was in the eye of the beholder (extrinsic), while another was internal (that usually sought by engineers).

The first principle in the Declaration of Interdependence states, "We increase return on investment by making continuous flow of value our focus." Flow of value means delivering value early and often during the initial development process (iterations) and then periodically over the life of the product (future releases).

The Agile Manifesto is written in the form "X over Y," for example "Individuals and interactions over processes and tools." This statement doesn't say that processes and tools are unimportant, but that individual and interactions are more important. Likewise, it's not that scope, schedule, and cost are unimportant, but that they are less important than business value and quality. The preponderance of today's measurement approaches say, either implicitly or explicitly, "Scope, schedule, and cost are more important than business value and quality."

> *A crucial problem with software is that we often let intrinsic quality slide to meet schedule or scope or cost demands. The customer may be satisfied—today, but over time customer satisfaction decreases as drastically as technical debt increases. The ability to deliver value over time can be directly linked to intrinsic quality.*

Why is technical (intrinsic) quality so important? Intrinsic quality has two components: reliability (correct functioning) and adaptability. First, does the software operate correctly (correct functioning is different from correct functionality, which is extrinsic quality) and second, is the software adaptable—does it deliver value today, and tomorrow?

Capers Jones' widely heralded book on software measurement concluded that "a cumulative defect removal rate of 95% on a project appears to be a nodal point where several other benefits accrue" (Jones 2008). For projects of similar size and type, these projects have the shortest schedules, have the lowest quantity of effort in terms of person-months, and have the highest levels of user satisfaction after release. Recent studies of agile organizations by Michael Mah have reached similar conclusions about the benefits of focusing on quality (Mah 2008).

The problem faced in many organizations is the mistaken idea that delivering high-quality software takes more time. In fact, as Jones' and Mah's data show (and agile teams experience), very high levels of quality actually act as development accelerators. A secondary problem is that technical debt caused by intrinsic quality problems may take several years to become significant. However, when these problems begin to manifest themselves, the problem increases exponentially, as was shown in Figure 9-7. Organizations think they are okay cutting quality corners because it doesn't catch up with them immediately, but when it does, the problem is often severe and expensive to fix. Nine-month release cycles become 10-month release cycles become 12, then 16, then…. Product managers focus on new features, and the lengthening product release cycles are blamed on decreasing development performance, not increasing product technical debt for which they have some responsibility.

Agile developers and testers know that reducing technical debt (increasing intrinsic quality) is important. Three intrinsic quality factors—the impact of code quality on testing time, error location dynamics, and error feedback ratio—can help explain technical debt.

Many people estimate testing time incorrectly—mostly because they don't understand testing. The rough guideline they may use is something like, "Well, it took five days to code it; I guess it will take about three days to test it." Although this rough estimate may work at times, testing time, in general, is not a function of coding time but of defect density. For example, as illustrated in Figure 13-2, take a coding effort that takes four developers 10 days and they produce four KLOC (thousand lines of code). Assuming a half day to find and fix a defect, the testing time for a team that produces a module with one defect per KLOC (an achievable level) is two days. Code produced that had 15 defects per KLOC (very possible with a team that does minimal unit testing nor any automated testing) would require 30 days of testing time!

> *High–defect density code can easily take 10–15 times longer to test. Because few project plans allow that much time, buggy software is the result.*

Figure 13-2
The Impact of Code Quality on Testing

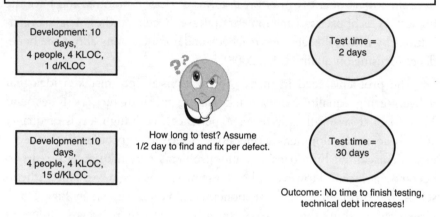

Development: 10 days, 4 people, 4 KLOC, 1 d/KLOC

How long to test? Assume 1/2 day to find and fix per defect.

Test time = 2 days

Development: 10 days, 4 people, 4 KLOC, 15 d/KLOC

Test time = 30 days

Outcome: No time to finish testing, technical debt increases!

Many development teams, and many managers, wonder why testing takes so long—and blame the testing team (the coding team made their freeze date!). But the greatest impact on testing time may not be testing team's perform-ance, but the development team's high defect density code.

A second testing issue is error-location dynamics. A number of years ago a large computer manufacturer did some studies of the time it took to find errors in software. The curve goes from 1–2 hours to find easier defects to over 50 hours for a small percentage of hard to find defects. Years ago, in one major airline reservation system, it took over six months to find a bug that brought both primary and secondary systems down. These hard-to-find bugs can be very disruptive because the emergencies they cause usually result in frantic activity to fix. One question this raises for testing is, "How much money can you spend looking for unfound defects?" The answers for a computer game and the space shuttle's avionics software would be much different. The agile practice of refactoring (both code and tests) can signifi-cantly decrease the percentage of hard-to-find bugs by improving code design, thereby reducing testing time. There will always be a curve of harder-to-find bugs, but the shape of the curve can be greatly altered if quality code is produced.

The final testing factor to explore is the error-feedback ratio, which is the number of new defects injected when fixing existing defects (e.g., 20 new defects generated in fixing 100 defects would be an error-feedback ratio of 20%). Several years ago Jerry Weinberg conducted studies on error-feedback ratio and found that a 20% difference in feedback ratio led to an 88% difference in completion time (bad enough), but the next 10% increase led to a 112% increase (Weinberg 1992).

Have you ever worked on a project in which the code never seemed to stabilize, no matter how much testing was done? If the code has a high defect density to begin with, then it will probably have a high error-feedback ratio also. Low-quality code also has worse error-location dynamics. These three factors (high defect density, lengthy error location curves, and high error-feedback ratios) lead to an inordinate amount of testing—testing that can never, no matter how much testing is done, result in a high-quality code base.

The moral to this whole story is that continuous value generation should be viewed from a product life cycle perspective that includes intrinsic quality. Organizations that focus entirely on customer satisfaction and extrinsic quality often wind up shortchanging intrinsic quality and loose significant "value" over a product's life cycle. Retaining customers over time depends, in part, on adapting to their changing business needs, so focusing on intrinsic quality becomes a key customer retention strategy.

Planning and Measuring

In a Cutter Business-IT Strategies report, Helen Pukszta (2006) reported, "I recently asked a colleague whether he would prefer to deliver a project somewhat late and over budget but rich with business benefits or one that is on time and under budget but of scant value to the business. He thought it was a tough call, and then went for the on-time scenario. Delivering on time and within budget is part of his IT department's performance metrics. Chasing after the elusive business value, over which he thought he had little control anyway, is not."

I once interviewed a project manager whose team's results were considered to be a failure. He had been given two hours to come up with his "project plan," and of course when the actual work was more extensive than he had imagined, the schedule slipped, but the expectations didn't. Subsequent metrics analysis of this project put it in the "above average" category when compared to industry norms for schedule.

The Standish Group's Chaos reports are heralded as verification that the software development community is in a sorry state of affairs and that we must all be unprofessional, undisciplined, and immature. If software is in such a sorry state of affairs, why is software the driving force behind nearly every technology—from the Web to bio-engineering? According to the Chaos reports, in 1994 82% of all projects were "challenged" or "failures." In 2001 we got better—only 72% were "not" successful. How can we reconcile the overwhelming intrusion of software into every nook and cranny of our corporate, governmental, and personal lives with a 72% "not successful" rate? We can't. Maybe it's time we seriously challenged these numbers.[1] I contend that while the Standish reports are NOT a good indicator of poor software development performance, they ARE a good indicator of systemic failure of our planning and measurement methods.

The first thing we need to do is look at the Chaos report's definitions of success and failure. In the reports, the definitions are Successful, in which the project is completed on time and on budget, with all the features and functions originally specified; Challenged, in which the project is completed and operational, but over-budget, late, and with fewer features and functions than initially specified; and Failed, in which the project is canceled before completion, or never implemented.

Why should project cancellation be considered a failure? In a certain number of cases the failure label is appropriate, but in many cases canceling a project becomes the right decision to make—and it's not a failure. Those who never cancel a project never take risks. Those that don't take risks won't survive. This isn't failure, this is good management.

According to the Chaos Report, 28% of projects were successful in their 2000 study. I'm surprised it's that high given that "success" means that time, budget, and scope plans had to be made. This definition of success

[1] Standish Group. *Chaos Reports*
(http://www.standishgroup.com/chaos_resources/chronicles.php).

leaves no room for changing business priorities. What if there is an absolute business priority that a project be delivered by some date and cost overruns are immaterial?

> *If we are ultimately to gain the full range of benefits of agile methods, if we are ultimately to grow truly agile, innovative organizations, then, as these stories show, we will have to alter our performance management systems.*

Having a "system" that leads managers, and others, into valuing "conformance to plan" while delivering "scant business value" will seriously impede agility, whether in projects or the entire enterprise. Conforming to plans is a budget-driven mentality—a mentality in which the budget, or plan, is sacrosanct. Never mind that the plan is months out of date and the competitive situation has changed three times since the plan was developed.

Adaptive Performance—Outcomes and Outputs

To grow an agile organization, we need a new measurement system, an Adaptive Performance Management System (APMS). Essentially, this system has one set of measurements oriented to outcomes—the business value created—and another set of measurements oriented to outputs—productivity, cost, and so on. The difference between these and traditional measurement systems is that on *outcomes* the strong link to quickly outdated plans is broken, and the *output* measures are geared to enabling learning and improvement by measuring relative performance across teams and not performance against a plan. Two key objectives of this APMS are

- To focus any enterprise group (team, project team, department, division, or company) on a set of desired strategic *outcomes*.
- To encourage those groups (project teams) to perform at high levels of *output*.

Measurement Issues

There are three measurement ideas critical to creating an adaptive organization:

- First, we must acknowledge that our performance measurement system impacts agility.
- Second, we must alter our obsession with time to an obsession for outcomes—that is, customer value.
- Third, we must separate the *outcome* performance measurement from the *output* performance measurement.

The business community wants agility, but it also wants stability—it wants certainty. Financial and project management measuring systems have grown up over decades around the concept of stability and certainty—plan the work and work the plan—a performance model that worked fine, or at least adequately, in times of less volatility.

Management wants their organizations to be mobile, agile, flexible, adaptive, but they also want predictability and reliability. Wall Street, in fact, demands predictability in earnings and revenues forecasts. There seems to be a core disconnect here: predictability or agility—pick one. In fact, companies need both, and herein lies the dilemma. The business world requires agility to be successful, but many companies are mired in predictability, in organizational structure, management style, and performance measurement systems. For agile methods to prosper, to extend agility past product teams to the organization as a whole, we first need to acknowledge that how we measure performance impacts agility.

We then have to move from a focus on change management to a focus on adaptation. When we examine a budgeting process that highlights variations from established numbers or a project management process in which deviations are considered mistakes to be corrected we are viewing change negatively. Our literature on change management is overwhelmingly filled with negatives, such as how difficult it is to change an organization's culture or processes. As the definition illustrates, to change is to be different from what we were before, and we resist being different.

Being adaptive creates an entirely different mindset. Adaptation is responding to change to meet some established goal within certain constraints or boundaries. Adaptation is a natural response to our world, to our environment. Evolution itself is an adaptive process. The business environment changes constantly and so we need to measure our response to those changes—our adaptability—to meet our goals within the context of those changes. Our budgeting and project performance management systems were designed to measure "conformance to plan (or budget)," not adaptability. These systems need to change, but not only at the project management level—they need to change throughout the organization.

Managers may be concerned, and this has happened in some organizations, that adaptability will become an excuse for any deviation from plans and all accountability will be lost. Two things should keep that from happening. First, focusing on value delivered through creating a releasable, high-quality product ensures performance from the customer/product management (outcome) perspective. Second, teams will measure against benchmarks (in the next section) so that management can monitor output performance. Adaptability should not become an excuse for poor performance.

When management has rigid expectations, then teams are actually discouraged from being flexible. The narrower the tolerance to variation, the greater the restrictions on adaptive behavior. The wider the tolerance to variation, the less the restrictions on adaptive behavior.[2]

> *The irony in accepting wider tolerances to variation is that performance in all dimensions usually improves! Michael Mah suggested we call this the "Predictability Paradox."*

Ironically, in a volatile environment, the tighter management tries to "control" the results, the more unpredictable they actually become. Conversely, when management can loosen the constraints and give teams the freedom to adapt, reliability has a better chance of happening. The key is focusing on the desired outcomes, not a restrictive plan.

[2] One type of variation can, and should, be reduced, and another can't. For example, better estimating skills can reduce variation given a certain set of information and assumptions, but they can't reduce variations caused by the fundamental uncertainty in the information.

When thinking about the predictability of traditional projects, Michael Mah had an interesting observation on the Standish report numbers that show such a high percentage of projects as failures (scope, schedule, cost variations). "What the Standish numbers might indicate is that at some point managers just ignore the plan because they know it doesn't reflect reality anymore." I would add that team members also begin to ignore plans because they realize how unrealistic and political they are.

The reason for this paradox is that success, particularly today, is a function of a team's ability to react to change, not their ability to plan and follow the plan. Teams' adaptability is a function of how performance is measured. If teams perceive they have wider tolerances in some performance measurement dimensions, it encourages them to be adaptive. If they are adaptive, they will actually have a better chance to meet all the project's objectives and measures.

In *Artful Making*, Rob Austin and Lee Devin (Austin 2003) describe a management style derived from Devin's work as a theater director. Plays evolve as actors learn their roles and interact with each other to create a unique production. Rehearsals are often chaotic and stressful, but one thing is absolutely predictable with a theatre play—it will open on schedule! Being agile and adaptable does not mean being unpredictable, but it does mean that the characteristics we want to predict should be carefully crafted, and furthermore, in a changing, unpredictable environment we need to limit how many characteristics we attempt to predict.

Actually, "predict" is the wrong name for what we are attempting. We are usually working toward a goal (which is a desired outcome, not necessarily a predicted outcome) that is to be achieved within some constraints (by a certain date, for example). With a play, no one sits down and estimates every detail activity, but the theatre season schedule does constrain the date. Budgets and project plans often get in the way of delivering to goals within constraints. They establish a false prediction, because they assume that if we follow the plan we will achieve the goal. In actuality, environmental changes and missed assumptions almost always require adaptation from the plan if there is any chance of the goal being achieved. Adaptation rather than adherence brings success.

Measurement Concepts

In looking for concepts on which to base an adaptive management system, two proved to be particularly useful—beyond budgeting from Jeremy Hope and Robin Fraser, and Rob Austin's views on performance measurement in organizations. Both have a distinctly agile or adaptive perspective, and both deal with measurement systems in general, not just project management.

Beyond Budgeting

In *Beyond Budgeting: How Managers Can Break Free from the Annual Performance Trap,* Jeremy Hope and Robin Fraser (Hope 2003) outline a measurement system, and in fact an adaptive, decentralized management style, that fits with an agile enterprise. Although Hope and Fraser discuss issues far beyond budgeting, they start with the issues surrounding traditional budgeting systems in organizations.

"Budgets have since been hijacked by a generation of financial engineers that have used them as remote control devices to 'manage by the numbers.' They have turned budgets into *fixed performance contracts* that force managers at all levels to commit to delivering specified financial outcomes, even though many of the variables underpinning those outcomes are beyond their control."

I would argue that the generation of "financial engineers" has been paralleled by a generation of "project administrators" who feed on the same ideas and have created a culture of "conformance to plan" performance measurement on projects. Both measurement systems suffer from the same problems:

- They are cumbersome and expensive
- They are out of kilter with the competitive environment
- "Gaming the numbers" is rampant

The budgeting process in many corporations begins six months prior to the year being budgeted for (it assumes annual budgets). The process is expensive and time consuming for every level of management in the organization. Similarly, project plans that involve reams of tasks, milestones, resource allocations, and network diagrams provide, as colleague Ken Orr once quipped, "a vast area of well documented ignorance." We spend time and money on excruciatingly detailed plans based on a fuzzy understanding of the project and significant uncertainty about the future.

> *"Some project leaders figure they have saved 95 percent of the time that used to be spent on budgeting and forecasting." (Hope and Fraser 2003).*

Second, these fixed budgets or plans are out of kilter with the competitive environment because things change and assumptions are invalidated. Hope and Fraser: "It is when the gap between key budget assumptions and emerging reality widens to the point at which the two bear little relation to each other that the problems begin."

> *Fixed targets and an agreed-upon plan may work for low-uncertainty projects and businesses, but for most, "fixed" plans act like a huge anchor on progress—they tie people to the past rather than the future.*

Third, in fixed performance contracts, whether budgets or project plans, "gaming the numbers" is rampant. In budgeting, every manager attempts to set minimum hurdles she will have to rise above to earn a high performance mark. Project plans are subjected to executive whims and project managers therefore try to build in additional time for contingencies.[3] One company reported in IT literature that it was on time, under budget, and met specifications 95% of the time. Is that good? Not if you are trying to innovate—it means you're not taking on enough risk or you are sandbagging on projects. Budgeting and estimating are often hog-tied by politics, and their relationship to real performance remain tenuous at best.

The solution to these problems with budgeting, according to Hope and Fraser, is to abandon the traditional budgeting process (as the author's case studies show multiple companies have done) and create a different kind of performance management system. This performance management system is

---

[3] Proponents of Critical Chain project management have shown that traditional schedules are rife with unnecessary estimating contingency.

based on Key Performance Indicators (KPIs) that establish strategic and tactical outcomes desired by companies and relative performance indicators that measure performance against internal and external benchmarks rather than fixed budgets or plans. These measurements are designed to answer two questions previously posed: Are we achieving our strategic and tactical goals as an organization? Are our people performing at the highest levels possible?

Furthermore, not only do Hope and Fraser outline an adaptive, rather than a prescriptive, system of performance management, but they also go on to show how this new-style measurement system fosters an adaptive management style—decentralized, collaborative, and innovative. Their adaptive measurement and management system is based on six common principles shown in Figure 13-3.

Figure 13-3
Beyond Budgeting Principles

Beyond Budgeting Principles

- Provide a governance framework based on clear principles and boundaries.
- Create a high-performance climate based on relative success.
- Give people freedom to make local decisions that are consistent with governance principles and the organization's goals. "Our cases have shown that although teams at every level need strategic direction, they don't need detailed plans (except those derived by the team to set their own course)."
- Place the responsibility for value creating decisions on front-line teams.
- Make people accountable for customer outcomes.
- Support open and ethical information systems.
                — Jeremy Hope & Robin Fraser (2003)

These principles are, not surprisingly, very compatible with the principles articulated by the Declaration of Interdependence presented in Chapter 1, "The Agile Revolution". The unique principle from Hope and Fraser that sparked ideas for the Adaptive Performance Management System is the one on relative measures. Relative measures enable mangers to focus on continuous value creation, not a fixed plan. To manage the business, they set targets on high-level KPIs (return-on-capital, cash flow, customer satisfaction). Staff "performance is evaluated and rewarded based on a formula related to how teams compare with benchmarks, peers, and prior years," say Hope and Fraser. The flawed fixed-performance contracts are replaced by relative improvement contracts that promote self-regulation within organizational units and teams. "This 'relative performance' approach focuses business unit mangers on maximizing profits at all times rather than playing games with the numbers, because there are not fixed targets that lead to irrational behavior."

> *"One of the primary benefits of managing without a plan or budget is that managers are able to focus all their attention on responding to changing events and providing value to customers and shareholders"* (Hope and Fraser 2003).

Hope and Fraser see this new approach to measurement as a key building block in converting organizations to be more adaptive. Companies "need to abandon fixed performance contracts, command-and-control management, the dependency culture, central resource allocation, the multilayered functional hierarchy, and the closed information systems."

> *"Effective empowerment is the product of freedom multiplied by capability"* (Hope and Fraser 2003).

Measuring Performance in Organizations

Performance measurement and management has proven to be much more difficult than people expect. Anyone undertaking the design of a performance management system would do well to read Rob Austin's *Measuring and Managing Performance in Organizations*, a sobering look into why measurement systems can go so awry (Austin 1996). Measurement "systems" are difficult, according to Austin, because "unlike mechanisms and organisms, organizations have subcomponents that realize they are being measured." In his introduction, Austin states that "if there is a single message that comes from this book, it is that trust, honesty, and good intentions are more efficient in many social contexts than verification, guile, and self-interest." It is the *intentions* of the managers who use the measurement systems that ultimately determine their veracity.

Metrics Program Failures

The metrics community within IT and software development companies has generally had a difficult time gaining traction. The failure rate of metrics implementation programs has been high—companies implement metrics programs with great fanfare, only to see them phased out over time as enthusiasm wanes.

One primary cause of this difficulty rises from inappropriate intentions, especially over time, that create dysfunctional measurement systems. Austin discusses the pattern of how measurement dysfunction occurs (see Figure 13-4). In the beginning, measurement systems tend to improve results because workers don't really understand the system, and therefore their course of action is to try to fulfill the intentions of the system. However, over time, added pressure to "improve," forces people to subvert the intentions to meet the measurement goal. Because there is always a disconnect between the desired outcome and the metric(s) used to achieve the outcome (for example, the disconnect between a desired business value outcome from a project and the measures of schedule and cost), over time the "measured performance trends upward; true performance declines sharply."

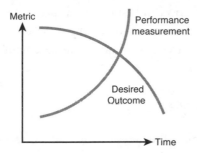

Figure 13-4
How Measurement Systems Become Dysfunctional

One company, whose managers were compensated according to Capability Maturity Model (CMM) levels achieved, provides a clear example of not measuring output, but input or process. (This should not be interpreted as a problem with the CMM, but one of its use.) Although a focus on process improvement measures may improve efficiency, it will have a great tendency to distract people from measuring effectiveness (outcomes). Why not a business value maturity model to use in conjunction with a process model? Intel has developed such a model with five levels similar to those of the CMM.[4] Using the two together gives organizations a balance between measuring process improvement and value improvement.

[4] Martin Curley, Director IT Innovation, Intel. Presentation at SPI Conference 2006, Dublin, Ireland.

> *Measuring and compensating staff for process improvement is a clear road to dysfunctional behavior if not combined with outcome measures that are understood to be more important.*

Many of the traditional project management metrics have made this trip from functional to dysfunctional. They no longer encourage true performance, but dysfunctional performance. Furthermore, dysfunction isn't necessarily eliminated by redesign of the system. In fact, in several case studies by Austin, "the implementation of more sophisticated measures caused more sophisticated dysfunctional reactions." Those being measured "can increase their rewards if they can successfully obliterate the correlation between true output and measured performance." Earned Value Analysis may be such a redesigned metric for project management performance. The more teams strive to achieve EVA targets, the further they are getting away from true business results. Measuring against results can be more difficult, less precise, fuzzier, and therefore both measurers and measurees shy away from outcomes measurement in favor of something more concrete. In so doing, the desired outcomes and the performance measurement systems diverge and become dysfunctional.

Two Management Styles

Self-organization implies a reliance on internal motivation of the team rather than external motivation (i.e., a measurement target). Austin calls this *delegatory* management as contrasted with *measurement-based* management. He goes on to say, that "measurement-based management is in conflict with delegatory management. There is a negative interaction because of the implicit message of distrust that a measurement system conveys by the fact of its existence." This may be a reason agile teams often feel out of sync with their management. They believe they are performing well—delivering customer value—but the measurements systems don't back that up.

There are two types, or intended uses, of measurement systems, although in practice it may be difficult to determine intentions and therefore tell them apart. Motivational measurement attempts to alter behavior and provoke greater effort from employees, whereas informational measurement provides insights into development and management processes over time. It is often difficult to implement the latter (informational measurements) without staff assuming the former (motivational measurement) is the real intention.

Says Austin, "the ideal to which organizations should aspire is one in which workers are internally motivated and measurement provides them with self-assessment information. Measurement and motivation are decoupled. The challenge for managers is to become more trusting, able to inspire and communicate, and willing to help rather than be helped." Delegatory (agile) system measurement should therefore be focused on two things: determining the value of output delivered to the customer and providing staff informational measurements with which they can do self-assessments to improve their own performance.

APMS Design Guidelines

Drawing from the ideas from Hope, Fraser, and Austin, the following were developed as guidelines for the Adaptive Performance Management System:

- Build the measurement system on a foundation of trust, honesty, and an intent to increase organizational value.
- Place the most emphasis on measuring outcomes, not inputs, even if the metrics are not as easy to obtain, nor as precise.
- Implement constraint metrics with broad tolerance for variations to encourage adaptation.
- Create output informational metrics that support people's innate internal motivational needs and provide them aggregate measures of overall progress.

The key to a successful transition to an agile organization, project, or enterprise is a focus on customer value rather than schedule, building collaborative project communities based on trust and respect, and learning from good feedback systems. Our measurement systems must support these focal points. The measurement system must ensure that the connection between business drivers (profit, ROI) and project deliverables is transparent.

Outcome Performance Metrics

The goal of outcome performance metrics is to provide assurances back to customers that they are obtaining value for their investment by measuring outcomes first and then performance against constraints. The key questions, which relate to the agile triangle in Figure 13-1, are

- Is the project community delivering a continuous stream of value to the customer?
- Is the project community delivering a high-quality product that can continue to deliver customer value in the future?
- Did the project community deliver within acceptable scope, schedule, and cost constraints?

Although plans, some detailed, may be needed by the team to coordinate the work and help to achieve the business outcomes, performance should be measured against the outcomes themselves. Some project managers complain that their performance should not be measured against business outcomes because they don't have any control over them. They argue that they should be measured only against scope, schedule, and cost because they do have some control over them. They may not have control, but they do have influence. Measuring the wrong thing, because you might have more control over it or because it's easier to measure, isn't a recipe for success.

Outcome measures are often both quantitative and qualitative, as is demonstrated in Balanced Scorecard systems. Even simple measures can be very effective: for example, a value measurement system called IRACIS—IR for increased revenue, AC for avoid cost, and IS for improved service. Whether the values for these are qualitative or quantitative, thinking of value in these three broad categories is helpful in thinking about outcomes rather than outputs.[5] Intel, as part of their business value maturity model, identified 17 standard measures of value—from headcount productivity to time-to-market.

[5] Another model for analyzing business value is Niel Nickolaisen's Purpose Alignment Model, which looks at market differentiation and mission criticality (Pixton 2009).

Ultimately, project success should be measured by outcome: Did the project deliver a releasable product that delivered on the business value, goals, and objectives? Whether a specific requirement defined in the beginning was implemented may be immaterial to success, if other requirements were subsequently determined to be of higher priority. Whether the project was delivered by the targeted date may be material or immaterial, depending upon decisions made by the sponsor and team during the project. One project may have a hard delivery date—a constraint—whereas another may not.

The three key questions to be answered by project performance metrics mentioned previously included current value, quality (future value), and constraints. Historically, project progress was measured by a Gantt chart that emphasizes schedule (the x-axis on such a report is time) and activities. The parking lot diagram shown in Chapter 10, in Figure 10-2, emphasizes value first (each box represents capabilities or stories that have been implemented and acceptance tested) and schedule second (dates in the bottom of the boxes). If we want managers and others to think differently about performance reporting, then we need to change the reporting mechanisms to reflect the most important characteristic—the outcomes, as do other reports shown in Chapter 10.

Constraints

Outcomes are a measure of business value. They may be expressed as a vision, an ROI target, and a set of capabilities that support that vision. In some circumstances, the outcomes may have a monetary value assigned (see capability valuation in Chapter 8). But businesses require more than outcomes themselves; they require that outcomes be generated within certain constraints to make them financially viable.

We need to understand constraints in three areas—scope, schedule, and cost. The adaptive measurement design guidelines lead us to a position of having as few narrow constraints as possible (to encourage adaptation), therefore only one of these three characteristics should be a "fixed" constraint and the others "flexible or accept" constraints—as defined in the tradeoff matrix in Chapter 6. For example, if the project's objective relates to a governmental requirement that must be met by some date, then the "fixed" constraint is schedule. The definition of a constraint is different from that for an estimate. An estimate is an expectation based on analysis of the work to be done. A constraint, which may be loosely based on an estimate, is a limit, a "not to exceed." Constraints should have broad tolerances to encourage flexibility and experimental design, and thereby innovation.

For example, if a team projected that their project would not meet a constraint date that had been designated "fixed," then a major red flag would be raised and either significant action or cancellation would ensue. However, if the cost was estimated to be $100,000, then the cost "flexible" constraint might be $100,000 +/- $25,000. The team would attempt to achieve a $100,000 cost, or less, but they would understand that the cost dimension had significant flexibility and that only if it exceeded $125,000 would the project need to be re-evaluated by the sponsor. Some might argue that this type of boundary setting would not keep enough pressure on team performance, but that's not the function of outcome metrics in this adaptive system. Their goal is to help deliver on a set of outcomes, in the face of changing circumstances, within certain constraints.

> *The tighter the constraints, the less flexibility the team has, and the less likely it is to deliver on the highest-priority outcomes.*

In looking at performance metrics in this way, we should not forget that value (outcome) is not independent from cost and schedule. A project's viability (ROI) might depend on delivering six high-level capabilities, constrained by a June delivery date (fixed) and a $250,000 +/- $50,000 cost (flexible). It may be that the revenue value of those capabilities decreases rapidly after June (for example, because of a competitor's expected product upgrade) such that the business case (ROI) decreases unacceptably after June. Similarly, if the cost exceeds the $300,000 constraint, the ROI decreases such that the project should be cancelled. Again, constraints are not unimportant, they are just of less importance than value and quality.

Community Responsibility

One of the important agile principles, one that rarely gets enough attention, is that the project community, as a whole, is responsible for performance. So project performance is not the sole responsibility of the development team, but of the entire project community—including the development team, the product team, and the project sponsor. This is particularly true when measuring outcomes. The product team and sponsor make critical priority and resource decisions during the project. When the sponsor, or other resource managers, shuffle people from project to project, they are making cross-project resource allocation decisions. Why, then, should a development team be judged for a resource loss over which they have no control? If the product team and product manager make priority decisions on features or stories throughout the project, why, then, would the development team be measured against the original requirements? In traditional project environments, the development team is saddled with a fixed plan, then further burdened with constant changes from both customers and management. They are then told to "conform to the plan anyway."

Product teams, development teams, and project sponsors must all be jointly committed to the project outcomes. Often in a traditional project the product team provides requirements and constraints to the development team, but they don't have direct accountability for outcomes. In an agile project the entire project community is an integrated team, all committed to the results.

Improving Decision Making

Outcomes and constraints are important for performance measurement, but they are also aids for effective decision making. If project communities must continually adapt to changing conditions, then the most critical process is the project community's decision-making process and the most critical inputs to that process are the decision-making criteria—both goals and constraints. So not only are goals and constraints the basis for project performance metrics, but they are critical to the constant decision making needed to adjust and adapt to changing conditions. If project management was like a manufacturing process, then project management would be about managing process flow, but it is not.

> *Project leadership is ultimately about two things: managing people and managing decisions.*

If success is measured as absolute conformance to each of the plan components, then on what basis can decisions about adapting be made? Project teams are driven to meet planned levels, even when they make no sense given the changes that have occurred during the project. If our goal is to guide decisions about adapting to change, then we need clear criteria for making those decisions.

Planning as a Guide

APMS put plans into a different perspective. Plans, including estimates of scope, schedule, and cost are still made—and are very useful, but their use is different. The key question becomes, "Given the planning we have done, are we relatively confident that the desired outcomes can be delivered within the specified constraints?" Plans are used to guide the team, but not to encase them in straightjackets. Teams will strive to deliver to the constraints, but delivering the desired outcomes will take precedence.

Again some will argue that projects get off track even with strictly followed plans, sometimes seriously off track, and that if we ease the constraints that we open ourselves up for even worse results. What these critics are basically saying is that they neither trust their teams nor consider them to be very smart. They are saying that a performance goal such as, "You must absolutely deliver this project within the estimate of $100,000 or heads will roll," is somehow superior to one that goes something like, "The estimated target cost for this project that we will strive to achieve is $100,000; however, the most critical constraint on this project is to deliver the set of capabilities defined by our June delivery schedule, so we are willing to spend up to $125,000 on this project if need be to achieve our desired outcomes." The target cost of this project is $100,000, but the constraint is different— $125,000. Teams and managers need to learn to deal with acceptable variations like this rather than demanding a single-point result.

Which statement above would motivate you? Which is more realistic? Which is liable to get better results? I believe the answer to all these questions is the second statement. I think today's workforce responds better to realistic goals that recognize the reality of change than to unrealistic single-valued numerics. David Spann made an astute comment about this example: "The real difference in the two statements in the paragraph above is the directive and punitive nature of the first and the intentional language of the second." Intention, to repeat one more time, is critical to the usefulness of any measurement system.

Output Performance Metrics

Becoming an adaptive, agile organization does not mean abandoning performance measurements; it means creating measurements that are meaningful within the context of continuously adapting to achieve outcomes. We want teams to increase productivity. We want teams to deliver faster. We want teams to deliver low-defect products. However, we won't achieve these goals by solely measuring conformance to plan, but *by measuring these characteristics directly and comparing progress against external and internal benchmarks.*

Measuring team performance against plan often leads to poor results. If a team is assigned to a project where the plan is heavily "padded or buffered" and they succeed, are they then a high-performance team? If a team is assigned to a project whose "plan" is completely and utterly unreasonable and they fail to achieve the plan, are they then a low-performance team? Wouldn't comparing team performance against realistic internal and external benchmarks be better? We want teams to improve their performance and, in an agile environment, we trust the teams to work on improving their own performance. Management's job is to provide "informational" metrics so that teams can measure their own performance and work on improving outputs.

Five Core Metrics

One way of doing this measurement is to use the SLIM model, developed by Lawrence Putnam and discussed in his book, written with Ware Myers, *Five Core Metrics: The Intelligence Behind Successful Software Management* (Putnam 2003). Michael Mah has worked with Putnam for years and their software product, plus their database of thousands of projects, provides a mechanism for both internal and external benchmarking.[6]

The five core metrics used by the SLIM model are

---

[6] There are other tools and approaches to measurement, but I am most familiar with Mah's work.

1. *Quantity of function*—That is, scope, measured in terms of user stories, use cases, requirements, or features (depending on a particular situation)[7]

2. *Productivity*—Expressed as functionality produced for the time and effort

3. *Time*—The duration of the project in calendar months

4. *Effort*—The amount of effort expended in person-months

5. *Reliability*—Expressed in terms of defect rate

Figure 13-5 shows how the data is gathered for this type of performance measurement and Figure 13-6 show comparisons between individual projects within an organization and trend lines that show industry averages for the specific type of software. Although scope, schedule, and cost are used in measuring both outcomes and outputs, they are used in different ways. In looking at outcome performance they are compared to plans, whereas in output performance they are compared to other projects. Both views aid in overall performance evaluation.

Figure 13-5
Gathering Metrics
Data

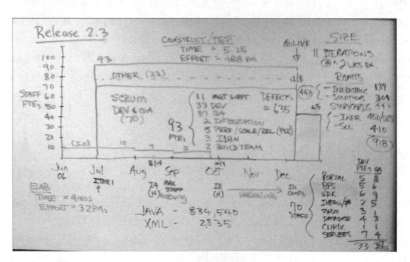

Graphic courtesy of Michael Mah

---

[7] These may be measured ultimately as objects, modules, classes, or lines of code.

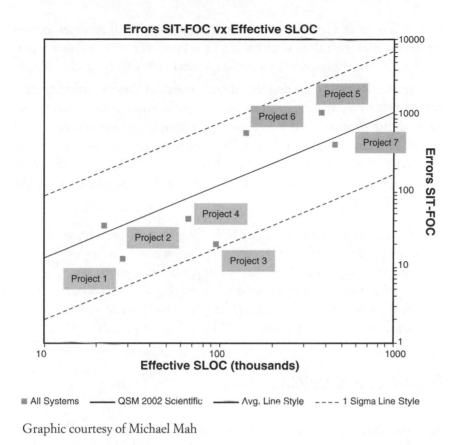

Figure 13-6
Project Performance
Comparisons

Graphic courtesy of Michael Mah

The data collection for these types of reports is straightforward and allows a team to

- Compare its progress over time against itself (Are we getting better?)
- Compare performance against other internal teams (How do we compare with others in our organization?)
- Compare performance against an external measure of like industries or projects (How do we compare with other companies?)

One of the clear advantages of measuring relative team performance rather than how well a team performed against a plan is that there are no upper limits to improvement (target). Because everything is relative, good teams will strive to get better and better, not just try to meet a target. Teams that have only to meet a fixed target tend to first, manipulate that target to their advantage, and second, to slack off after the target is reached. Relative performance keeps the internal pressure on teams to constantly excel.

Again, it's worth repeating that the intentions of these measurements is paramount. Comparing teams can lead to dysfunction such as destructive internal competition or poor resource optimization. Comparing against external benchmarks should be used as a learning opportunity and not as a basis for penalties. After the intentions become destructive rather than constructive, teams pick up on it very quickly and the measures produce the wrong behaviors.

> *"Knowledge work and design work in the information age has been sabotaged by manufacturing metrics. An accounting mindset, of measuring output over input (as in cost per function point), has placed all the emphasis on output measures that are primarily efficiency oriented and placed little emphasis on outcome measures, such as new product innovation" (Michael Mah, personal email).*

Outcomes and Outputs

Although the previous sections address outcome and output measures separately, in practice they cannot be viewed independently. For example, for a project in which significant innovation needed to occur and the technology was new and very complex, achieving the desired outcome requires innovation in both business value and technology implementation. Delivering on these outcomes could easily result in lower output measures (such as productivity).

If the intent of the output measurement system is learning, then the team should be able to answer the following question positively, with no negative repercussions. "Did we do the best job we could at delivering high-quality output given the particular situation on this project?" In a different environment, management might interpret the lower output measures negatively, as in "Why aren't your output numbers competitive with other teams?" When teams realize that output measures are dominating, they will opt for the easy way to make their numbers, and innovation and other outcome measures will suffer.

Many project managers, and even CIOs (based on the report from Helen Pukszta mentioned previously) don't believe they have any control over outcomes and that they should be measured only on outputs. Control isn't really the issue. The question people in the project community have to ask themselves is, "Do I have any *influence* on the project's outcomes?" Control, especially today, is illusive—in fact, we really don't have control over people and events. When people feel they are responsible only for outputs, outcomes will inevitably suffer. When people feel they have some influence over outcomes, that those outcomes are important, and that accountability for those outcomes is shared by the entire project community, they will act accordingly.

Unless we explicitly view outcomes as crucial and measure them in some objective way, be it quantitative or qualitative, output measures will dominate and cause desired performance and measured performance to move in opposite and dysfunctional directions.

Shortening the Tail

One final note on measuring performance is a metric that has proven effective in determining how "agile" organizations are: the length of the tail. The tail is the time period from "code slush" (true code freezes are rare) or "feature freeze" to RTM (release to manufacturing). This is the time period when companies do some or all of the following: beta testing, regression testing, product integration, integration testing, documentation, defect fixing. The worst "tail" I've encountered was 18 months—18 months from feature freeze to product release, and most of that time was spent in QA. Routinely I find software companies whose tail is 4–6 months of a 12-month release cycle.

> *Shortening the tail is a simple, powerful metric for measuring progress towards agility.*

The goal of aggressive agile teams is to produce shippable software every iteration, but most are far from this goal—especially if they have large, old legacy code bases. Think of everything a company might have to do to reduce a tail from six to three months (and less over time). They would have to learn how to do continuous integration across their entire product. They would have to improve their level of automated testing to drive regression and integration testing back into every iteration. They would have to improve the level of automated unit testing done by developers to reduce testing time at the end of iterations and releases. They would have to bring customers into the development process much earlier, not waiting until the end for beta testing. They would have to integrate documentation specialists into the team and produce documentation continuously during iterations. They would have to invest in systematic refactoring to reduce the technical debt and therefore reduce testing and defect fixing time.

You can probably think of more they would have to do. Each of these items would contribute in some way, large or small, to reducing the tail by days or weeks. For large products the tail might never be zero, but it could be small—maybe a month, as shown in Figure 13-7. Just think of the competitive disadvantage a company has when their delivery tail is 18 months, or even 6 months. That means that for 6 or 18 months prior to release few changes in the competitive environment could be incorporated into their products. Furthermore, it means that developers and QA staff are always out of sync—contributing to a gap, or chasm, between these two groups.

Figure 13-7
Shortening the Tail

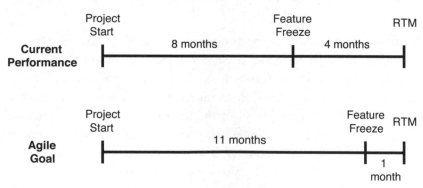

So here is one metric that embodies the quality values of agile development. It may work better in a software company than in an IT shop, but it can be used in both—a simple, powerful metric that drives behaviors in the direction you want the organization to go.

Final Thoughts

Some portfolio management systems classify IT projects into four broad categories—Infrastructure, Utility, Enhancement, and Frontier. Although projects in each category may require a degree of innovation, clearly the frontier (out in the West where the arrows are flying) projects are those that create new products, new business services, and new business processes. These frontier projects are the ones that require the closest coordination with the customer team, have less well-defined requirements, are higher risk—and have potentially the biggest payback.

In many organizations, frontier projects comprise only 10–20% of the portfolio budget and few people think of measuring success differently on this small percentage of projects, even if they are the most critical ones to their future. For most of the other 80–90% of the projects, completing them at the lowest cost may be the goal. In the traditional "a project is a project is a project" environment, all projects are measured in the same way—with schedule and cost dominating.

One could probably make a case for using an Adaptive Performance Management System on all projects because it makes sense to focus on value for any project (given that value may mean low-cost delivery for some projects). The word "adaptive" in APMS means just that: adapted to the project's required highest-value goal.

However, although it is highly desirable to use APMS with all projects—and will be necessary if you plan to create an agile enterprise—it is critical to use an APMS with those projects that are building the future of your organization: those that implement new products or services or processes that will create your future company. If you are creating the future, a couple of extra months or a few extra dollars (or euros, or pounds, or yen) will be insignificant. If you don't deliver value, if you don't deliver innovation—*that* will be significant. We cannot continue to ask teams to be innovative, to be flexible, to adapt to changing competitive conditions, and then measure their performance by forcing them into narrow measurement boxes.

> *We have to be as innovative with our measurement systems as we are with our development methodology.*

Finally, I want to return to one of the guidelines for APMS design:

> *Build the measurement system on a foundation of trust, honesty, and an intent to increase organizational value.*

Those who have studied the agile movement understand that these agile, adaptive, flexible approaches are really social and management movements. In *Adaptive Software Development*, I outlined the differences between what is typically known as a Command-Control style of management and what I called a Leadership-Collaboration style. Extreme Programming, Crystal, and Scrum all profess similar kinds of workplace social changes oriented to improving the human dimensions of our workplaces and thereby improving performance.

If we want adaptive organizations, we have to think long and hard about what success and performance mean and align our performance measures to the values of the management style we choose. We have to build our measurement systems on the right intentions—to illuminate, not to punish; to learn, not to repeat; to adapt, not to resist change. If we want to build adaptive organizations, then we have to abandon fixed-performance contracts for a measurement system that aligns with these new intentions.

Chapter 14

Reliable Innovation

In the end, the positive answers to two questions form the essence of Agile Project Management: "Are you delivering innovative products to your customers?" and "Are you excited about going to work every day?" Agilists want to build innovative products—products that test the limits of our abilities as individuals and teams—and create a work environment in which people, as individuals and in teams, can thrive.

Possibly the greatest barrier to becoming agile is dealing with the illusions of causality and certainty. In a production environment in which requirements and technology are relatively stable, we are better able to predict the future—to plan and expect conformance to that plan. However, as uncertainty in the external world increases, managers who have been successful in stable environments attempt to apply the same processes and performance measures to unstable environments. Their certainty—and the belief that if they just push hard enough they can "cause" the right results—is likely to result in failure rather than success.

> *Evolution itself—adapting to ecosystem changes—is an emergent process fueled by experimentation.*

Causality is easier to believe in than emergence; it's more tangible. Yet nature thrives on emergent results. Every individual action changes an ecosystem and fosters other changes in response. Just as a theatre play emerges from the interaction of actors, playwright, director, and the audience, a product emerges from the interaction of team members, the product and project leaders, customers, and competitors. But the illusion of certainty continues because in many organizations it's considered poor form to be other than certain. The certainty should be in the vision and the broad goals, not the specific path to reach that vision. When we confuse vision and path, we confuse causality and emergence.

New product development isn't Plan-Do but Envision-Explore. Where there is no uncertainty, no risk, there is no opportunity. Production projects are controlled by predicting scope, schedule, and cost. New product development projects are constrained by schedule and cost in order to deliver on vision. Scope is restrictive, vision expansive, yet vision isn't "anything goes." Poor visioning leads to uncontrolled experimentation in the same way that overly detailed requirements lead to rigid compliance.

It's important to remember that no product, and no organization, can be infinitely agile in all dimensions. Agility always occurs within certain boundaries—platform architectures for products, organizational frameworks for people. It balances structure and flexibility, dependence and autonomy. A restrictive architecture reduces a product's ability to respond to the product vision and market ecosystem, whereas too little architecture increases the likelihood of increased cost, duplication, and sub-optimization. A restrictive organizational framework reduces a team's ability to respond to changing conditions, whereas too little framework causes chaos and confusion.

The martial arts are all about balance. Whether defending or attacking, martial artists keep their bodies centered and in balance. Engineering artists should also be in balance. Finding that balance is key to agility, and it isn't easy; there isn't a formula. The balance point for every product, for every team, is different. Finding that balance point requires technical excellence that builds both quickness and agility. Skill, talent, and knowledge breed quickness—compelling people to go faster breeds hurrying. Agility can only be achieved through an unwavering focus on technical excellence.

The Changing Face of New Product Development

New product development—be it for industrial products, consumer products, or internal business processes—is being driven by two resolute forces: the continuing demand for innovation and the plunging cost of change (low-cost exploration). As the uncertainty about the outcome of a development effort increases, as the complexity of the interactions of design variables daunts cause-and-effect analysis, exploration through experimentation becomes the most effective and reliable mode of discovery. When we can conduct 1,000 experiments a day for $10 apiece, creating elaborate designs that would take a month to complete otherwise makes no sense. On the other hand, conducting 5,000 random experiments makes no sense either. Good experiments require good experimental design.

It is hard to overstate the impact of low-cost exploration on product development or the competitive advantage that will accrue to those companies that can adjust their development and managerial processes appropriately. A significant element of this strategy, even for hardware products, will involve software and the manipulation of bits rather than atoms, driving a low-cost exploration product development process that should strive to

- Fill products with "bits"
- Create a bit-oriented product development lifecycle (i.e., model and/or simulate products in software as far into the lifecycle as possible)
- Relentlessly drive down the cost of changing bits (low-cost iteration)
- Develop people and processes capable of the above strategies (agile people and processes)

Embedded software has rapidly become a critical piece of industrial products. Cell phones now boast a million or more lines of code. Automobiles have microprocessors for everything from fuel injection to transmission shifting. Airplanes are fly-by-wire, controlled completely electronically. In the past software supported hardware. In the future, it may be the other way around.

Software—developed well, of course—is more flexible than hardware. In fact, drastically shortening the product development lifecycle forces hardware engineers to lock in hardware designs earlier than they would like. Software's flexibility is often used to correct hardware problems or add new features after hardware designs are fixed. So the more "bits" there are in a product, in general, the better. As bits replace atoms, more product features can be developed faster and with greater flexibility.

But we can't drive a bit, or sit on one, or use one to hit a golf ball. At some point, atoms must be assembled into products that we can use. The critical question is, when do we assemble the atoms? A furniture manufacturer in West Virginia completes its entire product design process in software. At the end of the design phase, the software generates instructions to manufacturing robots, and the furniture parts are cut and assembled. The more chemical compound and biological response information is available in large databases, the further into the drug development process companies can go before lengthy and expensive activities such as animal testing have to begin. Simulations, modeling, and prototyping, for a wide array of products, are all increasingly being done in software prior to any physical assembly. As soon as physical assembly begins, flexibility suffers.

The point is that the longer teams can manipulate bits rather than atoms, the more effective the product development process can be. So two strategies are critical: increase the number of bits in products and manipulate bits rather than atoms as deep into the development process as possible.

Agile People and Processes Deliver Agile Products

There is, however, a caveat to the above strategies. A company's development and project management processes, and its executive support and performance measurements, must encourage experimentation, exploration, and low-cost iteration. Authors Moshe Rubinstein and Iris Firstenberg (1999) of the University of California write about "minding" organizations, a term that coincides with "adaptive." "The minding organization behaves like a living organism, in which adapting is central to vitality and survival.... Overly rigid and detailed planning must give way to a strategy that combines less planning and more adapting."

> *"Experimentation matters because it is through learning equally what works and what doesn't that people develop great new products, services, and entire businesses. But in spite of the lip service that is paid to 'testing' and 'learning from failure,' today's organizations, processes, and management of innovation often impede experimentation"*
> *(Harvard Business School professor Stefan Thomke 2003).*

Agile, adaptive project management and development will require a substantial cultural change within the development staff, project leadership, and executive ranks of organizations. There are individuals who excel in production environments: those who strive for repeatability and precision through the use of prescriptive processes and performance measures. Every organization requires production processes for a significant portion of its operations. But every organization also needs exploration processes: those that excel in delivering new products, new services, and new internal business initiatives. Unfortunately, the project cultures and management controls for exploration and production are usually at odds with each other, causing organizational schizophrenia. Great organizations will find a way to deal with both exploration and production processes. Others will languish behind.

So how do organizations deal with two distinct process models that have seemingly incompatible cultures? I think the answer lies in the word "adaptation." Adaptive cultures adjust to the situation, whereas production cultures have difficulty changing. When the business environment was more stable, production cultures could thrive.

> *As the pace of change accelerates, the mix of exploration versus production activity in organizations shifts, creating competitive advantage for those companies with predominantly adaptive cultures.*

Culture then identifies a critical piece of the agile vision, which might be expressed with a simple axiom: Don't work in Dilbert's company, and don't be Dilbert. Dilbert's company is the epitome of authoritarianism—the exact opposite of self-organizing. Dilbert complains, but he takes no responsibility for changing his environment. Dilbert and his cohorts lack self-discipline. Agile social architectures have both and thereby deliver innovative products and create great places to work. As Andrew Hill (2001) relates in his book about John Wooden and UCLA basketball, "The Bruins were built on speed, quickness, a tough man-to-man defense, a withering zone press, and a relentless fast break. Now, there may be some kid in America who grows up dreaming of playing slow-down, highly structured, Princeton-style basketball, but I've never met that kid. There was something intoxicating and captivating about the pace and attacking style of the Bruins." I think most product developers want to work on UCLA-style "agile" projects.

A grand vision? A utopian vision? An impractical vision? Possibly. I once received an email response to a message I posted on an online forum in which I argued that traditional project management is often authoritarian and high ceremony. "Jim, your sentence implies that authoritarianism and high ceremony are 'bad' things. Do we really care whether or not something is authoritarian, or should we judge it solely by its ability to deliver value to the customer?" My response was, "I care deeply." Delivering valuable products is important, and it's critical to project management success. No project team can exist for long without delivering value to its customers. But in the long run, how we deliver, how we interact at work, and how we treat each other as human beings are even more important.

Reliable Innovation

People and their interactions are critical to delivering quality products. And, just like Broadway plays always deliver on opening night, APM delivers on time and to the customer's vision more reliably than any other approach. Given the high degree of uncertainty on many new product efforts, given the changes in technology, given the ebb and flow of staff, reliable results are still obtainable. Given all the "maybes," agile project management and development still deliver, which is a tribute to the passion, drive, persistence, and ingenuity of team members.

When executives can articulate a product vision, agile teams deliver. When executives can establish reasonable cost and schedule boundaries, agile teams deliver. When customers and product managers can accept the consequences of their own demands on the product, agile teams deliver. When all participants can deal with the ambiguity of structure and flexibility, when they can focus on results and not activities, agile teams deliver.

Author Ed Yourdon (1999) writes about four kinds of death march projects: kamikaze, suicide, ugly, and mission impossible. Kamikaze projects are doomed from the start, but everyone agrees that the ride might be enjoyable, as in "technically interesting." On suicide projects everyone involved, from the engineers to the project leader, knows the project will fail and that it will be miserable to work on. Threatened job loss is the only reason to work on such a project. Ugly projects are those in which the project manager is willing to sacrifice others for his own glory. Long hours and a miserable working environment are sure to ensue. Mission impossible projects are doable, barely, with luck and exceptional effort. But mission impossible projects are also usually exciting—they are high-risk, high-reward projects.

If your project falls into one of the first three categories—kamikaze, suicide, or ugly—no project management process in the world—production, exploration, or otherwise—will help. Anyone who guarantees success for a particular process or methodology, under any conditions, for any project, is lying. Any executive who demands success, under any conditions, for any project, strangles her team's capability. However, if your project falls in the mission impossible category, hire Tom Cruise[1] and use agile project management and development.

APM isn't just a project management process, it is an organizational process. Agile teams won't survive in a hostile, death march environment. In a reasonable organizational environment, however, with executives and managers who understand the reality of marketplace uncertainty, agile teams will deliver more reliably than nonagile ones. They will turn the uncertainty of the marketplace and technology into the certainty of a working product.

Repeatable processes are specification based. They rely on minimal variations in both the process and the specification. Specification-based, strict change-controlled processes founder under uncertainty because when teams using repeatable processes encounter high rates of change, they fail to adapt rapidly enough.

Conversely, reliable processes work with exploration-based work because both product and process adapt to change. But adapting to change by itself isn't sufficient—over-response to change produces oscillation and chaos. The adaptations must be steered toward some goal: the product vision. Without a clear, well-articulated, continuously communicated vision, adapting to change can become a deadly spiral.

[1] Star of the *Mission Impossible* movies.

The fundamental nature of new product development cannot be escaped—it always involves uncertainty and risk. As the exploration factor goes up, as product teams push technology to the bleeding edge (and sometimes over it), as market forces change rapidly, no process, nor even the most brilliant team, can ensure success. Yet the right people and an agile, exploratory process offer, by far, the best chance at success. These projects are highly reliable because of the team's ability to adapt to the environment rather than follow a prescribed path.

The Value-Adding Project Leader

This book is about both project management and project leaders. Unfortunately, some agilists have been perceived as being anti-management and anti–project management. This is a Dilbert view of the world in which employees are the downtrodden and managers are the trodders. But high-performance agile teams (and organizations) create a balance between leaders and individual team members—a balance of self-organization with self-discipline. Agile teams are flexible, but not ad hoc—a difference that escapes cursory examinations. High-performance agile teams are highly self-disciplined; team members accept accountability, a development framework, and certain behavioral responsibilities as part of working in an environment that is open and flexible and delegates a high degree of decision making to them as individuals and as a team.

The agile project leader's style is one of leadership-collaboration rather than command-control. These leaders are critical to agile project success, and their role is very demanding. Leading is more difficult, and more rewarding, than commanding. Creating a collaborative work environment is more difficult, and more rewarding, than controlling. Both project and product leaders are the champions of the vision. They articulate it so that everyone understands it, and they nurture it so that no one forgets it. The vision has a customer focus—what delivers value to the customer—and a technical focus—championing the technical excellence that will continue to deliver value in the future. Leaders help the team focus on delivery while minimizing the distractions of compliance work.

Leadership also includes staff selection, staff development, and ongoing encouragement. Although others participate in these activities, the leader is accountable for them. Getting the right people on the bus, getting the wrong people off the bus, steering people toward roles that match their talents, developing both technical and behavioral skills, and encouraging people through frequent feedback are all time-consuming and critical activities for the project leader. But that's not all. Project leaders also help create an environment of "no fear" in which collaboration, interaction, participatory decision making, conflict resolution, fierce debate, and collegial respect can flourish. This is the hard part of APM—the people part—or what some deride as the "soft skills" part. The easier part deals with the so-called "hard skills": schedules, budgets, reports, release planning, and the like. Both are necessary to good project management, but the soft part is really the hard part, and the hard part is really the easy part. Got it?

And that's just the project leader's role within the team. She then has the task of working with the customer team, executives, and other stakeholders to set and meet their expectations and persuade them to participate as partners with the project team.

Given the uncertainty, ambiguity, speed, anxiety, and constant change of an agile project, the project leader's job zips constantly between mentor and moderator to decision maker and facilitator. It's never dull, and it's rarely part time. Watching hummingbirds fly is good training for the agile project leader.

Final Thoughts

During a tour of France, the German poet Heinrich Heine and his friend visited a cathedral. As they stood in admiration before the magnificent church, the friend asked Heinrich why people couldn't build like this anymore. The poet replied, "Friend, in those days people had convictions. We moderns have opinions. It takes more than opinions to build Gothic cathedrals" (Sweet 1982). And it takes more than opinions to build innovative products and adaptive organizations. We need deep convictions and resolute commitment if we hope to build great products and a better workplace. We need processes and practices grounded in core values and principles.

At the first Agile Development Conference in Salt Lake City in June 2003, the Executive Summit portion concluded with discussion groups being asked to identify the single most important factor to convey to senior executives. One team stated, and the others concurred, that the key factor in becoming agile is realizing that principles are more important than practices—that what we believe drives what we do.

Without concrete practices, principles are sterile; but without principles, practices have no life, no character, no heart. Great products arise from great teams—teams who are principled, who have character, who have heart, who have persistence, and who have courage. Although more than half of this book describes a lifecycle process and specific practices of APM, the other half is ultimately more important—the half that attempts to articulate the values and principles behind the processes and practices. We need modern-day conviction.

There is a great debate in historical circles: Do great men and women make history, or does history make them great? Why were there so many great leaders in the 1930s and 1940s? Churchill, Roosevelt, Montgomery, and Eisenhower all arose as leaders during this era. Did they make history, or did history make them?

We could apply similar reasoning to products: Do great product ideas make great teams, or do great teams make great products? Maybe there is a third alternative—they make each other. World War II, the ten years before it, and the ten years after it were years of tremendous uncertainty and risk. But these times helped people and countries crystallize what was important and what was not. At least for the democracies of the world, what was important was freeing the world from tyranny. That vision, plus superb execution, carried the day.

The conviction at the core of the agile movement is creating a better workplace, free from tyranny, arbitrariness, and authoritarianism. Not free from structure. Not free from responsibility. Not free from project leaders and executives making decisions. This conviction flows not only from wanting to create a progressive social architecture in which individuals can thrive, but also from the belief that agile social architectures produce the best, most innovative products. Where self-organization and self-discipline flourish, where processes are designed (and adapted) to support people rather than restrict them, where individual talents and skills are valued—great products emerge.

Bibliography

Adolph, Steve, and Paul Bramble, with Alistair Cockburn and Andy Pols. *Patterns for Effective Use Cases*. Boston: Addison-Wesley, 2003.

Ambler, Scott. *Agile Modeling: Effective Practices for Extreme Programming and the Unified Process*. New York: John Wiley & Sons, 2002.

Anderson, David J. *Agile Management for Software Engineering*. Upper Saddle River, NJ: Prentice Hall, 2004.

Austin, Rob. "Surviving Enterprise Systems: Adaptive Strategies for Managing Your Largest IT Investments." Cutter Consortium Business-IT Strategies Advisory Service, *Executive Report* 4, no. 4 (April 2001).

Austin, Rob. "Innovation Interruptus." Cutter Technology Trends and Impacts Advisory Service, *Executive Report* 4, no. 2 (February 2003).

Austin, Rob, and Lee Devin. *Artful Making: What Managers Need to Know About How Artists Work*. Upper Saddle River, NJ: Prentice Hall, 2003.

Bayer, Sam. "Customer-Focused Development: The Art and Science of Conversing with Customers." Cutter Consortium Agile Project Management Advisory Service, *Executive Report* 2, no. 4 (April 2001).

Beck, Kent. *Extreme Programming Explained: Embrace Change*. Boston: Addison-Wesley, 2000.

Benko, Cathleen and Warren McFarlan. *Connecting the Dots: Aligning Projects with Objectives in Unpredictable Times*. Boston: Harvard Business School Press, 2003.

Boehm, Barry. *Software Engineering Economics*. Englewood Cliffs, NJ: Prentice Hall, 1981.

Boehm, Barry, and Richard Turner. *Balancing Agility and Discipline*. Boston: Addison-Wesley, 2003.

Bogsnes, Bjarte, *Implementing Beyond Budgeting: Unlocking the Performance Potential*. Hoboken, NJ: John Wiley & Sons, 2009.

Bonabeau, Eric, and Christopher Meyer. "Swarm Intelligence: A Whole New Way to Think About Business." *Harvard Business Review* (May 2001), 106–14.

Bossidy, Larry, and Ram Charan. *Execution: The Discipline of Getting Things Done*. New York: Crown Business, 2002.

Brown, Shona L., and Kathleen M. Eisenhardt. *Competing on the Edge: Strategy as Structured Chaos*. Boston: Harvard Business School Press, 1998.

Buckingham, Marcus, and Curt Coffman. *First, Break All the Rules*. New York: Simon & Schuster, 1999.

Buckingham, Marcus, and Donald O. Clifton. *Now, Discover Your Strengths*. New York: Free Press, 2001.

Budeir, Robert. "GE Finds Its Inner Edison," *Technology Review* (October 2003), 46–50.

Cockburn, Alistair. *Surviving Object-Oriented Projects*. Reading, MA: Addison-Wesley, 1998.

Cockburn, Alistair. *Writing Effective Use Cases*. Boston: Addison-Wesley, 2000.

Cockburn, Alistair. *Crystal Clear: A Human-Powered Methodology for Small Teams*. Boston: Addison-Wesley, 2003.

Cockburn, Alistair. *Agile Software Development*. Boston: Addison-Wesley, 2006.

Cohn, Mike. *User Stories Applied*. Boston: Addison-Wesley, 2004.

Cohn, Mike. *Agile Estimating and Planning*. Upper Saddle River, NJ: Prentice Hall, 2006.

Collins, James C., and Jerry I. Porras. *Built to Last: Successful Habits of Visionary Companies*. New York: HarperBusiness, 1994.

Collins, Jim. *Good to Great: Why Some Companies Make the Leap...and Others Don't*. New York: HarperBusiness, 2001.

Cooper, Robert G. *Winning at New Products: Accelerating the Process from Idea to Launch*. 3d ed. Cambridge, MA: Perseus Publishing, 2001.

DeMarco, Tom. *Slack: Getting Past Burnout, Bustwork, and the Myth of Total Efficiency*. New York: Broadway Books, 2001.

DeMarco, Tom, and Tim Lister. *Peopleware: Productive Projects and Teams*. 2d ed. New York: Dorset House, 1999.

DeMarco, Tom, and Tim Lister. *Waltzing with Bears: Managing Risk on Software Projects*. New York: Dorset House, 2003.

Denne, and Jane Cleland-Huang. *Mark Software by Numbers: Low-Risk, High-Return Development*. Upper Saddle River, NJ: Prentice Hall, 2003.

Derby, Esther and Diana Larsen. *Agile Retrospectives: Making Good Teams Great*. Raleigh, NC: Pragmatic Bookshelf, 2006.

Dixon, Nancy. *Common Knowledge.* Boston: Harvard Business School Press, 2000.

Dove, Rick. *Response Ability: The Language, Structure, and Culture of the Agile Enterprise*. New York: John Wiley & Sons, 2001.

DSDM Consortium, with Jennifer Stapleton (editor). *DSDM: Business Focused Development*. Boston: Addison-Wesley, 2003.

Duward, K., and Li Sobek. "Toyota's Principles of Set-Based Concurrent Engineering." *Sloan Management Review* (Winter 1999): 67-83.

Eisenhardt, Kathleen M., and Donald N. Sull. "Strategy as Simple Rules." *Harvard Business Review* (January 2001), 106–116.

Fishman, Charles. "Engines of Democracy." *Fast Company*, Issue 28 (October 1999), 174.

Fowler, Martin. *Refactoring: Improving the Design of Existing Code*. Reading, MA: Addison-Wesley, 1999.

Fowler, Martin, and Jim Highsmith. "The Agile Manifesto." *Software Development* 9, no. 8 (August 2001), 28–32.

Frick, Don M., and Larry C. Spears, *On Becoming a Servant Leader: The Private Writings of Robert K. Greenleaf*. San Francisco: Jossey-Bass Publishers, 1996.

Gall, John. *Systemantics: How Systems Work and Especially How They Fail*. New York: Pocket Books/Quadrangle, 1975.

Gardner, Elizabeth. "Ultimate Analysis." *Bio-IT World* 2, no. 11 (November 2003), 39–44.

Goldman, Steven, Roger Nagel, and Kenneth Preiss. *Agile Competitors and Virtual Organizations: Strategies for Enriching the Customer*. New York: Van Nostrand Reinhold, 1995.

Goldratt, Eliyahu M., and Jeff Cox. *The Goal: Excellence in Manufacturing*. Croton-on-Hudson, N.Y.: North River Press, 1984.

Goldratt, Eliyahu M., and Jeff Cox. *Critical Chain*. Croton-on-Hudson, NY: North River Press, 1997.

Goranson, H. T. *The Agile Virtual Enterprise: Cases, Metrics, Tools*, Westport, CT: Quorum Books, 1999.

Haeckel, Stephan H. *Adaptive Enterprise: Creating and Leading Sense-and-Respond Organizations*. Boston: Harvard Business School Press, 1999.

Highsmith, James A., III. *Adaptive Software Development: A Collaborative Approach to Managing Complex Systems*. New York: Dorset House Publishing, 2000.

Highsmith, Jim. *Agile Software Development Ecosystems*. Boston: Addison-Wesley, 2002.

Hill, Andrew, with John Wooden. *Be Quick—But Don't Hurry: Finding Success in the Teachings of a Lifetime*. New York: Simon & Schuster, 2001.

Hock, Dee. *Birth of the Chaordic Age*. San Francisco: Berrett-Koehler Publishers, 1999.

Hodgson, Phillip, and Randall White. *Relax, It's Only Uncertainty: Lead the Way When the Way Is Changing*. London: Financial Times Prentice Hall, 2001.

Hohmann, Luke. *Beyond Software Architecture: Creating and Sustaining Winning Solutions*. Boston: Addison-Wesley, 2003.

Hope, Jeremy, and Robin Fraser. *Beyond Budgeting: How Managers Can Break Free from the Annual Performance Trap*. Boston: Harvard Business School Press, 2003.

Howell, Greg, and Lauri Koskela. "Reforming Project Management: The Role of Planning, Execution, and Controlling." In David Chua and Glenn Ballard (eds.), *Proceedings of the 9th International Group for Lean Construction Conference*, 185–198. Singapore: National University of Singapore, 2001.

Iansiti, Marco. *Technology Integration: Making Critical Choices in a Dynamic World*. Boston: Harvard Business School Press, 1998.

Jeffries, Ron, Ann Anderson, and Chet Hendrickson. *Extreme Programming Installed*. Boston: Addison-Wesley, 2001.

Jones, Capers. *Applied Software Measurement: Assuring Productivity and Quality*. 3d ed. New York: McGraw-Hill, 2008.

Jones, Capers. *Assessment and Control of Software Risks*. Englewood Cliffs: Yourdon Press, 1994.

Joyner, Tim. *Magellan*. Camden, ME: International Marine, 1992.

Kaner, Sam, with Lenny Lind, Catherine Toldi, Sarah Fisk, and Duane Berger. *Facilitator's Guide to Participatory Decision-Making*. Philadelphia: New Society Publishers, 1996.

Katzenbach, Jon R., and Douglas K. Smith. *The Wisdom of Teams: Creating the High-Performance Organization*. Boston: Harvard Business School Press, 1993.

Kelley, Tom. *The Art of Innovation*, New York: Currency Books, 2001.

Kennedy, Michael N. *Product Development for the Lean Enterprise: Why Toyota's System is Four Times More Productive and How You Can Implement It.* Richmond, VA: The Oaklea Press, 2003.

Kerth, Norman L. *Project Retrospectives*. New York: Dorset House, 2001

Larman, Craig. *Agile and Iterative Development: A Manager's Guide*. Boston: Addison-Wesley, 2004.

Larman, Craig, and Bas Vodde. *Scaling Lean & Agile Development*. Upper Saddle River, NJ: Addison-Wesley Professional, 2009.

Larson, Carl E., and Frank M. J. LaFasto, *Teamwork: What Must Go Right, What Can Go Wrong.* Newbury Park: Sage Publications, 1989.

Leffingwell, Dean. *Scaling Software Agility: Best Practices for Large Enterprises.* Upper Saddle River, NJ: Addison Wesley, 2007.

Lencioni, Patrick. *The Five Dysfunctions of a Team.* San Francisco: Jossey-Bass, 2002.

Mah, Michael. "How Agile Projects Measure Up, and What This Means to You." *Cutter Agile Product and Project Management Executive Report*, vol. 9, no.9, September, 2008.

Mathiassen, Lars, Jan Pries-Heje, and Ojelanki Ngwenyama. *Improving Software Organizations· From Principles to Practice.* Boston: Addison-Wesley, 2002.

Meyer, Christopher, and Stan Davis. *It's Alive: The Coming Convergence of Information, Biology, and Business.* New York: Crown Business, 2003.

Moore, Geoffrey A. *Crossing the Chasm: Marketing and Selling High-Tech Products to Mainstream Customers.* New York: HarperBusiness, 1991.

Moore, Geoffrey A. *Inside the Tornado: Marketing Strategies from Silicon Valley's Cutting Edge.* New York: HarperBusiness, 1995.

Pascale, Richard T., Mark Millemann, and Linda Gioja. *Surfing the Edge of Chaos: The Laws of Nature and the New Laws of Business.* New York: Crown Business, 2000.

Patterson, Kerry, Joseph Grenny, Ron McMillan, and Al Switzler. *Crucial Conversations: Tools for Talking When Stakes Are High.* New York: McGraw-Hill, 2002.

Petroski, Henry. *Evolution of Useful Things.* Reprint ed. New York: Vintage Books, 1994.

Petzinger, Thomas, Jr. *The New Pioneers: The Men and Women Who Are Transforming the Workplace and Marketplace.* New York: Simon & Schuster, 1999.

Pirsig, Robert. *Zen and the Art of Motorcycle Maintenance*. New York: Bantam Books, 1974.

Pixton, Pollyanna, Niel Nickolaisen, Todd Little, and Kent McDonald. *Stand Back and Deliver: Accelerating Business Transformation*, Boston: Addison Wesley, 2009.

Polikoff, Irene, Robert Coyne, and Ralph Hodgson. *Capability Cases: A Solution Envisioning Approach*. Upper Saddle River, NJ: Addision-Wesley, 2006.

Poppendieck, Mary, and Tom Poppendieck. *Lean Software Development: An Agile Toolkit*. Boston: Addison-Wesley, 2003.

Poppendieck, Mary, and Tom Poppendieck. *Implementing Lean Software Development*. Boston: Addison-Wesley, 2007.

Project Management Institute. *A Guide to the Project Management Body of Knowledge*. 2000 ed. New Square, PA: Project Management Institute, 2000.

Pukszta, Helen. "Rethinking Success and Failure in IT." *Cutter Business IT Strategies Advisory Service Executive Update*, vol. 9, no.6, June, 2006.

Putnam, Lawrence H., and Ware Myers. *Five Core Metrics: The Intelligence Behind Successful Software Management*. New York: Dorset House, 2003.

Reinertsen, Donald G. *Managing the Design Factory: A Product Developers Toolkit*. New York: Free Press, 1997.

Rubinstein, Moshe F., and Iris Firstenberg. *The Minding Organization: Bring the Future to the Present and Turn Creative Ideas into Business Solutions*. New York: John Wiley & Sons, 1999.

Rueping, Andreas. *Agile Documentation: A Pattern Guide to Producing Lightweight Documents for Software Projects*. New York: John Wiley & Sons, 2003.

Schrage, Michael. *No More Teams: Mastering the Dynamics of Creative Collaboration*. New York: Currency Doubleday, 1989.

Schrage, Michael. *Serious Play: How the World's Best Companies Simulate to Innovate*. Boston: Harvard Business School Press, 2000.

Schwaber, Ken, and Mike Beedle. *Agile Software Development with Scrum*. Upper Saddle River, NJ: Prentice Hall, 2002.

Sliger Michele, and Stacia Broderick. *The Software Project Manager's Bridge to Agility*. Upper Saddle River, NJ: Addison-Wesley Professional, 2008.

Smith, Preston G. *Flexible Product Development: Bringing Agility for Changing Markets*. San Fransisco: Josey-Bass, 2007.

Smith, Preston G., and Guy M. Merritt. *Proactive Risk Management: Controlling Uncertainty in Product Development*. New York: Productivity Press, 2002.

Sobek, Durward K., II, Allen C. Ward, and Jeffrey K. Liker. "Toyota's Principles of Set-Based Concurrent Engineering." *Sloan Management Review*

(Winter 1999). Quotes on pp. 205, 206 ©1999 by Massachusetts Institute of Technology. Reprinted by permission of the publisher. All rights reserved.

Stapleton, Jennifer. *DSDM: Business Focused Development 2nd Edition*. London: Addision-Wesley, 2003.

Sweet, Leonard I. "Not All Cats Are Gray: Beyond Liberalism's Uncertain Faith." *The Christian Century* (June 23–30, 1982), 721.

Tabaka, Jean. *Collaboration Explained: Facilitation Skills for Software Project Leaders*. Upper Saddle River, NJ: Addison-Wesley, 2006

Tate, Kevin. *Sustainable Software Development*. Upper Saddle River, NJ: Addison-Wesley, 2006.

Thomke, Stefan H. *Experimentation Matters: Unlocking the Potential of New Technologies for Innovation*. Boston: Harvard Business School Press, 2003.

Thomsett, Rob. *Radical Project Management*. Upper Saddle River, NJ: Prentice Hall, 2002.

Ulrich, William. "The New IT Organization." Cutter Consortium Business-IT Strategies Advisory Service, *Executive Report* 3, no. 7 (July 2003).

Verzuh, Eric. *The Fast Forward MBA in Project Management*. New York: John Wiley & Sons, 1999.

Waldrop, M. Mitchell. *Complexity: The Emerging Science at the Edge of Order and Chaos*. New York: Simon & Schuster, 1992.

Weinberg, Gerald M. *Quality Software Management Volume 1: Systems Thinking*. New York: Dorset House, 1992.

Wheelwright, Steven C., and Kim B. Clark. *Revolutionizing Product Development: Quantum Leaps in Speed, Efficiency, and Quality*. New York: The Free Press, 1992.

Wiegers, Karl E. *Software Requirements*. Redmond, WA: Microsoft Press, 1999.

Williams, Laurie, and Robert Kessler. *Pair Programming Illuminated*. Boston: Addison-Wesley, 2003.

Womack, James P., Daniel T. Jones, and Daniel Roos. *The Machine That Changed the World: The Story of Lean Production*. New York: HarperPerennial, 1990.

Womack, James P., and Daniel T. Jones. *Lean Thinking: Banish Waste and Create Wealth in Your Corporation*. New York: Simon & Schuster, 1996.

Wujec, Tom and Sandra Muscat. *Return on Imagination: Realizing the Power of Ideas*. London: Financial Times Prentice Hall, 2002.

Yourdon, Edward. *Death March: The Complete Software Developer's Guide to Surviving "Mission Impossible" Projects.* Upper Saddle River, NJ: Prentice Hall, 1999.

Index

C

calculating
  monetary value points, 176
  value points, 174-175
capabilities, 166-167
  timeboxing, 188-189
*Capability Cases: A Solution
  Envisioning Approach* (Polikoff,
  2005), 167
capacity, balancing with demand,
  159-161
CAS (Complex Adaptive Systems)
  theory, 25, 66-67
CFG (customer focus group) sessions,
  256-258
change cards, 191
change, responding to, 70-71
chaordic, 65
Chaos reports, 334-335
Charan, Ram, 32
Close phase (APM Delivery
  Framework), 22, 85, 268-269
CMM (Capability Maturity Model),
  343
coaching customers, 233-235
CoC (cost of change), 216
Cockburn, Alistair, 267, 281, 323
Coffman, Curt, 225
Cohn, Mike, 103, 139
collaboration, 248, 274
  daily stand-up meetings, 248-250
  encouraging, 55
    customer collaboration, 59
    participatory decision making,
      56-57
    shared space, 58-59
  product team interaction, 250-251
  versus coordination, 282

Collier, Ken, 16
Collins, Jim, 14, 50, 54, 61, 69, 113
community responsibility for
  performance, 348-349
comparing
  collaboration and coordination, 282
  value and priority, 177-178
complexity, impact on scaling, 276
compliance versus delivery, 43-44
compromise, 57
Concept phase of Enterprise-level
  Governance model, 316-318
consolidated development, 198-200
constraints on outcome performance
  measurement, 347-348
continuous feature delivery, 28
continuous innovation as APM
  objective, 10
continuous integration, 220-221
Cooper, Robert, 7
coordination versus collaboration, 282
core software project risks, 182
Coyne, Robert, 167
Critical Chain Project Management,
  194
critical participants, 116
customer collaboration, 59
customers, 115
  coaching, 233-235
  versus stakeholders, 30

D

daily stand-up meetings, 248-250
decision framing, 238-240
decision making, 240-244
  and leadership, 245
  delay-based, 247

E

H

Hill, Andrew, 42, 363
Hock, Dee, 65, 226
Hodgson, Phillip, 49
Hodgson, Ralph, 167
Hope, Jeremy, 339
Howell, Greg, 32
Human Genome Project, 9
hyper-development and release, 200

I

Iansiti, Marco, 221
ICS (Inter-team Commitment Story)
    cards, 191
    large agile projects, scaling,
        299-302
Immelt, Jeffrey, 31
Implementing Beyond Budgeting
    (Bognes, 2009), 328
improved time-to-market as APM
    objective, 11
improving decision making, 349-350
increasing productivity, 181-182
indecision, impact on projects, 184
individual capabilities, developing,
    232-233
informational measurement, 344
innovation, 30-31
integrating principles, 86-87
intrinsic quality, 330-333
IRACIS-IR, 346
ISO certification, requirements
    for, 43
iteration, story-level, 208
iteration 0, 147
Iteration Management Layer
    (Agile Enterprise Framework), 80

iteration planning, 164, 206
    iteration length, 210-212
    task size, determining, 209
iteration process, monitoring, 213
iterations 1-N, 148-152
iterative development, 35-37

J-K

Johnson, Jim, 145
kamikaze projects, 365
Kanban, 197-198
Kaner, Sam, 240
Kelley, Tom, 58
Kennedy, Michael, 38, 126, 205
knowledge sharing, effect on large
    team building, 287-290
Koskela, Lauri, 32
KPIs (key performance indicators),
    341

L

LaFasto, Frank, 48, 117, 237
large projects
    large agile teams, building
        backlogs, 296-297
        collaboration/coordination
            design, 281-284
        decision-making design,
            284-287
        ICSs, 299-302
        knowledge sharing and
            documentation, 287-290
        multi-level release plans, 297-298
        organizational design, 279-281
        process discipline, 294
        product architecture, 295

W

X-Y-Z